Series in Anxiety and Related Disorders

Series Editor
Martin M. Antony
Ryerson University Dept. Psycholog, Toronto, Ontario, Canada

For further volumes:
http://www.springer.com/series/6926

Brenda K. Wiederhold • Stéphane Bouchard

Advances in Virtual Reality and Anxiety Disorders

 Springer

Brenda K. Wiederhold
Virtual Reality Medical Center
San Diego
California
USA

Stéphane Bouchard
Université du Québec en Outaouais
Gatineau
Québec
Canada

ISBN 978-1-4899-8022-9   ISBN 978-1-4899-8023-6 (eBook)
DOI 10.1007/978-1-4899-8023-6
Springer New York Heidelberg Dordrecht London

Library of Congress Control Number: 2014940172

© Springer Science+Business Media New York 2014
This work is subject to copyright. All rights are reserved by the Publisher, whether the whole or part of the material is concerned, specifically the rights of translation, reprinting, reuse of illustrations, recitation, broadcasting, reproduction on microfilms or in any other physical way, and transmission or information storage and retrieval, electronic adaptation, computer software, or by similar or dissimilar methodology now known or hereafter developed. Exempted from this legal reservation are brief excerpts in connection with reviews or scholarly analysis or material supplied specifically for the purpose of being entered and executed on a computer system, for exclusive use by the purchaser of the work. Duplication of this publication or parts thereof is permitted only under the provisions of the Copyright Law of the Publisher's location, in its current version, and permission for use must always be obtained from Springer. Permissions for use may be obtained through RightsLink at the Copyright Clearance Center. Violations are liable to prosecution under the respective Copyright Law.
The use of general descriptive names, registered names, trademarks, service marks, etc. in this publication does not imply, even in the absence of a specific statement, that such names are exempt from the relevant protective laws and regulations and therefore free for general use.
While the advice and information in this book are believed to be true and accurate at the date of publication, neither the authors nor the editors nor the publisher can accept any legal responsibility for any errors or omissions that may be made. The publisher makes no warranty, express or implied, with respect to the material contained herein.

Printed on acid-free paper

Springer is part of Springer Science+Business Media (www.springer.com)

Contents

Part I General Concepts

1 **Introduction** 3
   Brenda K. Wiederhold and Mark D. Wiederhold

2 **Presence** 9
   Giuseppe Riva, Fabrizia Mantovani and Stéphane Bouchard

3 **Sickness in Virtual Reality** 35
   Sarah Sharples, Gary Burnett and Sue Cobb

Part II Anxiety Disorders

4 **Fear of Flying (Aviophobia): Efficacy and Methodological
   Lessons Learned from Outcome Trials** 65
   Brenda K. Wiederhold, Stéphane Bouchard and Claudie Loranger

5 **Arachnophobia and Fear of Other Insects: Efficacy and
   Lessons Learned from Treatment Process** 91
   Stéphane Bouchard, Brenda K. Wiederhold and Jessie Bossé

6 **Fear of Heights (Acrophobia): Efficacy and Lessons Learned
   from Psychophysiological Data** 119
   Stéphane Bouchard, Brenda K. Wiederhold and Jessie Bossé

7 **Claustrophobia: Efficacy and Treatment Protocols** 145
   Stéphane Bouchard, Brenda K. Wiederhold and Claudie Loranger

8 **Panic Disorder, Agoraphobia, and Driving Phobia: Lessons
   Learned From Efficacy Studies** 163
   Cristina Botella, Azucena García-Palacios,
   Rosa Baños and Soledad Quero

9 **Social Anxiety Disorder: Efficacy and Virtual Humans** 187
   Stéphane Bouchard, Jessie Bossé, Claudie Loranger
   and Évelyne Klinger

10 **Virtual Reality for Posttraumatic Stress Disorder** 211
   Brenda K. Wiederhold and Mark D. Wiederhold

11 **Generalized Anxiety Disorder and Obsessive–Compulsive
   Disorder: Efficacy and the Development of Virtual Environments** ... 235
   Tanya Guitard, Mylène Laforest and Stéphane Bouchard

Part III Conclusions

12 **A Case Example of a Virtual Reality Clinic** 261
   Brenda K. Wiederhold and Mark D. Wiederhold

13 **Conclusions: The Present and the Future of Virtual Reality
   in the Treatment of Anxiety Disorders** 265
   Giuseppe Riva and Claudia Repetto

Index 285

Contributors

Professor Rosa Baños, Ph.D. Evaluación y Tratamientos Psicológicos

Jessie Bossé, B.A., Ph.D. Cand. Université du Québec en Outaouais

Professor Cristina Botella, Ph.D. Laboratorio de Psicología y Tecnología

Professor Gary Burnett, Ph.D. Florida State University

Professor Sue Cobb, Ph.D. University of Nottingham

Professor Azucena García-Palacios, Ph.D. Universitat Jaume I

Dr. Tanya Guitard, Ph.D. Université du Québec à Montréal

Dr. Évelyne Klinger Eng., Ph.D. HDR École supérieure d'informatique, électronique, automatique

Dr. Mylene Laforest, Ph.D. Université d'Ottawa

Claudie Loranger, B.A., Ph.D. Cand. Université du Québec en Outaouais

Professor Fabrizia Mantovani, Ph.D. Università degli Studi di Milano-Bicocca

Professor Soledad Quero, Ph.D. Universitat Jaume I

Dr. Claudia Repetto, Ph.D. Università Cattolica del Sacro Cuore

Professor Giuseppe Riva, Ph.D. Istituto Auxologico Italiano, Università Cattolica, Milan

Professor Sarah Sharples, Ph.D. University of Nottingham

Professor Mark D. Wiederhold, M.D., Ph.D., FACP Virtual Reality Medical Center

Part I
General Concepts

Chapter 1
Introduction

Brenda K. Wiederhold and Mark D. Wiederhold

1.1 Virtual Reality

1.1.1 What is Virtual Reality?

Virtual reality (VR) may be defined as a set of computer technologies, which, when combined, provide an interface to an interactive, computer-generated world. In particular, VR provides an immersive environment, allowing the user to actually feel present in a three-dimensional computer-generated world, transported to another reality. The VR application enables users to navigate and interact with a three-dimensional computer-generated (and computer-maintained) environment in real time, with the user's actions and reactions being experienced in the present moment.

1.1.2 VR for Clinical Use

Virtual environments (VEs) became available for clinical use in behavioral health care in the mid-1990s. Initially, their application was limited by a lack of inexpensive, easy-to-maintain, and easy-to-use personal computer (PC)-based systems. The expensive, high-powered computational systems that were previously required were out of reach for most practicing clinicians. With the development of PC-based platforms and more user-friendly programming software, more clinicians became attracted to the use of this technology in their clinical practices and more universities began to explore VR's use in its research projects. We are now, as well, encouraged by the ability to transport many of these systems to laptop computers, Internet-based platforms, and more mobile platforms such as the iPad and iPhone. These trends all point to the ability to provide prevention and treatment services more conveniently and cost-effectively to a wider segment of the population.

Areas in which VR treatments have proven quite successful include the treatment of anxiety disorders, including specific phobias, panic disorder, agoraphobia, social phobia, and posttraumatic stress disorder; neuropsychological evaluation, testing, and rehabilitation; distraction for acute medical and dental procedures and chronic pain; and eating disorders and obesity treatment. Well over 1000 publications from centers around the world exist in the scientific literature. Results indicate that VEs may have multiple advantages for anxiety disorder's treatment when compared to conventional therapies. Given that VR can be used to conduct exposure (often referred to in this book as *in virtuo* exposure), where all the senses are stimulated in a controlled fashion, this makes intuitive sense as well.

Despite these results and two decades of research, there is still no widespread dissemination of VR. Clinicians need to be made aware of the advantages and of training programs, which will allow them to learn how to effectively integrate these new technologies into their everyday practice.

1.1.3 VR in the Treatment of Anxiety Disorders

The basic psychotherapeutic approach to treating specific phobias is exposure therapy, sometimes in combination with other procedures such as relaxation or cognitive components. Exposure therapy is most often performed in one of three basic ways: (1) In vivo exposure, which involves having the patient confront actual real-life phobic situations. (2) Imaginal exposure, which involves having the patient visualize the phobic situation using mental imagery. (3) VR exposure (also referred to as *in virtuo* exposure), which involves placing the patients in the computer-generated environment where all their senses are stimulated. The weaknesses of imaginal exposure include the difficulty many patients experience when trying to elicit images of the anxiety-evoking stimuli (Kosslyn et al. 1984). In addition, many patients, approximately 25%, drop out of in vivo treatment (or never begin) because they are too afraid of facing the threatening phobic object (Marks and O'Sullivan 1988).

VR exposure addresses some of these weaknesses by providing stimuli for patients who experience difficulty imagining scenes and by providing a less overwhelming starting point for those too phobic to experience real-life situations. Unlike in vivo exposure, VR can be performed in the privacy of a therapist's office, thus avoiding public outings and violation of patient confidentiality. VR can also generate stimuli of much greater magnitude than standard in vivo techniques, such as motor vehicle scenarios for those suffering from fear of driving after a crash or violent flight turbulence for those afraid to fly. Since VR is under the control of both the patient and the therapist, it may in some instances, be a safer starting point than in vivo and, at the same time, more realistic than imaginal therapy. The ability to control an artificial environment and introduce a set of stimuli can provide additional capabilities to standard office-based psychotherapy, leading to greater creativity and flexibility in exploring and understanding a patient's individual problems, concerns, and underlying health-related issues.

To readers concerned with the initial costs of VR systems, it should be noted that traditional treatments of anxiety disorders often utilize physiological monitoring. Many of these physiology systems are comparable to the cost of a VR system. Given the typical monetary and time expenditure associated with treating anxiety disorders, investing between US$ 5 and 10,000 in a VR system is not prohibitive relative to the reduced treatment time and cost and the increased efficacy of the treatment itself.

1.2 Anxiety Disorders

1.2.1 Prevalence and Economic Costs of Anxiety Disorders

Anxiety disorders are the most common mental health disorders in both the USA and Europe, with lifetime prevalence rates of 28.8% in the USA (Kessler et al. 2005) and approximately 15% in Europe. One category of anxiety disorders, specific phobias, are more common than major depression, alcohol abuse, or alcohol dependence. Anxiety disorders as well are the second most common psychiatric diagnosis given in primary care settings in Europe and the USA (Sansone and Sansone 2010). Additionally, 33% of patients presenting with chest pain, abdominal pain, or insomnia actually have an anxiety disorder, as do 25% of those with fatigue, headache, or joint or limb pain (Sherman 1997). The average person with an anxiety disorder will have ten encounters with the health-care system before a correct diagnosis is given, increasing health-care costs and contributing to frustration on the part of both the patient and the physician. Women, individuals under age 45, separated and divorced persons, and individuals in lower socioeconomic groups are among those who suffer the highest incidence of anxiety disorders and also among the groups least likely to be able to afford appropriate treatment (Regier et al. 1990).

Long viewed by clinicians as particularly challenging to treat and requiring extensive long-term therapy, with the advent of managed care and health-care reform, clinicians are being pressured to become more efficient in their treatment of patients with anxiety disorders. Over US$ 147 billion was spent on mental health in the USA in 1990. Of this amount, the largest portion of mental health-care dollars, US$ 47 billion (32%), was spent to treat anxiety disorders.

In 1997, costs related to anxiety disorders were estimated at US$ 15 billion in direct costs, including medical, administrative, and research costs, and US$ 50 billion in indirect costs, such as lost or reduced productivity, illness, and death (Sobel and Ornstein 1997).

1.2.2 Treatment of Anxiety Disorders

A large-scale study by Goisman et al. (1993) compared the utilization patterns of the following methods for the treatment of anxiety disorders: behavioral (relaxation, exposure, modeling/role play), cognitive (thought stopping, mental distraction, thought recording), medication, psychodynamic, family therapy, and biofeedback. This study confirmed the results of earlier studies' findings that behavioral treatments for anxiety disorders are widely underutilized in spite of research that proves their efficacy for treating these types of disorders. In addition, it was found that the most common behavioral techniques utilized were relaxation and imaginal exposure, both of which are less effective than in vivo exposure. All behavioral techniques were utilized less frequently than psychodynamic psychotherapy, a modality that is of unproven efficacy in the treatment of anxiety disorders. Medications were also utilized more frequently than cognitive-behavioral interventions and often in concert with other treatments. There are good meta-analyses that support the combined use of pharmacological agents with cognitive-behavioral therapy (CBT)-based therapies. There are interesting pilot studies that have combined other forms of drug therapy and VR therapies. Goisman's study confirms that wider dissemination of behavioral methods relative to the treatment of anxiety disorders is merited. One way to understand the underutilization of in vivo exposure in particular is the general inconvenience and greater cost of in vivo exposure. This technique requires that therapists accompany patients into anxiety-provoking situations in the real world at great cost to the patient and with great time expenditure on the part of both therapist and patient. A further complication with in vivo exposure is that severely anxious or phobic patients may be unwilling or very resistant to the intensity of in vivo exposure. VR technology offers a means by which therapists can provide in-office in vivo treatment to patients suffering from a variety of anxiety disorders, thus eliminating many of the complications of real-world in vivo exposure. Given that in vivo exposure is one of the most powerful treatments, especially for specific anxiety disorders and phobias, VR-enhanced psychotherapy (also called VR graded exposure therapy or VRGET) offers practitioners an additional clinically proven and efficient treatment tool.

1.3 Goals and Contents of this Book

1.3.1 Goals

The main goal of this book is to provide information on the applicability of VR to the treatment of anxiety disorders. The authors explain what VR is, what type of technology it involves, and how it is applied in clinical practice. The book describes practical, hands-on strategies and interventions designed to guide therapists through each step of the treatment process for each of the specific anxiety disorders.

1.3.2 Contents

The book begins with Chap. 1, which provides a short summary of the prevalence, economic costs, and treatment of anxiety disorders and gives an overview of VR and its clinical applications. The remainder of the book is broken down into three parts.

Part I, consisting of Chaps. 1, 2, and 3, provides the reader a greater understanding of VR as a technology: its history, some basic concepts, and its use in treating anxiety disorders. Chapter 2 defines further the VR terms of "presence" and "immersion" and discusses their applicability to the clinical use of VR. Chapter 3 provides an overview of side effects that may be encountered by a small percentage of those who use VR, focusing on cybersickness.

Part II (Chaps. 4–11) is intended as a user's guide to help clinicians understand how VR is implemented in the treatment of anxiety disorders, with each chapter dedicated to a different disorder. The chapters follow a similar format and present key components of the disorder, efficacy studies, and how the addition of VR into clinical protocols has been employed. Key issues related to the following specific anxiety disorders are discussed: aviophobia; arachnophobia; acrophobia; claustrophobia; panic disorder, agoraphobia and driving; social phobia; posttraumatic stress disorder generalized anxiety disorder; and obsessive–compulsive disorder. To note, Chap. 8 discusses panic, agoraphobia, and driving. We have included driving in this chapter as many of the patients who present for treatment for their panic disorder and agoraphobia have as part of their disability an inability to drive. The VR driving scenarios are therefore used as part of their treatment. Posttraumatic stress disorder (PTSD) due to motor vehicle accidents is included separately in Chap. 10, which is dedicated to PTSD.

You may notice the variance in chapter length in Part II. The differences in length reflect the ease by which these disorders lend themselves to VR therapy, as well as the amount of research and clinical work that has been completed in these areas.

Part III continues with clinical applications and practical issues for those wishing to incorporate VR into their clinical practice. Chapter 12 discusses a case example of a VR clinic model, transitioning technologies from the laboratory setting into an applied clinical use. Chapter 13 sets forth conclusions, future trends, and new areas of investigation.

Although VR has been in practice for diagnosing, assessing, and treating anxiety disorders for almost two decades, the practice is still not widespread. We, as the pioneers, have been careful not to oversell results, but have maintained that VR is an adjunct to traditional therapy skills and judgment.

References

Goisman, R. M., Rogers, M. P., Steketee, G. S., Warshaw, M. G., Cuneo, P., & Keller, M. B. (1993). Utilization of behavioral methods in a multicenter anxiety disorders study. *Journal of Clinical Psychiatry, 54,* 213–218.

Kessler R., Berglund, P., Demler, O., Jin, R., Merikangas, KR, & Walters EE. (2005). Lifetime prevalence and age-of-onset distributions of DSM-IV disorders in the National Comorbidity Survey Replication. *Archives of General Psychiatry, 62*(6), 593–602.

Kosslyn, S. M., Brunn, J., Cave, K. R., & Wallach, R. W. (1984). Individual differences in mental imagery ability: A computational analysis. *Cognition, 18,* 195–243.

Marks, I., & Sullivan G. (1988). Drugs and psychological treatments for agoraphobia/panic and obsessive compulsive disorders: a review. *British Journal of Psychiatry, 153,* 650–658.

Sansone, R.A., & Sansone, L.A., (2010) Psychiatric disorders: A global look at facts and figures. *Psychiatry, 7*(12), 16–19.

Regier, D. A., Narrow, W. E. & Rae, D. S. (1990). The epidemiology of anxiety disorders: the Epidemiologic Catchment Area (ECA) experience. *Journal of Psychiatric Research, 24* (suppl. 2), 3–14.

Sherman, C. (1997). Multiple Somatic symptoms may signal anxiety, depression. *Internal Medicine News,* May 15, p. 21.

Sobel, D & Orstein R. (1997). The cost of anxiety. *Mind/Body Health Newsletter. 6,* p. 7.

Chapter 2
Presence

Giuseppe Riva, Fabrizia Mantovani and Stéphane Bouchard

2.1 Introduction

Virtual reality (VR) literature includes many descriptions of users reacting to a virtual environment (VE) in instinctual ways that suggest they believe, at least for a short time, that they were "immersed" and even "present" in the synthetic experience. Following the definitions introduced by Slater et al. (1996): "Presence is a state of consciousness, a state of being [in an environment]…while immersion is related to the quantity and quality of sensory data that is from that environment" (p. 22).

Specifically, immersion is generally understood to be a product of technology that facilitates the production of the multimodal sensory "input" to the user (Burdea et al. 1996) while presence is defined as the psychological perception of being "there," within a VE (Heeter 1992).

However, as commented by Biocca (1999), and agreed by most researchers in the area, "while the design of virtual reality technology has brought the theoretical issue of presence to the fore, few theorists argue that the experience of presence suddenly emerged with the arrival of virtual reality" (p. 121). So, what is presence? And what is its possible impact in virtual exposure therapy?

For instance, does a strong sense of presence cause patients to better engage and modify emotions and cognitive processes they have already developed in a real environment? Will the skills and the competences acquired in the virtual world transfer to a corresponding real experience? This chapter will try to provide some answers to these questions.

2.2 Two Definitions of Presence: Media Presence and Inner Presence

Presence depends on how an individual interprets the VE, or integrates the multimodal information as a function of his/her biological and individual cognitive predisposition (van der Straaten and Shuemie 2000).

In a review, Christine Youngblut (2007) examined 127 research papers related to presence. These papers investigated the relationship between the sense of presence in virtual worlds and over 60 media characteristics. Table 2.1 reports the particular characteristics that have been found to influence the experience of presence. The reported data can provide direction for system developers and may also provide insight into differences that can be expected using different media.

These data clearly underline that visual cues are not the only ones relevant to presence. A large study examined 322 subjects' responses to multisensory cues in a virtual world (Dinh et al. 1999). The results showed that tactile, olfactory, and auditory cues were actually more effective than visual stimuli in increasing the sense of presence. It is important, too, to keep in mind that the content and context of the virtual experience also affect the quality of presence and immersion. In a recent experiment, Gorini and colleagues (2010) analyzed the contribution of media form (i.e., the physical immersion with or without the use of the HMD) and media content (i.e., the presence or absence of a contextualizing narrative) in influencing the users' sense of presence during the exploration of a virtual hospital. Their data clearly show that both media form and media content have a significant impact on the subjects' sense of presence.

In this view, the illusion of presence requires: (1) the processing of multimodal input (i.e., visual, tactile, auditory, kinesthetic, olfactory) from the virtual experience to be combined to form coherent perceptual categories—that is, the virtual experience be recognized as "real"; (2) the integration of this multimodal integration to be processed in an egocentric reference frame—that is, the user feels that he or she is within the environment as opposed to observing it from a third-person perspective; and (3) the ability to give a meaning to the multimodal input—that is, the virtual experience be recognized as "meaningful" and "relevant."

Due to the complexity of the topic, and the interest in this concept, different attempts to define presence and to explain its role are available in the literature (Waterworth et al. 2012). In general, as underlined by Lombard and Jones (Lombard and Jones 2006): "the first and most basic distinction among definitions of presence concerns the issue of technology" (p. 25).

One group of researchers describes the sense of presence as *media presence*, a function of our experience of a given medium (IJsselsteijn et al. 2000; Lombard and Ditton 1997; Loomis 1992; Marsh et al. 2001; Sadowski and Stanney 2002; Schloerb 1995; Sheridan 1992, 1996).

The main outcome of this approach is the *perceptual illusion of nonmediation* (Lombard and Ditton 1997) definition of presence. Following it, presence is produced by means of the disappearance of the medium from the conscious attention of the subject. The main advantage of this approach is its predictive value: The level of presence is reduced by the experience of mediation during the action. The main limitation of this vision is what is not said. What is presence for? Is it a specific cognitive process? What is its role in our daily experience? It is important to note that these questions are unanswered even for the relationship between presence and media. As underlined by Lee (2004b), "Presence scholars may find it surprising and even disturbing that there have been limited attempts to explain the fundamental

2.2 Two Definitions of Presence: Media Presence and Inner Presence

Table 2.1 Effects of media to presence. (Adapted from Youngblut 2007)

Audio	
Audio cues	•
Audio sources, nature of	•
Audio sources, number of	♦
Aural rendering quality	•
Collision detection, audio	♦
HRTF	♦
Sound rotation, direction	•
Sound rotation, velocity	•
Spatialized audio	❑
Olfactory	
Olfactory cues	♦
Tactile	
Collision detection, haptic	♦
Collision detection, tactile	♦
Haptic force feedback	♦
Tactile cues	♦
Video	
Visual detail	
Color	♦
Dynamic shadows	•
Rendering quality	•
Scene realism	❑
Texture mapping, use of	♦
Texture mapping, quality	♦
Visual display	
Latency, visual	♦
Device, CAVE-HMD-monitor	❑
Device, HMD-monitor	❑
Device, projector-screen-monitor	♦
Device, other	♦
Field of view	♦
Frame rate	♦
Resolution	♦
Stereopsis	♦
Update rate	❑
Visual representation	
Behavioral realism	♦
Fidelity of body	♦
Fidelity of hand	♦
Moving between worlds	♦
Navigation method	❑

CAVE C-automatic virtual environment, *HRTF* head related transfer functions, *HMD* head-mounted display

Key: • single experiment with consistent findings, ♦ different experiments with consistent findings, ❑ replicated experiments with consistent findings reason *why* human beings can feel presence when they use media and/or simulation technologies" (p. 496).

To address these questions, a second group of researchers considers presence as *inner presence*—the feeling of being located in a perceived external world around the self (Revonsuo 2006; Riva et al. 2011; Waterworth et al. 2010). In this view, presence is a broad psychological phenomenon, not necessarily linked to the experience of a medium, whose goal is the control of the individual and social activity (Baños et al. 1999, 2000; Lee 2004a, 2004b; Mantovani and Riva 1999; Marsh et al. 2001; Moore et al. 2002; Riva 2009; Riva and Davide 2001; Riva et al. 2003; Schubert et al. 2001; Spagnolli and Gamberini 2002; Spagnolli et al. 2003; Waterworth and Waterworth 2001, 2003; Zahoric and Jenison 1998). In this chapter, we support this second vision, starting from the following broad statements:

- The content of consciousness is the content of a simulated world in our brain (Metzinger 2009; Revonsuo 2006).
- Presence refers to the part of the contents of consciousness that relate to the current time and place in which the body is located (Biocca 1997; Biocca and Nowak 2001; Metzinger 2009; Riva 2006; Waterworth et al. 2010).
- The psychology of presence is related to human action and its organization in the environment (Marsh 2003; Riva 2009; Riva et al. 2003).
- The feeling of presence is not the same in all the situations (virtual or real), but it can be different in relation to the characteristics of the physical, social, and cultural space the subject is in (Mantovani and Riva 1999, 2001; Mantovani and Spagnolli 2000).
- A circular interaction exists between presence and emotions: On the one hand, the feeling of presence is greater in "emotion-inducing" environments; on the other hand, the emotional state is influenced by the level of presence (Bouchard et al. 2008; Riva 2011; Riva et al. 2007).
- Presence alone is not enough to guarantee a positive clinical outcome in VR exposure therapy: The technology behind the virtual stimuli has to be "transparent" enough to enable the activation of the fear structure. Once this threshold is passed, there is no direct effect of the level of presence on the efficacy of desensitization (Côte and Bouchard 2009; Price and Anderson 2007).

2.3 Our Brain Is a Simulation: Linking Consciousness and Presence

A series of recent discoveries from cognitive sciences suggests that the mind has to be understood in the context of its relationship to a physical body that interacts with the world. Hence human cognition, rather than being centralized, abstract, and sharply distinct from peripheral input and output modules, has deep roots in sensorimotor processing.

An example of this trend is the recent discovery of neuronal resonance processes activated by the simple observation of others. Rizzolatti and colleagues found that a functional cluster of premotor neurons (F5c-PF) contains *mirror neurons*, a class of neurons that are activated both during the execution of purposeful, goal-related hand actions, and during the observation of similar actions performed by another individual (Gallese et al. 1996; Rizzolatti et al. 1996).

The general framework outlined by the above results was used by simulation theorists—for example, Lawrence Barsalou, Vittorio Gallese, Alvin Goldman, Jane Heal, Susan Hurley, Marc Jeannerod, Guenter Knoblich, and Margaret Wilson—to support the following view: The mirror system instantiates simulation of transitive actions used to map the goals and purposes of others' actions (Barsalou 2003; Gallese 2005). As clearly explained by Wilson and Knoblich (2005), this is the outcome of an implicit/covert, subpersonal process:

> The various brain areas involved in translating perceived human movement into corresponding motor programs collectively act as an emulator, internally simulating the ongoing perceived movement... The present proposal suggests that, in tasks requiring fast action coordination, the emulator derives predictions about the future course of others' actions, which could be integrated with the actions one is currently planning. (pp. 468–469)

According to this approach, action and perception are more closely linked than has traditionally been assumed. Specifically, for the *Common Coding Theory* (Hommel et al. 2001), the cognitive representations for perceived events (perception) and intended or to-be-generated events (action) are formed by a common representational domain: Actions are coded in terms of the perceivable effects they should generate. For this reason, when an effect is intended, the movement that produces this effect as perceptual input is automatically activated, because actions and their effects are stored in a common representational domain.

In simpler words, the brain has its own VR system that is used in both action planning and action understanding. If this is true, how can we distinguish between the virtual action planning and the real action? The answer is easy: using presence. In his book *Inner Presence*, Revuonso (2006) clearly states:

"To be conscious is to have the sense of presence in a world... To have contents of consciousness is to have patterns of phenomenological experience present... In the philosophy of presence, consciousness is an organized whole of transparent surrogates of virtual objects that are immediately present for us in the here-and-now of subjective experience. " (pp. 126–129). In this view, to be directly present right here or for an object to be directly present for me requires some form of "acquaintance": a direct awareness based on a nonpropositional knowledge or nonconceptual content (Fox 1994).

This view is surprisingly near to the vision of presence as the *perceptual illusion of nonmediation* (Lombard and Ditton 1997) introduced before. In both cases, presence is related to a direct experience.

However, while in the Lombard and Ditton definition the mediation is given by the used medium (VR), in Revuonso's view (2006), *the mediation is given by the body*: The experience of the body is our first VR system. This vision is shared by many cognitive scientists. For instance, Andy Clark (2008) underlines that:

> The infant, like the VR-exploring adult, must learn how to use initially unresponsive hands, arms, and legs to obtain its goals.... With time and practice enough bodily fluency is achieved to make the wider world itself directly available as a kind of unmediated arena

for embodied action.... At such moments the body has become "transparent equipment"... that is not the focus of attention in use. (p. 10)

Moreover, different neurological disorders clearly support this view, showing how the direct experience of presence in our body is the result of different and separable subcomponents that can be altered in some way (Metzinger 2009): *agency, ownership, and location*:

- *Autopagnosia (agency)*: It is a neurological disease characterized by the inability to recognize or orient any part of one's own body, caused by a parietal lobe lesion (Sirigu et al. 1991): A patient with Autopagnosia is not able to use his/her own body.
- *Anarchic Hand (ownership)*: It is a neurological disease in which patients are aware of the actions of their anarchic hand but do not attribute its intentional behavior to themselves (it is not "owned" by them) (Della Sala 2006): The anarchic hand is not present to the patient who owns it.
- *Hemispatial Neglect (location)*: It is a neurological disease characterized by a deficit in attention to and awareness of one side of space. For example, a stroke affecting the right parietal lobe of the brain can lead to neglect for the left side of the visual field, causing a patient with neglect to behave as if the left side of sensory space is nonexistent: A patient with left neglect will not be present in the left part of a room.

Recently, different authors showed that it is possible to induce an illusory perception of a fake limb (Slater et al. 2009; Perez-Marcos et al. 2009) as a part of our own body, by altering the normal association between touch and its visual correlate. It is even possible to generate a body transfer illusion (Slater et al. 2009): Slater and colleagues substituted the experience of male subjects' own bodies with a life-sized virtual human female body. This was demonstrated subjectively by questionnaire and physiologically through heart-rate deceleration in response to a threat to the virtual body (Slater et al. 2009).

2.4 What Is Presence: a Neuro-Psychological Approach

As we have seen before, Lombard and Ditton defined presence as the *perceptual illusion of nonmediation* (Lombard and Ditton 1997), linking it to the experience of a medium:

An illusion of nonmediation occurs when a person fails to perceive or acknowledge the existence of a medium in his/her communication environment and responds as he/she would if the medium were not there.... Presence in this view cannot occur unless a person is using a medium.

However, in the previous paragraph, we suggested that the outcome of many recent neurological studies considers the body as the first medium, through which we articulate ourselves and engage with others. Moreover, recent studies on peripersonal

2.4 What Is Presence: a Neuro-Psychological Approach

space demonstrated that tool-mediated actions modify the multisensory coding of near peripersonal space (Farné et al. 2007; Gamberini et al. 2008): The active use of a tool to physically and effectively interact with objects in the distant space appears to produce a spatial extension of the multisensory perihand space corresponding to the whole length of the tool. *In other words, through the successful enaction of the subject's intentions using the tool, he/she becomes physically present in the tool* (Riva 2009).

These studies confirm that the subject locates himself/herself in an external space according to the action he can do in it (Riva and Mantovani 2012). As suggested by Zahoric and Jenison (Zahoric and Jenison 1998): "presence is tantamount to successfully supported action in the environment" (p. 87, italics in the original).

In other words, the subject is "present" in a space if he/she can act in it. Moreover, the subject is "present" in the space—real or virtual—where he/she can act. Interestingly, what we need for presence are both the affordance for action (the possibility of acting) and its enaction (the possibility of successfully acting).

The first suggestion this framework offers to the developers of virtual worlds is that for presence *action is more important than perception* (Riva 2008): I am more present in a perceptually poor VE (e.g., a textual multi user display) where I can act in many different ways than in a lifelike VE where I cannot do anything.

Another consequence of this framework is the need to better understand what "acting successfully" means (Riva et al. 2011). We can start from the definition of *agency*: "the power to alter at will one's perceptual inputs" (Russell 1996). But how can we define our will? A simple answer to this question is: through intentions. Following this line of reasoning, *presence can be defined as the nonmediated (prereflexive) perception of using the body to successfully transforming intentions into actions (enaction).*

A possible criticism to this definition is the following: "I may be asked to repair a computer, and I may be unable to fix it. This does not mean that I am not present in the environment (real or virtual) where the computer and I are."

This objection makes sense if we use the folk psychology definition of intention: The intention of an agent performing an action is his/her specific purpose in doing so. However, the latest cognitive studies clearly show that *any behavior is the result of a complex intentional chain that cannot be analyzed at a single level* (Pacherie 2006; Searle 1983).

According to the *dynamic theory of intentions* presented by Pacherie (2006, 2008) and the *activity theory* introduced by Leont'ev and disseminated by Kaptelinin and Nardi (Kaptelinin and Nardi 2006; Leontjev 1978), repairing a computer is driven by a higher objective (e.g., obtaining the money for paying a new car) and is the result of lower-level operations (e.g., removing the hard disk or the central processing unit (CPU), cleaning them, etc.), each driven by specific purposes.

So, for an intention that failed (repairing the computer), many others were successful (removing the hard disk, cleaning it, etc.) inducing presence (Riva 2009, 2010).

Specifically, the *dynamic theory of intentions* identifies three different "levels" or "forms" of intentions (Fig. 2.1), characterized by different roles and contents:

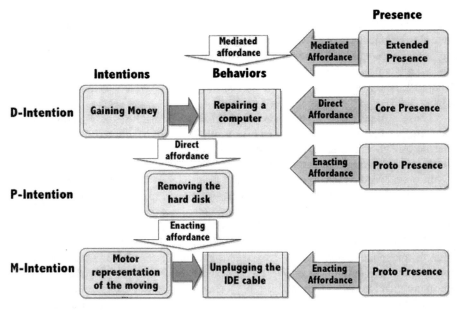

Fig. 2.1 The intentional chain

distal intentions (D-intentions), proximal intentions (P-intentions), and motor intentions (M-intentions):
- *D-intentions (future-directed intentions)*: These high-level intentions act both as intra- and interpersonal coordinators, and as prompters of practical reasoning about means and plans: In the activity, "obtaining a Ph.D. in psychology" described in Fig. 2.2, "helping others to solve problems" is a D-intention, the object that drives the activity of the subject.
- *P-intentions (present-directed intentions)*: These intentions are responsible for high-level (conscious) forms of guidance and monitoring. They have to ensure that the imagined actions become current through situational control of their unfolding: In the activity described in Fig. 2.1, "preparing the dissertation" is a P-intention.
- *M-intentions (motor intentions)*: These intentions are responsible for low-level (unconscious) forms of guidance and monitoring: We may not be aware of them and have only partial access to their content. Further, their contents are not propositional: In the activity described in Fig. 2.2, the motor representations required to write using the keyboard are M-intentions.

Any intentional level has its own role: the rational (D-intentions), situational (P-intention), and motor (M-intention) guidance and control of action. They form an intentional cascade (Pacherie 2006, 2008) in which higher intentions generate lower intentions.

2.4 What Is Presence: a Neuro-Psychological Approach

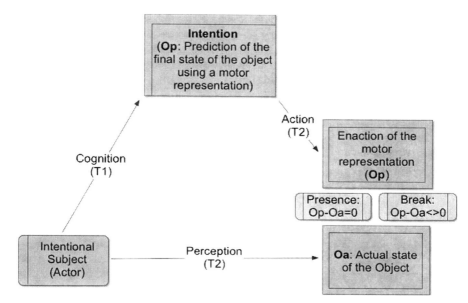

Fig. 2.2 The feeling of presence

This view suggests that the ability to feel "present" in a VR system—a medium—basically does not differ from the ability to feel "present" in our body. When the subject is present during agency—i.e., he/she is able to successfully enact his/her intentions—he/she locates himself/herself in the physical and cultural space in which the action occurs.

Moreover, it also suggests that even in the real world the feeling of presence will be different according to the ability of the subject to enact his/her intentions within an external environment. For instance, I am in a restaurant for a formal dinner with some colleagues in a Korean restaurant, but I do not know how to use the chopsticks I have near my dish. In this situation, I am physically there, but the lack of knowledge puts me outside, at least partially, from the social and cultural space of the "formal Korean dinner." The result is a reduced presence and a limitation in my agency: I am not able to enact my intention (pick up some rice) using the chopsticks, so I do not use them to avoid mistakes.

Finally, in this view, presence can be described as a sophisticated but unconscious form of monitoring of action and experience: The self perceives the variations in the feeling of presence and tunes its activity accordingly. From a computational viewpoint, the experience of presence is achieved through a forward–inverse model (Blackemore and Decety 2001) (Fig. 2.2):

- First, the agent produces the motor command for achieving a desired state given the current state of the system and the current state of the environment.

- Second, an efference copy of the motor command is fed to a forward dynamic model that generates a prediction of the consequences of performing this motor command.
- Third, the predicted state is compared with the actual sensory feedback. Errors derived from the difference between the desired state and the actual state can be used to update the model and improve performance.

The results of the comparison (which occurs at a subpersonal level) between the sensory prediction and the sensory consequences of the act can then be utilized to determine both the agent of the action and to track any possible variation in its course. If no variations are perceived, the self is able to concentrate on the action and not on its monitoring. As suggested by *the simulation theorists* (Knoblich et al. 2005; Wilson and Knoblich 2005), the brain instantiates a sophisticated simulation, based on motor codes, of the outcome of an action and uses this to evaluate its course.

For this reason, the feeling of presence—*the prereflexive perception that the agent's intentions are successfully enacted*—is not separated by the experience of the subject, but *is directly related to it*. It corresponds to what Heidegger (Heidegger 1959) defined as "the interrupted moment of our habitual standard, comfortable *being-in-the-world.*" A higher feeling of presence is experienced by the self as a better quality of action and experience (Zahoric and Jenison 1998). In fact, the subject perceives consciously only *significant variations* in the feeling of presence: *breakdowns* and *optimal experiences* (Riva 2006).

Why do we consciously track presence variations? Riva and colleagues suggest that it is a sophisticated evolutionary tool used to control the quality of behavior. Specifically, the subject tries to overcome any breakdown in its activity and searches for engaging and rewarding activities (optimal experiences). It provides both the motivation and the guiding principle for successful action. According to Csikszentmihalyi (1975, 1990), individuals preferentially engage in opportunities for action associated with a positive, complex, and rewarding state of consciousness, defined by him as "optimal experience" or "flow." There are exceptional situations in which the activity of the subject is characterized by a higher level of presence than in most others. In these situations the subject experiences a full sense of control and experiential immersion (Morganti and Riva 2004; Riva 2004; Waterworth et al. 2003).

When this experience is associated with a positive emotional state, it constitutes a flow state. An example of flow is the case where a professional athlete is playing exceptionally well (positive emotion) and achieves a state of mind where nothing else is attended to but the game (high level of presence).

2.4.1 The Layers of Presence

Even if presence is a unitary feeling, on the process side it can be divided into three different layers/subprocesses (Riva et al. 2004), phylogenetically different, that correspond reasonably well (see Fig. 2.3) to the three levels of intentions identified by Pacherie in her dynamic theory of intentions (Pacherie 2006):

2.4 What Is Presence: a Neuro-Psychological Approach

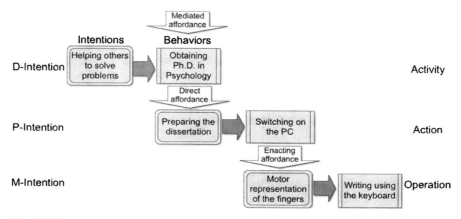

Fig. 2.3 The layers of presence

- Proto presence (Self vs. nonself—M-intentions)
- Core presence (Self vs. present external world—P-intentions)
- Extended presence (Self vs. possible/future external world—D-intentions)

We define *proto presence* more precisely as the process of internal/external separation *related to the level of perception–action coupling (self vs. nonself)*. The more the organism is able to correctly couple perceptions and movements, the more it differentiates itself from the external world, thus increasing its probability of surviving. Proto presence is based on proprioception and other ways of knowing bodily orientation in the world. In a virtual world, this is sometimes known as "spatial presence" and requires the tracking of body parts and appropriate and rapid updating of displays, for example, in response to head movements. Proto presence allows the enaction of M-intentions only.

Core presence can be described as *the activity of selective attention made by the self on perceptions (self vs. present external world)*: The more the organism is able to focus on its sensorial experience by leaving the remaining neural processes in the background, the more it is able to identify events of the present moment and the direct affordances offered by the current external world, increasing its probability of surviving. Core presence allows the enaction of M-intentions and P-intentions only. Core presence in media is based largely on vividness of perceptible displays. This is equivalent to "sensory presence" and requires good quality, preferably stereographic, graphics and other displays.

The role of *extended presence* is to *verify the relevance to the self of possible/future events in the external world (self vs. possible/future external world)*. The more the self is able to forecast possible/future experiences, the more it will be able to identify relevant ones, increasing the possibility of surviving. Extended presence allows the enaction of M-intentions, P-intentions, and D-intentions. Following Sperber and Wilson's approach (Sperber and Wilson 1995), an input is relevant when its processing yields a positive cognitive effect, a worthwhile difference to the self's representation of the world. Extended presence requires intellectually and/or emotionally significant content. So, reality judgment influences the level of extended presence—a real event is more relevant than a fictitious one.

As underlined by Dillon and colleagues (2003), converging lines of evidence from different perspectives and methodologies support this three-layered view of presence. In their analysis, they identified three dimensions common to all the different perspectives: a "spatial" dimension (M-intentions), relating to how consistent the media experience is with the real world, "naturalness" (P-intentions), and an "engagement" dimension (D-intentions).

This view has two main consequences (Riva 2009). On the one hand, the role of the different layers will be related to the complexity of the activity done: the more complex the activity, the more layers will be needed to produce a high level of presence (Fig. 2.3). At the lower level—motor intention (e.g., grasping a ball)—proto presence is enough to induce a satisfying feeling of presence. At the higher level—distal intention (e.g., improving stress management)—the media experience has to support all three layers (e.g., allowing movement, *proto presence*; allowing interaction with the environment, *core presence*; giving a sense to the experience, *extended presence*).

On the other hand, subjects with different intentions will not experience the same level of presence, even when immersed in the same VE: This means that understanding and supporting the intentions of the user will improve his/her presence in a virtual world. Moreover, maximal presence is achieved when the environment is able to support the full intentional chain of the user.

2.5 Measuring Presence

As a consequence of the existence of a bidirectional relationship between presence and emotions, much research has also been done for the task of determining possibilities for reliable measurement of the concept. Approaching the concept from different perspectives, researchers have, as a consequence, developed different methods of measuring presence. These attempts are discussed here under two major types (for a full list of the different tools available check here: http://www.peachbit.org/?q=node/114): *subjective self-reports and objective measures*.

2.5.1 Subjective Measurements of Presence

To date, the majority of methods developed to measure presence have relied on subjective measurements using self-report. Subjective measures of presence include distinct forms of evaluation (Coelho et al.2006): *questionnaires* (e.g., from 1 to 10, what level of "being there" did this VE offer?); *paired comparative method* (e.g., which system offered more presence?); and *comparative method by similari-*

2.5 Measuring Presence

ties (e.g., put this light as bright as the strength of presence you have experimented in this VR system).

Postexperience questionnaires are the most frequently used measure of presence. Many different questionnaires have been developed depending on the author's conceptualization of presence and their context of application. Some studies have used only one general item addressing presence, while others have tried to develop questionnaires reflecting the multidimensional structure of presence presumed by the authors. The most used questionnaires are presented and discussed below.

Witmer and Singer (Witmer et al. 2005; Witmer and Singer 1998) developed and validated the *presence questionnaire* (PQ), which includes 29 items measured through a 7-point Likert scale, that measures presence after using a VR system via causal factors. The questionnaire has gained a significant level of acceptance and has been tested across a number of studies. A factor analysis suggested four subscales (Witmer et al. 2005):

- *Involvement, 12 items*: how the VR interface is natural to the user and facilitates the user's ability to control activities in the environment
- *Sensory fidelity, 6 items*: the perceived quality of the VR interface and the extent to which it does not interfere with activities in the VE
- *Adaptation/immersion, 8 items*: the perceived proficiency of interacting with and operating in the VE and how quickly the user adjust to the VE experience
- *Interface quality, 3 items*: the quality of the visual and control interfaces

The magnitudes of the correlations among the factors indicate moderately strong relationships among the four factors (Witmer et al. 2005). Within these relationships, sensory fidelity items seem to be more closely related to involvement, whereas interface quality items appear to be more closely related to adaptation/immersion, even though there is a moderately strong relationship between the involvement and adaptation/immersion factors. All four subscales measure user's perception of display system features.

A second well-known scale is the ITC-sense of presence inventory (ITC-SOPI). It is a state questionnaire measure that focuses on users' experiences of media, with no reference to objective system parameters (Lessiter et al. 2001). It has been translated in many languages and used in studies covering a wide range of media. The ITC-SOPI, including 44 items measured through a 5-point Likert scale, has four factors:

- *Sense of physical space, 19 items*: a sense of being located in a physical space depicted by the media system
- *Engagement, 13 items*: a sense of involvement with the narrative/content of the mediated environment
- *Ecological validity, 5 items*: a sense of naturalness and believability of the depiction of the environment itself and events within the environment
- *Negative effects, 6 items*: the negative experiences associated to an immersive media, such as eyestrain, headache, or sickness

A third popular scale is the igroup presence questionnaire (IPQ). It is a state questionnaire that describes presence as the outcome of two different components: spatial presence and involvement (Schubert et al. 2001). It has been translated in different languages and extensively used in VR studies. The IPQ, including 14 items measured through a 5-point Likert scale, has three factors:

- *Spatial presence, 5 items*: a sense of being located in the physical space created by the media system
- *Involvement, 4 items*: a sense of attention and engagement with the narrative/content of the mediated environment
- *Realness, 4 items*: a sense of naturalness and believability (reality judgment) of the VE itself and events within the environment

A final scale is the reality judgment and presence questionnaire (RJPQ). It is a state questionnaire designed to assess both presence and reality judgment (Baños et al. 2000). The RJPQ, including 18 items (there is also a longer version containing 77 items), measured through a 10-point scale (from 0 "not at all," to 10 "absolutely"), has three factors:

- *Reality judgment, eight items*: the realism attributed to the virtual experience
- *Internal/external correspondence, six items*: the ability of the subject in transforming intentions in actions within the virtual experience
- *Attention/absorption, four items*: the level of concentration, attention to a limited field of stimuli, and loss of a sense of the pass of time

Some researchers are also using very short presence scales based on three, two, or even a single item, both during and after the VR experience. For instance, Barfield and Weghorst (1993) used three items measured through a 10-point rating scale. Items address "the sense of being there," "the sense of inclusion in the virtual world," and "sense of presence in the virtual world." Later, Slater et al. (1994) adapted these items to address "the sense of being there," "the extent to which the VE becomes more real than reality," and "the extent to which the VE is thought of as a place visited." More recently, Bouchard and colleagues (2004) used a single item to evaluate the level of experienced presence.

The reliability of these brief measures of presence may be questioned. A few items do not fully address all the subtleties of the presence construct discussed in this chapter and, therefore, more items would probably be warranted. However, assessing users' subjective feeling while immersed, without distracting them too much, required the maximum reduction to the number of questions that could be asked. To paraphrase Wanous and Hudy (2001), research is now challenging the assumption that the reliability of single-item measures cannot be estimated and that, if it could be estimated, it would be unacceptably low. Bouchard et al. (2004) examined the test–retest reliability of a single-item measure of presence and found a test–retest of 0.81. and 0.83 when users were immersed in two different environments. The content, face validity, and sensitivity of the brief measure were also confirmed. Yet, studies are still needed to compare very short measures with the longer questionnaires presented before.

In order to subjectively assess presence, it is also possible to ask the participant to compare magnitudes in different modes. Sound and presence are sometimes used as an example. In this case, the subject elevates the amplitude of a sound to the level of presence he felt in the VR environment. Although this method has many methodological difficulties, it is considered to be an adequate quantitative measure of presence (Coelho et al. 2006).

A variant of the comparison method is the "break in presence" approach (Slater and Steed 2000). This approach is based on the idea that a participant experiencing VR technology interprets the stimuli coming from the environment as belonging either to the virtual or to the real world. Slater and Steed (2000) suggested that the participant switches between the two interpretations throughout the experience, and that a measure of presence could be obtained if the amount of time that the participant spent interpreting the stimuli coming from the virtual world could be estimated. They proposed to do this estimation by looking for "breaks"—those times when the participants realized they were in the real world. The main limitation of this approach is its oversimplification: It does not address the layered structure of presence discussed before. For example, it does not account for mixed perceptions where the participant simultaneously holds and even partially responds to both (real and virtual) interpretations, as noted by Spagnolli and Gamberini (2002, 2005).

2.5.2 Objective Presence Measurements

Studies in the general area of objective measurement are necessary to better describe the concept of presence instead of relying exclusively on verbal report, much like in the field of anxiety, where physiological, behavioral, and subjective responses are often measured.

Objective performance measures have the advantage of not interfering with the task. For this reason, many researchers are orienting their efforts towards physiological indices of presence (Meehan et al. 2002). Specifically, the use of different neurophysiologic responses like cardiac frequency, skin's electric conductance (galvanic skin response, GSR), reflex motor behaviors, and VR-event-evoked cortical responses were suggested as objective measures corroborative of presence. For example, Meehan and colleagues (2005) conducted four experiments to compare participants' physiological reactions to a nonthreatening virtual room and their reactions to a stressful virtual height situation. They found that change in heart rate was a reliable index of presence, significantly correlated with self-report questionnaires. Change in skin conductance did to a lesser extent, and that change in skin temperature did not.

However, when developing physiological measures of presence, one should not confound presence with emotions (e.g., when facing a virtual snake, an increase in heart rate would reflect fear, not presence) and one should look for similarities in physiological response to virtual and physical stimuli, not differences (e.g., differences in physiological responses or in electroencephalographic (EEG) patterns in reaction to a virtual and a physical snake would indicate that the illusion of nonmediation is incomplete).

Specifically, two cautions must be raised when using physiological measures. First, it is important not to confound presence and anxiety. As correctly noted by Meehan and colleagues (2005): "Although, change in heart rate satisfied the requirements for a presence measure for our VE, which evokes a strong reaction, it may not for less stressful VEs. To determine whether physiological reaction can more generally measure presence, a wider range of VEs must be tested, including less stressful, nonstressful, and relaxing environments" (pp. 253–254). Increases in heart rate or skin conductance are well-recognized measures of anxiety, not presence. They are signs of anxiety and, at best, proxy measures of presence in anxiety-related contexts. Thus, changes in these physiological parameters cannot be specifically associated with presence.

Second, in agreement with the vision of presence discussed before, we can argue that being totally present in a VE should be characterized by the *lack* of significant difference in physiological reaction when comparing a virtual and a physical situation. If the VR is completely perceived as real, then why should the immersion lead to a different physiological state than an *in vivo* experience? Following this line of reasoning, the search of a physiological marker of presence should mean comparing a mediated and a nonmediated experience and looking for physiological parameter that is specific to presence (i.e., not a proxy measure), but is not significantly different.

A difference in physiology on a specific marker of presence between the *in virtuo* and the *in vivo* experience should be the sign of a poor feeling of presence, not the opposite. This is much like looking for a needle in a haystack. Other innovative strategies to objectively assess presence have been developed, such as the fractal computations of eye-gaze behavior (Renaud et al. 2002, 2007).

The European project "PRESENCCIA—Presence: Research Encompassing Sensory Enhancement, Neuroscience, Cerebral-Computer Interfaces and Application" (http://www.presenccia.org) has tried to identify a neural and physiological characterization of presence. Specifically, the project carried out different psychophysiological and brain-imaging studies to identify the physiological and neuronal signatures associated with switches between different presence states. The key goal was to implement functional MRI (fMRI) experiments, using event-related designs, where the presence state (or switches in state of presence) is indexed by (1) phenomenological report from subjects and (2) a change in bodily state indexed by independent psychophysiological markers.

An outcome of this work is a paper recently published by Jäncke and colleagues (2009). The paper suggests that presence is associated with activation of a distributed network, which includes the dorsal and ventral visual stream, the parietal cortex, the premotor cortex, mesial temporal areas, the brainstem, and the thalamus. Moreover, the paper also suggests that the dorsolateral prefrontal cortex (DLPFC) is a key node of the network as it modulates the activity of the network and the associated experience of presence. In more detail (Baumgartner et al. 2008), the right DLPFC controlled the sense of presence by downregulating the activation in the egocentric dorsal visual processing stream, while the left DLPFC upregulated widespread areas of the medial prefrontal cortex known to be involved in self-reflective and stimulus-independent thoughts.

In a different fMRI study, Bouchard et al. (2010) tried to identify brain areas associated with presence. Clear and significant results were obtained in one specific region, the parahippocampal cortex. In 2008, Bar et al. (2008) published results showing that this area mediates the representation and processing of contextual associations. The parahippocampus provides contextual meaning of scenes and places. These results suggest that contextual processing is involved in determining where events are happening in a VE, or where the person is during the immersion in VR.

Multiple channels of communication link the DLPFC and the hippocampus via the parahippocampal gyrus, subiculum, presubiculum, and adjacent transitional cortices. Goldman-Rakic and colleagues (1984) argue that each of these prefrontal projections may carry highly specific information into the hippocampus, whereas the reciprocal projections may allow retrieval by prefrontal cortex of memories stored in the hippocampus.

A possible explanation of these data is that the parahippocampus is associated with proto presence, and more specifically, with the location, or *there*, portion of the concept, that is, the contextual meaning of the experience felt when being immersed in VR. On the other hand DLPFC may be associated with higher layers of presence—core presence and extended presence—that require integration of sensory and mnemonic information and the regulation of intellectual function and action. This may also explain why DLPFC is not activated in children's brain during a VR experience (Baumgartner et al. 2008).

2.6 Conclusions: Presence and Treatment Outcome

2.6.1 *Presence and Emotions*

One of the most important effects of presence for clinical practice is that a virtual experience may evoke the same reactions and emotions as a real experience. For instance, Slater and colleagues (2006) used VR to reproduce the Stanley Milgram's 1960s experimental approach: The participants were invited to administer a series of word association memory tests to a female virtual human (avatar) representing the stranger. When the avatar gave an incorrect answer, the participants were instructed to administer an "electric shock" to her, increasing the voltage each time. The avatar then responded with increasing discomfort and protests, eventually demanding termination of the experiment. Their results show that in spite of the fact that all participants knew for sure that neither the avatar nor the shocks were real, the participants who saw and heard her tended to respond to the situation at the subjective, behavioral, and physiological levels as if it were real. As noted by the researchers (Slater et al. 2006): "In the debriefing interviews many said that they were surprised by their own responses, and all said that it had produced negative feelings

– for some this was a direct feeling, in others it was mediated through a 'what if it were real?' feeling. Others said that they continually had to reassure themselves that nothing was really happening, and it was only on that basis that they could continue giving the shocks."

Experimental manipulations of emotions and presence have been conducted. Bouchard and colleagues (Bouchard et al. 2008) immersed adults suffering from snake phobia into a VE where anxiety was experimentally induced, or not, by manipulating the apprehension of the participants and keeping the content of the immersions identical. Using a single-item measure of presence, the results showed that presence was significantly higher when participants were anxious during the immersion than in the baseline or the nonanxious immersion.

Baños et al. (2005) compared the sense of presence between virtual and imaginary environments. Participants were randomly assigned to one of the two conditions (imagined vs. virtual spaces) and the subjective sense of presence was measured in three moments (beginning, middle, and end). Results showed that the participants in "imagery" spaces indicated a decrease of their sense of presence, whereas the opposite occurs in participants in "virtual" spaces.

Michaud et al. (2004) experimentally manipulated presence in a sample of heights phobics who had to take an elevator and perform tasks on a scaffold outside of a 15-story building. When the immersion in the VE was conducted in a high-presence setting, the level of anxiety was significantly higher than when the immersion was conducted in a low-presence setting.

Riva and colleagues (2007) also analyzed the possible use of VR as an affective medium, focusing on the relationship between presence and emotions. Their data showed a circular interaction between presence and emotions: While the feeling of presence was greater in the "emotional" environments, the emotional state was influenced by the level of presence. Taken together, these results, in agreement with the model presented before, underline the existence of a bidirectional relationship between presence and emotions.

As stated, the higher the presence, the higher the intensity of emotions the user experiences. Therefore, if the focus is on designing applications capable of eliciting emotions with the goal of reducing or modifying them (as in psychological therapy), the environments must be able to induce a high feeling of presence through a full support to the intentions of the user. However, the opposite could also be claimed: the higher the intensity of the emotions and feelings, the higher the presence and reality judgment. From this point of view, the focus for psychological treatment would lie on designing relevant environments, providing intellectually and/or emotionally significant content for the specific sample involved in the treatment. For instance, a recent study by Gorini and colleagues (2009) comparing a sample of 20 Mexican participants—8 living in El Tepeyac, a small rural and isolated Mexican village characterized by a very primitive culture, and 12 high-civilized inhabitants of Mexico City—clearly showed that VR exposure to a relaxing environment has different physiological and psychological effects according to the cultural and technological background of the users.

A study by Bouchard et al. (2006) studied presence using a VE designed to treat specific phobias (musophobia) with VR. Participants in both conditions were immersed in the same VE containing a rodent, yet in one condition they were deceived and led to believe that they were actually being immersed in real time in a physical room with a rodent. The deception used a blend of mixed videoconference-VR technologies, display of high-tech hardware relaying the videoconference and the VR computers, and false instructions stating that they were "currently live in the real room" or that they were "seeing a fake 3D copy of a room." Presence was significantly higher when participants were told they were seeing the "real" room that was being projected in the HMD in real time (Bouchard et al. 2006). This study confirmed the possibility of manipulating presence without changing any objective properties of the VE.

2.6.2 Presence and Exposure

According to Wiederhold and Wiederhold (1999, 2005, 2006), the quality of presence that is felt in the VE may be related to the efficacy of exposure-based treatment. This hypothesis is very appealing, especially since some people do not seem to react emotionally to VEs (e.g., Walshe et al. 2003). In order to relate presence and patient's emotional involvement in VR therapies, Wiederhold and Wiederhold (1999), starting from their clinical observations made during nearly 500 VR exposure therapy sessions with patients, affirmed that individuals receiving VR treatment should be classified into four functional groups.

The first subgroup exhibits high subjective and objective arousal to the VE. Such individuals are described as (Wiederhold and Wiederhold 1999): "highly phobic" and "capable of becoming highly immersed in the VR environment" (p. 163). The second subgroup of individuals evidences a high level of physiological arousal, but a low level of subjective arousal. These individuals may show significant decreases, for example, in autonomic arousal while not reporting any change in subjective discomfort (or may deny becoming anxious when exposed to virtual stimuli despite measurable increase in physiological arousal). A third subgroup evidences high levels of subjective arousal but objective indices of physiological arousal are nominal. Wiederhold and Wiederhold suggested this may occur in situations where the individual may have something to gain by inaccurately reporting his or her level of anxiety (e.g., secondary gain issues, if litigation is pending, and so forth). A fourth group, and one not often seen in treatment, includes individuals who are not able to immerse themselves in the virtual world. These participants do not report feeling present in the VE and do not benefit from *in virtuo* exposure, unless the therapist can help these participants moving into the first subgroup.

In sum, because individual patients exhibit wide variation in their responses to VEs, presence alone is not enough to guarantee a positive clinical outcome. This statement has been recently confirmed by different researches.

Price and Anderson (2007) explored the relation between presence, anxiety, and treatment outcome in a clinical study that used a virtual airplane to treat individuals with fear of flying. The results supported presence as a conduit that enabled phobic anxiety to be expressed during exposure to a VE. Nevertheless, presence was not supported as contributing to treatment outcome: Feeling present during exposure may be necessary, but not sufficient to achieve benefit from VR therapy. These results echoed findings from Krijn and colleagues (2004), who compared the efficacy of a highly immersive CAVE-like system and the less immersive but more affordable HMD technology. They reported more presence and more anxiety in the CAVE system, but no difference in treatment outcome.

These data do not mean that Wiederhold and Wiederhold's (2005) hypothesis that *"the efficacy of VR is related to the quality of presence"* (p. 77, italics added) is erroneous. Patients in the fourth subgroup of the Wiederhold's classification did not become present and did not feel any anxiety in VR. Their experience suggests instead that, at least for anxiety disorders, presence should be viewed as a moderator, not a mediator. Quero and colleagues (Quero et al. 2008) treated 107 phobics with *in virtuo* exposure and used a regression analysis to assess the relationship between change in fear/avoidance and presence. Considering the degree of fear and avoidance as dependent variables, in both cases they obtained as a predictor variable *the influence of the quality of the software in the reality judgment and presence*.

Their data suggest that the technology behind the virtual stimuli has to be "transparent" enough to enable the activation of the fear structure: a minimal level of presence is necessary to trigger the anxiety reaction. But for treatment outcome, what matters is to change the mental representations from threat to nonthreat. Once this threshold is passed, there is no direct effect of the level of presence on the efficacy of desensitization. Recently, Côté and Bouchard (2009) investigated the cognitive mechanisms associated with therapeutic change after a VR exposure treatment. The analyses showed that changes in perceived self-efficacy and dysfunctional beliefs were the best predictors of change.

References

Baños, R. M., Botella, C., García-Palacios, A., Villa, H., Perpiñá, C., & Alcañiz, M. (2000). Presence and reality judgment in virtual environments: A unitary construct? *Cyberpsychology & Behavior, 3*(3), 327–355.

Baños, R. M., Botella, C., Guerrero, B., Liaño, V., Alcañiz, M., & Rey, B. (2005). The third pole of the sense of presence: Comparing virtual and imagery spaces. *PsychNology Journal, 3*(1), 90–100. http://www.psychology.org/pnj103(101)_banos_botella_guerriero_liano_alcaniz_rey_abstract.html.

Baños, R. M., Botella, C., & Perpiña, C. (1999). Virtual reality and psychopathology. *Cyberpsychology & Behavior, 2*(4), 283–292.

Bar, M., Aminoff, E., & Schacter, D. L. (2008). Scenes unseen: The parahippocampal cortex intrinsically subserves contextual associations, not scenes or places per se. *Journal of Neuroscience, 28*(34), 8539–8544.

Barfield, W., & Weghorst, S. (1993). The sense of presence within virtual environments: A conceptual framework. In G. Salvendy & M. Smith (Eds.), *Human-computer interaction: Applications and case studies* (pp. 699–704). Amsterdam: Elsevier.

Barsalou, L. W. (2003). Situated simulation in the human conceptual system. *Language and Cognitive Processes, 18,* 513–562.

References

Baumgartner, T., Speck, D., Wettstein, D., Masnari, O., Beeli, G., & Jäncke, L. (2008). Feeling present in arousing virtual reality worlds: Prefrontal brain regions differentially orchestrate presence experience in adults and children. *Frontiers in Human Neuroscience, 2*(8). http://www.frontiersin.org/neuroscience/humanneuroscience/paper/10.3389/neuro.3309/3008.2008/.

Biocca, F. (1997). The Cyborg's Dilemma: Progressive embodiment in virtual environments. *Journal of Computer Mediated-Communication [Online], 3*(2). http://jcmc.indiana.edu/vol3/issue2/biocca2.html.

Biocca, F. (1999). The Cyborg's Dilemma: Progressive embodiment in virtual environments. In J. P. Marsh, B. Gorayska, & J. L. Mey (Eds.), *Humane interfaces: Questions of method and practice in cognitive technology* (pp. 113–142). Amsterdam: Elsevier.

Biocca, F., & Nowak, K. (2001). Plugging your body into the telecommunication system: Mediated embodiment, media interfaces, and social virtual environments. In D. Atkin & C. Lin (Eds.), *Communication Technology and Society* (pp. 407–447). Cresskill: Hampton Press.

Blackemore, S. J., & Decety, J. (2001). From the perception of action to the understanding of intention. *Nature Reviews Neuroscience, 2*, 561–567.

Bouchard, S., Dumoulin, S., Labonte-Chartrand, G., Robillard, G., & Renaud, P. (2006). Perceived realism has a significant impact on the feeling of presence. *Cyberpsychology & Behavior, 9*(6), 660.

Bouchard, S., Robillard, G., St-Jacques, J., Dumoulin, S., Patry, M. J., & Renaud, P. (2004). Reliability and validity of a single item measure of presence in VR. *IEEE International Workshop on Haptic Virtual Environments and Their Applications, 3*, 59–61.

Bouchard, S., St-Jacques, J., Robillard, G., & Renaud, L. (2008). Anxiety increases the feeling of presence in virtual reality. *Presence: Teleoperators & Virtual Environments, 17*(4), 376–391.

Bouchard, S., Talbot, J., Ledoux, A. A., Phillips, J., Cantamesse, M., & Robillard, G. (2010). Presence is just an illusion: Using fMRI to locate the brain area responsible to the meaning given to places. *Studies in Health Technology and Informatics, 154*, 193–196.

Burdea, G., Richard, P., & Coiffet, P. (1996). Multimodal virtual reality: Input–output devices, system integration, and human factors. *International Journal of Human Computer Interaction, 8*(1), 5–24.

Clark, A. (2008). *Supersizing the mind: Embodiment, action and cognitive extension.* Oxford: Oxford University Press.

Coelho, C., Tichon, J., Hine, T. J., Wallis, G., & Riva, G. (2006). Media presence and inner presence: The sense of presence in virtual reality technologies. In G. Riva, M. T. Anguera, B. K. Wiederhold, & F. Mantovani (Eds.), *From communication to presence: Cognition, emotions and culture towards the ultimate communicative experience. Festschrift in honor of Luigi Anolli* (pp. 25–45). Amsterdam: IOS Press. http://www.emergingcommunication.com/volume8.html.

Cote, S., & Bouchard, S. (2009). Cognitive mechanisms underlying virtual reality exposure. *Cyberpsychology and Behaviour, 12*(2), 121–129.

Csikszentmihalyi, M. (1975). *Beyond boredom and anxiety.* San Francisco: Jossey-Bass.

Csikszentmihalyi, M. (1990). *Flow: The psychology of optimal experience.* New York: Harper Collins.

Dillon, C., Freeman, J., & Keogh, E. (2003). *Dimension of presence and components of emotion.* Paper presented at the Presence 2003, Aalborg, Denmark.

Dinh, H. Q., Walker, N., Song, C., Kobayashi, A., & Hodges, L. F. (1999). *Evaluating the importance of multi-sensory input on memory and the sense of presence in virtual environments.* Paper presented at the IEEE Virtual Reality Conference 99.

Farné, A., Serino, A., & Làdavas, E. (2007). Dynamic size-change of perihand space following tool-use: Determinants and spatial characteristics revealed through cross-modal extinction. *Cortex; a journal devoted to the study of the nervous system and behavior, 43*, 436–443.

Fox, I. (1994). Our knowledge of the internal world. *Philosophical Topics, 22*, 59–106.

Gallese, V. (2005). Embodied simulation: From neurons to phenomenal experience. *Phenomenology and the Cognitive Sciences, 4*, 23–48.

Gallese, V., Fadiga, L., Fogassi, L., & Rizzolatti, G. (1996). Action recognition in the premotor cortex. *Brain, 119*, 593–609.

Gamberini, L., Seraglia, B., & Priftis, K. (2008). Processing of peripersonal and extrapersonal space using tools: Evidence from visual line bisection in real and virtual environments. *Neuropsychologia, 46*(5), 1298–1304.

Goldman-Rakic, P. S., Selemon, L. D., & Schwartz, M. L. (1984). Dual pathways connecting the dorsolateral prefrontal cortex with the hippocampal formation and parahippocampal cortex in the rhesus monkey. *Neuroscience, 12*(3), 719–743.

Gorini, A., Mosso, J. L., Mosso, D., Pineda, E., Ruiz, N. L., Ramiez, M., et al. (2009). Emotional response to virtual reality exposure across different cultures: The role of the attribution process. *Cyberpsychology & Behaviour, 12*(6), 699–705.

Gorini, A., Capideville, C. S., De Leo, G., Mantovani, F., & Riva, G. (2010). The role of immersion and narrative in mediated presence: The virtual hospital experience. *Cyberpsychology, Behavior and Social Networks.* doi:10.1089/cyber.2010.0100.

Heeter, C. (1992). Being there: The subjective experience of presence. *Presence: Teleoperators and Virtual Environments, 1*(2), 262–271.

Heidegger, M. (1959). *Unterwegs zur sprache.* Neske: Pfullingen.

Hommel, B., Müsseler, J., Aschersleben, G., & Prinz, W. (2001). The theory of event coding (TEC): A framework for perception and action planning. *Behavioral and Brain Sciences, 24*(5), 849–937.

IJsselsteijn, W. A., de Ridder, H., Freeman, J., & Avons, S. E. (2000). *Presence: Concept, determinants and measurement.* Paper presented at the Human Vision and Electronic Imaging V, San Jose, USA.

Jäncke, L., Cheetham, M., & Baumgartner, T. (2009). Virtual reality and the role of the prefrontal cortex in adults and children. *Frontiers in Neuroscience, 3*(1), 52–59.

Kaptelinin, V., & Nardi, B. (2006). *Acting with technology: Activity theory and interaction design.* Cambridge. MA: MIT Press.

Knoblich, G., Thornton, I., Grosjean, M., & Shiffrar, M. (Eds.). (2005). *Human body perception from the inside out.* New York: Oxford University Press.

Krijn, M., Emmelkamp, P. M., Olafsson, R. P., & Biemond, R. (2004). Virtual reality exposure therapy of anxiety disorders: A review. *Clinical Psychological Review, 24*(3), 259–281.

Lee, K. M. (2004a). Presence, explicated. *Journal of Communication, 14*, 27–50.

Lee, K. M. (2004b). Why presence occurs: Evolutionary psychology, media equation, and presence. *Presence, 13*(4), 494–505.

Leontjev, A. N. (1978). *Activity, consciousness, and personality.* Englewood: Prentice-Hall. http://marxists.org/archive/leontev/works/1978/ch3.htm.

Lessiter, J., Freeman, J., Keogh, E., & Davidoff, J. (2001). A cross-media presence questionnaire: The ITC-sense of presence inventory. *Presence: Teleoperators, and Virtual Environments, 10*(3), 282–297.

Lombard, M., & Ditton, T. (1997). At the heart of it all: The concept of presence. *Journal of Computer Mediated-Communication [Online], 3*(2). http://www.ascusc.org/jcmc/vol3/issue2/lombard.html.

Lombard, M., & Jones, M. T. (2006). *Defining presence.* Paper presented at the Presence 2006—The Ninth International Workshop on Presence, Cleveland, OH, USA.

Loomis, J. M. (1992). Distal attribution and presence. *Presence, Teleoperators, and Virtual Environments, 1*(1), 113–118.

Mantovani, G., & Riva, G. (1999). "Real" presence: How different ontologies generate different criteria for presence, telepresence, and virtual presence. *Presence, Teleoperators, and Virtual Environments, 8*(5), 538–548.

Mantovani, G., & Riva, G. (2001). Building a bridge between different scientific communities: On Sheridan's eclectic ontology of presence. *Presence: Teleoperators and Virtual Environments, 8,* 538–548.

Mantovani, G., & Spagnolli, A. (2000). Imagination and culture: What is it like being in the cyberspace? *Mind, Culture, & Activity, 7*(3), 217–226.

Marsh, T. (2003). Staying there: An activity-based approach to narrative design and evaluation as an antidote to virtual corpsing. In G. Riva, F. Davide, & W. A. IJsselsteijn (Eds.), *Being there:*

Concepts, effects and measurements of user presence in synthetic environments (pp. 85–96). Amsterdam: IOS Press.

Marsh, T., Wright, P., & Smith, S. (2001). Evaluation for the design of experience in virtual environments: Modeling breakdown of interaction and illusion. *Cyberpsychology & Behavior, 4*(2), 225–238.

Meehan, M., Insko, B., Whitton, M., & Brooks, F. P. (2002). Physiological measures of presence in stressful virtual environments. *ACM Transactions on Graphics, 21*(3), 645–652.

Meehan, M., Razzaque, S., Insko, B., Whitton, M., & Brooks, F. P. Jr. (2005). Review of four studies on the use of physiological reaction as a measure of presence in stressful virtual environments. *Applied Psychophysiology and Biofeedback, 30*(3), 239–258.

Metzinger, T. (2009). *The ego tunnel: The science of the mind and the myth of the self*. New York: Basic Books.

Michaud, M., Bouchard, S., Dumoulin, S., Zhong, X. W., & Renaud, P. (2004). Manipulating presence and its impact on anxiety. *Cyberpsychology & Behavior, 7*(3), 297–298.

Moore, K., Wiederhold, B. K., Wiederhold, M. D., & Riva, G. (2002). Panic and agoraphobia in a virtual world. *Cyberpsychology & Behavior, 5*(3), 197–202.

Morganti, F., & Riva, G. (2004). Ambient intelligence in rehabilitation. In G. Riva, F. Davide, F. Vatalaro, & M. Alcañiz (Eds.), *Ambient intelligence: The evolution of technology, communication and cognition towards the future of the human-computer interaction* (pp. 283–295). Amsterdam: IOS Press. http://www.emergingcommunication.com/volume6.html.

Pacherie, E. (2006). Toward a dynamic theory of intentions. In S. Pockett, W. P. Banks & S. Gallagher (Eds.), *Does consciousness cause behavior?* (pp. 145–167). Cambridge: MIT Press.

Pacherie, E. (2008). The phenomenology of action: A conceptual framework. *Cognition, 107*(1), 179–217.

Perez-Marcos, D., Slater, M., & Sanchez-Vives, M. V. (2009). Inducing a virtual hand ownership illusion through a brain-computer interface. *Neuroreport, 20*(6), 589–594.

Price, M., & Anderson, P. (2007). The role of presence in virtual reality exposure therapy. *Journal of Anxiety and Disorders, 21*(5), 742–751.

Quero, S., Salvador, S., Baños, R. M., Garcia-Palacios, A., Botella, C., & Serrano, B. (2008). *Components of presence and reality judgment as predictors of treatment efficacy*. Paper presented at the Presence 2009, Padova, Italy.

Renaud, P., Bouchard, S., & Proulx, R. (2002). Behavioral avoidance dynamics in the presence of a virtual spider. *IEEE Transactions on Information Technology in Biomedicine, 6*(3), 235–243.

Renaud, P., Chartier, S., Albert, G., Décarie, J., Cournoyer, L., & Bouchard, S. (2007). Presence as determined by fractal perceptual-motor dynamics. *Cyberpsychology & Behavior, 10*(1), 122–130.

Revonsuo, A. (2006). *Inner presence, consciousness as a biological phenomenon*. Cambridge: MIT Press.

Riva, G. (2004). The psychology of ambient intelligence: Activity, situation and presence. In G. Riva, F. Davide, F. Vatalaro, & M. Alcañiz (Eds.), *Ambient intelligence: The evolution of technology, communication and cognition towards the future of the human-computer interaction* (pp. 19–34). Amsterdam: IOS Press. http://www.emergingcommunication.com/volume6.html.

Riva, G. (2006). Being-in-the-world-with: Presence meets social and cognitive neuroscience. In G. Riva, M. T. Anguera, B. K. Wiederhold, & F. Mantovani (Eds.), *From communication to presence: Cognition, emotions and culture towards the ultimate communicative experience. Festschrift in honor of Luigi Anolli* (pp. 47–80). Amsterdam: IOS Press. http://www.emergingcommunication.com/volume8.html.

Riva, G. (2008). From virtual to real body: Virtual reality as embodied technology. *Journal of Cybertherapy and Rehabiliation, 1*(1), 7–22.

Riva, G. (2009). Is presence a technology issue? Some insights from cognitive sciences. *Virtual Reality, 13*(3), 59–69.

Riva, G. (2010). Dall'intenzione, all'azione, all'interazione: Il ruolo di "presenza" e "presenza sociale". In F. Morganti, A. Carassa, & G. Riva (Eds.), *Intersoggettivitã e interazione: Un dialogo fra scienze cognitive, scienze sociali e neuroscienze* (pp. 136–177). Torino: Bollati Boringhieri.

Riva, G. (2011). Presence, actions and emotions: A theoretical framework. *Annual Review of CyberTherapy and Telemedicine, 9*, 2–5.

Riva, G., & Davide, F. (Eds.). (2001). *Communications through virtual technologies: Identity, community and technology in the communication age.* Amsterdam: IOS Press. http://www.emergingcommunication.com/volume1.html.

Riva, G., & Mantovani, F. (2012). From the body to the tools and back: A general framework for presence in mediated interactions. *Interacting with Computers.* doi:10.1016/j.intcom.2012.1004.1007.

Riva, G., Davide, F., & IJsselsteijn, W. A. (Eds.). (2003). *Being there: Concepts, effects and measurements of user presence in synthetic environments.* Amsterdam: IOS Press. http://www.emergingcommunication.com/volume5.html.

Riva, G., Loreti, P., Lunghi, M., Vatalaro, F., & Davide, F. (2003). Presence in 2010: The emergence of ambient intelligence. In G. Riva, F. Davide, & W. A. IJsselsteijn (Eds.), *Being there: Concepts, effects and measurements of user presence in synthetic environments* (pp. 59–82). Amsterdam: IOS Press.

Riva, G., Waterworth, J. A., & Waterworth, E. L. (2004). The layers of presence: A bio-cultural approach to understanding presence in natural and mediated environments. *Cyberpsychology & Behavior, 7*(4), 405–419.

Riva, G., Mantovani, F., Capideville, C. S., Preziosa, A., Morganti, F., Villani, D., et al. (2007). Affective interactions using virtual reality: The link between presence and emotions. *Cyberpsychology and Behavior, 10*(1), 45–56.

Riva, G., Waterworth, J. A., Waterworth, E. L., & Mantovani, F. (2011). From intention to action: The role of presence. *New Ideas in Psychology, 29*(1), 24–37.

Rizzolatti, G., Fadiga, L., Gallese, V., & Fogassi, L. (1996). Premotor cortex and the recognition of motor actions. *Cognitive Brain Research, 3*, 131–141.

Russell, J. A. (1996). *Agency: Its role in mental development.* Hove: Erlbaum.

Sadowski, W. J., & Stanney, K. M. (2002). Measuring and managing presence in virtual environments. In K. M. Stanney (Ed.), *Handbook of virtual environments technology.* Mahwah: Lawrence Erlbaum Associates.

Schloerb, D. (1995). A quantitative measure of telepresence. *Presence: Teleoperators, and Virtual Environments, 4*(1), 64–80.

Schubert, T., Friedman, F., & Regenbrecht, H. (2001). The experience of presence: Factor analytic insights. *Presence: Teleoperators, and Virtual Environments, 10*(3), 266–281.

Searle, J. (1983). *Intentionality: An essay in the philosophy of mind.* New York: Cambridge University Press.

Sheridan, T. B. (1992). Musing on telepresence and virtual presence. *Presence, Teleoperators, and Virtual Environments, 1*, 120–125.

Sheridan, T. B. (1996). Further musing on the psychophysics of presence. *Presence, Teleoperators, and Virtual Environments, 5*, 241–246.

Sirigu, A., Grafman, J., Bressler, K., & Sunderland, T. (1991). Multiple representations contribute to body knowledge processing: Evidence from a case of autotopagnosia. *Brain: a journal of neurology, 114*(1), 629–642.

Slater, M., & Steed, A. (2000). A virtual presence counter. *Presence: Teleoperators, and Virtual Environments, 9*(5), 413–434.

Slater, M., Steed, A., & Chrysanthou, Y. (2002). *Computer graphics and virtual environments: From realism to real-time.* Harlow, Essex: Pearson

Slater, M., Antley, A., Davison, A., Swapp, D., Guger, C., Barker, C., et al. (2006). A virtual reprise of the Stanley Milgram obedience experiments. *PLoS One, 1*, e39.

Slater, M., Perez-Marcos, D., Ehrsson, H. H., & Sanchez-Vives, M. V. (2009). Inducing illusory ownership of a virtual body. *Frontiers in Neuroscience, 3*(2), 214–220.

Slater, M., Usoh, M., & Steed, A. (1994). Depth of presence in virtual environments. *Presence: Teleoperators and Virtual Environments, 1*(3), 130–144.

References

Spagnolli, A., & Gamberini, L. (2002). *Immersion/emersion: Presence in hybrid environments*. Paper presented at the Presence 2002: Fifth Annual International Workshop, 9–11 October, Porto, Portugal.

Spagnolli, A., & Gamberini, L. (2005). A place for presence. Understanding the human involvement in mediated interactive environments. *Psychology Journal, 3*(1), 6–15. http://www.psychology.org/article801.htm.

Spagnolli, A., Gamberini, L., & Gasparini, D. (2003). Situated breakdown analysis for the evaluation of a virtual environment. *Psychology Journal, 1*(1). http://www.psychology.org/File/PSYCHOLOGY_JOURNAL_1_1_SPAGNOLLI.pdf.

Sperber, D., & Wilson, D. (1995). *Relevance: Communication and cognition* (2nd ed.). Oxford: Blackwell.

Walshe, D. G., Lewis, E. J., Kim, S. I., O'Sullivan, K., & Wiederhold, B. K. (2003). Exploring the use of computer games and virtual reality in exposure therapy for fear of driving following a motor vehicle accident. *Cyberpsychology & Behaviour, 6*(3), 329–334.

Wanous, J. P., & Hudy, M. J. (2001). Single-item reliability: A replication and extension. *Organizational Research Methods, 4*(4), 361–375.

Waterworth, J. A., & Waterworth, E. L. (2001). Focus, locus, and sensus: The three dimensions of virtual experience. *Cyberpsychology and Behavior, 4*(2), 203–213.

Waterworth, J. A., & Waterworth, E. L. (2003). The meaning of presence. *Presence-Connect, 3*(2). http://presence.cs.ucl.ac.uk/presenceconnect/articles/Feb2003/jwworthFeb1020031217/jwworthFeb1020031217.html.

Waterworth, E. L., Häggkvist, M., Jalkanen, K., Olsson, S., Waterworth, J. A., & H., W. (2003). The exploratorium: An environment to explore your feelings. *Psychology Journal, 1*(3), 189–201. http://www.psychology.org/File/PSYCHOLOGY_JOURNAL_181_183_WATERWORTH.pdf.

Waterworth, J. A., Waterworth, E. L., Mantovani, F., & Riva, G. (2010). On feeling (the) present: An evolutionary account of the sense of presence in physical and electronically-mediated environments. *Journal of Consciousness Studies, 17*(1–2), 167–178.

Waterworth, J. A., Waterworth, E. L., Mantovani, F., & Riva, G. (2012). Special issue: Presence and interaction. *Interacting with Computer*. doi:10.1016/j.intcom.2012.1005.1003.

Wiederhold, B. K., & Wiederhold, M. D. (1999). Clinical observations during virtual reality therapy for specific phobias. *Cyberpsychology & Behavior, 2*(2), 161–168.

Wiederhold, B. K., & Wiederhold, M. D. (2005). *Virtual reality therapy for anxiety disorders: Advances in evaluation and treatment*. Washington, DC: American Psychological Association.

Wiederhold, B. K., & Wiederhold, M. D. (2006). Communication and experience in clinical psychology and neurorehabilitation: The use of virtual reality driving simulators. In G. Riva, M. T. Anguera, B. K. Wiederhold, & F. Mantovani (Eds.), *From communication to presence: Cognition, emotion and culture towards the ultimate communicative experience* (pp. 262–275). Amsterdam: IOS Press. http://www.emergingcommunication.com/volume8.html.

Wilson, M., & Knoblich, G. (2005). The case for motor involvement in perceiving conspecifics. *Psychological Bulletin, 131*(3), 460–473.

Witmer, B. G., & Singer, M. J. (1998). Measuring presence in virtual environments: A presence questionnaire. *Presence: Teleoperators & Virtual Environments, 7*(3), 225–240.

Witmer, B. G., Jerome, C. J., & Singer, M. J. (2005). The factor structure of the presence questionnaire. *Presence: Teleoperators & Virtual Environments, 14*(3), 298–312.

Youngblut, C. (2007). *D-3411: What a decade of experiments reveals about factors that influence the sense of presence: Latest findings*. Alexandria: Institute for Defense Analysis.

Zahoric, P., & Jenison, R. L. (1998). Presence as being-in-the-world. *Presence, Teleoperators, and Virtual Environments, 7*(1), 78–89.

Chapter 3
Sickness in Virtual Reality

Sarah Sharples, Gary Burnett and Sue Cobb

3.1 Introduction

This book demonstrates the potential of VR in a number of contexts, and in particular, the treatment of anxiety disorders. However, since the 1990s, it has been observed that there may be some unintended consequences, or side effects, of using VR technologies in a variety of forms. This needs to be carefully considered if VR is to be widely implemented as a treatment or therapy—if there are unintended consequences, then users must be clearly informed of risks, and trained in methods to minimise their occurrence and prevalence; therapists must understand the indicators that suggest that a participant is experiencing side-effects; and the system should be designed to limit negative effects, whilst not compromising the intended therapeutic effects of VR use.

The most commonly observed immersion side effect of VR use has been sickness, sometimes termed "cybersickness". This chapter provides an overview of work that has examined the nature of these effects, their causes and prevalence, and, critically for the implementation of VR for treatment of anxiety, how to minimise their impact on the effectiveness of implemented VR systems.

3.1.1 Introduction to Simulator Sickness and VR-related Side Effects

The concept of simulator sickness has been observed and studied for many years in the context of flight simulation (Kennedy et al. 1992). Since the early 1990s, work in the area of virtual reality (VR) and virtual environment (VE) has examined the nature of the unintended side effects that may result from using these new and continually developing technologies and systems. Of these, sickness-type symptoms have been most often noted (Nichols et al. 1997; Sharples et al. 2008), but other effects to have been observed include postural instability (Cobb and Nichols 1998; Smart et al. 2002; Stoffregen and Smart 1998; Stoffregen et al. 2000) and visual fatigue (Kuze and Ukai 2008). The collection of effects experienced when using

VR systems was described by Cobb et al. (1999) as including a variety of effects that could be considered both "negative" (such as sickness or fatigue), "positive" (such as enjoyment or transfer of training) as well as effects that can be either positive or negative, depending on the context. For example, an increase in heart rate could be positive if an indicator of arousal resulting from enjoyment of a game or negative if associated with experiencing unintended stress or panics (Nichols and Patel 2002). It is reasonable to expect that positive effects will usually be the *intended* experience resulting from use of VR applications, particularly where the purpose of use is geared towards a beneficial outcome (for example, improving patient mobility in a physical VR rehabilitation task or assisting a person in returning to driving following involvement in a major road traffic accident). Incidental positive experiences may serve to enhance or support the intended positive effect (e.g. if patients find the VR activity fun to do, they will be more motivated to use the application). As an emerging technology, one that comprises a range of hardware of software elements, including the facility to fully or partially immerse a viewer, there is potential for users to experience a variety of negative effects including sickness, disorientation, visual fatigue and physical discomfort. These *unintended* effects of using immersive VR are the focus of this chapter and they will collectively be described as "exposure side effects". However, sickness remains the most widely researched of these effects, and therefore provides the focus for the rest of this chapter.

Stanney and Kennedy (2009) conclude, after reviewing work from a range of authors, that 80–95 % of participants will experience some level of unintended side effects when viewing a VE via a head-mounted display (HMD). Our own research has investigated a range of methods of presentation of VEs, including projection technologies, and suggests that 60–70 % of participants experience an increase in sickness symptoms from pre–post use (Sharples et al. 2008). For *early* VR systems, we found that for exposures of around 20–30 min, about 5 % of participants experienced symptoms so severe that they asked to drop out of their period of VR use (Cobb et al. 1999; see also page 110 and Bouchard et al. 2009 for more information relevant to people suffering from anxiety disorders). It is worth noting that exposure side effects are due to a variety of causes including individual susceptibility, aspects of the VE design and user activities performed, and size and weight of VR hardware used, and so changes in computing technology and user experiences of three dimensional (3D), interactive and immersive games may result in a change of prevalence of reported symptoms and side effects over time. For example, a study of user experience in a locomotion task in an immersive VE indicated that textured visual scenes resulted in a higher incidence of sickness than less complex images (Jaeger and Mourant 2001); these authors suggest that this effect could diminish as the quality of computer graphics improves. It is likely that some exposure side effects are either partially or completely influenced by the characteristics of technology (e.g. lag in display update or low resolution) and thus may reduce with advances in technology. However, as will be discussed later in this chapter, the fundamental conflict between the visual and vestibular senses remains, and, if sensory conflict theory is the primary causative mechanism of sickness symptoms, then these will occur even with continuing developments in technology quality and capability.

3.1 Introduction

Whilst the role of the display used to present the VE clearly affects the effects experienced, it is important to note that sickness symptoms are not only found in 3D HMD or projection type displays. Ujike et al. (2008) report on an incident where 36 out of 294 Junior High School students in Japan were treated in hospital for motion sickness symptoms after viewing a 20-min video shot using a hand-held video camera and displayed on a school projection screen.

The theory most often used to explain the occurrence of sickness is sensory conflict theory (Reason and Brand 1975). The following section provides a brief outline of this theory, summarises its application to VR and considers other theories that have been proposed to explain the experience of sickness when using a VE.

3.1.2 Sensory Conflict Theory

A number of theories have been proposed to explain the cause of motion sickness symptoms since they were first noted on sea voyages hundreds of years ago. It is generally accepted that an intact vestibular system is required in order for motion sickness to be experienced (Bos et al. 2008; Bouyer and Watt 1996). Reason and Brand (1975) report that between 1945 and 1960, the dominant theory was that motion sickness was caused by an excessive stimulation of the vestibular system (vestibular "overstimulation" theory). However, the observation of visually induced motion sickness (e.g. Benfari 1964) in simulators and large screen cinemas, implicated the involvement of the visual system in the production of sickness symptoms.

The most widely accepted theory of motion sickness that has been applied to simulator and VR use is sensory conflict theory (Groen and Bos 2008; Nichols and Patel 2002; Reason and Brand 1975; Stanney and Kennedy 2009). Simulator sickness is a specific type of motion sickness which is primarily visually induced (Hettinger and Riccio 1992). Whilst the main symptoms of motion sickness tend to be nausea, vomiting and retching, and extreme drowsiness in the case of sea sickness, other symptoms such as pallor, sweating, salivation, apathy, headache, stomach awareness, disorientation, blurred vision, postural instability and residual after-effects tend to be more prominent in people experiencing simulator sickness (Kennedy et al. 1992).

Sensory conflict theory proposes that symptoms occur as a result of conflict between signals received by the three major spatial senses—the visual system, the vestibular system and non-vestibular proprioception. The two pairs of conflicting receptors proposed are (Reason and Brand 1975):

1. **Visual–inertial conflict** where discrepancies exist between the sense modalities of vision and both the vestibular senses and non-vestibular proprioceptors.
2. **Canal–otolith conflict** where conflict occurs within the vestibular system, between the otoliths, which signal the head's position with relation to gravitational force, and the canals which sense angular movement of the head, and are unaffected by gravity.

Three types of conflict can occur within these pairings:

- **Type I**: When A and B simultaneously signal contradictory or uncorrelated information
- **Type II**: When A signals in the absence of an expected B signal
- **Type III**: When B signals in the absence of an expected A signal

Kennedy et al. (1992) suggested that the strong similarities between flight simulators and VEs should lead to the same types of problems experienced in simulators being seen in

> any VE in which a compelling sense of presence and self-motion throughout the simulated environment are experienced by the user. Kennedy et al. (1992)

On the basis of this, it can be assumed that as different types and qualities of VR system may actually produce different levels of presence and self-motion, different levels and types of sensory conflict may be experienced. Groen and Bos (2008) extend this thought, proposing that simulator sickness profiles may be affected by the motion frequency in a driving simulator and Stanney and Kennedy (2009) summarise a number of factors that affect simulator stimulus intensity, including rate of visual flow, number of degrees of freedom (DOF) of movement control and field of view.

It may be the case, however, that VR-induced sickness cannot be accounted for by any single one of the types of conflict suggested by Reason and Brand's (1975) model of sensory-conflict patterns. Instead, there is a combination of type II and type III visual–inertial conflict. Type II conflict, where visual information which is not backed up by corresponding vestibular information provided, occurs during any movement which is controlled by a device which does not provide any feedback to the vestibular system. In the use of VR systems, this usually occurs when the user experiences vection (perceived self-motion induced by visual stimuli) during forwards and backwards movement (or ascending and descending movement), which is primarily controlled by use of a 3D mouse. However, the extent of physical movement possible in VR systems varies considerably depending on the set up—in some VR systems, the user may have freely tracked movement, whereas in others, that movement may be more restricted. Findings from Suma et al. (2009) appear to contradict the implied prediction from this, where higher sickness was found in a "natural" walking condition compared with gaze-directed simulated walking—in other words, the condition with the larger vestibular input, which would be expected to have a lower level of conflict, elicited a higher level of symptoms.

In contrast, type III conflict occurs when the head is moved (i.e. vestibular information is provided), but the expected visual information is not instantly provided to back up the changes in the vestibular system due to the lag in response of the visual display.

A VR user will also receive input to the proprioceptive senses. Proprioception is defined as

> a general term used to cover all those sensory systems that are involved in providing information about position, location, and orientation and movement of the body (and its parts).

3.1 Introduction

The two primary groups of proprioceptors are those in the vestibular system of the inner ear, and the kinaesthetic and cutaneous systems (collectively, the somatosenses). Reber (1985)

A condition unique to VR occurs when the information given by the proprioceptive senses with respect to the position of the hand with relation to the body may not tally with that given by the image of the virtual hand on the HMD display. For example, the restricted field of view means that a user has to be directly looking at their hand to see it, and the apparent reach distance of the user may be different to the actual reach distance normally experienced. Therefore, it can be seen that rather than the information from each of the systems actually conflicting, it tends to be the case that there are shortcomings in the signals so the magnitude of each type of signal from the spatial senses is different to that which would normally be expected. This does still, however, result in the conflict between expectation and reality, which produces symptoms of sickness.

Sensory conflict theory also explains the phenomenon of adaptation. Adaptation describes the fact that

> prolonged exposure to any one type of provocative stimulus leads to a diminution and eventual disappearance of the signs and symptoms in most people ... without any alteration in the properties of the provocative stimulus. Reason and Brand (1975)

This is explained by the change in expectation as the user becomes accustomed to the new pattern of sensory conflict and any change in behaviour or response required. If adaptation is completed successfully, then symptoms may be encountered on return to the original environment. One example of this is the *mal de debarquement*—the feeling of unsteadiness and postural disorientation experienced by passengers on stepping ashore after long sea voyages (Reason and Brand 1975).

However, the sensory conflict theory has been criticised, leading to the proposal of new theories. McCauley and Sharkey (1992) report that sensory conflict theory succeeds more in post hoc explanation than in predictive power. They suggest that stimulation of electrical activity in the vestibular nuclei, the specific role of vection (e.g. Bonato et al. (2009)), or the "poison hypothesis", referring to the notion that an effect of poisons involves disturbed coordination of sensory inputs, may be involved in the causation of VR-induced sickness symptoms. This last suggestion in particular is more difficult to apply to VE use— the assumption is that the lack of coordination between sensory inputs is physiologically interpreted as a sign that poison has been ingested and sickness symptoms therefore occur.

Gary Riccio and Thomas Stoffregen have criticised the sensory conflict theory more severely (Riccio and Stoffregen 1991; Stoffregen and Riccio 1991). They argue on an ecological basis that the sensory conflict theory would require a highly specialised neural subsystem specifically devoted to the generation of motion sickness. The reason such a specialised system would be required is to recognise the vast number of situations that occur where sensory conflict, but not sickness, occurs (e.g. the conflict between separate images from each eye is used as information in stereopsis rather than a cue for motion sickness). In addition, situations where a novel combination of sensory inputs is encountered do not always lead to sickness—questioning the role of expectancy in sensory conflict theory.

These issues led Riccio and Stoffregen (1991) to present an ecological theory of motion sickness. They claimed:

> Motion sickness results from prolonged instability in the control of posture. [Ecological theory] is a claim about behaviour rather than sensory stimulation. Riccio and Stoffregen (1991)

Postural control strategies take into account both changing environmental conditions and the goals of behaviour. Postural stability is also proposed to be a necessary precursor to sickness, with prolonged instability producing a greater likelihood and intensity of symptoms than a short moment of instability (such as a sudden fall). More recent work (Bonnet et al. 2008) has obtained additional data to support this theory.

Warwick-Evans and Beaumont (1995) attempted to experimentally compare the sensory conflict and ecological theories of motion sickness. This involved showing two speeds of videotape of a walk round campus to participants. Participant movement was restricted whilst viewing the video. Sensory conflict would predict that the higher speed video would lead to more conflict therefore more sickness. Ecological theory would predict that postural instability preceded sickness. However, there were few signs of postural instability, although motion sickness symptoms were widespread. Moreover, a greater number of symptoms were observed in the normal viewing condition than in the fast viewing condition, so no conclusive evidence for either theory was obtained.

Finally, Kennedy et al. (1995) note that an additional problem is the experience of fatigue symptoms. These may occur after other symptoms have dissipated and therefore have implications for post-immersion activities. This is similar to the concept of "Sopite Syndrome" that has been noted in sea travellers (Kennedy et al. 1995). Kennedy et al. (1995) examined the individual symptoms of drowsiness and fatigue in a quantitative meta-analysis of data from a population of simulator users and found that nearly 50% experienced these sopite symptoms. This result indicated that these effects can result from visual stimulation alone, and that vestibular stimulation is not required, as had been previously thought. These findings raise the possibility that drowsiness as a result of VR use could be a problem.

The theory of sensory conflict, and its derivatives, still dominates the literature and provides the basis of most analysis of incidence of sickness symptoms associated with VR use. The remainder of this chapter assumes that sensory conflict, notwithstanding its limitations, provides the basis for understanding of causation of sickness. Furthermore, the chapter considers in detail how we can measure sickness, influential factors on sickness and appropriate strategies for management of sickness.

3.2 Measuring Sickness

Both objective and subjective measures can be used to measure levels of simulator sickness. Some research has applied physiological monitoring techniques, including use of EEG measurement (Park et al. 2008), blood pressure and heart rate

(Sugita et al. 2008). Measurement of postural stability has also been applied (e.g. Cobb and Nichols (1998), but the most frequently applied measures are subjective report tools, in particular the simulator sickness questionnaire (SSQ) (Kennedy et al. 1993).

3.2.1 Simulator Sickness Questionnaire (Kennedy et al. 1993)

The SSQ was derived from the Pensacola Motion Sickness Questionnaire (MSQ) developed to study motion sickness from a previously used MSQ. The original questionnaire included 25–30 symptoms identified as being associated with or predictive of motion sickness onset, and providing a measure of degree of severity of experience of the sickness. However, Kennedy and colleagues noted distinct differences between the experience of simulator sickness and motion sickness (notably the lower severity and prevalence of simulator sickness, and the different symptom profiles associated with this). It was also noted that simulator sickness was polygenic and polysymptomatic, and that any measure should accommodate this (Kennedy and Fowlkes 1992). Thus, a new tool was developed to measure this phenomenon. From a set of factor analyses, three sub-factors and a general factor were identified. A scoring method was also devised to ensure that participants experiencing no symptoms had a score of 0, and that the standard deviation of scores was 15 (these data were based on a sample of 1200 simulator users). It is important to note that Bouchard et al. (2007, 2011) commented that the SSQ factors were originally derived with a military population, and in their own examination of factors found evidence for two distinct (with no cross-loading) factors of nausea and disorientation. Table 3.1 shows the factors identified in the original development of the SSQ (Kennedy et al. 1993).

This divides symptom scores into three subscales—symptoms associated with feelings of nausea and related neurovegetative problems, oculomotor disturbances and disorientation, ataxia and vertigo (Kennedy and Drexler 1994). The consistent use of the SSQ across a range of research studies allows profiles from different systems and technologies to be compared.

The SSQ produces a profile of symptoms that shows the relative prominence of each of the three types of symptoms—comparison of profiles can be used to examine the nature of different types of sickness and provide evidence about the potential causative influences on sickness. For example, if oculomotor symptoms were observed to predominate, it might be assumed that there were problems with the visual presentation of stimuli.

However, McCauley and Sharkey (1992) point out a number of problems with measuring motion sickness, including the variety of symptoms experienced, the fact that symptomatology is internal, non-observable and subjective, the large individual differences in symptom profiles and general susceptibility and the fact that a constellation of symptoms develops over time periods ranging from a few minutes to several hours. In addition, it is important to screen participants in some way before exposure to VR stimuli, to allow clear inference that any symptoms measured on

Table 3.1 Factors associated with simulator sickness (Kennedy et al. 1993)

SSQ symptom	Weight		
	Nausea	Oculomotor	Disorientation
General discomfort	1	1	
Fatigue		1	
Headache		1	
Eyestrain		1	
Difficulty focusing		1	1
Increased salivation	1		
Sweating	1		
Nausea	1		1
Difficulty concentrating	1	1	
Fullness of head			1
Blurred vision		1	1
Dizzy (eyes open)			1
Dizzy (eyes closed)			1
Vertigo			1
Stomach awareness	1		
Burping	1		
TOTAL	[1]	[2]	[3]
Score			
$N = [1] \times 9.54$			
$O = [2] \times 7.58$			
$D = [3] 13.92$			
$TS = [1] + [2] + [3] \times 3.74$			

the SSQ post exposure are due to the VR treatment alone and not any pre-existing levels of discomfort.

These concerns, along with our own desire to develop a deeper understanding of the patterns of development of symptoms for users of VEs, led us to develop a shorter tool—the short symptoms checklist (SSC) (Nichols et al. 1997).

3.2.2 Short Symptoms Checklist (Nichols 1999; Nichols et al. 1997)

The SSC was intended to be a shorter version of the SSQ, incorporating the variety of symptoms that contribute to simulator sickness, but which would only take about 30 s to verbally administer, and therefore could be used as a continuous monitoring tool.

Six symptoms were selected—these were chosen to reflect the different aspects of VR-induced sickness. The six symptoms were:

- Headache
- Eyestrain
- Blurred vision
- Dizziness (eyes open)

3.2 Measuring Sickness

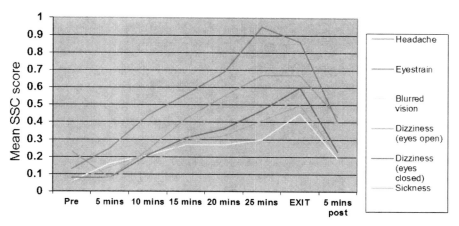

Fig. 3.1 SSC results for a participant sample ($N=79$) who experienced a 30 min period of use of a HMD based VR system (scale from 0 = no symptom at all to 10 = unbearable level of symptom)

- Dizziness (eyes closed)
- Sickness

In early versions of the tool, responses were made on an ordinal scale—1 = not at all, 2 = slightly, 3 = moderately, 4 = definitely, 5 = severely—but in later versions, this was revised to an 11-point numerical scale, with the anchors of 0 = not at all, 10 = unbearable level of symptom.

This use of the tool provides the potential to yield a large set of data which can be classified along four dimensions:

- Time of symptom occurrence
- Type of symptom
- Severity of symptom
- Number of people experiencing the symptoms

However, of course, the use of the checklist *during* a period of VR use may distract the user, and affect their experience with the technology, potentially inducing a "break in presence" (Slater 2002).

Figure 3.1 shows an example of the data elicited using the SSC over an entire experimental sample, and Fig. 3.2 shows data obtained from participants who exited a period of VR use early. Although the mean scores demonstrate that overall the level of symptoms experienced is low, the trend of increasing symptom level over time is apparent. In addition, the higher mean level of symptoms experienced by those participants who experienced symptoms so severe that they asked for their period of exposure to be ended is apparent.

Administration of the SSC allowed us to monitor the sickness symptoms of a large set of participants over a series of trials conducted over several years. We now tend to use this tool when we are concerned that an exposure may be particularly likely to provoke symptoms, and use it to monitor symptom levels—our informal

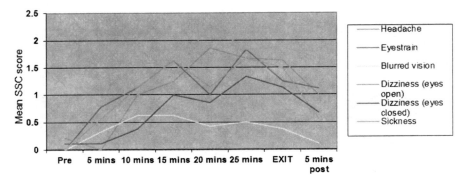

Fig. 3.2 SSC scores for participants who exited early ($N=9$, one participant exited after 6 min; the other eight exited between 19–28.5 min)

"rule of thumb" is that any participant who reports a symptom level of 4 on any SSC subscale is likely to be experiencing reasonably uncomfortable levels of symptoms and is important to monitor closely and perhaps specifically enquire as to whether they are happy to continue; whilst it is acknowledged that this may predispose participants to report or introspect on their symptom levels, it is felt by our research team that for such levels of symptoms, it is more ethically important to ensure that the participant is not subjected to an uncomfortable experience than to preserve experimental integrity in these circumstances.

3.3 Factors Influencing Sickness in VR

Nichols et al. (1997) categorised the influential factors on sickness and other side effects in VR as being associated with the VR system (e.g. display characteristics, field of view, input devices), VE design (e.g. content, sound, interactivity and permitted movement), task characteristics (e.g. duration of exposure, training, circumstances of use) and user characteristics (e.g. age, gender, health, experience and attitudes). Much research has been conducted since to examine the nature of the influence of these factors in detail. The following sections consider some of this work and comments on the relevance of these factors for those designing systems to be implemented when using VR to treat anxiety.

3.3.1 Characteristics of VR System

The nature of VR displays has changed considerably over the past 20 years, and continues to evolve. Whereas in the 1990s, the marketplace was dominated by head-mounted-display-type technologies, since around the year 2000, displays have tended to be based around projection technologies, and, if stereoscopic viewing is

3.3 Factors Influencing Sickness in VR

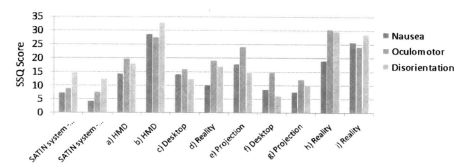

Fig. 3.3 SSQ data obtained from a series of administrations after a variety of periods of VR use with a range of types of display (N ranges from 8 to 79; displays include both monoscopic and stereoscopic display types)

required, shutter glasses are increasingly being used in a range of contexts. Research that we have conducted (Sharples et al. 2008) has collected subjective symptom reports in a variety of display types—Fig. 3.3 summarises these data. The two left-hand columns include data obtained as part of the EU-funded project SATIN, which examined the use of stereoscopic display technology for viewing early-stage prototypes in product design. The exposures for these data were around 10 min, as opposed to 20–30 min for the rest of the data on the graph, and the level of vection experienced by participants was low; these two factors are felt to particularly contribute the overall lower level of symptoms experienced by these participants. The different display types refer to:

- SATIN: A multimodal system using stereoscopic display on a projected screen, with representations of objects in front of the participant. In this application, the participants did not have a large requirement to experience self-motion, as they were manipulating the object being viewed, rather than their own position.
- HMD: A V8 stereoscopic HMD was used to display a range of tasks being completed within a Virtual Factory (conditions a and b).
- Desktop: The Virtual Factory task was presented on a monoscopic standard CRT monitor (conditions c and f).
- Reality: The Virtual Factory was presented on a wrap-around monoscopic high-resolution screen display in a dedicated theatre (built to seat 20–30 viewers; conditions d, h and i).

Projection: The Virtual Factory was displayed on a monoscopic projection screen (conditions e and g). It is interesting to note that for many of conditions a to i, oculomotor symptoms predominate. Kennedy and Fowlkes (1992) also noted that a larger field of view may increase the levels of symptoms experienced.

Input devices and their design may also influence side effects experienced. This influence is likely to take one of the two forms. Firstly, the design of the input device may influence the DOF of control provided to a user—Stanney and Kennedy (2009) report that complete movement control (6 DOF) can be expected to lead to

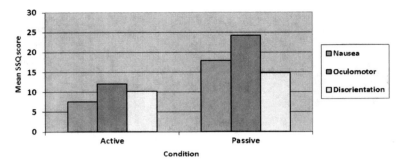

Fig. 3.4 Comparison of SSQ scores for active and passive control in a VE (*N*=31)

2.5 times more dropouts than streamlined control for example. Secondly, the design of the input device, and its resultant ease of use, may influence the participant's ability to accurately and smoothly move around an environment; for example, a more "jerky" movement may increase experienced sensation of vection, lead to disorientation or distress on the part of the participant, thus contributing to sickness symptoms. Making an input device easy or intuitive to use may reduce the unnecessary movement in the visual scene that may result from such "unskilled" movement.

3.3.2 Characteristics of Virtual Environments

The characteristics of a VE can very broadly be classified as associated with environment *content* or *interaction*. The impact of content is likely to be closely associated with the experience of vection, as mentioned previously—a higher number of objects, particularly if passed in the peripheral vision by the participant, whilst moving through an environment, is likely to lead to a higher level of symptoms being experienced. Therefore, designers of VEs should consider carefully whether the participant is actually required to move through an environment, or whether therapeutic aims can be achieved whilst the participant is reasonably static. This may of course lead to a trade-off between effective treatment, experience of presence (as discussed by Nichols et al. (2000a) the relationships between presence and sickness is not straightforward) face validity of the experience (a higher level of detail in an environment may lead to a higher level of perceived realism of the experience) and any negative effects experienced.

One particular aspect of VE design that has been examined is level of control on the part of the user (although of course this aspect could be considered to straddle the categories of VE design and task circumstances) (Fig. 3.4). Stanney and Hash (1998) and Sharples et al. (2008) demonstrated that passive observers of VEs experienced a higher level of symptoms; this finding emphasises the importance of the role of expectation in sensory conflict. This finding is particularly pertinent when we consider many common scenarios of use of VR technology seen in collaborative decision making—the authors have frequently observed situations where a new design is visualised by a group of people, one of whom is wearing a tracked display system such as shutter glasses, or controlling movement via a joystick, whereas the other observers simply view the visual display from the point of view of the primary viewer. This may also have implications for therapists—if a patient is receiving therapy in a VE, a therapist may wish to observe their experience (indeed, good ethical practice may well demand this); in this case, the therapist may be the passive viewer. Alternatively, if the therapist is in control of movement, the passive nature of viewing by the participant may increase any negative symptoms that they experience. This can perhaps be managed by the therapist providing a verbal commentary, warning the participant of the movement (and thus conflict) that they are likely to expect, or the participant themselves providing verbal instructions to the therapist, although, whilst sensory conflict theory may suggest this, there is not to our knowledge experimental data that would reinforce our suggestion that this verbal interaction could minimise symptoms. Indeed, whilst research and development exploring the use of VR systems and related technology for rehabilitation has been ongoing for over 15 years, very few have reported any side effects (Cobb and Sharkey 2007). One study did measure SSQ in healthy participants who were trialling two types of VR platforms used to display a variety of tasks to be used for neurological rehabilitation. Three types of motor-coordination games (Birds and Balls, Soccer and Snowboarding) and exploration of a virtual office environment were assessed when viewed via a GX video projection observed, although there was a significant difference between the conditions (with higher level of symptoms reported following HMD than projection screen use). The authors concluded that the observed low SSQ scores resulted from the relatively short exposure durations (less than 5 min per trial) and that observed differences between conditions was due to display type (with the HMD producing more short term side effects) and the nature of the task (dynamic vs. static activities).

3.3.3 Task Characteristics

The task characteristics, or circumstances of use, may also affect experience of exposure side effects. Stanney and Kennedy (2009) and So and Yuen (2007) report that adverse effects increase with duration of exposure to a VR stimulus, but it is known that for some participants, effects can be experienced quite quickly, and certainly within the first 10–15 min of use. Howarth and Hodder (2008) and Bailenson and Yee (2006) have investigated habituation over repeated uses of VR and demonstrated that symptoms do decrease with repeated exposures, and that a time gap of between 1 and 7 days is sufficient to yield symptom reduction (although Stanney and Kennedy (2009) report evidence that does not completely concur with this finding). Due to the general lack of studies in this area, there is as yet no confirmed recommendation regarding the maximum time period for duration of immersion. In our own work, we recommend a maximum exposure of 30 min, and recommend for exposures of more than 20 min that symptoms are monitored using the short symptom checklist every 5 min. This is supported by the findings from Regan (1994) that participants experienced progressively higher symptom levels in exposure duration above 20 min and Lampton et al. (1994) who found that symptoms increased with immersion exposure time, with severe sickness symptoms reported at 40 min. Kennedy et al. (2000) reviewed sickness data collected from 938 case reports collected during 11 years of studies examining symptoms experienced by military personnel when using helicopter flight simulators. Four exposure duration times were examined: 0–1, 1–2, 2–3, and >3 h. The results found that total sickness reported did increase with length of exposure. However, they also found that reported sickness decreased with repeated exposures. This supports the suggestion that adaptation to the stimulus reduces adverse effects. In a study of 60 participants performing an immersive locomotion task, comparison of reported symptoms after three different exposure times (<15, 16–20 and >20 min) identified higher symptoms with longer exposure duration (Jaeger and Mourant 2001). These authors suggest that symptoms increase up to durations of 30 min after which adaptation may take effect to reduce the experience of symptoms.

Other aspects of task circumstances that have been examined include seated versus standing viewing (Merhi et al. 2007) demonstrating that sickness was more common for participants who were seated.

3.3.4 Participant Characteristics

Participant characteristics have been demonstrated to have an effect on experience of symptoms. Females tend to experience a higher level of symptoms than males (Emoto et al. 2008; Jaeger and Mourant 2001; Stanney and Kennedy 2009), and there have been some suggestions that those aged between 2 and 12 appear to be most susceptible to higher levels of symptoms(Stanney and Kennedy 2009), although Arns and Cerney (2005) suggest a more complex relationship between age and symptoms may exist. We have also identified the possibility that those who suffer from migraines are susceptible to high levels of symptoms (Nichols et al. 2000b) and found a relationship between self-reported motion sickness susceptibility and experience of VR-induced sickness symptoms (Nichols 1999). In addition, Nichols (1999) found a strong correlation between two exposures to VR use, where the first exposure was only 10 min long—this suggests that it may be appropriate to expose participants to a short period of VR use, monitor their symptoms, and for those who report symptoms after a short time (e.g. 5–10 min), exhibit caution (e.g. consistent monitoring, with particular attention to be paid to any consistent increases in symptoms) in recommending any VR-based therapy.

When using participant characteristics as a selection basis, caution must be demonstrated. Therefore, a combination of selection criteria and gradual introduction to stimuli may be appropriate.

3.4 Management of Sickness in VR Systems

There are a number of strategies that can be employed in an effort to minimise the negative effects experienced by a VR participant, particularly in a therapeutic context. These can be grouped as associated with VR/VE design, appropriate procedures when applying the VR therapy, and, if appropriate, selection criteria for participants.

3.4.1 VR/VE Design

From a technical perspective, lag between participant input (via body movement or input device activation) should be minimised to limit the extent of type III visual–inertial conflict. This type of conflict can also be minimised via the provision of as much feedback as possible to a participant's proprioceptive senses. The designer should also consider whether a large, enveloping field of view is required for a system—if it is felt to be acceptable to not have complete occlusion of the real world during VR use, then the retention of a real-world frame of reference may reduce the prevalence of symptoms. Similarly, the combination of a wide field of view and large number of objects, combined with requirement for movement through the VE by the participant, will contribute to a sense of vection, and is likely to increase sickness. It is also important to consider whether a participant or therapist will be in active control of their movement—allowing a user to retain control of the VE will help to reduce sickness symptoms.

3.4.2 Implementation Procedures for VR/VE Therapy

Nichols et al. (2000) describe a set of reported strategies that participants adopted in an attempt to minimise their negative experience of symptoms. These can be used as the basis for observing participants and looking for what Stanney and Kennedy (2009) term "red flags". The behaviours adopted by participants experiencing symptoms include:

- Looking away from the main point of interest, or looking to the floor
- Squinting of the eyes, or closing the eyes (this of course may be difficult to observe if a participant is wearing an enveloping HMD)
- Shifting of focal point on the screen (e.g. choosing to look at the corners of the screen)
- Rubbing eyes or blinking
- Changing sitting, standing, body or head position
- Restricting head movement
- Fidgeting
- Using a deliberate calming strategy, such as controlling breathing or sucking thumb

In addition, a participant who is experiencing symptoms may demonstrate observable sway, sweating or hold their hand to their head to relieve discomfort, although it is important to be aware of any of the effects of a successful treatment (e.g. sweating due to the effort exercised in overcoming a fear) could potentially be confused with a symptom of exposure side effects (e.g. sweating due to developing sickness symptoms). In such cases, it is important to monitor symptoms using a tool such as the SSC. Ultimately, it is recommended that any participant who is noted to demonstrate any of the above behaviours is closely monitored, and directly asked if they are happy to continue their period of use of VR.

Training of participants may also enable participants to minimise the symptoms that they experience. Training in use of the input device can minimise the occurrence of jerky movements that may create unnecessary vection that could increase the symptoms experienced. Welch and Sampanes (2008) agree and provide some insight into the specific perceptual motor elements that could be considered in such a training programme. Smither et al. (2008) demonstrate that adaptation training from one VE may transfer to another.

It is also important to clearly inform participants of any negative effects that they might experience. Whilst this may predispose them to report a higher level of symptoms experienced, from an ethical perspective, it is vital that participants feel appropriately empowered to report any negative effects that they experience, and that they are able to stop their period of VR use at any time. We also recommend that participants who experience sickness symptoms during a study wait 30 min, or until symptoms have subsided as demonstrated by their response to the SSC, before leaving the experimental laboratory (to allow for continued informal observation). Finally, we require that all participants wait at least 30 min after exposure before carrying out safety-critical tasks, such as driving or operating machinery.

3.4.3 Selection of Participants

The selection of participants for therapeutic treatment using VR presents a small ethical dilemma—if it is felt that a therapy is of benefit, then it would be unethical to preclude an individual from having the opportunity to receive that therapy. However, the negative effects that they experience whilst undergoing therapy may negate the positive effects. Therefore, each therapeutic treatment should consider selection criteria on a case-by-case basis. Care should also be taken to ensure that the participant is fit to enter the VE. Administration of the SSQ should be conducted before immersion to assess whether participants have any symptoms. This may well be the case for participants with anxiety disorders due to apprehension about conducting the study (Bouchard et al. 2009). If symptoms are present, the participant should be given time to calm down before engaging in the study.

There is a need to develop methods to identify susceptible individuals without requiring them to experience sickness. Some methods employed by the authors in their past research do appear to provide an indication of who may be likely to experience exposure side effects—notably motion sickness susceptibility, VR attitude,

3.4 Management of Sickness in VR Systems

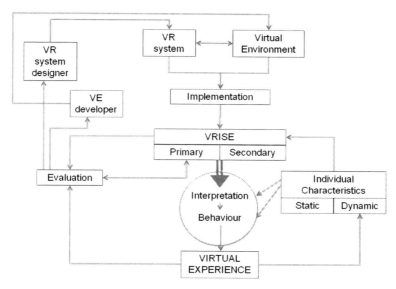

Fig. 3.5 Model for management of exposure side effects (Nichols and Patel 2002)

performance on previous use of VR, and headache/migraine history (Nichols et al. 2000b). These methods should be used to identify susceptible individuals, who should particularly be informed about the negative effects of VR. It may also be appropriate to limit initial periods of exposure. Stanney and Kennedy (2009) also note that females may be more susceptible to sickness than males. It is also important that a participant is in their normal state of health before commencing the use of VR, as our experience has suggested that those who have consumed alcohol the night before, or who are suffering from mild cold or flu symptoms may experience a higher level of symptoms as a result.

3.4.4 Model of Management of Exposure Side Effects

Figure 3.5 presents a model that describes the different stakeholders and processes involved in the management of Virtual Reality Induced Symptoms and Effects (VRISE) which can be applied to the exposure side effects discussed in this chapter. Firstly, it is important to remember that the participant who has used VR, for example as part of a therapeutic treatment, takes away with them what can be termed the "virtual experience". This concept captures all of the elements associated with that experience—any positive impact of training, rehabilitation or familiarisation; any enjoyment, thrill or happiness they experienced whilst using the system, and any side effects that are experienced. Whilst methods such as the SSQ can measure specific effects such as VR-induced sickness, the participant takes away the combined impact of all effects, positive and negative, that have been experienced. This can be likened to the experience of a fairground ride—someone might feel slightly queasy after going on a ride, but the excitement that they experienced during the ride will often override any negative feelings they might have had. This virtual experience may well have an effect on what have been termed "dynamic" individual characteristics, where dynamic refers to a characteristic that can change under the influence of an experience or input. An example of a dynamic characteristic could be attitude for example, and, in the context of therapy, the aim of an application might be explicitly to change such a characteristic. For example, in the case of VR to treat arachnophobia, the participant characteristic of interest would be "level of fear of spiders"—this characteristic would be changed (reduced) by successful treatment using VR. This concept of the dynamic characteristic can also be used to articulate the impact of training a participant. A participant who is trained in using an input device will be more skilled, their movement through the environment will be more smooth, and they may as a result experience less sensory conflict and thus experience a lower level of symptoms.

The model also represents the role of the VR and VE design, and their associated designers or developers, in influencing symptoms experienced. The distinction between primary and secondary VRISE is intended to articulate the difference between intended (primary) effects and normally unintended effects that were not the main goal of the use (secondary).

3.4.5 Guidance

There are a number of general guidelines that can be applied to all periods of VR exposure, where extra care and attention must be taken with participants whom are likely to be more susceptible. These guidelines include:

- Education about potential negative effects of VR use, with the aim of minimising anxiety and apprehension about the experience
- Designing VEs so that the minimum level of symptom-provoking elements is present for susceptible individuals
- Informing participants about appropriate behaviour strategies that may minimise negative symptoms but not detract from their experience of using the VE, including training in use of input devices
- Where possible, allowing participants control over their movement around the VE
- Monitoring of VR participants, and providing assurance that they may terminate their period of exposure at any time (this point should particularly be emphasised for susceptible individuals)
- Education of people responsible for monitoring VR participants about possible physiological signs and behaviours that participants who are experiencing negative symptoms may exhibit (e.g. sweating, pallor, fidgeting with HMD, looking away from display, closing eyes)

In addition, on the basis of previous findings relating to habituation (see, Hill and Howarth 2000), it may be appropriate for participants to undergo a series of short introductory VE exposures.

There may be a small subset of VR users who, despite all appropriate precautions being taken, will always experience negative symptoms of VR use. For example, research into migraineurs (Nichols et al. 2000b) suggests that this may be one group of users for whom this is the case; therefore, until further research is completed, migraine-susceptible individuals should use VR with caution.

3.5 Driving Simulator Sickness

3.5.1 Introduction

Driving simulators can be seen as a specific type of VR and VE in which sickness symptoms may arise. They have become increasingly popular in recent years, largely due to decreases in hardware and software costs in combination with increasing concerns over ethical, safety and liability issues for on-road studies. As such, they offer an interesting case study application in which to consider the prevalence of sickness in an established application area, known risk factors and recommended remediation strategies. This section presents a case study illustrating how sickness has been managed and understood in work conducted using our driving simulator in the Human Factors Research Group at the University of Nottingham.

Driving simulators are used for a wide range of different purposes, including training and assessment (especially for professional drivers), education (e.g. for young drivers), rehabilitation (e.g. for those who have experienced a stroke), as well as research and development (e.g. investigating the distraction of in-car devices). Of specific relevance to this book, simulators have been used extensively in the treatment of people suffering from driving-related phobias (e.g. panic disorder following involvement in a serious road traffic accident)—e.g. Wald and Taylor (2003), Walshe et al. (2005), and Wiederhold and Wiederhold (2010).

Simulators vary considerably according to their fidelity, that is, the faithfulness with which they represent reality. Some driving simulators may offer extremely basic desktop environments in which only rudimentary aspects of driving are maintained (e.g. a purely visual tracking task). In contrast, other driving simulators may possess highly immersive visual–audio environments utilising multiple projections and surround sound. The most expensive driving simulators aim to mimic aspects of motion for driving (including low-and high-amplitude vibration and the various forces experienced during the longitudinal and lateral control of a vehicle).

Many authors have argued that driving simulators provide a safe, controlled and cost-effective environment in which a wide range of data can be collected and visualised (McGehee et al. 2000; Reed and Green 1999). Nevertheless, potential disadvantages are well known in this area, notably concerning validity (do drivers behave

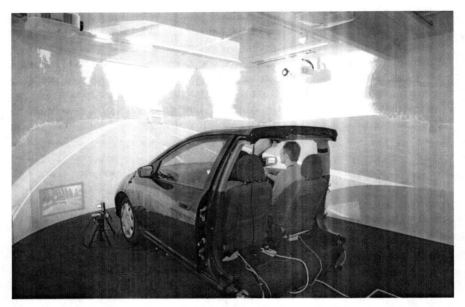

Fig. 3.6 The Human Factors Research Group driving simulator at the University of Nottingham

in the simulator as they do in the real world?) and sickness rates. Not surprisingly, this section focuses on the second issue, although it will become apparent later that the two problems are inextricably linked.

At Nottingham, we have approximately 7 years experience in the use of what would generally be termed a mid-fidelity driving simulator (Fig. 3.6). This includes a real-car cabin with existing primary controls, together with an immersive visual environment (270° wrap-around projection, rear projection and side mirror displays, plus reconfigurable dashboard display). Surround sound speakers provide road and traffic noise, whilst low-amplitude vibration is provided through the driver's seat and pedals. The simulator is primarily used in research to investigate the design issues for new technology within vehicles. By means of illustration, specific studies have addressed: the impact of vehicle navigation systems on environmental learning (Burnett and Lee 2005; Oliver and Burnett 2008); the design of touchpad user interfaces for vehicles (Burnett and Lee 2005; Burnett et al. 2010); and the relationship between information content for Head-Up Displays and narrowing of peripheral vision (Burnett and Donker 2010).

3.5.2 *Importance of Understanding Sickness in Driving Simulators*

It is worth considering at this point why sickness is a particular concern for driving simulators. Obviously, we do not want our study participants or trainees to suffer the symptoms associated with sickness—however, other factors are important too. There are concerns for research purposes that issues of sickness can compromise the representativeness of a sample. In other words, as a result of preselection and attrition rates, a study may have a group of people who are significantly different to the target population. In this respect, potential individual factors that may influence sickness susceptibility and therefore bias a sample include age, gender, and computing experience (see later). Indeed, some researchers have actively avoided recruiting older drivers for simulator studies in the belief that sickness rates are higher for these individuals (Srinivasan and Jovanis 1997). Individual differences perhaps carry an even greater significance if driving simulators are being considered as mandatory assessment tools (Mullen et al. 2010) or to aid specific people (as will be the case for those suffering from driving-related phobias).

There are also issues concerning the relationship between a driver's behaviour in a simulator and the occurrence of sickness symptoms. When the symptoms of sickness commence, drivers may exhibit alternative unrealistic behaviours in an attempt to cope with or alleviate symptoms, for example, slowing down, closing eyes whilst cornering and so on. Such behaviour are further examples of Stanney and Kennedy's (2009) "red flags" and will clearly impact on the validity of research studies and assessment results as well as potential transfer of training.

3.5.3 Prevalence of Sickness

It can be very difficult to make sensible conclusions regarding the prevalence of sickness in driving simulators. This is largely a result of varying configurations of simulator and contexts in which they are used. In addition, any figures quoted are often confounded to an extent by how researchers have defined "sickness". For instance, Mullen et al. (2010) claim that the incidence of sickness (measured by onset of symptoms) for driving simulators are usually in the order of 10% and are typically lower than those encountered in other VEs. Nevertheless, in a report on sickness symptoms by Roe et al. (2007), values for sickness (measured by dropout rates) were reported to range from 0 to 19% for different studies. In our own research, attrition rates for studies in the driving simulator have been low. Indeed, to date there have been no dropouts for studies utilising motorway (highway) driving scenarios. Nevertheless, there has been some experience of sickness (approx. 5% dropout rates) for studies requiring urban/town driving. This trend appears to be in line with the conclusions of Roe et al. (2007) who found that sickness rates were highest in studies where there were greater steering and braking activity.

Several papers have found that the type of sickness experienced in driving simulators is qualitatively different to that experienced in more traditional VEs. As noted by Stanney et al. (1997), there are arguably different "strains" of motion sickness that we need to understand for alternative VEs. Utilising the Kennedy et al. (1993)

questionnaire, authors have typically encountered higher incidence of oculomotor sickness symptoms (eyestrain, blurred vision, headaches, etc.), in relation to those concerning disorientation or nausea. The common explanation for such symptoms is the high degree of vection that can be experienced when "driving" in a simulator, that is, the illusion of self-motion. Indeed, evidence for such a phenomenon can be found in the fact that a positive correlation has been found between sickness scores and the speed of driving required (Mourant and Thattachery 2000).

3.5.4 Risk Factors

Three risk factors are widely regarded as having an impact on driving simulator sickness, simulator design (fidelity), types of exposure (task) and individual differences (susceptibility) (Roe et al. 2007)

With respect to fidelity issues, there are many variables involved and it can be difficult to draw firm conclusions from previous studies. Nevertheless, from a practical perspective, it is clear that developers of driving simulators often face three questions (Green et al. 2003). These questions are of significance, primarily because of the costs and space implications associated with different decisions. Moreover, the questions often highlight the trade-offs associated with the need for validity in a simulator versus the need to minimise sickness.

1. Should a simulator use a wrap-around screen ($\geq 180°$ front field of view) or a single screen (approx. 60–90° front field of view)? Not surprisingly, research here has demonstrated increased sickness rates for the more immersive VEs (Lin 2002), largely due to increased optic flow. However, such environments are also associated with greater sense of presence and validity of results (Jamson 2001; Lin 2002).
2. Should a simulator utilise a real-vehicle cabin or a desktop environment? A study conducted at our facility (Burnett et al. 2007) considered this issue and found that ratings of oculomotor discomfort were lower for participants who were enclosed within a car cabin, as opposed to sitting at a desk. It was hypothesised that a combination of issues may have contributed to this result, including differences in reference points between configurations (floor and car), and variations in optic flow. In this case, there was evidence that greater validity was also associated with the real-vehicle set-up.
3. Should a simulator provide motion cues (e.g. through a moving platform) or be static (often termed a fixed-base simulator)? Very little open research has been conducted on this topic, perhaps because (a) vehicle manufacturers presently operate the majority of motion-based driving simulators and (b) there is considerable self-interest to not prove a sickness problem for motion. Nevertheless, there are indications from other areas of simulation that sickness can be more severe for motion-based simulators when compared with fixed-base simulators (Burki-Cohen et al. 1998; Jaeger and Mourant 2001). Such findings could be explained as a type III conflict (i.e. conflict within a sense—vestibular information is provided, but this does not wholly match expectations for this

sense) being more influential for sickness than a type II conflict (i.e. conflict across senses—vestibular information not provided, whereas visual inputs suggest movement to an individual).

Some task issues have been mentioned above which act as risk factors (e.g. requirement for turns, driving speed). One key additional factor concerns exposure time, notably the individual drive times and overall time spent in a simulator. In this respect, research has suggested that sickness symptoms do increase with the duration of an individual trial within a driving simulator (Min et al. 2004), but that an increase in the number of repeat exposures leads to a reduction in sickness (Teasdale et al. 2009). In other words, to enable users of a simulator to adapt to the novel "driving" experience, it is better to use a greater number of short duration trials (drives) within a simulator. For our own simulator, we generally aim not to require participants to drive for any longer than 10 min in one individual trial.

Research concerning the susceptibility of different driver groups to sickness in simulators often highlights conflicting results across the literature. For instance, with respect to the effects of age, some researchers have noted increased incidence of sickness for older drivers (e.g. Park et al. 2006), whereas others have not found such differences (Mourant and Thattachery 2000). Similarly, gender differences have been noted by some (Mourant and Thattachery 2000; Park et al. 2006) but not by others (Lee et al. 1997). Finally, some authors have noted that frequent users of computer games are less susceptible to sickness than those with reduced experience (Bigoin et al. 2007). In an MSc project conducted in our group, no such difference was found (Mowforth 2005).

Confounding variables associated with the simulator configurations involved, the tasks included and sample sizes would lead to variations in study results and conclusions. Clearly, this is an area requiring extensive, coordinated and controlled research, rather than one-off studies. Selective interpretation of the current literature has led to a conclusion amongst many users of simulators that older females are the greatest risk group. As noted above, such potential misconceptions are important, since they often influence recruitment strategies.

3.5.5 Remediation Strategies

To reduce the likelihood of sickness in driving simulators, there are various strategies that researchers, trainers and assessors can utilise. As discussed above, the design of the simulator itself and the nature of tasks utilised are important. In addition, it is common practice for driving simulator users to screen participants for propensity towards sickness (Green et al. 2003). Individual characteristics included in screening vary, but often include those noted in the wider VR research that have been shown to predict sickness rates, including severe travel sickness, migraines, and epilepsy (Cobb et al. 1999). In the driving simulator area, there is evidence that an individual's perception of their susceptibility to motion and simulator sickness is a reliable predictor of sickness (Wesley et al. 2005).

A robust protocol for simulator sickness can also include various mitigation and contingency strategies, although there appears to be limited research addressing this specifically for the driving situation. In one interesting paper, it was found that acupressure wrist bands (generally used to alleviate motion and morning sickness) reduced oculomotor sickness ratings for older people using a driving simulator (Wesley et al. 2005). The authors felt that a placebo effect may have contributed to the results, although they recommend further research takes place to understand the exact mechanisms involved.

In our own research, we commonly observe participant for signs of sickness (sweating, burping, etc.) and deal carefully with sickness should it arise (e.g. having quite, cool place away from the simulator to relax, drinking water, etc.). In our own studies, we are also mindful of the potential impact of sickness on actual driving behaviour following a simulator study. Consequently, we request that participants do not drive for a minimum of 30 min after a study and sign forms before they leave our facility indicating that any symptoms of sickness they may have had in a study have now subsided.

3.6 Conclusions

This chapter provides an overview of the theoretical context of experience of exposure side effects and VR-induced sickness (or cybersickness) in particular. Sensory conflict theory provides a basis for explanation of most phenomena associated with sickness, but needs further development if it is to be used effectively as a tool for predicting the extent to which a particular VR-based treatment will elicit symptoms. Some guidelines for the effective management of exposure side effects are presented, with the aim of supporting those considering implementation of VR/VE in therapeutic contexts, and in particular, the treatment of anxiety disorders. A large enough proportion of the population experience symptoms for it to be important not to ignore the likelihood of these symptoms occurring, but appropriate and careful management of implementation of VR should minimise the impact of these symptoms as far as practicable.

References

Arns, L. L., & Cerney, M. M. (2005). The relationship between age and incidence of cybersickness among immersive environment users. In proceedings of the IEEE virtual reality conference, pp. 267–268.

Bailenson, J. N., & Yee, N. (2006). A longitudinal study, of task performance, head movements, subjective report, simulator sickness, and transformed social interaction in collaborative virtual environments. *Presence-Teleoperators and Virtual Environments, 15*(6), 699–716.

Benfari, R. C. (1964). Perceptual vertigo: A dimensional study. *Perceptual and Motor Skills, 18*, 633–639.

References

Bigoin, N., Porte, J., Kurtiko, I., & Kavatli, M. (2007). *Effects of depth cues on simulator sickness*. Paper presented at the first international conference on immersive telecommunications, Verona, Italy.

Bonato, F., Bubka, A., & Paumisano, S. (2009). Combined pitch and roll and cybersickness in a virtual environment. *Aviation Space and Environmental Medicine, 80*(11), 941–945. doi:10.3357/Asem.2394.2009.

Bonnet, C. T., Faugloire, E., Riley, M. A., Bardy, B. G., & Stoffregen, T. A. (2008). Self-induced motion sickness and body movement during passive restraint. *Ecological Psychology, 20*(2), 121–145. doi:10.1080/10407410801949289.

Bos, J. E., Bles, W., & Groen, E. L. (2008). A theory on visually induced motion sickness. *Displays, 29*(2), 47–57. doi:10.1016/j.displa.2007.09.002.

Bouchard, S., St-Jacques, J., Renaud, P., & Wiederhold, B.K. (2009). Side effects of immersions in virtual reality for people suffering from anxiety disorders. *Journal of Cybertherapy and Rehabilitation, 2* (2), 127–137.

Bouchard, S. Robillard, G., Renaud, P., & Bernier, F. (2011). Exploring new dimensions in the assessment of virtual reality induced side-effects. *Journal of Computer and Information Technology, 1* (3), 20–32.

Bouchard, S., Robillard, G., & Renaud, P. (2007). Revising the factor structure of the simulator sickness questionnaire. *Annual Review of Cybertherapy and Telemedicine, 5,* 117–122.

Bouyer, L. J. G., & Watt, D. G. D. (1996). "Torso rotation" experiments. 1. Adaptation to motion sickness does not correlate with changes in VOR gain. *Journal of Vestibular Research-Equilibrium & Orientation, 6*(5), 367–375.

Burki-Cohen, J., Soja, N. N., & Longridge, T. (1998). Simulator platform motion-the need revisited. *International Journal of Aviation Psychology, 8*(3), 293–317.

Burnett, G. E., & Donker, R. (2010). Evaluating the impact of head-up display complexity on peripheral detection performance: A driving simulator study. *Advances in Transportation Studies, 22,* 19–33.

Burnett, G. E., & Lee, K. (2005). *The effect of vehicle navigation systems on the formation of cognitive maps traffic and transport psychology: Theory and application* (pp. 407–418). Amsterdam: Elsevier.

Burnett, G. E., Irune, A., & Mowforth, A. (2007). Driving simulator and validity: How important is it to use real car cabins? *Advances in Transportation Studies, 13,* 33–42.

Burnett, G. E., Millen, L., Lawson, G., & Pickering, C. (2010). Investigating design issues for the use of touchpad technology within vehicles. *Advances in Transportation Studies.*

Cobb, S. V. G., & Nichols, S. C. (1998). Static posture tests for the assessment of postural instability after virtual environment use. *Brain Research Bulletin, 47*(5), 459–464.

Cobb, S. V. G., Nichols, S., Ramsey, A., & Wilson, J. R. (1999). Virtual reality-induced symptoms and effects (VRISE). *Presence-Teleoperators and Virtual Environments, 8*(2), 169–186.

Cobb, S. V., & Sharkey, P. M. (2007). A decade of research and development in disability, virtual reality and associated technologies: Review of ICDVRAT 1996–2006. Retrieved from http://www.ijvr.org/issues/issue2-2007/6.pdf.

Emoto, M., Sugawara, M., & Nojiri, Y. (2008). Viewing angle dependency of visually-induced motion sickness in viewing wide-field images by subjective and autonomic nervous indices. *Displays, 29*(2), 90–99. doi:10.1016/j.displa.2007.09.010.

Green, P., Nowakowski, C., Mayer, K., & Tsimhoni, O. (2003). *Audio-visual system design recommendations from experience with the umtri driving simulator.* Paper presented at the driving simulator conference North America. Dearborn, MI: Ford Motor Company.

Groen, E. L., & Bos, J. E. (2008). Simulator sickness depends on frequency of the simulator motion mismatch: An observation. *Presence-Teleoperators and Virtual Environments, 17*(6), 584–593.

Hettinger, L. J., & Riccio, G. E. (1992). Visually induced motion sickness in virtual environments. *Presence:Teleoperators and Virtual Environments, 1*(3), 306–310.

Hill, K., & Howarth, P. A. (2000). Habituation to the side effects of immersion in a virtual environment. *Displays, 21*(1), 25–30.

Howarth, P. A., & Hodder, S. G. (2008). Characteristics of habituation to motion in a virtual environment. *Displays, 29*(2), 117–123. doi:10.1016/j.displa.2007.09.009.

Jaeger, B. K., & Mourant, R. R. (2001). *Comparison of simulator sickness using static and dynamic walking simulators.* Paper presented at the Human Factors and Ergonomics Society Annual Meeting.

Jamson, H. (2001). *Image characteristics and their effect on driving simulator validity.* Paper presented at the International driving symposium on Human Factors in driver assessment, training and vehicle design, Iowa.

Kennedy, R. S., & Drexler, J. M. (1994). *Methodological and measurement issues for identification of engineering features contributing to virtual reality sickness.* Paper presented at the IMAGE VII conference, Tuscon, Arizona, 12–17 June 1994.

Kennedy, R. S., & Fowlkes, J. E. (1992). Simulator sickness is polygenic and polysymptomatic: Implications for research. *International Journal of Aviation Psychology, 2*(1), 23–28.

Kennedy, R. S., Lane, M. E., Lilienthal, M. G., Berbaum, K. S., & Hettinger, L. J. (1992). Profile analysis of simulator sickness symptoms: Application to virtual environment systems. *Presence-Teleoperators and Virtual Environments, 1*(3), 295–301.

Kennedy, R. S., Lane, N. E., Berbaum, K. S., & Lilienthal, M. G. (1993). Simulator sickness questionnaire: An enhanced method for quantifying simulator sickness. *International Journal of Aviation Psychology, 3*(3), 203–220.

Kennedy, R. S., Massey, C. J., & Lilienthal, M. G. (1995). Incidences of fatigue and drowsiness reports from three dozen simulators: relevance for the sopite syndrome. Paper presented at the first workshop on simulation and interaction in virtual environments (SIVE '95), University of Iowa, Iowa City, IA, USA.

Kennedy, R. S., Stanney, K. M., & Dunlap, W. P. (2000). Duration and exposure to virtual environments: Sickness curves during and across sessions. *Presence: Teleoperators and Virtual Environments, 9*(5), 463–472.

Kuze, J., & Ukai, K. (2008). Subjective evaluation of visual fatigue caused by motion images. *Displays, 29*(2), 159–166. doi:10.1016/j.displa.2007.09.007.

Lampton, D. R., Knerr, B. W., Goldberg, S. L., Bliss, J. P., Moshell, J. M., & Blau, B. S. (1994). The virtual environment performance assessment battery (VEPAB): Development and evaluation. *Presence: Teleoperators and Virtual Environments, 3*(2), 145–157.

Lee, G.C.H., Yoo, Y., & Jones, S. (1997). Investigation of driving performance, vection, postural sway, and simulator sickness in a fixed-based driving simulator. *Computers and Industrial Engineering, 33*(3–4), 533–536.

Lin et al. (2002). Effects of field of view on presence, enjoyment, memory, and simulator sickness in a virtual environment. Paper presented at the IEEE virtual reality conference (VR 2002).

McCauley, M. E., & Sharkey, T. J. (1992). Cybersickness: Perception of motion in virtual environments. *Presence: Teleoperators and Virtual Environments, 1*(3), 311–318.

McGehee, D. V., Mazzae, E. N., Baldwin, G. H. S. (2000). *Driver reaction time in crash avoidance research: validation of a driving simulator study on a test track.* Paper presented at the XIVth triennial congress of the international ergonomics association (IEA).

Merhi, O., Faugloire, E., Flanagan, M., & Stoffregen, T. A. (2007). Motion sickness, console video games, and head-mounted displays. *Human Factors, 49*(5), 920–934. doi:10.1518/001872007×230262.

Min, B. C., Chung, S. C., Min, Y. K., & Sakamoto, K. (2004). Psychophysiological evaluation of simulator sickness evoked by a graphic simulator. *Applied Ergonomics, 35*(6), 549–556.

Mourant, R. R., & Thattachery, T. R. (2000). *Simulator sickness in a virtual environments driving simulator.* Paper presented at the IEA/HFES 2000 congress.

Mowforth, A. (2005). *An investigation into the role of presence as a means of validating driving simulators.* MSc information technology dissertation. University of Nottingham.

Mullen, N. W., Weaver, B., Riendeau, J. A., Morrison, L. E., & Bédard, M. (2010). Driving performance and susceptibility to simulator sickness: Are they related? *American Journal of Occupational Therapy, 64*(2), 288–295.

References

Nichols, S. (1999). *Virtual reality induced symptoms and effects: Theoretical and methodological issues*. Ph.D., University of Nottingham.

Nichols, S., & Patel, H. (2002). Health and safety implications of virtual reality: A review of empirical evidence. *Applied Ergonomics, 33*(3), 251–271. doi:Pii S0003-6870(02)00020-0.

Nichols, S., Cobb, S., & Wilson, J. R. (1997). Health and safety implications of virtual environments: Measurement issues. *Presence-Teleoperators and Virtual Environments, 6*(6), 667–675.

Nichols, S., Haldane, C., & Wilson, J. R. (2000a). Measurement of presence and its consequences in virtual environments. *International Journal of Human-Computer Studies, 52*(3), 471–491.

Nichols, S., Ramsey, A. D., Cobb, S., Neale, H., D'Cruz, M., & Wilson, J. R. (2000b). *Incidence of virtual reality induced symptoms and effects (VRISE) in desktop and projection screen display systems*. HSE Contract Research Report.

Oliver, K., & Burnett, G. E. (2008). *Learning-oriented vehicle navigation systems: A preliminary investigation in a driving simulator*. Paper presented at the ACM conference on Mobile Human-Computer Interaction, Amsterdam.

Park, G. D., Allen, R. W., Fiorentino, D., Rosenthal, T. J., & Cook, M. L. (2006). *Simulator sickness scores according to symptom susceptibility, age, and gender for an older driver assessment study*. Paper presented at the human factors and ergonomics society annual meeting.

Park, J. R., Lim, D. W., Lee, S. Y., Lee, H. W., Choi, M. H., & Chung, S. C. (2008). Long-term study of simulator sickness: Differences in EEG response due to individual sensitivity. *International Journal of Neuroscience, 118*(6), 857–865. doi:10.1080/00207450701239459.

Reason, J. T., & Brand, J. J. (1975). *Motion sickness*. San Diego: Academic.

Reber, A. S. (1985). *Dictionary of psychology*. London: Penguin Books.

Reed, M. P., & Green, P. A. (1999). Comparison of driving performance on-road and in a low-cost simulator using a concurrent telephone dialling task. *Ergonomics, 42*(8), 1015–1037.

Regan, E. C. (1994). *Some human factors issues in immersive virtual reality*. APRE Report 94R027, UK, Defence Research Agency.

Riccio, G. E., & Stoffregen, T. A. (1991). An ecological theory of motion sickness and postural instability. *Ecological Psychology, 3*(3), 195–240.

Roe, C., Brown, T., & Watson, G. (2007). *Factors associated with simulator sickness in a high-fidelity driving simulator*. Paper presented at the driving simulator conference (DSC2007), Iowa City.

Sharples, S., Cobb, S., Moody, A., & Wilson, J. R. (2008). Virtual reality induced symptoms and effects (VRISE): Comparison of head mounted display (HMD), desktop and projection display systems. *Displays, 29*(2), 58–69. doi:10.1016/j.displa.2007.09.005.

Slater, M. (2002). Presence and the sixth sense. *Presence-Teleoperators and Virtual Environments, 11*(4), 435–439.

Smart, L. J., Stoffregen, T. A., & Bardy, B. G. (2002). Visually induced motion sickness predicted by postural instability. *Human Factors, 44*(3), 451–465.

Smither, J. A. A., Mouloua, M., & Kennedy, R. (2008). Reducing symptoms of visually induced motion sickness through perceptual training. *International Journal of Aviation Psychology, 18*(4), 326–339. doi:10.1080/10508410802346921.

So, R. H. Y., & Yuen, S. L. (2007). *Comparing symptoms of visually induced motion sickness among viewers of four similar virtual environments with different color*. In proceedings of the IEEE virtual reality conference, vol. 4563, pp. 386–391.

Srinivasan, R., & Jovanis, P. P. (1997). Effect of in-vehicle route guidance systems on driver workload and choice of vehicle speed: Findings from a driving simulator experiment. In Y. I. Noy (Ed.), *Ergonomics and safety of intelligent driver interfaces*. Athens, Greece: LEA publishers.

Stanney, K., M., Kennedy, R.M., & Drexler, J.M. (1997). Cybersickness is not simulator sickness. *Proceedings of the Human Factors and Ergonomics Society Annual Meeting, 41*(2), 1138–1142.

Stanney, K. M., & Hash, P. (1998). Locus of user-initiated control in virtual environments: Influences on cybersickness. *Presence-Teleoperators and Virtual Environments, 7*(5), 447–459.

Stanney, K. M., Kennedy, R. S. (2009). Simulation sickness. In D. A. Vincenzi, J. A. Wise, M. Mouloua, & P. A. Hancock (Eds.), *Human factors in simulation and training*. Boca Raton: CRC Press.

Stoffregen, T. A., & Riccio, G. E. (1991). An ecological critique of the sensory conflict theory of motion sickness. *Ecological Psychology, 3*(3), 159–194.

Stoffregen, T. A., & Smart, L. J. (1998). Postural instability precedes motion sickness. *Brain Research Bulletin, 47*(5), 437–448.

Stoffregen, T. A., Hettinger, L. J., Haas, M. W., Roe, M. M., & Smart, L. J. (2000). Postural instability and motion sickness in a fixed-base flight simulator. *Human Factors, 42*(3), 458–469.

Sugita, N., Yoshizawa, M., Tanaka, A., Abe, K., Chiba, S., Yambe, T., et al. (2008). Quantitative evaluation of effects of visually-induced motion sickness based on causal coherence functions between blood pressure and heart rate. *Displays, 29*(2), 167–175. doi:10.1016/j.dispia.2007.09.017.

Suma, E. A., Finkelstein, S. L., Reid, M., Ulinski, A., & Hodges, L. F. (2009). *Real walking increases simulator sickness in navigationally complex virtual environments*. In proceedings of the IEEE virtual reality conference, pp 245–246.

Teasdale, N., Lavallière, M., & Tremblay, M. (2009). *Multiple exposition to a driving simulator reduces simulator symptoms for elderly drivers*. Paper presented at the fifth international driving symposium on human factors in driver assessment, training and vehicle design, Big Sky, Montana.

Ujike, H., Ukai, K., & Nihei, K. (2008). Survey on motion sickness-like symptoms provoked by viewing a video movie during junior high school class. *Displays, 29*(2), 81–89. doi:10.1016/j.displa.2007.09.003.

Wald, J., & Taylor, S. (2003). Preliminary research on the efficacy of virtual reality exposure therapy to treat driving phobia. *CyberPsychology & Behavior, 6*(5), 459–465.

Walshe, D., Lewis, E., O'Sullivan, K., & Kim, S. I. (2005). Virtually driving: Are the driving environments "Real Enough" for exposure therapy with accident victims? An explorative study. *CyberPsychology & Behavior, 8*(6), 532–537.

Warwick-Evans, L., & Beaumont, S. (1995). An experimental evaluation of sensory conflict versus postural control theories of motion sickness. *Ecological Psychology, 7*(3), 163–179.

Welch, R. B., & Sampanes, A. C. (2008). Adapting to virtual environments: Visual-motor skill acquisition versus perceptual recalibration. *Displays, 29*(2), 152–158. doi:10.1016/j.displa.2007.09.013.

Wesley, A. D., Sayer, T. D., & Tengler, S. (2005). *Can Sea Bands be used to mitigate simulator sickness?* Paper presented at the third international driving symposium on human factors in driver assessment, training and vehicle design, Park City, Utah.

Wiederhold, B. K., & Wiederhold, M. D. (2010). Virtual reality treatment of posttraumatic stress disorder due to motor vehicle accident. *Cyberpsychology, Behavior, and Social Networking, 13*(1), 21–27.

Part II
Anxiety Disorders

Chapter 4
Fear of Flying (Aviophobia): Efficacy and Methodological Lessons Learned from Outcome Trials

Brenda K. Wiederhold, Stéphane Bouchard and Claudie Loranger

4.1 Key Variables Involved in this Disorder

The pathological fear of flying, also called aviophobia, falls under the subtype of specific situational phobias in the Diagnostic and Statistical Manual of Mental Disorders-IV (DSM-IV) (APA 2000) or under specific (isolated) phobia in the International Classification of Diseases (ICD)-10 (World Health Organization 1992). The term fear of flying was actually coined during World War II and referred to the mixture of fear and anxiety seen in aviators involved in combat (Joseph and Kulkarni 2003). People presenting for treatment for the pathological fear of flying may have either a well-defined specific phobia or their fear of flying may be part of another anxiety disorder (Brown 1996) such as panic disorder with agoraphobia, posttraumatic stress disorder, or claustrophobia. People suffering from the specific phobia of flying are afraid of events directly related to the flying experience (crashing, losing control of themselves, not having control over the situation, having a panic attack in planes, turbulence, etc.), whereas those with panic disorder with agoraphobia suffer from a more general fear of having an uncued and unexpected panic attack (APA 2000), those with claustrophobia are more afraid of suffocating or being confined to an enclosed space, and people with posttraumatic stress disorder have a more complex pattern of fears following exposure to a traumatic event (such as a plane crash) characterized by re-experiencing the traumatic event (flashbacks, distressing dreams, etc.), persistent avoidance of stimuli associated with the trauma, and hyperarousal. Some people suffering from aviophobia do actually fly, but with extreme discomfort or by using drugs like benzodiazepines or alcohol to deal with their anxiety (Greist and Greist 1981). Aviophobia is also characterized by negative cognitions when thinking about the flying experience (Möller et al. 1998), unproductive coping strategies such as self-blame, rumination, or catastrophizing (Kraaij et al. 2003), and significant anticipatory anxiety observed, for example, when planning trips and vacations, buying plane tickets, going to the airport, or waiting in the boarding area.

In a 1997 study by van Gerwen et al. with 419 people seeking treatment for fear of flying, the authors found that only a minority had never flown, suggesting that lack of experience with flying may not be the most frequent cause of aviophobia.

In their sample, van Gerwen et al. (1997) discovered that the reasons most patients often reported for being afraid of flying were, in descending order of frequency: fear of an accident, claustrophobia, the need for control over the situation, fear of heights, and fear of losing control over oneself. Some patients also mentioned being afraid of water.

Despite the fact that air transportation is safer than driving, an estimated 10–25 % of the general population in industrialized countries are affected by fear of flying, although this fear may not always reach the intensity required to meet DSM or ICD criteria for classification as a specific phobia (Agras et al. 1969; Dean and Whitaker 1982; van Gerwen and Diekstra 2000). Fredrickson et al. (1996) found that aviophobia affected 1.8 % of males and 3.2 % of females in their sample of 1000 individuals in the USA. A large epidemiologic survey conducted with >43,000 Americans reported similar data, with 2.9 % of the adult population suffering from aviophobia (Stinson et al. 2007). Fear of flying not only results in social stigmatization for some but may also result in loss of job opportunities due to an inability to travel. If these figures are accurate, the cost to the US airline industry in 1982 was estimated at $ 1.6 billion (Dean and Whitaker 1982; Roberts 1989).

4.2 Description of most Significant Efficacy Studies Using Traditional Approaches

Exposure is the most commonly used method for treating aviophobia, either in the form of systematic desensitization, stress inoculation training, flooding, imaginal or in vivo, or a mixture of all these forms. The study by Solyom et al. (1973) is the first controlled study conducted with a civilian population. Forty participants were assigned to one of four treatments: exposure through habituation, systematic desensitization, aversion relief, or group psychotherapy. Post treatment, all three forms of exposure therapies were shown to be equally effective in reducing fear of flying and significantly superior to the more general psychotherapy approach. However, these differences disappeared at follow-up.

Since then, several subsequent controlled studies have shown that exposure-based treatments are effective for fear of flying (Beckham et al. 1990; Denholtz and Mann 1975; Denholtz et al. 1978; Doctor et al. 1990; Haug et al. 1987; Howard et al. 1983). The strongest study was conducted by van Gerwen et al. (2006). These researchers randomly assigned 150 people suffering from aviophobia to one of three conditions: a waiting list, 12 h of behavioral therapy, or 20 h of cognitive–behavioral therapy (CBT). All participants except those in the waiting list received individual therapy sessions that included relaxation training, breathing retraining, and sitting in a stationary commercial aircraft for a mocked simulation, in addition to group therapy sessions (with a trained pilot as co-therapist), which included objective information about aircrafts and flying, coping skills, how to get prepared for a flight and an in vivo exposure session with a stationary Boeing 737, plus two

4.2 Description of most Significant Efficacy Studies Using Traditional Approaches

flights in a large flight training simulator[1] and two 1-h flights. The cognitive treatment program also included training in cognitive therapy (mostly about cognitive restructuring for anxiety and panic attacks) and practicing cognitive restructuring during the flight simulations. A booster session occurred at the 3-month follow-up. Statistical analyses conducted post therapy revealed that both treatments were significantly superior to the waiting list on all measures (all effect-sizes were large), and that treatment gains were maintained at the 6- and 12-month follow-ups. All participants in the cognitive condition and 49 out of 50 participants in the behavioral condition agreed to engage in the in vivo flight planned as part of the therapy, while none of the participants in the waiting list condition agreed when offered. After 6 and 12 months, all who received treatment were flying on their own. Participants in the cognitive–behavioral condition performed better on all fear-of-flying questionnaires, suggesting that learning how to restructure manifestations of anxiety and panic attacks can boost treatment efficacy.

Other studies have attempted to approximate flight experiences through advanced audiovisual sensations. As early as 1975, Denholtz and Mann used a series of scenes related to flying to create a film described as an "automated audiovisual program." This automated audiovisual program was used in conjunction with a combination of techniques (systematic desensitization, modeling, and positive reinforcement) to treat flight phobics. Despite problems with dropouts, their results suggest that using audiovisual stimuli could be useful to conduct exposure or systematic desensitization. More recently, Bornas et al. (2001) tested a computer-assisted fear-of-flying treatment. A hierarchy of 65 photographs (still images) with matching sounds (actual recordings) depicts situations such as going to a travel agency, packing at home, going to the airport, waiting for takeoff, watching the safety demonstration inside a plane, taking-off, announcing landing, reentering the airport terminal, etc. A sequence of pictures and sounds related to airplane accidents is also included in the computer program. The computer program displays the images on a projection screen while the patients wear stereo headphones and expose themselves to the stimuli. For their study, Bornas et al. (2001) assigned 50 people afraid of flying to either: (a) a waiting list, (b) computer-assisted exposure therapy, or (c) a combined treatment including watching a video providing information about various aspects of flying, an informational brochure, and a general relaxation training session followed by the computer-assisted exposure. After the computer-assisted exposure therapy, 93.4% of patients actually took a flight, compared to 11.8% on the waiting list. None of the participants receiving the combined treatment agreed to fly after the information and relaxation portion of their therapy, and surprisingly, only 50% of the participants in this condition agreed to fly after completing the computer-assisted exposure portion of their therapy. On questionnaire data, the analyses revealed that participants who only received the computer-assisted therapy improved

---

[1] Since such a simulator is a mocked copy of an airplane controlled by hydraulic systems and it does not meet the definition of virtual reality provided in the first chapter (e.g., no 3D computer-generated and computer-maintained stimuli), this study is not included in the section on VR outcome trials.

significantly more than those who received the combined treatment, who in turn improved significantly more than those in the waiting list did. This study suggests that simple information and relaxation may not be sufficient to help aviophobics, but it is difficult to explain why adding these components could reduce the efficacy of the computer-assisted therapy.

Öst et al. (1997) raised an important methodological issue about the use of posttreatment flight as an outcome measure. Öst et al. (1997) noted that relying solely on having people take an airplane flight post treatment is a questionable measure of outcome given that many patients do not have the opportunity to complete a pretreatment flight as a baseline measure. Without a baseline rate, it is impossible to measure change. Also, many individuals can fly with extreme discomfort and anxiety. Therefore, a flight should be offered at pretreatment to exclude participants who can actually fly and the posttreatment flight should be carefully designed to avoid standardization problems such as the use of medication, alcohol, or sense of security gained by flying accompanied by a therapist.

4.3 Description of most Significant Efficacy Studies Using Virtual Reality Approaches

Using virtual reality (VR) to conduct exposure is attractive because of the cost-efficiency and simplicity relative to in vivo exposure. For example, the therapist and patient do not have to drive to the airport, there is no need to buy airplane tickets, patient and therapist behaviors do not raise the suspicions of airport security personnel, the therapist has total control over the stimuli that the patient will be exposed to, and situations such as takeoff and landing can be repeated over and over again.

Compared with studies using *in virtuo* exposure to treat other anxiety disorders, there are manifestly more published studies on the application of VR in the treatment of fear of flying. Many randomized controlled trials have been published by a number of independent research groups. In every case, the VR intervention has yielded significant treatment effects. But first, let us mention some case studies using *in virtuo* exposure to successfully treat fear of flying that have appeared in the literature, although they vary widely in terms of their quality and reliance on questionnaires to measure outcome (Hodges et al. 1996; Kahan 2000; North et al. 1997; Rothbaum et al. 1996, 1997). For example, Klein (1998, 1999) reported five case studies in separate publications. In each case, clinical change was reported either based on Subjective Units of Disturbance Scale (SUDS) or other forms of self-report. The patient in the study by the Hodges and Rothbaum group was a 42-year-old female who had grown increasingly fearful of flying over the previous 5 years and who had not been able to fly at all for the previous 2 years. The patient first received seven sessions of anxiety management techniques, followed by six sessions of *in virtuo* exposure in a virtual airplane. The patient showed important decreases on all self-report measures after learning anxiety management techniques and further improvements after *in virtuo* exposure. She even completed a posttreatment flight. North, North, and Coble (1996) reported on a 42-year-old male who also received

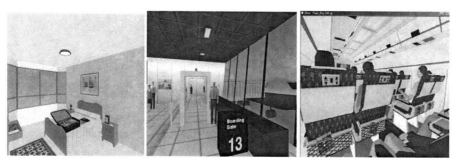

Fig. 4.1 Screenshots of the virtual environment developed by Previ and used by Botella et al. Images reproduced with permission from C. Botella

in virtuo exposure therapy for his fear of heights. Rather than an aircraft, a virtual helicopter was used with this patient, and a virtual therapist was also present in the virtual environment. He was given five sessions of *in virtuo* exposure and was administered only SUDS ratings. He has flown successfully several times after therapy. Wiederhold et al. (1998) also described the case of a patient who received four sessions of *in virtuo* exposure in a virtual airplane. In this study, physiological responses were measured along with self-report questionnaires. Heart rate, peripheral skin temperature, respiration rate, skin conductance, and brain wave activity were measured during a 5-min eyes-closed baseline period, a 20-min VR flight, and a 5-min eyes-closed recovery period. During the first session, skin resistance decreased between 34 and 36% during various parts of the flight compared to baseline levels, indicating significant anxiety or physiological arousal. During the fourth session, the patient was able to stabilize her skin resistance levels and actually had an increase in skin resistance, which was 57% above baseline by the end of the VR flight, confirming her state of relaxation with physiological indices. Post therapy, the patient was able to take a flight, with no medication or alcohol needed. In Spain, Baños et al. (2002) and Botella et al. (2004) also reported clinical case series of four and nine participants, respectively, and successfully treated with seven to eight sessions of *in virtuo* exposure (see Fig. 4.1). A pioneering aspect of the studies from the Spanish group of researchers is that the virtual environment includes not only a virtual flight but also a bedroom where the patient can experience the anticipatory anxiety of packing the luggage and a virtual airport where the patient can go through a check-in and boarding process (see Fig. 4.2). All of these important case studies paved the way for more robust outcome studies.

In 1999, Wiederhold published the results of the first randomized controlled clinical trial conducted with 30 participants suffering from aviophobia (see also Wiederhold et al. 2002). Participants were randomly assigned to one of three conditions: (a) *in virtuo* exposure, (b) *in virtuo* exposure plus physiological feedback, and (c) a control condition based on systematic desensitization using imaginal exposure. As is the case with most outcome studies on *in virtuo* exposure for fear of flying, participants were excluded from the study if they presented with a history of heart

Fig. 4.2 Screenshots of the virtual environment developed by Virtually Better and used by Rothbaum et al. © Copyright Virtually Better, Inc. All rights reserved

disease, migraines, seizures, or concurrent diagnosis of severe mental disorders, such as psychosis or major depressive disorder. The hardware equipment used at the time to conduct *in virtuo* exposure was a Pentium II 300 MHz personal computer, a MRG4 head-mounted display (HMD) from Liquid Image™, an Insidetrack head tracker from Polhemus™, and an office chair with a subwoofer and an attached airplane seatbelt. The software provided the user with the feeling of being seated in the window seat on a commercial airplane. Every step of a flight was recreated, including being parked on the tarmac, taxiing, messages from the pilot or crew members, taking off, the sound of landing gears raising and locking into place, flying in good conditions, flying in turbulence, landing, etc.

All 30 participants received two sessions of anxiety management skills training (diaphragmatic breathing retraining, relaxation training), plus six sessions of exposure-based therapy. In the control condition, an individualized hierarchy was developed to conduct the systematic desensitization with imaginal exposure. For the *in virtuo* exposure plus physiological feedback condition, the therapist verbally presented feedback after *in virtuo* exposure about participants' skin resistance levels while immersed in the virtual environment. Feedback was also displayed on a computer monitor pre-, during, and post VR immersion for heart rate, skin conductance, peripheral skin temperature, respiration rate, and brain wave activity.

Statistical analyses from the analysis of variances (ANOVAs) revealed that, on fear of flying questionnaires, all three treatment conditions improved significantly over time and none was superior to the others. The SUDS levels reported during therapy decreased significantly during treatment for the two *in virtuo* exposure conditions compared to the imaginal exposure condition, with the *in virtuo* exposure alone showing significantly lower SUDs during the last therapy session compared to the *in virtuo* exposure plus physiological feedback. When contacted 3 months post therapy to assess if patients took a flight on their own (see Fig. 4.3), a significantly higher number of participants flew on their own without medication in both groups who received *in virtuo* exposure. However, the group receiving *in virtuo* exposure plus physiological feedback had a higher number of participants (100%) who could fly compared to the *in virtuo* alone group (80%).

Wiederhold and Wiederhold (2005) reported an interesting anecdote about two cases that received the systematic desensitization with imaginal exposure. One participant, wanting very desperately to fly, was offered six additional sessions of

4.3 Description of most Significant Efficacy Studies Using Virtual Reality Approaches

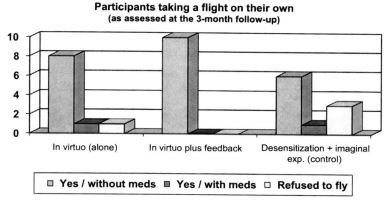

Fig. 4.3 Adapted from Wiederhold (1999)

imaginal exposure and biofeedback training after discontinuing the research study. This resulted in the participant being able to fly on his own, although still with the help of a prescription medication. After reporting an inability to fly when contacted at 3-month follow-up, a second participant received *in virtuo* exposure with physiological feedback. After completing six exposure sessions, the participant was able to fly successfully without the use of prescription medication or alcohol and with considerably less anxiety than had previously been experienced. The addition of physiological feedback to exposure may have its advantages. According to Wiederhold and Wiederhold (2000), taking physiological measures allows the therapist to see if patients' physiology is in concordance with their subjective report of anxiety. Participants reporting high levels of anxiety that are not accompanied with physiological arousal may represent patients who are more difficult to treat. It is also possible that observing measurable and objective improvements could increase participants' perceived self-efficacy to cope with their aviophobia.

Wiederhold and Wiederhold (2003) followed up with the participants 3 years post therapy and were able to contact all participants who received *in virtuo* exposure and seven out of ten of those who received systematic desensitization with imaginal exposure. They found that the number of participants who were still flying on their own without medication was 60% in the *in virtuo* exposure condition, 100% in the *in virtuo* exposure plus physiological feedback condition, and 10% in the systematic desensitization with imaginal exposure condition. An additional 30% of those in the *in virtuo* exposure alone condition and 60% of those in the systematic desensitization with imaginal exposure condition were flying with the use of medication.

Rothbaum and her group conducted two distinct controlled trials confirming the efficacy of *in virtuo* exposure in the treatment of aviophobia. In Rothbaum et al. (2000), all 49 participants recruited had flown before and were reliably diagnosed, using a semi-structured clinical interview, as suffering from either specific phobia of flying, panic disorder with agoraphobia, or agoraphobia without a history of panic disorder in which flying was the feared stimulus. They were randomly assigned

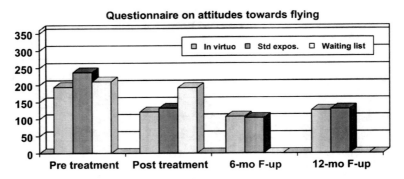

Fig. 4.4 Adapted from Rothbaum et al. (2000)

to (a) *in virtuo* exposure, (b) standard exposure (in vivo exposure in the airport, in vivo exposure in a stationary airplane, and imaginal exposure while in the stationary airplane), or (c) a wait-list control group. The same VR software was used for this study as was used for the Wiederhold (1999) study and the difference in hardware lies essentially in the HMD used (VR6 from Virtual Research System™).

Forty-nine participants began the study, with 45 completing treatment. Participants received eight individual treatment sessions over a period of 6 weeks, with four sessions consisting of breathing retraining, cognitive restructuring, and thought-stopping techniques. This was followed by four sessions of exposure. As shown in Fig. 4.4, results indicated that the exposure groups were largely equivalent in treatment effects and superior to the wait-list control group. Post test, both exposure conditions were not significantly different from one another but significantly superior to the waiting list in terms of taking a graduation flight (3-h round-trip), with 53% of participants in the *in virtuo* exposure condition, 67% of participants in the standard exposure condition, and 7% of participants on the waiting list actually taking the flight. At the 6-month follow-up, 79% of VR participants and 69% of real-life exposure participants gave self-reports of having flown since the graduation flight. In total, in both exposure conditions 93% of participants had flown at least once, either on their own or at the graduation flight. In 2002, Rothbaum et al. reported the results from a 12-month follow-up. They were able to contact 80% of the participants who received a treatment. No significant differences were found between the two treatment groups at follow-up on any of the outcome measures. At that time, 92 and 93% of participants in the *in virtuo* and the standard exposure conditions, respectively, had flown since the graduation flight.

In 2006, Rothbaum et al. (2006) replicated their study with a new sample of 75 participants (25 completers per condition out of 83 initially enrolled). The treatment was essentially the same, as well as the software; the computer was slightly more powerful and the HMD was lighter and more immersive (VFX-3D by IIS-VR™). Analyses included an intent-to-treat approach as well as traditional completer analyses. Statistical analyses confirmed that (a) both standard exposure and *in virtuo* exposure were superior to the waiting list and (b) the differences between the two

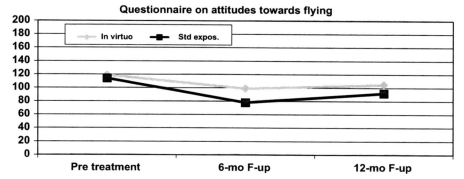

Fig. 4.5 Adapted from Rothbaum et al. (2006)

forms of exposure were far from being significant. Post treatment, 76% of participants in both exposure conditions participated in the graduation flight, compared to 20% from the waiting list. Once participants on the waiting list were reassigned to the experimental conditions and treated, the comparisons between the treatment involving *in virtuo* and standard exposure revealed that effect sizes were small to trivial. These results further support the lack of significant difference between both forms of exposure. At the 6-month follow-up, 71 and 76% of the participants in the *in virtuo* and standard exposure conditions, respectively, did not meet the diagnostic criteria for specific aviophobia (Fig. 4.5).

In an interesting follow-up, Anderson et al. (2006) contacted the participants from the Rothbaum et al. (2000) and (2006) clinical trials to test if treatment gains were maintained after the September 11, 2001 terrorist attack. Their analyses revealed that patients who completed therapy maintained or improved their treatment gains and that the difference between standard exposure and *in virtuo* exposure remains trivial. Kim et al. (2008) also found that patients were still using the skills taught in therapy and that cognitive restructuring and self-exposure were more useful than breathing skills.

Some clinical studies have reported on the feasibility of using *in virtuo* exposure in private practice settings. For example, Klein (1998, 1999) and Kahan et al. (2000) reported treating patients with success. Both groups combined *in virtuo* exposure with other cognitive–behavioral techniques, such as anxiety management. This raised the issue of effectiveness, as opposed to efficacy, of VR-based therapies. What effectiveness studies lose in internal validity (e.g., strict selection criteria, high standardization of treatment delivery, elaborated control conditions), they gain in external validity (i.e., more similar to what is used in clinical settings). There is an increasing need for effectiveness studies (Stirman et al. 2005) to follow efficacy studies in order to document the implementation of evidence-based treatment in routine clinical practice. An open trial for effectiveness was conducted in a collaborative effort from Wiederhold and Bouchard's clinics (Robillard et al. 2004). A total of 53 aviophobics suffering from various comorbid disorders received between eight and ten therapy sessions with therapists who varied greatly in their experience with VR and using different hardware and software configurations. Their results showed a statistically significant reduction of score on the Fear of Flying Questionnaire and the Questionnaire on Attitudes towards Flying, with large effect sizes (>0.60). Since fear of flying is a heterogeneous disorder, Kahan et al. (2000) conducted a small effectiveness study in order to document if patients suffering only from the fear of crashing benefited more from *in virtuo* exposure compared to those presenting more varied fears, such as claustrophobia, fear of heights, or fear of panicking. Although no statistical analyses were performed, their results suggest that both types of aviophobics benefited equally from, on average 5.75, sessions of therapy. Given the methodological limitations of this study, a replication with a larger sample accompanied with statistical analyses is warranted.

Given that most treatment packages of *in virtuo* exposure include relaxation training, the results from a study conducted in Germany by Mühlberger et al. (2001) are especially important. In order to assess whether fear reduction observed during *in virtuo* exposure is stronger than fear reduction induced by relaxation, they immersed each of their 30 aviophobics in a 6-min VR test flight, randomly assigned them to relaxation training or *in virtuo* exposure for about an hour and a half, and then immersed them again in a 6-min VR test flight. Both the test flights and the exposure flights were conducted in a virtual environment using a VR4 HMD by Virtual Research Systems™, a Fast Track motion tracker from Polhemus Corporation™, and a motion base from Symtech Corporation™ simulating acceleration, deceleration, and turbulence (see Fig. 4.6; see Boyd et al. (2013) for an example of a more complex simulator). The VR systems worked on extremely high performance and expensive Silicon Graphics computers. The virtual environment consisted of the inside of a Boeing 737 and the participant was seated at the window seat with a virtual passenger seated in the aisle seat. The virtual flight included steps such as taxiing, taking-off, ascending, two periods of air turbulence, descending, and landing. The most important differences between the test flight and the exposure flight were the duration of the experience (only the first 6 min of the flight versus repeating the entire 16-min flight four times), the auditory stimulation (none was provided during the test flight), and the air turbulence (occurring only in the exposure flight). Mühlberger et al. (2001) found that (a) the virtual test flight induced anxiety (as measured with self-report and physiological indices), (b) habituation occurred within and between *in virtuo* exposure sessions, (c) self-report measures of fear of flying significantly decreased in both conditions when comparing self-report questionnaires completed before the first test flight and after the second test flight, and, most importantly, (d) *in virtuo* exposure leads to significantly stronger improvements than relaxation training on SUDS ratings and skin conductance during the post-test flight, as well as avoidance of flying ratings. The latter differences were still significant at the 3-month follow-up. The difference in efficacy between the two conditions was not significant for all measures, but this study still highlights that *in virtuo* exposure reduces fear more effectively than plain relaxation training. In terms of physiology, the findings for within session habituation were significant only for the skin conductance measure, not heart rate, while between-session habituation was noted on both physiological indices.

4.3 Description of most Significant Efficacy Studies Using Virtual Reality Approaches 75

Fig. 4.6 Picture of the seat used to simulate motion in Mühlberger et al.. Image reproduced with permission from A. Mühlberger

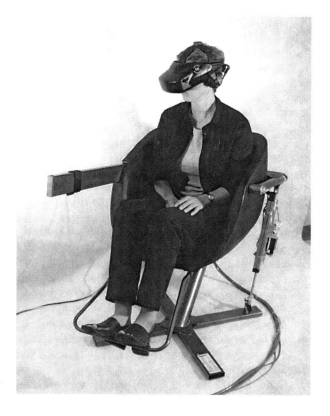

In trying to further dismantle active ingredients in exposure packages for fear of flying, Mühlberger et al. (2003) examined the treatment effects of motion simulation by assigning 47 flight phobics to one of four treatment conditions: (a) cognitive therapy, (b) cognitive therapy plus *in virtuo* exposure without motion simulation, (c) cognitive therapy plus *in virtuo* exposure with motion simulation, and (d) a wait-list control. The therapy session (lasting 140 min for the treatment involving exposure and 60 min for the treatment involving only cognitive restructuring) consisted of identifying and analyzing catastrophic cognitions and discussing concepts related to anxiety and exposure and, for participants in conditions (b) and (c) performing four consecutive flights in VR using the same hardware and software as Mühlberger et al. (2001). Statistical analyses revealed that both *in virtuo* exposure conditions were significantly superior to the waiting list on post-therapy and follow-up questionnaires measuring fear and avoidance of flying. They also revealed that, most of the time, cognitive therapy alone was less effective than *in virtuo* exposure, with cognitive therapy alone not differing significantly from the waiting list on any measure post treatment and at follow-up. However, no differences were found in the rate of participants who agreed to book their own flight after the therapy or at the follow-up. Even more interesting are the comparisons with artificial motion during *in virtuo* exposure. Simulating motions and vibrations did not significantly increase

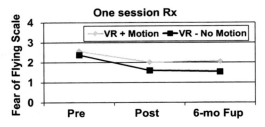

Fig. 4.7 From Mühlberger. (Data from personal communication, 2005)

treatment efficacy compared to *in virtuo* exposure without the hydraulic devices post treatment and at follow-up, as measured by questionnaire or booking actual flights (see Fig. 4.7).

The technologies involved in the studies described previously were immersive and used an HMD to foster the feeling of presence. In 2011, a Spanish research team (Tortella-Feliu et al. 2011) conducted a study with 60 flying phobics to compare three computer-based exposure systems: (a) a virtual environment displayed on HMD without motion tracking and operated by the therapist, (b) an Internet-based software displaying images on a computer screen operated by the patient while the therapist is in the room and intervenes only to address technical problems, and (c) the same Internet-based software self-administered online at the clinic but without the presence of the therapist. The Internet-based software provided photos and associated sounds displayed on a personal computer following a progressive hierarchy. For the three forms of treatment, a maximum of six 1-h, twice-weekly sessions were established. Interestingly, all three treatments were equally effective at significantly reduced fear of flying both at post treatment and at 1-year follow-up. The success rate measured by taking an actual flight post therapy was 50 % for the Internet-based program delivered in the presence of a therapist, 62 % for the same program self-administered, and 79 % for the treatment using the virtual environment. None of the differences between the three treatments, including for the graduation flight, reached statistical significance post treatment or at follow-up. These results have three implications. First, one may wonder to what extent the addition of motion tracking would have improved treatment efficacy. Motion tracking would make the experience more immersive and facilitate the feeling of presence through multisensory integration. Second, it seems possible to have interesting successes even with technology, which is not very immersive (an issue discussed in more detail in Chaps. 5 and 6). This does not mean that the strength of the immersion is not important, but rather that the relationship between immersiveness, presence, and treatment outcome is probably not linear (see Chap. 2). Third, this study paves the way for VR applications that can be self-administered. In order to improve our understanding of the strengths and weaknesses of clinical trials used for flying phobia, Mühlberger et al. (2006) completed another study with exposure in VR delivered during only one session and using their pneumatic motion system. The aim of the study was to assess the impact of the graduation flight, which is a common behavioral measure of treatment success. Participants were randomly assigned to two conditions for their graduation flight: either accompanied or alone. In the first condition, participants met with the therapist and other patients at the airport and flew together, although they did not sit next to each other. Participants in the second condition had to complete the graduation flight alone. Results show a highly significant reduction of fear of flying after the therapy session for both groups before the graduation flight. Only 67 % of the participants agreed to fly post treatment in the condition where they were alone, compared to 87 % when accompanied. The difference was not statistically significant, but it may suggest a motivational advantage of being accompanied. Treatment credibility was also related to treatment outcome. What is most interesting is the comparison between those who completed the behavioral avoidance test (BAT) and those who did not. Although there was no difference between completers and non-completers of the BAT post treatment, those who did not complete the BAT showed a worsening of their fear of flying. The advantage of performing the graduation flight remained significant at the 1-year follow-up. Several reasons could be formulated to explain the results (e.g., completing the BAT may serve as an additional in vivo exposure session or boost self-efficacy, refusing to perform the graduation flight may have a deleterious effect on self-efficacy or fear, non-completers may have refused the BAT because they had already worsened), but it raises nevertheless the question of the potential therapeutic effect of a BAT.

In general, results from Maltby et al. (2002) are less supportive of the efficacy of *in virtuo* exposure. Maltby et al. (2002) assigned 45 aviophobics who refused to fly in a pretreatment screening test to either a treatment including *in virtuo* exposure or an attention-placebo condition. Maltby et al.'s (2002) hardware included a Pentium II computer, a joystick to walk in the virtual environment, and a V6 HMD from Virtual Research™. It is not mentioned in the paper if they used any form of head tracking, a factor that might have significantly hindered the feeling of presence. Their VR software consisted of ten scenes including an empty hallway, an airport terminal, walking to a small non-commercial airplane, taking-off, flying in smooth, turbulent or stormy conditions, etc. Their treatment protocol for the *in virtuo* exposure condition lasted five individual sessions over 3 weeks and consisted of training in anxiety management skills, relaxation, information about the safety and mechanics of flying, cognitive restructuring, and graded *in virtuo* exposure. The control condition consisted of a credible attention-placebo: five group meetings where patients received education about the safety and mechanics of flying and discussed each other's flying histories. After completing the self-report measures post treatment, a graduation flight was offered to the participants. As opposed to other VR studies, the graduation flight was performed in a small noncommercial airplane where each participant was alone with a therapist and the pilot, the flight lasted for 10–20 min, and the patients remained in control over when to enter the aircraft, takeoff, and land.

Maltby et al.'s (2002) results showed large pre–post differences in measures of subjective flight anxiety in both groups. Participants in the treatment condition improved significantly more on in-flight anxiety, anticipatory flight anxiety, somatic anxiety, and cognitive anxiety compared to the placebo condition, but not in generalized flight anxiety. Clinically significant change in in-flight anxiety was significantly higher in those receiving treatment (70 %) compared to the placebo (22 %). The same pattern of result was observed for anticipatory flight anxiety. However, the difference in posttreatment test-flight was not significant, with 65 % of participants in the treatment condition and 57 % of the patients in the placebo condition completing the graduation flight. The high number of patients who completed the graduation flight in the placebo condition may be related to the information provided during the group meeting, or to nonspecific factors embedded in the task, such as retaining some control over the flight, the small size of the aircraft, the loyalty to the therapist (even if it was not the one treating the patient), self-disclosure, etc. But being able to fly, even once, probably had a strong therapeutic impact on participants in the control condition. Indeed, the statistical analyses revealed that their scores on the self-report measures significantly improved at the 6-month follow-up, to the point that they were not significantly different from those of the participants in the treatment condition.

A study on *in virtuo* exposure for fear of flying was conducted by Krijn et al. (2007) in an attempt to differentiate the impact of *in virtuo* exposure and CBT, as well as to document how these interventions impact a 2-day group CBT program. They recruited adults suffering from a specific phobia of flying based on *DSM-IV*'s criteria. They recruited 86 participants, but several dropped out, including 12 due to the *in virtuo* condition because the environment did not induce any anxiety, and one due to VR-induced side effects (other dropouts were mostly in the control condition). Every participant received a self-help book, which included psychoeducation about airplanes and cognitive–behavioral coping skills, and were assigned to one of the three following experimental conditions: (a) control (just reading the book), (b) individual *in virtuo* exposure therapy (four 60-min weekly sessions of exposure only), and (c) individual CBT (two to four 60-min weekly sessions of relaxation and cognitive restructuring, plus some in vivo exposure). After 5 weeks, participants in the control condition were tested and reassigned to the active treatment conditions. In *both* conditions with active treatment, patients suffering from claustrophobia or acrophobia received up to two sessions of exposure. Following the individual therapies, participants received 2 days of intensive group therapy according to van Gerwen et al.'s (2006) treatment program. Interestingly, all patients paid to receive their therapy. Measures were taken at the start of the study, after the individual therapies, and after the group therapy. To conduct *in virtuo* exposure, the researchers used a Pentium-II computer (generating the images at a low 15–20 frames/s), a stereoscopic Visette Pro™ HMD, and a Flock of Bird™ 6-dof motion tracker. The research team also developed two virtual environments specific to the fear of flying (see Fig. 4.8) and an extensive interface allowing the therapist to manipulate several factors such as the number of passenger in the airplane, the user's position, etc. (Gunawan et al. 2004). In the virtual Schipol airport, the users could see a check-in terminal and move within a 1-m^2 area. In the airplane environment, the user was seated in an aircraft seat that vibrated during takeoff, turbulence, and landing. Virtual environments for the fear of heights (see Chap. 6 on acrophobia) and for claustrophobia were also used. Treatment outcome was measured with two self-report measures of subjective anxiety and somatic/cognitive symptoms. No behavior avoidance/approach test was used, but presence was assessed at each therapy session.

4.3 Description of most Significant Efficacy Studies Using Virtual Reality Approaches

Fig. 4.8 Screenshots from the VR software developed by Delft University and used in Krijn et al. (2007). Images courtesy of Delft University of Technology, The Netherlands

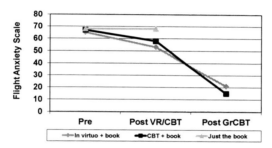

Fig. 4.9 Adapted from Krijn et al. (2007)

Results of the Krijn et al. (2007, see Fig. 4.9) study revealed several interesting findings. First, both forms of active treatment were significantly superior to the control condition after the four therapy sessions. Second, the difference in efficacy between the two active treatments was very small and nonsignificant, supporting the idea that they were both equally effective. However, the effect-sizes of both treatment approaches were moderate. These results were generally similar when analyses were performed with those who only completed the individual treatments and with intent-to-treat analyses. Third, the addition of the 2-day intensive group treatment led to further improvements that were very important and statistically significant. Lastly, participants who received the individual cognitive–behavior intervention fared significantly better at the end of the study than those who received *in virtuo* exposure. The authors raised several interesting issues in discussing their results. The efficacy of their individual treatment was lower than other clinical trials on fear of flying. This may be influenced by the rather brief duration of their therapy, by spending therapy time working on acrophobia and claustrophobia instead of aviophobia and by the potentially low level of anxiety induced by the environments (29 % of the initial participants in the *in virtuo* condition did not experience anxiety and had to be excluded). When looking at the impact of individual treatments on the intensive package, the additional training in relaxation and cognitive restructuring may have been more fruitful in preparing the patients for a comprehensive set of interventions that includes in vivo exposure than preparing the patients for *in virtuo* exposure. In sum, this study raises interesting questions about dismantling treatment, studying treatment duration, addressing comorbid issues explicitly in the treatment protocol, performing direct comparisons between in vivo and *in virtuo* exposures, and assessing the incremental advantages of these two forms of exposure.

In order to further our understanding of the learning mechanisms involved in emotional processing during exposure-based treatments, Meyerbroeker et al. (2012) conducted a placebo-controlled trial with a clinical sample of participants suffering from fear of flying. Their intention was to measure the potential of yohimbine hydrochloride to enhance the extinction of fear. Because the stimuli used for exposure *in virtuo* are similar for each patient, using this technology to conduct outcome trials on pharmacological augmentation strategies standardizes the treatments and strengthens the methodology. In Meyerbroeker et al.'s research (2012), participants had to take yohimbine or placebo an hour prior to the sessions (one training session and four therapy sessions). Therapy sessions consisted of two 25-min periods of *in virtuo* exposure and were preceded by instructions about anxiety hierarchy and the general rationale of the therapy, but no cognitive restructuring took place. Although participants improved significantly on measures of flight anxiety from pretreatment to posttreatment, the results did not support the enhancing effects of yohimbine. No significant differences between the yohimbine and placebo groups were found, even though assessment of noradrenaline levels confirmed the impact of the experimental manipulation. In addition to adding confidence in the effectiveness of using VR to treat flying phobia, this study illustrates how this technology could be used to improve the standardization and homogeneity of clinical experimental manipulations.

4.4 Available Software

At least four software programs are commercially available, from Previ (http://www.previsl.com/ing), Virtually Better Inc. (http://www.virtuallybetter.com), Virtual Reality Medical Center (http://www.vrphobia.com), and CleVr (www.clevr.net). The Previ software includes anticipatory anxiety scenes—packing a suitcase in a bedroom, listening to the radio, watching the weather outside, sitting in the terminal listening to other flights being announced, hearing other waiting passengers discussing the flight, seeing other planes takeoff outside the airport terminal windows, and viewing the weather (good or bad) during daytime or nighttime. The flight then includes a radio, which can be turned on or off and tuned to different stations, a drop-down screen that shows a flight attendant giving safety instructions, a magazine that can be taken from the seatback and "flipped through," a window whose covering can be opened or closed, and a seatbelt that can be fastened and unfastened. The passenger cabin is filled with people, and the participant has the choice of choosing to be represented with a male or female body. The flight goes through engines on, taxi, takeoff, air turbulence, flying in good weather, flying over the ocean, and landing. By moving their head, users can look around the virtual world,

Fig. 4.10 Screenshots of the virtual environment developed by Virtual Reality Medical Center

and joystick navigation is also provided. The Virtually Better Inc. software has been available in different versions over the years and includes a passenger cabin where one is seated in the left window seat over the wing. The person can look around the cabin by turning his or her head. The cabin was empty in most of the early versions, including only the patient on board the virtual plane, but more recent versions include passengers. The flight goes through engines off, engines on, taxi, takeoff, air turbulence, flying in good weather, and landing. Using the keyboard, the therapist can activate a chime or lightening strikes and navigate directly to selected steps in the flight. The system comes with an amplifier and a platform with two bass shakers transmitting loud noises and vibrations. With some work, the audio files of the messages from the captain and the crew can be replaced with "in house" recordings, allowing the use the software in languages other than English.

Virtual Reality Medical Center's (VRMC's) software includes environments for both anticipatory anxiety and fear of flying (see Fig. 4.10). The patient can view scenes of a busy airport and interact with ticket agents and security guards, before entering the virtual plane. The "passenger" then experiences takeoff, hears the captain and flight attendants make announcements, and can gaze out the window viewing clouds and the plane's wing as well as viewing the interior of the plane and other passengers, before landing again safely in the treatment room. The therapist can trigger visual and audio stimuli to simulate different weather patterns and plane movements and the patient can choose either a daytime or nighttime flight, as well as a male or female avatar. The patient sits in real airplane seats with built-in motors atop a subwoofer platform during the therapy sessions to make the experience truly immersive. Created by a multidisciplinary team of computer scientists, therapists, and graphic artists, the end user (in this case the patient with a fear of flying) also provided valuable input on what stimuli were most important for inclusion.

Engineers have also conducted research on the design and usability of VR software. Brinkman et al. (2010) used an extremely versatile computer interface that allows adjusting several conditions of a virtual flight. They reported that therapists would, on occasion, make mistakes when using a complex interface. For example, therapists would play inappropriate sounds, such as a pilot giving information about the height of the plane while actually taking off. For this reason, they suggested that designers of virtual environments move away from a *simulation-oriented* user interface that provides many options to make the experience realistic and flexible, to a *treatment-oriented* user interface that is simple and intuitive for therapists. More specifically, Brinkman et al. (2010) propose new design guidelines: (1) provide therapists with automated exposure scenarios, (2) provide therapists with an integrated timeline (representation of the different phases in the scenario, recorded anxiety scores, comment flags, events to come, and those already taken place) and the current position on the timeline, (3) design for error prevention (by hiding inappropriate simulation events), (4) provide therapists with predefined comment flags to record events in the session, and (5) when the position of the patient is fixed in the virtual environment, therapists do not need an additional viewpoint displaying where the patient is in the virtual environment. The authors suggest these solutions could increase therapists' confidence in using the system and reduce therapists' task load. Fortunately, designers of clinical virtual environments commercially available have now integrated these suggestions to simplify the task of the therapists.

A common question about the use of virtual environment is about the necessity to adapt or contextualize the environment and the treatment protocol to cultural differences. This question has not been thoroughly empirically explored. Although flying is an experience that shares many similarities across cultures, translation of audio files and text material required to understand the situation seems logical a priori. Additionally, taking a flight where all instructions from the flight attendants and pilot are provided in a foreign language may actually be more frightening to some patients than hearing them in their native language. Other details may be relevant for patients, such as the style of airplanes, signs in the airport, local expressions, physical appearance of other passengers, etc. Cardenas-Lopez et al. (2009) conducted a pilot study with Mexican patients using a virtual environment designed in Spain. Their results provide clinical impressions supporting the effectiveness of the virtual environment.

4.5 Relevant Findings from Studies Using VR Approaches

Overall, results from outcome studies are supportive of the efficacy of *in virtuo* exposure for the treatment of aviophobia. Studies comparing the efficacy of *in virtuo* exposure to waiting list and standard treatments show that *in virtuo* exposure is clearly superior to no treatment and effect sizes comparing both treatments suggest that the differences between the two are very small, if any exist at all. Comparisons with control conditions including active therapeutic ingredients are less clear but still suggest that the efficacy of *in virtuo* exposure can be compared with that of state-of-the-art CBT (Meyerbroeker and Emmelkamp 2010; Opris et al. 2012). Using VR to conduct exposure can be considered as a reliable technique to be used in the treatment of aviophobia (Da Costa et al. 2008). A variety of VR software, treatment packages, and methodologies have been used, some like the Rothbaum's group with large samples and direct replication of their findings and others like the Wiederhold's group with long-term follow-up.

Except for the dismantling studies from Mühlberger et al. (2001, 2003), every study used rather inexpensive computers that are not considered powerful by current standards. All of the HMDs used in the studies are now outdated and are

4.5 Relevant Findings from Studies Using VR Approaches

Fig. 4.11 Picture of a patient in an airplane seat, accompanied with her therapist. Reproduced with permission from S. Bouchard

surpassed by less expensive, lighter, and more powerful units. Some clinicians are using aircraft seats to seat the patient (see Fig. 4.11). This may increase the sense of presence by providing a more credible physical context for the immersion, and by having patients engaged in behaviors, they would perform in physical reality, such as buckling-up. Patients also often grab the armrests, as they would do in actual flights. However, no study has been conducted to document if using airplane seats has any significant impact on the therapy.

In terms of presence, Price (2006) treated 35 aviophobics and tested whether the feeling of presence is related to anxiety felt during *in virtuo* exposure. This doctoral thesis found a significant and linear relationship between anxiety assessed regularly during the immersion and presence, as measured with the Presence Questionnaire (Witmer and Singer 1998). This relationship remained significant after controlling statistically for pretreatment scores on measures of fear of flying. Bouchard et al. (2006) used residualized change scores in multiple regression analyses and showed that age, immersive tendencies assessed at pretreatment, and presence assessed regularly during therapy sessions significantly predicted treatment outcome on the Fear of Flying Questionnaire (Adj $R^2 = 0.58$, $p < 0.001$) and the Questionnaires on Attitudes towards Flying (Adj $R^2 = 0.61$, $p < 0.001$).

The length of the treatment varies from four to, in general, eight sessions and the majority of researchers used treatment packages combining a variety of anxiety management techniques such as relaxation and breathing retraining. Treatment invariably begins with objective information about airplanes, the mechanics of flying and the rationale for exposure. In their seminal book on cognitive therapy, Beck and Emery (1985) offered examples of the need to provide information to reduce patient's anxiety, such as the actuarial estimation that if a person could only die as the result of a plane crash, that person would live to be a million years old (p. 202). Brown (1996) and Antony and Swinson (2000) are useful sources of information for therapists about factual information regarding the mechanics of flying and an-

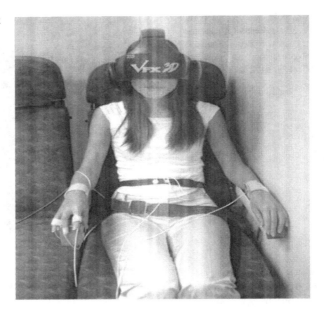

Fig. 4.12 Picture of a patient doing biofeedback while immersed in virtual reality. Reproduced with permission from B. Wiederhold

swers to patients' questions. In some cases, the patients are instructed to apply their new coping skills during *in virtuo* exposure. Wiederhold et al. (1998) even used biofeedback to monitor patients' abilities to control their anxiety (see Fig. 4.12), an approach followed by other researchers (e.g., Reiner 2003). It is also possible to use coping self-statements and other techniques while the patient is immersed in VR, but it is important not to use these strategies when they become safety-seeking behaviors. However, isolating the role of various treatment strategies is still inconclusive and more research is needed in this area. Based on Mühlberger et al. (2003), the lack of motion accompanying virtual flights does not seem to have a clinically significant impact, at least in terms of efficacy (Fig. 4.7).

During *in virtuo* exposure, the therapist usually has patients regularly rate their SUDS level to monitor whether the anxiety level is at the expected level and if it decreases progressively. It is again important to pay attention to patients' avoidance and safety-seeking strategies (Bouchard et al. 2012). For example, some patients will keep looking out of the window to monitor what is happening to the aircraft, while others will avoid looking outside to see that the plane is up in the air. These two instances can be easily picked up by an attentive therapist, but other potential avoidance strategies should also be monitored. Narrative context could also be used to increase the level of fear (Bouchard et al. 2012), especially if the patient appears to be suggestible. In that sense, it is useful to exploit all the possibilities of the software as well as the patient's imagination. For example, it could be useful to boost anxiety by suggesting that the pilot is sick today, the engines were repaired just before the flight, or bad weather is forecasted for the ongoing trip. The therapist can also mention the loud noise made by the landing gear being locked into place or focus on specific issues that the patient is afraid of (claustrophobic cognitions, panic sensations, etc.). From a methodological standpoint, it is important to echo the Öst et al. (1997) observation about the use of a posttreatment flight as a behavioral test. Although it is a very attractive outcome measure, it was used differently from one study to another, and with different results. In one study (Maltby et al. 2002), participants were excluded if they agreed to fly pre-therapy, while most other studies do not use this as an exclusion criterion. Some researchers offered free flights (e.g., Maltby et al. 2002), others shared the costs with the participants (e.g., Rothbaum et al. 2000), and others asked if participants booked a flight on their own (e.g., Kahan et al. 2000). For practical reasons, the flights were often performed in groups of patients accompanied by a therapist. Most of the time, but not always, the flights were in a commercial airliner and of a sufficient length to stir apprehension. Only a few studies assessed specifically whether the participants flew without medication (e.g., Wiederhold 1999). All of these differences make comparisons difficult, and in some instances, participants assigned to the control condition might have been tempted to push their limits and "try it out."

No study explicitly assessed VR-induced side effects (cybersickness). Informal reports from researchers contend that VR immersion causes very few cybersickness symptoms with fear of flying. Users' motion remains rather limited as participants in the virtual airplane simply turn their heads to look around the cabin or out the window. Maltby et al. (2002) are the only ones to report a case of cybersickness sufficiently severe to exclude the participant from the study. It is not mentioned how cybersickness was measured if the patient confounded it with symptoms of anxiety or when it occurred (e.g., while walking in the virtual hallway or when seated in the plane). Systematic measurement of VR-induced side effects should be performed routinely, at least until there is data confirming the safety of this application of VR.

4.6 Conclusion

This chapter describes a significant number of outcome trials. Based on these accumulating evidences, it seems difficult to believe that conducting exposure in VR is not effective. Research on VR is an international endeavor, with trials on fear of flying being conducted in the USA, Spain, Germany, Canada, France, the Netherlands, and other countries. Each study has its own methodological assets, such as the use of BAT measures, a variety of control conditions, long follow-up, independent replication, etc. There are even dismantling studies looking at the role of some treatment components (e.g., relaxation, immersion augmented by hydraulic systems). Some methodological improvement could be included if additional outcome studies are designed, such as the systematic use of treatment manuals, anti-exposure instructions given to patients to discourage them from practicing between sessions (e.g., going to the airport on their own), more detailed documentation of VR-induced side effects, and conducting some statistical analyses with the inclusion of dropouts (intent-to-treat analyses). Nevertheless, the data are supporting the idea that VR offers practical advantages, since in vivo exposure and large-scale flight simulators (such as in van Gerwen et al. 2006, for example) are expensive and not available to most therapists.

References

Agras, S., Sylvester, D., & Oliveau, D. (1969). The epidemiology of common fears and phobias. *Comprehensive Psychiatry, 10,* 151–156.

American Psychiatric Association (APA). (2000). *Diagnostic and statistical manual of mental disorders fourth edition text revision.* Washington, DC: American Psychiatric Association.

Anderson, P., Jacobs, C. H., Lindner, G. K., Edwards, S., Zimand, E., Hodges, L. F., & Rothbaum, B. O. (2006). Cognitive behavior therapy for fear of flying: Sustainability of treatment gains after september 11. *Behavior Therapy, 37,* 91–97.

Antony, M. M., & Swinson, R. P. (2000). *Phobic disorders and panic in adults: A guide to assessment and treatment.* Washington, DC: American Psychiatric Association.

Baños, R. M., Botella, C., Perpiñá, C., Alcañiz, M., Lozano, J. A., Osma, J., & Gallardo, M. (2002). Virtual reality treatment of flying phobia. *IEEE Transactions on Information Technology in Biomedicine, 6*(3), 206–212.

Beck, A. T., & Emery, G. (1985). *Anxiety disorders and phobias: A cognitive perspective.* USA: HarperCollins.

Beckham, J. C., Vrana, S. R., May, J. G., Gustafson, D. J., & Smith, G. R. (1990). Emotional processing and fear measurement synchrony as indicators of treatment outcome in fear of flying. *Journal of Behavior Therapy and Experimental Psychiatry, 21*(3), 153–162.

Bornas, X., Tortella-Feliu, M., Llabrés, J., & Fullana, M. A. (2001). Computer-assisted exposure treatment for flight phobia: A controlled study. *Psychotherapy Research, 11*(3), 259–273.

Botella, C., Osma, J., Garcia-Palacios, A., Quero, S., & Baños, R. M. (2004). Treatment of flying phobia using virtual reality: Data from a 1-year follow-up using a multiple baseline design. *Clinical Psychology and Psychotherapy, 11,* 311–323.

Bouchard, S., Robillard, G., & Dumoulin, S. (2006). *Why would VR works in the treatment of anxiety disorders?* Oral presentation at the 36th Annual Congress of the European Association for Behavioral and Cognitive Therapy (EABCT), Paris (France), 20–23 Sept.

Bouchard, S., Robillard, G., Larouche, S., & Loranger, C. (2012). Description of a treatment manual for in virtuo exposure with specific phobia. In C. Eichenberg (Ed.), *Virtual reality in psychological, medical and pedagogical applications* (Chap. 4, pp 82–108). Rijeka: InTech.

Boyd, D., Wetterneck, C., & Hart, J. (2013). Potential utility of full motion flight simulators for treatment of individuals with fear of flying. *Aviation, Space, and Environmental Medicine, 84*(3), 264–265.

Brinkman, W.-P., van der Mast, C., Sandino, G., Gunawan, L. T., & Emmelkamp, P. M. G. (2010). The therapist user interface of a virtual reality exposure therapy system in the treatment of fear of flying. *Interacting with Computers, 22,* 299–310.

Brown, D. (1996). *Flying without fear.* Oakland: New Harbinger Publications.

Cardenas-Lopez, G., Botella, C., Quero, S., Moreyra, L., De La Rosa, A., & Munoz, S. (2009). A cross-cultural validation of VR treatment system for flying phobia in the Mexican population. *Annual Review of Cybertherapy and Telemedicine, 144,* 141–144.

Da Costa, R. T., Sardinha, A., & Nardi, A. E. (2008). Virtual reality exposure in the treatment of fear of flying. *Aviation, Space, and Environmental Medicine, 79*(9), 899–903.

Dean, R. D., & Whitaker, K. M. (1982). Fear of flying: Impact on the US air travel industry. *Journal of Travel Research, 21,* 7–17.

Denholtz, M. S., & Mann, E. T. (1975). An automated audiovisual treatment of phobias administered by non-professionals. *Journal of Behavior Therapy and Experimental Psychiatry, 6,* 111–115.

Denholtz, M. S., Hall, L. A., & Mann, E. (1978). Automated treatment for flight phobia: A 3 1/2-year follow-up. *American Journal of Psychiatry, 135*(11), 1340–1343.

Doctor, R. M., McVarish, C., & Boone, R. P. (1990). Long-term behavioral treatment effects for the fear of flying. *Phobia Practice and Research Journal, 2,* 3–14.

Fredrickson, M., Annas, P., Fischer, H., & Wik, G. (1996). Gender and age differences in the prevalence of specific fears and phobias. *Behaviour Research and Therapy, 26,* 241–244.

References

Greist, J. H., & Greist, G. L. (1981). *Fearless flying: A passenger guide to modern airline travel.* Chicago: Nelson Hall.
Gunawan, L. T., van der Mast, C., Neerincx, M. A., Emmelkamp, P. M. G., & Krijn, M. (2004). *Usability of the therapist's user interface in virtual reality exposure therapy for fear of flying.* Euromedia 2004, Hasselt, Belgium, 19–21 April.
Haug, T., Brenne, L., Johnsen, B. H., Berntzen, D., Gotestam, K., & Hugdahl, K. (1987). A three-systems analysis of fear of flying: A comparison of a consonant vs. a non-consonant treatment method. *Behaviour Research and Therapy, 25*(3), 187–194.
Hodges, L. F., Rothbaum, B. O., Watson, B. A., Kessler, G. D., & Opdyke, D. (1996). Virtually conquering fear of flying. *IEEE Computer Graphics and Applications, 16*(6), 42–49.
Howard, W. A., Murphy, S. M., & Clarke, J. C. (1983). The nature and treatment of fear of flying: A controlled investigation. *Behavior Therapy, 14*, 557–567.
Joseph, C., & Kulkarni, J. S. (2003). Fear of flying: A review. *Journal of Aerospace Medicine, 47*(2), 21–31.
Kahan, M. (2000). Integration of psychodynamic and cognitive-behavioral therapy in a virtual environment. *Cyberpsychology & Behavior, 3*(2), 179–184.
Kahan, M., Tanzer, J., Darvin, D., & Borer, F. (2000). Virtual reality-assisted cognitive-behavioral treatment for fear of flying: Acute treatment and follow-up. *Cyberpsychology & Behavior, 3*(3), 387–392.
Kim, S., Palin, F., Anderson, P., Edwards, S., Lindner, G., & Rothbaum, B. O. (2008). Use of skills learned in CBT for fear of flying: Managing flying anxiety after september 11th. *Journal of Anxiety Disorders, 22*(2), 301–309.
Klein, R. A. (1998). Virtual reality exposure therapy (fear of flying): From a private practice perspective. *Cyberpsychology & Behavior, 1*(3), 311–316.
Klein, R. A. (1999). Virtual reality exposure therapy in the treatment of fear of flying. *Journal of Contemporary Psychotherapy, 30*(2), 195–208.
Kraaij, V., Garnefski, N., & van Gerwen, L. (2003). Cognitive coping and anxiety symptoms among people who seek help for fear of flying. *Aviation, Space, and Environment Medicine, 74*(3), 273–277.
Krijn, M., Emmelkamp, P. M. G., Olapsson, R. P., Bouwman, M., van Gerven, L. J., Spinhoven, P., Schuemie, M. J., & van der Mast, C. A. P. G. (2007). Fear of flying treatment methods: Virtual reality exposure vs cognitive behavioural therapy. *Aviation, Space, and Environmental Medicine, 78*, 121–128.
Maltby, N., Kirsch, I., Mayers, M., & Allen, G. J. (2002). Virtual reality exposure therapy for the treatment of fear of flying: A controlled investigation. *Journal of Consulting and Clinical Psychology, 70*(5), 1112–1118.
Meyerbroeker, K., & Emmelkamp, P. M. G. (2010). Virtual reality exposure therapy in anxiety disorders: A systematic review of process-and-outcome studies. *Depression and Anxiety, 2 7*, 933–944.
Meyerbroeker, K., Powers, M. B., van Stegeren, A., & Emmelkamp, P. M. G. (2012). Does yohimbine hydrochloride facilitate fear extinction in virtual reality treatment of fear of flying? A randomized placebo-controlled trial. *Psychotherapy and Psychosomatics, 81*(1), 29–37.
Möller, A. T., Nortje, C., & Helders, S. B. (1998). Irrational cognitions and the fear of flying. *Journal of Rationale-Emotive and Cognitive-Behavior Therapy, 16*(2), 135–148.
Mühlberger, A., Hermann, M. J., Wiedemann, G., Ellgring, H., & Pauli, P. (2001). Repeated exposure of flight phobics to flights in virtual reality. *Behaviour Research and Therapy, 39*, 1033–1050.
Mühlberger, A., Wiedemann, G., & Pauli, P. (2003). Efficacy of one-session virtual reality exposure treatment for fear of flying. *Psychotherapy Research, 13*(3), 323–336.
Mühlberger, A. (2005). Personnal communication.
Mühlberger, A., Weik, A., Pauli, P., & Wiedemann, G. (2006). One-session virtual reality exposure treatment for fear of flying: 1-year follow-up and graduation flight accompaniment effects. *Psychotherapy Research, 16*(1), 26–40.

North, M. M., North, S. M., & Coble, J. R. (1996). Virtual environments psychotherapy: A case study of fear of flying disorder. *Presence, 5*(4), 1–5.
North, M., North, S., & Coble, J. R. (1997). Virtual reality therapy for fear of flying (letters to the editor). *American Journal of Psychiatry, 154*(1), 130.
Opris, D., Pintea, S., Garcia-Palacios, A., Botella, C., Szamoskozi, S., & David, D. (2012). Virtual reality exposure therapy in anxiety disorders: A quantitative meta-analysis. *Depression and Anxiety, 29*, 85–93.
Öst, L. G., Brandberg, M., & Alm, T. (1997). One versus five sessions of exposure in the treatment of flying phobia. *Behaviour Research and Therapy, 35*, 987–996.
Price, M. (2006). *The relation of presence and virtual reality exposure for treatment of flying phobia.* Master thesis, College of Arts and Sciences, Georgia State University.
Reiner, R. H. (2003). Dual utilization of GSR feedback with virtual reality treatment to reduce fear of flying. Behavioral Associates, http://www.behavioralassociates.com/news_story_08.asp. Accessed 18 Jan 2003.
Roberts, R. J. (1989). Passenger fear of flying: Behavioral treatment with extensive in-vivo exposure and group support. *Aviation, Space, and Environmental Medicine, 60*, 342–348.
Robillard, G., Wiederhold, B. K., Wiederhold, M. D., Larouche, S., & Bouchard, S. (2004). *An open trial to confirm the external validity of virtual reality exposure treatment of fear of flying.* Poster presented at the 38th Annual convention of the Association for the Advancement of Behavior Therapy, New Orleans, LA, 17–21 Nov.
Rothbaum, B. O., Hodges, L., Watson, B. A., Kessler, G. D., & Opdyke, D. (1996). Virtual reality exposure therapy in the treatment of fear of flying: A case report. *Behaviour Research and Therapy, 34*(5/6), 477–481.
Rothbaum, B. O., Hodges, L., & Kooper, R. (1997). Virtual reality exposure therapy. *Journal of Psychotherapy Practice and Research, 6*(3), 291–296.
Rothbaum, B. O., Hodges, L., Smith, S., Lee, J. H., & Price, L. (2000). A controlled study of virtual reality exposure therapy for the fear of flying. *Journal of Consulting and Clinical Psychology, 68*(6), 1020–1026.
Rothbaum, B. O., Anderson, P., Zimand, E., Hodges, L., Lang, D., & Wilson, J. (2006). Virtual reality exposure therapy and standard (in vivo) exposure therapy in the treatment of fear of flying. *Behavior Therapy, 37*, 80–90.
Solyom, L., Shugar, R., Bryntwick, S., & Solyom, C. (1973). Treatment of fear of flying. *American Journal of Psychiatry, 130*(4), 423–427.
Stinson, F. S., Dawson, D. A., Chou, S. P., Smith, S., Goldstein, R. B., Ruan, W. J., & Grant, B. F. (2007). The epidemiology of DSM-IV specific phobia in the USA: Results from the national epidemiologic survey on alcohol and related conditions. *Psychological Medicine, 37*, 1047–1059.
Stirman, S. W., DeRubeis, R. J., Crits-Christoph, P., & Rothman, A. (2005). Can the randomized controlled trial literature generalize to nonrandomized patients? *Journal of Consulting and Clinical Psychology, 73*, 127–135.
Tortella-Feliu, M., Botella, C., Llabrés, J., Bretón-López, J. M., del Amo, A. R., Baños, R. M., & Gelabert, J. M. (2011). Virtual reality versus computer-aided exposure treatments for fear of flying. *Behavior Modification, 35*(1), 3–30.
van Gerwen, L. J., & Diekstra, R. F. W. (2000). Fear of flying treatment programs for passengers: An international review. *Aviations, Space and Environmental Medicine, 71*(4), 430–437.
van Gerwen, L. J., Spinhoven, P., Diekstra, R. F., & van Dyck, R. (1997). People who seek help for fear of flying: Typology of flying phobics. *Behavior Therapy, 28*, 237–251.
van Gerwen, L. J., Spinhoven, P., & van Dyck, R. (2006). Behavioral and cognitive group treatment for fear of flying: A randomized controlled trial. *Journal of Behavior Therapy, 37*, 358–371.
Wiederhold, B. K. (1999). *A comparison of imaginal exposure and virtual reality exposure for the treatment of fear of flying.* Doctoral dissertation, California School of Professional Psychology, 1999, Dissertations Abstracts International.
Wiederhold, B. K., & Wiederhold, M. D. (2000). Lessons learned from 600 virtual reality sessions. *Cyberpsychology & Behavior, 3*(3), 393–400.

References

Wiederhold, B. K., & Wiederhold, M. D. (2003). Three-year follow-up for virtual reality exposure for fear of flying. *Cyberpsychology & Behavior, 6*(4), 441–445.

Wiederhold, B. K., & Wiederhold, M. D. (2005). *Virtual reality therapy for anxiety disorders: Advances in evaluation and treatment.* Washington, DC: American Psychological Association Press.

Wiederhold, B. K., Gevirtz, R., & Wiederhold, M. D. (1998). Fear of flying: A case report using virtual reality therapy with physiological monitoring. *Cyberpsychology & Behavior, 1*(2), 97–104.

Wiederhold, B. K., Jang, D. P., Gevirtz, R. G., Kim, S. I., Kim, I. Y., & Wiederhold, M. D. (2002). The treatment of fear of flying: A controlled study of imaginal and virtual reality graded exposure therapy. *IEEE Transactions on Information Technology in Biomedicine, 6*(3), 218–223.

Witmer, B. G., & Singer, M. J. (1998). Measuring presence in virtual environments: A presence questionnaire. *Presence: Teleoperators and Virtual Environments, 7*(3), 225–240.

World Health Organization. (1992). *The ICD-10 classification of mental and behavioural disorders.* Geneva: WHO.

Chapter 5
Arachnophobia and Fear of Other Insects: Efficacy and Lessons Learned from Treatment Process

Stéphane Bouchard, Brenda K. Wiederhold and Jessie Bossé

5.1 Key Variables Involved in Animal Phobia

The pathological fear of animals, spiders, bugs, mice, cats, or snakes, among others, can be severe enough to be considered a specific phobia according to the *Diagnostic and Statistical Manual of Mental Disorders Fourth Edition* (DSM-IV) and the International Classification of Diseases 10 (ICD-10) classifications (APA 2000; WHO 1992). It falls under the animal subtype in both classifications. Using data from the Epidemiological Catchment Area Survey, Bourdon et al. (1988) revealed that the lifetime prevalence of specific phobias of spiders, bugs, mice, and snakes is about 7 % among women and 2 % among men. Using more reliable estimates from the National Comorbidity Survey, Curtis et al. (1998) found a lifetime prevalence rate of animal phobia of 5.7 % and the lifetime of non-pathological fears of animals to be around 25.8 %. Fredrickson et al. (1996) reported the point prevalence rate (actual rates of prevalence at the time of assessment) of specific phobias to be 5.5 % for snake phobia and 3.5 % for spider phobia. More recently, a large epidemiological study conducted in the USA reported a prevalence rate of 4.7 % for animal subtype-specific phobia in the general population (Stinson et al. 2007). Since the large majority of studies using virtual reality (VR) have been conducted on the specific phobia of spiders, the theoretical context of this chapter will focus mostly on arachnophobia. However, VR studies on animal phobia in general will be described here.

People suffering from arachnophobia show marked, persistent, and excessive anxiety upon actual or anticipated exposure to spiders and avoid spiders and situations in which they might encounter a spider. Animal phobias normally begin in childhood and affect twice as many women as men, although men may underreport their fears (Öst 1987; Fredrickson et al. 1996; Curtis et al. 1998).

Because fear of spiders is so prevalent and easy to induce, arachnophobia has been studied extensively in experimental research. This led to important findings for our understanding of the nature and treatment of phobias. These findings raise issues that are important to VR applications as well. Let us take disgust, for example. Research on anxiety disorders, and on phobias in general, has typically focused on perceived danger or perceived threat. In 1986, Watts (1986) suggested that disgust was probably involved in arachnophobia. Indeed, disgust is now more and more recognized as an important element in some specific phobias such as fear of bugs, snakes, or spiders (McNally 2002). For example, Woody et al. (2005) used the intensity of disgust and anxiety to predict avoidance during a series of behavior avoidance tasks with a tarantula in a cage and a pen that had been touched (contaminated) in the cage by the tarantula. Among their 115 participants, the intensity of disgust was a significant and stronger predictor of avoidance than level of anxiety, both for avoidance of the tarantula and the contaminated pen. In addition, twice as many participants avoided the contaminated pen among the highly fearful participants compared to the less fearful participants. These results are in line with findings from Mulkens et al. (1996) where only 25% of their phobic participants agreed to eat a cookie that a spider had walked across, compared to 71% of their non-phobic participants. These experimental studies illustrate how arachnophobic avoidance is related to disgust and not only perceived threat. Smiths et al. (2002) also showed that changes in disgust and fear are partially independent from each other, while Edwards and Salkovskis (2006) further revealed that fear magnifies the reaction of disgust but that disgust does not enhance fear. All these findings highlight for VR designers the importance of stimuli that elicit fear and disgust in the development of virtual environments. They also alert therapists to which cues they must draw a patient's attention to during exposure therapy and the relationship between these cues.

Given that specific phobia is the simplest of the anxiety disorders in terms of fear and avoidance, researchers have also used fear of spiders to study neurological correlates of phobias and their treatment. Studies have shown that fear is an alarm reaction that involves specific neural areas of the brain such as the limbic system, the prefrontal cortex, and the hippocampus (Phillips et al. 2003). For example, using functional magnetic resonance imaging (fMRI) with participants suffering from spider phobia, Larson et al. (2006) found a strong but brief reaction of the amygdala, suggesting that this area of the brain may be more involved in the rapid detection of threat and initial processing of fear than in the sustained processing of threat. Other studies conducted with spider phobics using fMRI have shown that exposure-based therapy leads to significant change in brain functioning (Paquette et al. 2003; Straube et al. 2006). For example, Schienle et al. (2009) investigated the long-term effects of exposure-based cognitive behavioral therapy (CBT) on brain activation in spider phobics using fMRI technology. Ten patients underwent an fMRI session 6 months after successfully completing CBT to treat spider phobia. Patients were exposed to phobic relevant pictures while brain activation was being monitored. Results from the fMRI at the 6-month follow-up showed an increased activation in the medial orbitofrontal cortex, a region of the brain involved in the representation of positive reinforcers, and a decreased activation in the lateral orbitofrontal cortex, an area implicated in the processing of negative stimulations. These results illustrate how exposure-based treatments can allow learning new associations with the lack of threat. Patients learned to perceive the phobic-relevant stimulus as rewarding, probably because their interaction with the spider during therapy led to positive affect and a sense of accomplishment. In that same fashion, they learned that there were no negative consequences associated with their interaction with the spider.

Addressing the neurophysiology of fears is important because it could help therapists understand that the treatment mechanism of exposure involves changing: (a) the automatic association between spider and threat/disgust (an operation involving the amygdala, among other brain areas), (b) mental representations of these associations that have been learned and are stored in the memory (an operation involving the hippocampus, among other areas), and the contribution of reflexive processes (an operation involving the prefrontal cortex, among other areas).

Studying spider phobia has also helped scientists understand the treatment mechanism behind exposure. To quote Powers et al. (2006), "As compared to early conceptualizations of extinction as the systematic *unlearning* of a learned association, modern learning theory now conceptualizes extinction as the acquisition of *new learning*" (p. 109; see also Bouton 2007 and Abramowitz 2013 for a detailed review on learning and Powers et al. 2006 and Abramowitz et al. 2011 for clinical applications). The psychological mechanism behind exposure is therefore conceptualized as the active development and learning of safe associations with the feared stimuli rather than as a passive weakening, or unlearning, of previous associations with threat (and probably disgust, although this is much less studied). According to Bouton (2007), both the learned associations developed during the acquisition of the fear and the learned associations developed during therapy remain after extinction. Thus, an additional strategy to increase the generalization of new learning outside of the therapist's office is to vary the contexts in which the patient is exposed to the feared stimuli. Otherwise, facing feared stimuli in a new context can cause a patient to rely on previously learned dysfunctional associations, rather than on the more functional ones learned in therapy, and therefore relapse. The study by Mineka et al. (1999) conducted with spider phobics provides a nice example of the importance of context on the generalization of treatment gains. They treated 36 arachnophobics with in vivo exposure in either one of two therapy contexts that differed based on: therapist's gender and clothing, room size, salient visual cues in the two rooms, room location, and size and color of the exposure tools such as the terrarium for the tarantula. Participants were retested with a behavior avoidance test 1 week post therapy either in the same context in which they received their therapy or in the other context. Participants tested in the novel context showed significantly more anxiety during the test compared to those retested in the same context where they received their therapy. This finding has been replicated using slightly different methodologies (Mystkowski et al. 2002, 2003; Vansteenwegen et al. 2007). Mystkowski et al. (2006) even showed that mentally reinstating the therapy context (remembering what happened and what was learned) before being tested in the novel setting is beneficial for the patients. To support the idea that exposure will be most effective when the therapy maximizes the salience of threat disconfirmation, Wolitsky et al. (2005) showed that height phobics benefited more from therapy when they adopted anti-phobic or paradoxical behaviors such as running towards the balcony of a high place or leaning over the edge of a balcony without holding the railing. Even if this study was not conducted with spider phobics, the conclusion remains: One key mechanism behind exposure is to develop new associations with safety (or, at least, with non-threat). This also raises a potential advantage of

VR, which is helping arachnophobic patients perform anti-phobic behavior that is difficult or impossible to do otherwise, such as holding a tarantula, facing dozens of spiders at the same time, or encountering exaggeratedly large spiders. Mineka and Thomas (1999) also highlighted that simply changing the direct associations with threat and safety is incomplete. They argued for the importance of developing new mental representations that one can cope by increasing perceived self-efficacy. Increased perceived self-efficacy is an important factor in anxiety (Bandura 1986) and may contribute to explaining the generalization effect.

Using evidence-based knowledge about the treatment mechanism for specific phobia is essential in the development of virtual environments and in conducting any form of exposure, including *in virtuo* exposure (Otto and Hofmann 2010; Bouchard et al. 2012; Abramowitz 2013). For example, based on the information presented in the paragraphs above, it would be important for generalization to vary the characteristics of the virtual spiders, along with the virtual locations where the patients are exposed to virtual spiders. Virtual locations depicting situations where patients would usually encounter a spider, such as a kitchen, bedroom, patio, or backyard with a picnic table, should lead to better generalization than less common virtual locations such as a cavern or a virtual room with no furniture. To maximize learning new associations with safety and high self-efficacy, distraction should not interfere with cognitive and emotional processing. Research on the effect of distraction on exposure has been inconsistent, with most studies showing that distraction reduces treatment efficacy and some reporting no detrimental effects. These apparently contradictory findings are in fact all pointing in one direction: The distraction should not interfere with the learning of adaptive safety associations with the stimuli and with regard to self-efficacy (Powers et al. 2006; Richards et al. 2006; Telch 2004). For example, engaging in stimulus-relevant conversations while maintaining visual attention to a spider during exposure will not hinder the efficacy of exposure (Johnstone and Page 2004), but focusing visually on a stimulus irrelevant to spiders will be detrimental (Mohlman and Zinbarg 2000).

5.2 Description of Significant Efficacy Studies Using Non-VR Approaches

Early treatment of arachnophobia included imaginal flooding and implosion (Marshall et al. 1977) or systematic desensitization (Rachman 1966). With empirical data showing that the key ingredient in those forms of therapy was the systematic exposure to the feared stimuli, clinicians progressively shifted their efforts towards exposure itself. Regrettably, no large-scale randomized control trial for spider phobia has yet been conducted using a passive (i.e., waiting list) or nonspecific (i.e., placebo) control condition. Based on the assumption that results of controlled studies documenting the efficacy of in vivo exposure with other forms of phobia (see Öst 1997 for an overview of controlled studies) can be extended to arachnophobia, several outcome studies used active treatments or different forms of exposure as control conditions. For example, Hellström and Öst (1995) used four different controls to test against the efficacy of a 3-h in vivo exposure session conducted with a therapist: (a) a treatment manual specifically targeting arachnophobia, to be used at home; (b) a treatment manual specifically targeting arachnophobia, to be used at the clinic; (c) a treatment manual nonspecific to arachnophobia, to be used at home; and (d) a treatment manual nonspecific to arachnophobia, to be used at the clinic. Note that for all four control conditions, the treatment was delivered without the assistance of a therapist and participants had to plan for two 2-h therapy sessions on their own. Their 52 participants were assessed with behavioral, physiological, and self-report measures at pretreatment, posttreatment, and 1-year follow-up. At the follow-up, the success rate of in vivo exposure therapy reached 80%, compared to 63% for the specific manual applied at the clinic, 10% for the general manual applied at the clinic, 10% for the specific manual applied at home, and 9% for the general manual applied at home. Nine of the ten participants in the one session of in vivo exposure were able to reach the maximum score on the behavioral avoidance test (BAT; i.e., holding a spider in their hands for 20 s). Öst et al. (1991) reported that a 3-h session of in vivo exposure with a therapist helped 71% of participants suffering from spider phobia reach a clinically significant improvement, compared to 6% of participants performing self-directed exposure at home over weeks. Other studies have supported the efficacy of one session of intense in vivo exposure (e.g., Götestam 2002), or that exposure delivered in a group is an effective alternative to individual exposure (Öst et al. 1997). It is important to note that the one-session exposure treatments used guided mastery, which is a slightly more intensive form of exposure. In this case, the therapist first conducts an individualized case conceptualization in a session preceding exposure. The exposure itself is used like a series of behavioral tests, conducted to weaken dysfunctional beliefs, as opposed to simple exposure. The therapist also models approach behaviors. This approach enables the therapist to try moving faster along the hierarchy within the 3-h session, with the explicit rationale that exposure must be continued at home after the session (Öst 1997).

One research group from the University of Tasmania in Australia used a computer program to conduct vicarious exposure (Smith et al. 1997; Gilroy et al. 2000). Their computer-aided vicarious exposure software (see Fig. 5.1) allows the patient to help a character on a computer screen face the feared stimuli.[1] In one controlled study, Gilroy et al. (2000) randomly assigned 45 spider phobics to either computer-aided vicarious exposure, therapist-delivered in vivo exposure, or relaxation placebo. They found that both active treatments were effective and superior to placebo on all measures posttreatment and at follow-up. Live graded exposure was superior

---

[1] This form of computer-assisted exposure is not described in the section on *in virtuo* exposure because: (a) the authors themselves do not claim that their treatment is a form of VR, (b) the depth of the real-time interactivity is limited, (c) the user consciously remains in the physical office of the therapist, controlling the actions of someone else in the synthetic environment, (d) the immersion properties of the system are significantly weaker than what is found in VR, and (e) the acronym CAVE refers here to "computer-aided vicarious exposure" and not to the C-Automated Virtual Environment.

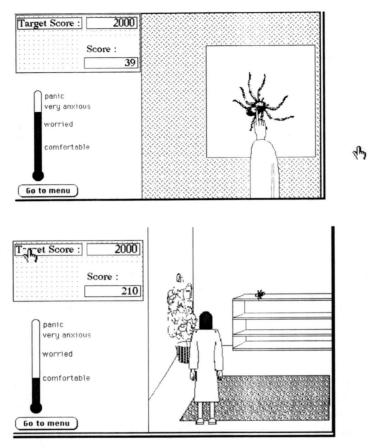

Fig. 5.1 Images from the computer-aided vicarious exposure program developed at the University of Tasmania. Reproduced with permission from professor Ken Kirkby

to computer-aided vicarious exposure only on the behavior avoidance test at posttreatment. All other posttreatment comparisons were nonsignificant and, at follow-up, all comparisons including the BAT were nonsignificant. A 33-month follow-up supported the lack of difference between both forms of exposure (Gilroy et al. 2003). However, results on the BAT were rather low at posttreatment and follow-up, with participants completing on average only half of the avoidance/approach task (i.e., partially opening a container with a live spider). It raises some doubts about the overall efficacy of the treatments. Another study from the same group (Heading et al. 2001) revealed less promising results, with the computer-assisted vicarious exposure being significantly less effective than in vivo and not significantly different from the waiting list. A study with 28 children aged 10–17 also suggested that in vivo exposure was more effective than the use of their computer software (Dewis et al. 2001). Nevertheless, this line of research addressed vicarious exposure, an

5.3 Description of the Studies Using VR Approaches to Treat Arachnophobia

Fig. 5.2 Picture of Hunter Hoffman with a patient looking at a spider in Spider World. Note the patient trying to touch a toy spider. The HMD displayed in this picture is not the one used by Carlin et al. (1997). Photo by Stephen Dagadakis, copyright Hunter Hoffman, UW, www.vrpain.com

option that is used less systematically by therapists but that could be beneficial for highly phobic patients.

5.3 Description of the Studies Using VR Approaches to Treat Arachnophobia

The first study published on the use of *in virtuo* exposure to treat the specific phobia of spiders is from Carlin et al. (1997). They provided 12 weekly sessions of a treatment consisting essentially of *in virtuo* exposure and deep muscle relaxation to a 37-year-old woman who had been severely arachnophobic for 20 years. The *in virtuo* exposure consisted of five 5-min immersions, with breaks between each immersion, during therapy sessions lasting about 50 min each. The length of the immersion was kept brief in the hope of reducing cybersickness. Two virtual spiders were used. After four therapy sessions, tactile cues were added by having the patient touch a furry toy spider with her physical hand while she would see her virtual hand touching the virtual spider (i.e., tactile augmentation; see Fig. 5.2). The therapy led to a decrease in subjective anxiety within and between exposure sessions, a reduction in scores on a self-report instrument, and reports of a reduction of dysfunctional behaviors. A 1-year follow-up indicated that treatment gains were still intact (Hoffman 1998).

To further study the impact of tactile augmentation, Hoffman et al. (2003) conducted a study with a pooled sample of eight arachnophobics and 28 fearful, yet non-phobic university students. The diagnosis of specific phobia was made according to DSM-IV criteria and the fear of the non-phobics had to reach one standard deviation above the mean of their classmates on the Fear of Spiders Questionnaire (Szymanski and O'Donohue 1995) to qualify for the study. They randomly assigned the phobic and the non-phobic participants to either no treatment, *in virtuo* exposure without tactile augmentation, or *in virtuo* exposure with tactile augmentation. The

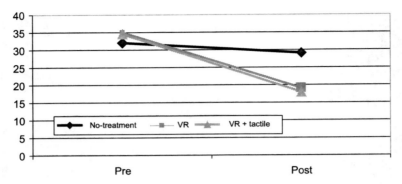

Fig. 5.3 Results from Hoffman et al. (2003) on a modified version of the Fear of Spider Questionnaire

treatment consisted of three 1-h therapy sessions delivered over 1 week. The VR environment was the same as Carlin et al. (1997) and, except for the computer, the hardware was the same as well, with a dVisor head-mounted display (HMD) from Division™, a Polhemus motion tracker (for the head, the hand, and the toy spider), and a Silicon Graphics computer. Results on a modified version of the Fear of Spider Questionnaire revealed that both forms of treatment led to improvements that are significantly superior to the no-treatment condition but not significantly different from one another (see Fig. 5.3). A different pattern of results was found on the level of anxiety felt during the behavior avoidance test, with VR plus tactile augmentation being significantly more effective than VR without tactile augmentation, the latter not being significantly different from the no-treatment controls. For the distance on the BAT, both treatments were found to be effective when compared to the control condition, with the tactile augmentation group performing significantly better (on average, getting as close as 6 in. to a live tarantula in a closed terrarium) than the VR without tactile augmentation (on average, getting as close as 2.5 ft to a live tarantula in a closed terrarium). Given the small number of clinically phobic participants (three in each treatment group) and the divergences between the three outcome measures, it is difficult to draw confident conclusions about the usefulness of the tactile augmentation. Nevertheless, the Hoffman et al. (2003) hypothesis that adding tactile feedback may lead to stronger emotional processing for spider phobics seems sound. In light of the literature on the importance of disgust and the advantage of varying contexts to foster generalization, tactile augmentation may be very useful clinically to help patients touch or kill spiders.

In a more controlled study, Garcia-Palacios et al. (2002) assigned 23 adults who were clinically phobic of spiders according to DSM-IV criteria to a wait-list control condition or an *in virtuo* exposure treatment. The therapy was flexible in length (from three to ten sessions, for an average of four 1-h sessions) and consisted essentially of exposure while immersed in VR. The first therapy sessions were conducted without tactile augmentation. After patients were able to face a virtual spider drifting from a vase to the floor, tactile augmentation was introduced. Patients were encouraged to touch the virtual spider with their virtual hand, while at the same time

5.3 Description of the Studies Using VR Approaches to Treat Arachnophobia

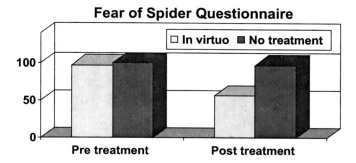

Fig. 5.4 Results from Garcia-Palacios et al. (2002) on the Fear of Spider Questionnaire

their physical hand was actually touching the furry toy spider. The hardware and software were the same as in Hoffman et al. (2003), except for a different HMD (V8 from Virtual Research™). Results showed significant differences from pre- to posttherapy for the treatment group only on measures such as a BAT, level of anxiety felt during the BAT, clinician's ratings of severity, and the Fear of Spider Questionnaire (see Fig. 5.4). At pretreatment, people who received *in virtuo* exposure were on average only able to approach to within 3 m from a closed terrarium containing a large tarantula, while at posttreatment they were able to touch the closed terrarium with their hands.

Given the high cost of the VR hardware and software used by Hoffman and his team, Bouchard et al. (2006) developed a VR environment using the 3D game Half-Life™. Actually, they did not use the game itself, which is a violent first-person shooter game, but the game engine. A game engine is the core software component that allows developing and running a computer or a video game. Some powerful game engines are available for free, either on the web or on the CD-ROM of the game itself. It is therefore possible to modify the game to some extent (this is legal as long as the modified product is not used for profit[2]). They developed a VR environment with five rooms containing spiders that were progressively more frightening in terms of number, size, and behaviors (see Fig. 5.5 for screenshots). Because of restrictions imposed by the technology and resources available at the time, the researchers had to use graphic material and computer programs already available within the game (e.g., color of the walls, behavior of the spiders). The software cost about US$ 50 in 2000, and the virtual environments took about 2 weeks of programming. To test this beta version of the VR environment, 11 spider phobics received four weekly therapy sessions of 90 min in which they followed a written treatment manual. The first therapy session included presentation of psychoeducational material about arachnophobia and its treatment plus a first VR immersion in an environment devoid of spiders. The following three sessions included *in virtuo* exposure only, except for the last 20 min of the final session, where relapse prevention was addressed. The hardware used was also more affordable than in previous studies. It included a Pentium III computer, an I-Glass HMD from IO-Display™, an Intertrax2

---

[2] See the end-user license agreement of each software program for details.

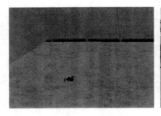  

Fig. 5.5 Screenshots from the first VR environment developed at UQO using Half-Life™ 3D game engine. Reproduced with permission from S. Bouchard

Fig. 5.6 Three screenshots from the second VR environment developed at UQO using the Max Payne™ 3D game engine (taken in Level 1, Level 3, and with the largest spider found in Level 3). Reproduced with permission from S. Bouchard

from Intersense™, and a joystick. Results of this uncontrolled study were promising, as all measures significantly decreased from pre- to posttreatment. However, clinical observations showed the necessity to improve the software significantly (e.g., use a more natural environment than a concrete basement with a military look, improve the virtual spiders by refining their appearance, making them look more realistic and diversifying their behavior, etc.).

The largest randomized control trial for arachnophobia so far was conducted by Michaliszyn et al. (2010) using a second VR software program developed at Université du Québec en Outaouais (UQO) with the 3D-game engine Max Payne™ (see Fig. 5.6). Thirty-two spider phobics were recruited and assigned to eight 90-min sessions of in vivo or *in virtuo* exposure. Half of the sample had previously been assigned to a waiting list before receiving their treatment. The researchers used the same treatment manual as the Bouchard et al. (2006) study initiated 5 years earlier, but the hardware was newer and slightly more powerful than before. Two live house spiders were used for in vivo exposure. Results showed significant improvements from pre- to posttreatment, with no difference between the two treatment groups and stability of the results over the 3-month follow-up. The scores of both conditions at the BAT show that on average participants in each condition were able to touch a terrarium containing a live tarantula and put their hands into it (see Fig. 5.7). The authors noted that three participants did not experience any fear

5.3 Description of the Studies Using VR Approaches to Treat Arachnophobia

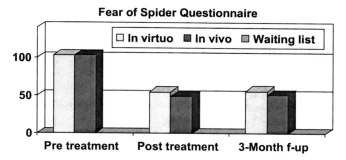

Fig. 5.7 Results from Michaliszyn et al. (2010) on the Fear of Spider Questionnaire

in the virtual environment and one felt significant cybersickness, which is precious information usually omitted in outcome studies on VR.

In order to document the impact of *in virtuo* exposure on psychophysiological and information processing measures and to explore the treatment process of *in virtuo* exposure, Côté and Bouchard (2005) studied 28 adults suffering from spider phobia according to the DSM-IV (APA 2000). Their hypotheses were that: (a) treatment would have an impact not only on self-report and behavioral measures but also on physiological and information processing indices, and (b) the treatment mechanism of *in virtuo* exposure would involve change in dysfunctional beliefs, self-efficacy, and information processing. Their intention was not to conduct an efficacy study but rather to confirm that change did occur in order to find out what would predict outcome. The treatment and the hardware were similar to Bouchard et al. (2006), except for the addition of one session of *in virtuo* exposure to the treatment manual, the use of a more powerful computer, and a slightly better HMD. The researchers used the software developed at UQO based on the experience previously learned during the pilot study with Half-Life™ (Bouchard et al. 2006), a program that was also used by Michaliszyn et al. (2010) with a few additional therapy sessions. In addition to questionnaires like the Fear of Spider Questionnaire (Szymanski and O'Donohue 1995), patients completed measures of dysfunctional beliefs towards spiders and of perceived self-efficacy to confront various situations involving spiders. They also performed a behavior avoidance test while their heart-rate variability was measured. Finally, the participants completed a non-lexical emotional Stroop task where pictures of spiders (threat stimuli), cows (neutral-control stimuli), and rabbits (positive-control stimuli) were presented on a computer monitor covered by a colored filter. Participants had to push a button corresponding to the color of the screen as fast as they could when they saw the pictures (see Fig. 5.8). The pictorial Stroop task engages cognitive resources in two competitive processes, i.e., perceiving the color and perceiving the feared stimuli. The interference created by images of spiders, compared to images of rabbits and cows, expresses the activation of an emotional processing specific to spiders. At posttreatment, changes on all variables were statistically significant, with patients able to remain seated <50 cm away from a live tarantula in an open terrarium. The originality of the analyses presented in this paper show that *in virtuo* exposure led to significant changes in cardiac response

Fig. 5.8 Illustration of images used in the pictorial emotional Stroop task by Côté and Bouchard (2005). Reproduced with permission from S. Bouchard

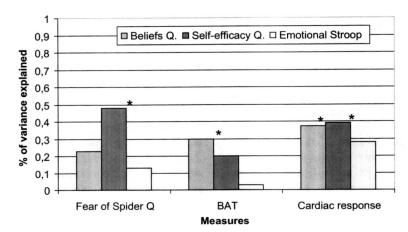

Fig. 5.9 Percentage of variance explained by three predictors (beliefs, self-efficacy, and emotional processing) on three outcome measures (global, behavioral, and physiological) for *in virtuo* exposure for fear of spiders. Note: * indicates predictors that were significant

during the BAT as well as in the emotional processing of the feared stimuli. Slight symptoms of VR-induced side effects (cybersickness) were observed during the immersions but they decreased significantly over the course of treatment. The feeling of presence was high and only minor changes in this measure were reported over time.

In a second paper dedicated to the analysis of treatment mechanism, Côté and Bouchard (2009) used residualized change scores to find the best predictors of improvement on the Fear of Spider Questionnaire (i.e., a general measure of outcome), on the performance on the BAT (i.e., a behavioral measure of outcome), and on the cardiac response during the last minute of the BAT (i.e., a physiological measure of outcome). Results revealed an interesting pattern, where change in perceived self-efficacy was the strongest predictor of improvement on the Fear of Spider Questionnaire, change in beliefs was the strongest predictor of improvement on the BAT, and change in both self-efficacy and beliefs predicted improvement in cardiac response when performing the BAT (see Fig. 5.9). Change in information processing never significantly predicted improvement. These results shed some light on the treatment mechanism of in vivo exposure. It is also interesting to see that changes in beliefs and self-efficacy that occur when facing virtual stimuli predict changes in behavioral and physiological performance on a BAT.

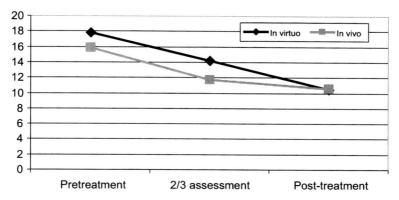

Fig. 5.10 Results of 31 children on a modified version of the Fear of Spider Questionnaire when measured after four sessions of either *in virtuo* or *in vivo* exposure and after one final session of *in vivo* exposure

5.3.1 In Virtuo *Exposure with Children*

In virtuo exposure may be especially useful with children. Children may be attracted by the "coolness" of VR, which could increase the likelihood that they will enroll in exposure-based therapies. In a pilot study, Bouchard et al. (2007, 2011) used the pilot VR environment developed at UQO with Half-Life™ and treated nine clinically phobic children. The four-session treatment was adapted to children but otherwise similar to other studies conducted at UQO. The researchers used a multiple baseline across subject design and administered questionnaires at pre- and posttreatment. Statistical analyses revealed significant improvement on all measures of phobia. Visual analyses of weekly reports of children's fear of spiders show that improvements followed the introduction of the treatment. However, the visual analyses also showed that there was still room for improvement as many children were not rating their fear at 0%.

A larger study from St-Jacques et al. (2006) was conducted to test the hypothesis that using *in virtuo* exposure would increase children's motivation for therapy compared to in vivo exposure. They recruited 31 children aged 8–15 who were clinically phobic of spiders. Participants were assessed at pretreatment, randomly assigned to either four sessions of *in virtuo* exposure or four sessions of in vivo exposure, and reassessed, and then they all received one session of in vivo exposure. Treatment manuals adapted for children were provided to children and parents to inform them of the principles guiding the therapy and underlying exposure, as well as to ascertain that therapy was delivered as planned. Adherence to the treatments protocols was confirmed by random spot checks of audio recordings of therapy sessions. In terms of efficacy at the end of the therapy, the statistical analyses could not detect any significant difference between both forms of therapy (see Fig. 5.10 for results on a modified version of the Fear of Spider Questionnaire). Albeit nonsignificant, examination of effect sizes of the differences between both conditions from pretreatment to the time everyone participated in the last session with in vivo exposure revealed a medium effect. This suggests that a larger sample could have detected significant differences, and thus that the addition of one in vivo exposure session could be beneficial. But most surprisingly, and contrary to the researcher's hypotheses, *in virtuo* exposure did not increase children's motivation towards therapy. In general, children had a relatively strong self-determined motivation to engage in exposure-based therapy. Pre-therapy and weekly assessments of motivation were lower in the *in virtuo* exposure, although these differences were not statistically significant. The researchers raised several ad hoc hypotheses to explain their results, one possibility being that children in the *in virtuo* condition were more afraid of what the virtual spiders could look like and could do in the VR environment. This is probably due to their fertile imagination (i.e., some kids were afraid that spiders would be huge or aggressive) and highlights the importance of preparing children more carefully than adults about what to expect during *in virtuo* exposure. This hypothesis was confirmed by Silva et al. (2011). As part of an attraction in a science museum depicting a virtual environment used to treat phobias, they compared the apprehension of 533 people during an immersion in VR, just before opening doors that would lead to a spider or a rabbit. Results revealed significantly less apprehension in adults compared to younger participants. The lesson learned from this study is that therapists should describe to young participants what will happen in the virtual environment, how frightening, disgusting, or large the virtual spiders will be, and what the therapist will do.

Another important finding from St-Jacques et al. (2006), this study is the demonstration that treatment motivation, more specifically integrated extrinsic motivation, is a significant predictor of success ($sr^2 = 0.49$, $p < 0.01$). Given the importance of motivating children to come and stay in therapy, in addition to the enticing effect of VR for children, more research should be conducted on the power of VR to increase treatment motivation.

One of the most recent VR studies for arachnophobia treatment has explored how memory consolidation might be enhanced by sleep (Kleim et al. 2013). Although it is well established that memory consolidation after learning is benefitted by sleep, this has not yet been researched in an emotional learning paradigm in psychotherapy. Eighty subjects were recruited and a total of 50 who met inclusion criteria underwent one-session VR exposure treatment. Exposure was done in a protocol similar to the one used in a VR exposure study for acrophobia (de Quervain et al. 2011). Following exposure, participants were assigned to either a sleep or wake condition. Participants in the sleep condition were then taken to a different room in the lab to sleep for 90 min. Those in the wake condition watched a neutral National Geographic film for 90 min. After the 90-min lapse, all participants completed a BAT. They then returned to the lab 1 week later and completed a second BAT and questionnaires. Results indicated that sleep improves therapeutic effectiveness, with participants showing a greater reduction in both subjective anxiety and spider-related cognitions at 1-week follow-up as compared to patients who had not napped.

This study provided an initial exploration into the clinical application of memory research. Some patients do not benefit from exposure therapy or benefit only

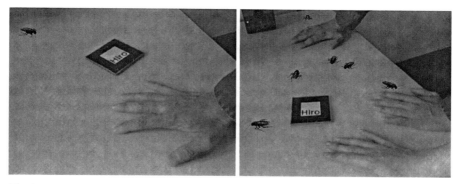

Fig. 5.11 Reproduction of what a user can see in Botella et al. (2005) augmented reality program for the specific phobia of cockroaches. Note that everything seen by the participant through the HMD is the physical reality, including the therapist's and the participant's hands, except for the cockroaches that are virtual. Reproduced with permission from C. Botella

to have the phobia later return (Craske and Mystkowski 2006). Napping after a therapy session may be one avenue by which exposure-based treatments can be enhanced to increase response rates.

5.3.2 In Virtuo *Exposure for Other Animal Phobias*

Snake phobia (ophidiophobia) is more prevalent than arachnophobia, but it has received much less attention from researchers in the field of VR. Only one research team has developed a VR environment for snake phobics (see Parrott et al. 2004). This environment allows the user to see pictures of snakes, then snakes in several cages or outdoors, and finally to handle a fiber optic-based 3D bend and twist tubular sensor mimicking the curvature and feel of a virtual snake, an approach that resembles the Hoffman et al. (2003) tactile augmentation. The authors only mentioned that pilot testing with one patient was positive.

Botella et al. (2005) took advantage of an innovative technique to develop an environment to treat the specific phobia of cockroaches. They used augmented reality (AR), a technology where the user wears a HMD that allows them to see physical reality while virtual replicas of cockroaches are superimposed upon it (see Fig. 5.11). The authors report results from one single case where a 26-year-old woman meeting the DSM-IV diagnosis of specific phobia of cockroaches was treated with 1 h of exposure using the augmented reality system. After 2 months of baseline self-monitoring for an AB single-case research design, the introduction of treatment led to an immediate and clear improvement. After the intensive therapy session, the patient was able to open a terrarium and hold a cockroach using a piece of cardboard. Results were maintained at the 2-month follow-up. More recently, a group of researchers combined the use of a "serious game" to AR to treat phobias (Botella et al. 2011). In a pilot study with a 25-year-old woman diagnosed with cockroach phobia, Botella et al. (2011) used a mobile phone application to create a game called *The Cockroach Game* where the user interacts with the insect shown on screen, at different intensity levels, while trying to complete a puzzle. The only subject to this study was instructed to play the game 9 days before undergoing a 1-hour-long intensive exposure session using AR. Once the exposure session was completed, the subject was encouraged to resume playing the game for another 9 days. Results suggest that: (a) the use of a serious game before undergoing an exposure session helped the patients by reducing her fear and avoidance, (b) a single AR exposure session led to a reduction in levels of fear, avoidance, and catastrophic beliefs while providing higher BAT scores, and (c) assessment at the end of the experimental trial showed that levels of fear, avoidance, and catastrophic thoughts continued to decrease during the following 9 days of playing the game. An improved version called *The Catch Me Game,* which uses a slightly different technology, is now being tested. Results with non-phobic participants are very encouraging (Wrzesien et al. 2013) and data are now being collected on a clinical sample.

5.4 Available Software

There are very few VR programs commercially available to treat the specific phobia of spiders, snakes, cockroaches, or small animals. In Virtuo (www.invirtuo.com) distributes virtual environments developed for phobias of spiders, snakes, dogs, and cats. Each environment allows users to face insects or animals of different sizes and shapes in various indoor and outdoor contexts. Virtually Better (www.virtuallybetter.com) also offers a virtual environment for spider phobia.

With specific phobias, therapists may be interested by simpler virtual environments, either available for free (e.g., see http://labpsicom.ulusofona.pt for a suite of free virtual environments) or that can be built by the therapist using free development software. For example, the early VR environments developed at UQO by modifying 3D games are available for free download on the Cyberpsychology Lab's website (w3.uqo.ca/cyberpsy). The two most significant drawbacks of these programs are that: (a) the user must buy a legal copy of the game before installing the modified version, (since versions of the game that are generally available on the market are more recent but incompatible with previous versions; old versions are difficult to find) and (b) there is no technical support to assist the user for troubleshooting and fixing technical problems. The issue of keeping software versions updated is a significant one. For example, the VR environment developed with Max Payne™ used in Côté and Bouchard (2005) was built using Windows 98. As versions of Windows evolved, updates and patches were needed. The company distributing the game does not support these old versions anymore and integrating new trackers and peripherals that require the latest versions of Windows or need updated drivers may not be possible. The apparent planned obsolescence of a computer operating system, or constant evolution and lack of support of past versions, is actually putting a significant toll on developers. The latest virtual environment for spider phobia offered by In Virtuo was built for Windows XP. While it was modified to run on Windows 7, Microsoft came up with Windows 8, making the virtual environment incompatible with the latest version. Due to necessity of keeping the version up to date which requires an investment of time and money, it makes the use of freely distributed virtual environments very cumbersome. For the same reason, technical support is often unavailable with freely distributed virtual environments. Unless the therapist has sufficient time and technical skills, using free virtual environments often ends up being a frustrating experience.

A mid-term alternative is to use free or inexpensive software that allows building and modifying your own environment. For example, NeuroVR (www.neurovr2.org) is a free program that comes with a basic library of virtual scenes and objects and can be customized to put a spider, a cockroach, or a snake on the table of a virtual kitchen. And it is user-friendly. For example, it has been used by bachelor degree students in psychology in courses delivered by the first author of this chapter. As their main assignment, students have to create a new treatment for a mental disorder of their choice, develop a therapeutic protocol, and build the required virtual environment. This can be done with no skills in computer programming and basic knowledge in managing files and editing images. There is a community of NeuroVR users who can help providing technical support. Although many researchers use this software to create efficient applications, the options remain limited and the visual quality of the final product is not as attractive as virtual environments developed with more expensive 3D editing and rendering software.

5.5 Relevant Findings from Studies Using Virtual Reality Approaches

Outcome studies on *in virtuo* treatment of specific phobias of spiders, snakes, and cockroaches are in general methodologically less robust than what can be found for phobia of flying or heights, an observation that is similar for research on the effectiveness of in vivo exposure (Öst 1997). Three studies compared the efficacy of *in virtuo* exposure to a control condition (Garcia-Palacios et al. 2002; Hoffman et al. 2003; Michaliszyn et al. 2006). In all three cases, VR was more effective than no treatment, except for one of three variables in Hoffman et al. (2003) where the participants who did not have the tactile feedback performed just like the controls on the level of fear felt during the BAT. The efficacy of *in virtuo* exposure in controlled studies mirrors the observations from less controlled studies (Meyerbröker and Emmelkamp 2010; Opris et al. 2012). Michaliszyn et al. (2006) paid attention to effect sizes of the comparison between treatments and did not find meaningful differences between *in virtuo* and in vivo exposure. Only one controlled study tested VR with children and no significant difference was found at posttreatment, although effect sizes suggest that the addition of one in vivo session to the VR treatment may be beneficial. Two innovative studies used AR for the fear of cockroaches (Botella et al. 2005, 2011). As mentioned above, the 2011 study integrated the usage of a serious game before and after a 1-hour-long exposition session. Although these two studies are uncontrolled case studies, the results highlight the potential of this technology. The patients' improvements have been documented by multiple sources, such as self-reports (e.g., Fear of Spider Questionnaire), physiological measures (e.g., heart rate variability), automatic information processing (e.g., emotional Stroop task), and behavioral measures. However, long-term follow-ups are needed to confirm claims about treatment efficacy. The advantages of AR for exposure with people suffering from animal phobia are significant, in terms of both costs and generalizability. The cost of developing a virtual environment is significantly reduced if the developers only have to create and animate one object. With VR, the virtual spider has to be placed somewhere, on a virtual table which is in a virtual kitchen, surrounded with other virtual objects that make the visual experience credible. Augmented reality requires that the 3D object be overlaid on objects present in the physical reality so that the developer only has to provide the virtual insect of an animal. A study comparing people's reactions to 3D spiders presented in augmented reality or in VR using a HMD technology or a fully immersive virtual room (Baus et al. 2011) revealed that all three technologies were as effective in inducing anxiety. In addition to cost, the other advantage is that when AR will become portable and simpler to use, patients will be able bring the virtual spider home and project it in several places that would be useful for exposure. Most of the behavior avoidance tests involved approaching a live tarantula in a terrarium. In some cases, a perfect score on the test would involve touching or holding the tarantula, which may be considered extreme by some people. It may also be more difficult than BAT used in often-cited studies on in vivo exposure, such as Öst's work, where house spiders were used. At posttreatment, patients were (on average) able to get very close to the tarantula, either with the lid of the terrarium open or by touching it if closed, sometimes to the point of putting their hands in the terrarium. However, the use of more similar BAT in terms of difficulty and hierarchy would help when comparing the efficacy of different treatment protocols. A tentative comparison of pre- and posttreatment scores on the Fear of Spider Questionnaire between studies using *in virtuo* exposure, and with published studies using in vivo exposure (e.g., Murris and Merkelbach 1996), reveals that the severity of scores at pretreatment are comparable across studies, and that improvement from pre to post are similar to what is found in classical studies using in vivo exposure (e.g., all effect sizes were >2).

To test if VR may be used as an assessment and diagnostic tool, Mühlberger et al. (2008) designed a virtual BAT to study the interaction between physiological fear responses, approach behavior, reported fear, and other subjective measures related to fear of spiders. During their behavior avoidance test, the participant was immersed in VR using a HDM in monoscopic display, and the approach behavior of the participant towards the virtual spider was carefully measured in centimeters. Patients underwent the test before and after undergoing eight very brief (1 min) *in virtuo* exposure sessions in the same virtual environment but with a spider that looked different (i.e., using a different texture). Subjective measures were also taken. Participants showed a reduction in negative beliefs regarding spiders, lower subjective fear, and an increase in approach behavior towards the spider. The documented change in approach behavior suggests the possibility of using avoidance of virtual spiders as an assessment tool. This is only a preliminary step that it needs to be substantiated with concomitant validity (e.g., with an in vivo BAT), information about reliability, and using a different environment for the BAT and the exposure treatment. But it remains an interesting avenue that could provide a wide range of stimuli that would be very practical for therapists (e.g., the possibility to switch in a few clicks a BAT for dogs, cats, snake, cows, etc.). Another interesting finding from this study was the observed lack of significant change in heart rate and significant increase in skin conductance from the pre to the post-exposure BAT. What this means is that even though participants approached the virtual spider more closely at the post-exposure BAT, they did so with the same level of physiological fear than in the pre-exposure BAT. Mühlberger et al. (2008) hypothesised that physiological responses was still high as a result of closer approach behavior. Nevertheless, these results are typical examples of desynchrony and discordance among modes of responses (Haynes and O'Brian 2000) and are replicating observations by Côté and Bouchard (2005). Treatment protocols vary in duration, from 3 to 12 h, with an average around four or five 1-h sessions. Although the 3-h/one-session treatment protocol validated by Öst is intended to be a first step that should be followed by self-directed exposure at home post therapy, it has received extended empirical support. However, only one controlled study (Hoffman et al. 2003) and two single case studies (Botella et al. 2005, 2011) successfully condensed VR therapy to that extent. Research on the frequency and spacing between therapy sessions has been prolific with in vivo exposure and should be addressed with *in virtuo* exposure as well. For example, no study has tried to replicate the findings from Rowe and Craske (1998) that frequent exposure-based therapy sessions early in therapy, followed by progressively spaced the sessions, will be more effective than evenly spaced weekly therapy sessions.

Within therapy sessions, the treatment protocols do not usually keep the patient immersed in VR for the entire duration of the exposure session (see Bouchard et al. 2012 for more details). In the first VR study, Carlin et al. (1997) paused every 5 min to reduce the risks of VR-induced side effects. Indeed, looking into the HMD for long periods of time may create eyestrain due to accommodation fatigue. However, stopping the exposure after 5 min was not done in subsequent studies. To reduce the possibility of eyestrain, it is suggested to take breaks roughly every 20 min and remove the HMD (Stanney et al. 2002), although these breaks must be adjusted in order to allow anxiety to decrease significantly during the exposure session.

During therapy sessions, almost every treatment protocol devoted the majority of the time to *in virtuo* exposure. This is different from treatment protocols used for some other anxiety disorders (e.g., fear of flying, social anxiety disorder), where significant therapy time was often allocated to additional therapeutic strategies. Cognitive restructuring, breathing retraining, or other coping strategies were not explicitly taught to arachnophobic patients, at least not in studies using a written treatment manual. Patients were not encouraged to conduct self-exposure exercises at home, either in vivo (for methodological purposes, such as keeping treatment as purely VR as possible) or *in virtuo* (for practical reasons). The lack of homework is important to notice since homework is included in traditional in vivo exposure therapies. In clinical practice, therapists may want to add take-home exercises, and some portable and immersive applications using iPads are now being tested (Bouchard et al. 2012). In terms of hardware, every VR environment now works on affordable computers and with a wide range of VR devices, from the most expensive to the most affordable. Only two studies report the presence of VR-induced side effects (see Chap. 3 for more information about cybersickness). Apart from one patient where cybersickness was significant, other participants generally experienced no or very slight side effects. Further research is needed to ascertain if these symptoms are more related to the anxiety felt during exposure than to VR, if they are caused by patient's characteristics or the mere immersion in VR, or if they are specific to the environment used (e.g., users had to move and walk a lot more in the virtual environments for arachnophobia than they do in a virtual airplane). A few studies are actually raising concerns about the overlap between symptoms of anxiety and VR-induced side effects (Bouchard et al. 2009, 2011). First, Bouchard et al. (2009) reported normative data on the Simulator Sickness Questionnaire and observed that: (a) most participants report only slight signs of negative side effects post immersion, (b) many phobic patients report symptoms that are on the list of this questionnaire before any immersion in VR, and (c) the original scoring method, factor structure, and norms of the questionnaire may not be appropriate for samples of phobic patients. In 2011, the same research team (Bouchard et al 2011) pursued their investigations and questioned whether at least two items of the Simulator Sickness Questionnaire were not inflated by anxiety (i.e., general discomfort and difficulty concentrating) and only four items were totally independent of anxiety.

Given the growing body of data on disgust, researchers in VR should measure this construct more often in their outcome studies. Practically, therapists seem to be including this variable in their therapy, as they often draw a patient's attention towards aspects of spiders and their behavior that are more relevant to disgust than fear (e.g., spider web, the "grace" of spiders walking, furry texture, or shape of the legs).

One significant advantage of using VR to conduct exposure is the possibility to vary the context. As documented in the introduction of this chapter, varying contextual information during the learning of new associations with lack of threat is important for generalization and prevention of relapse (Power et al. 2006; Otto and Hofmann 2010). So far, only one study has been conducted on the impact of systematically varying the context of *in virtuo* exposure (Shiban et al. 2013). Shiban et al. (2013) used a very well-controlled experimental paradigm where they exposed *in virtuo* spider phobics to a spider in an empty room for one session that lasted less than an hour, using a HMD and a 6-dof motion tracker. Participants were randomly assigned to five brief *in virtuo* exposure exercises in a room that either: (a) remained exactly the same color (walls, floor, roof, and lighting) for all exercices or (b) changed color for each exercise. A pre- and post-session BAT involving a live tarantula revealed significantly more improvement in participants who were exposed to the virtual spider in different contexts for each immersion compared to those exposed in a single context. The level of fear experienced during and between the exercises was also related to the change in contexts, with greater within session reduction of fear for those treated in a variety of contexts. Because the experiment involved only changing the color of the room, it is highly probable that more important variations in context (e.g., exposure exercises in the kitchen, in the bedroom, on the porch, on the grass) would have an even stronger impact. More work on this topic should be conducted also to orient developers of VR environments to the kind of scenarios that must be developed. For now, VR environments for specific phobias include several varieties of feared stimuli that are encountered in a variety of locations while they are engaged in a variety of behaviors. To what extent does this variety of contexts facilitate generalization? It is worthy to note that in the environment developed using the game Max Payne, the behaviors of the virtual spiders were not realistic. Even if it was not detrimental for the therapy, this deserves to be studied more often since it does not allow patients to learn how spiders really behave.

It is practical to use arachnophobia for conducting experimental research in VR, just as it is the case with in vivo exposure. Two studies have tackled the task of investigating the treatment mechanism of *in virtuo* exposure. Hoffman et al. (2003) revealed that adding a tactile feeling may increase treatment efficacy. It remains to be seen whether the increase in efficacy would be caused by the increase in the feeling of presence, or if it relates more to the inclusion of an additional context (the feeling of touch) or an additional sensory modality, to increases in self-efficacy, to the development of stronger anti-phobic behavior, or to more tangible evidences of the lack of danger. More experimental research on this topic is warranted. The study by Côté and Bouchard (2005) showed that even if spiders are virtual, in vivo exposure initiates change in process variables such as dysfunctional beliefs, self-efficacy, and an emotional Stroop task. However, only changes in dysfunctional beliefs and self-efficacy predicted treatment outcome. The emotional Stroop task is often used as an index of changes in the fear structure, a concept relevant to Foa and Kozak's (1986) emotional processing theory. This influential theory in the field of anxiety disorders is often cited as the explanation for the effectiveness of *in virtuo* exposure (North et al. 1996). However, in light of the current conceptualization of the mechanisms involved in exposure illustrated in the introduction of this chapter, Côté and Bouchard's (2009) results may illustrate the learning of safe associations with the feared stimuli in terms of perceived consequences (involving threat or disgust) and perceived self-efficacy, along with fear structures that are not so much modified as inhibited but still present to some extent. Further experimental studies are needed to explain why the emotional Stroop task did not predict outcome (Côté and Bouchard 2009). Nevertheless, knowing that change in beliefs and self-efficacy are key predictors of outcome is clinically very important to therapists using VR. Therapists must use patients' gains in therapy to foster their perceived self-efficacy, guide patients' attention to events that disprove their dysfunctional beliefs, and conduct post-exposure reviews of what has been learned during the immersion. The contribution of self-efficacy to therapeutic success may also explain the advantage of using biofeedback during *in virtuo* exposure for fear of flying (Wiederhold 1999).

No study has yet documented the neurological correlate of improvements after VR therapy. It is assumed that *in virtuo* exposure is simply a different form of exposure which aims to develop new mental associations between the stimuli and lack of danger. It therefore remains to be tested whether *in virtuo* exposure involves change in the same brain areas as in vivo exposure. However, a few studies conducted with claustrophobics used VR to fully standardize the exposure treatment and test the efficacy of a drug that can boost the occurrence of emotional learning in the limbic system (see Ressler et al. 2004 in the following chapters)

It is commonly believed that VR is an innovative form of therapy that could make exposure-based therapies more attractive to patients, or at least make exposure more acceptable. Two studies performed by Garcia-Palacios et al. (2001) confirm people's preference for *in virtuo* exposure over in vivo exposure. In the first study, 87 undergraduate students scoring high on a brief assessment of fear of spiders were provided standardized information about in vivo and *in virtuo* exposure and asked to indicate their willingness to receive each form of therapy. When asked if they would consider several sessions of free treatment, 17.4% said they would definitely not engage in in vivo exposure, compared to only 4.6% who said they would definitely not try VR. On a forced-choice question, 81% chose *in virtuo* exposure compared to only 19% who chose in vivo. In the second study, they used the same methodology with 75 students highly fearful of spiders to contrast their preferences between multiple sessions of *in virtuo* exposure compared to one 3-h session of in vivo exposure. In this case, 34.7% said they would definitely not do in vivo exposure, compared to 8% who said they would not do *in virtuo* exposure. On the forced-choice question, 89.2% chose VR with only 10.8% choosing in vivo. However, these results were obtained with adults. When St-Jacques et al. (2006) compared children's actual motivation towards therapy just after they have been told that they would receive *in virtuo* or in vivo exposure therapy, results were slightly different. Motivation was not different for the *in virtuo* condition. This finding may very well be due to children entertaining frightening expectations about what could happen during VR exposure. It could also be explained by methodological differences between Garcia-Palacios' and St-Jacque's studies. One measured what type of therapy adults would chose if they were to seek treatment and the other one measured motivation of children already seeking treatment. Still, it raises the possibility that acceptance and attractiveness of *in virtuo* exposure could be more complex with children than originally thought.

5.6 Conclusion

The overall results of completed research validate the potential of *in virtuo* exposure to treat arachnophobia. If one wants to rigorously prove that *in virtuo* exposure is specifically effective for spider phobia, then additional trials are needed. The current ones are very good but can be criticized on the grounds of control conditions, sample size, or long-term follow-ups. But considered in the general context of validating VR for the treatment of specific phobias, the current studies are adding significant support to the growing body of evidence that *in virtuo* exposure is an effective treatment. Some researchers are also developing new applications of VR to other insects (cockroaches) and animals (snakes), so further outcome studies are expected.

A useful contribution to VR studies with people suffering from arachnophobia is for examining variables related to treatment process. Tactile feedback may increase the efficacy of VR treatment. What remains to be seen is whether this is because it increases the feeling of presence or if it is via other mechanisms such as self-efficacy or the addition of physical motor approach or avoidance response of the arm towards the spider. Changes in cognitive information processing were also observed but did not predict treatment outcome. Rather, treatment success appears to be related to change in dysfunctional beliefs and self-efficacy. Given the importance of varying the contexts of exposure to maximize its effectiveness, it is interesting to note that most VR environments were developed with variety in mind. Finally, VR appears to be an attractive form of therapy, an asset that still needs to be studied more thoroughly.

Since it is easy to find spiders for therapy, one may wonder why researchers found an interest in the use of VR. Many VR studies were conducted with arachnophobia for methodological reasons. First, given the availability of spiders, researchers could compare *in virtuo* exposure with the gold-standard in vivo exposure. This is not possible with fear of flying, for example, where the exposure program can hardly be provided entirely in vivo with actual flights. Second, the availability of spiders also facilitates the use of safe, simple, and affordable BAT. VR also offers to the therapist a degree of control and variety of contexts that is impossible to have even with live spiders. Fourth, the possibility to use physical and virtual spiders is a significant asset for experimental research on factors that make VR effective. Finally, it seemed natural for researchers to begin clinical research on VR with more circumscribed disorders and then move on to study phobias where physical stimuli cannot be used in vivo (e.g., fear of thunderstorm) and to more complex anxiety disorders such as social anxiety or panic disorder.

References

Abramowitz, J. S. (2013). The practice of exposure therapy: Relevance of cognitive-behavioral theory and extinction theory. *Behavior Therapy, 44*, 548–558.

Abramowitz, J. S., Deacon, B. J., & Whiteside, S. P. H. (2011). *Exposure therapy for anxiety. Principles and practice.* New York: Guilford.

American Psychiatric Association: APA. (2000). *Diagnostic and statistical manual of mental disorders fourth edition text revision.* Washington: American Psychiatric Association.

Bandura, A. (1986). *Social foundations of thoughts and action: A social cognitive theory.* Englewoods Cliffs: Prentice Hall.

Baus, O., Bouchard, S., Gougeon, V., & Roucaut, F.-X. (2011). Comparison of anxiety in response to virtual spiders while immersed in augmented reality, head-mounted display, or CAVE-like system. *Journal of Cybertherapy and Rehabilitation, 4*(2), 171–174.

Botella, C. M., Juan, M. C., Baños, R. M., Alcañiz, M., Guillén, V., & Rey, B. (2005). Mixing realities? An application of augmented reality for the treatment of cockroach phobia. *Cyber Psychology & Behavior, 8*(2), 162–171.

Botella, C., Breton-López, J., Quero, S., Baños, R. M., García-Palacios, A., Zaragoza, I., & Alcaniz, M. (2011). Treating cockroach phobia using a serious game on a mobile phone and augmented reality exposure: A single case study. *Computers in Human Behavior, 27*, 217–217.

Bouchard, S. (2011). Could virtual reality be effective in treating children with phobias? *Expert Review of Neurotherapeutics, 11*(2), 207–213.
Bouchard, S., Côté, S., Robillard, G., St-Jacques, J., & Renaud, P. (2006). Effectiveness of virtual reality exposure in the treatment of arachnophobia using 3D games. *Technology and Health Care, 14*(1), 19–27.
Bouchard, S., St-Jacques, J., Robillard, G., & Renaud, P. (2007). Efficacité d'un traitement d'exposition en réalité virtuelle pour le traitement de l'arachnophobie chez l'enfant: Une étude pilote. *Journal de Thérapie Comportementale et Cognitive, 17*(3),101–108.
Bouchard, S., St-Jacques, J., Renaud, P., & Wiederhold, B. K. (2009). Side effects of immersions in virtual reality for people suffering from anxiety disorders. *Journal of Cybertherapy and Rehabilitation, 2*(2), 127–137.
Bouchard, S., Robillard, G., Renaud, P., & Bernier, F. (2011). Exploring new dimensions in the assessment of virtual reality induced side-effects. *Journal of Computer and Information Technology, 1*(3), 20–32.
Bouchard, S., Robillard, G., Larouche, S., & Loranger, C. (2012). Description of a treatment manual for in virtuo exposure with specific phobia. In C. Eichenberg (ed.), *Virtual reality in psychological, medical and pedagogical applications* (ch. 4, pp. 82–108). Rijeka: InTech.
Bourdon, K. H., Boyd, J. H., Rae, D. S., & Burns, B. J. (1988). Gender differences in phobias: Results of a ECA community survey. *Journal of Anxiety Disorders, 2*, 227–241.
Bouton, M. E. (2007). *Learning and behaviour: A contemporary synthesis.* Sunderland: Sinauer.
Carlin, A. S., Hoffman, H. G., & Weghorst, S. (1997). Virtual reality and tactile augmentation in the treatment of spider phobia: A case report. *Behaviour Research & Therapy, 35*(2), 153–158.
Côté, S., & Bouchard, S. (2005). Documenting the efficacy of virtual reality exposure with psychophysiological and information processing measures. *Applied Psychophysiology and Biofeedback, 30*(3), 217–232.
Côté, S., & Bouchard, S. (2009). Cognitive mechanisms underlying virtual reality exposure. *Cyberpsychology & Behavior, 12*(2), 121–129.
Craske, M. G., & Mystkowski, J. L. (2006). Exposure therapy and extinction: clinical studies. In D. H. M. G. Craske & D. Vansteenwegen (Eds.), *Fear and learning: Basic science to clnical application* (pp. 217–234). Washington: American Psychological Assoication.
Curtis, G.C., Magee, W.J., Eaton, W.W., Wittchen, H.-U., & Kessler, R.C. (1998). Specific fears and phobias: Epidemiology and classification. *British Journal of Psychiatry, 173*, 212.
de Quervain, D.F.G., Bentz, D., Michael, T., Bolt, O., Wiederhold, B.K., Margraf, J., & Wilhelm, F.H. (2011). Glucocorticoids enhance extinction-based psychotherapy. *Proceedings of the National Academy of Science U S A, 108*, 6621–6625.
Dewis, L. M., Kirkby, K. C., Martin, F., Daniels, B. A., Gilroy, L. J., & Menzies, R. G. (2001). Computer-aided vicarious exposure versus live graded exposure for spider phobia in children. *Journal of Behavior Therapy, 32*, 17.
Edwards, S., & Salkovskis, P. M. (2006). An experimental demonstration that fear, but not disgust, is associated with return of fear in phobias. *Anxiety Disorders, 20*, 58–71.
Foa, E. B., & Kozak, M. J. (1986). Emotional processing of fear: Exposure to corrective information. *Psychological Bulletin, 99*, 20–35.
Fredrickson, M., Annas, P., Fischer, H., & Wik, G. (1996). Gender and age differences in the prevalence of specific fears and phobias. *Behaviour Research & Therapy, 26*, 241–244.
Garcia-Palacios, A., Hoffman, H., See, S. K., Tsai, A., & Botella, C. (2001). Redefining therapeutic success with virtual reality exposure therapy. *Cyber Psychology and Behavior, 4*(3), 341–348.
Garcia-Palacios, A., Hoffman, H., Carlin, A., Furness III, T. A., & Botella, C. (2002). Virtual reality in the treatment of spider phobia: A controlled study. *Behaviour Research and Therapy, 40*, 983.
Gilroy, L. J., Kirby, K. C., Daniels, B. A., Menzies, R. G., & Montgomery, I. M. (2000). Controlled comparison of computer-aided vicarious exposure versus live exposure in the treatment of spider phobia. *Behavior Therapy, 31*(4), 733–744.
Gilroy, L. J., Kirkby, K. C., Daniels, B. A., Menzies, R. G., & Montgomery, I. M. (2003). Long-term follow-up of computer-aided vicarious exposure versus live graded exposure in the treatment of spider phobia. *Behavior Therapy, 34*, 65.

Götestam, K.G. (2002). One session group treatment of spider phobia by direct or modelled exposure. *Cognitive Behaviour Therapy, 31*(1), 18–24.
Haynes, S. N., & O'Brien, W.H. (2000). *Principles and practice of behavioral assessment.* New York: Kluwer.
Heading, K., Kirkby, K. C., Martin, F., Daniels, B. A., Gilroy, L. J., & Menzies, R. G. (2001). Controlled comparison of single-session treatments for spider phobia: Live graded exposure alone versus computer-aided vicarious exposure. *Behaviour Change, 18,* 103–113.
Hellström, K., & Öst, L.-G. (1995). One-session therapist directed exposure vs two forms of manual directed self-exposure in the treatment of spider phobia. *Behaviour Research and Therapy, 33*(8), 959–965.
Hoffman, H. (1998). VR: A new tool for interdisciplinary psychology research *Cyber Psychology and Behavior, 1*(2), 195–200.
Hoffman, H., Garcia-Palacios, A., Carlin, A., Furness III, T. A., & Botella, C. (2003). Interfaces that heal: Coupling real and virtual objects to treat spider phobia. *International Journal of Human-Computer Interaction, 16*(2), 283–300.
Johnstone, K. A., & Page, A. C. (2004). Attention to phobic stimuli during exposure: The effect of distraction on anxiety reduction, self-efficacy and perceived control. *Behaviour Research and Therapy, 42,* 249.
Kleim, B., Wilhelm, F. H., Temp, L., Margraf, J., Wiederhold, B. K., & Rasch, B. (2013). Sleep enhances exposure therapy. *Psychological Medicine, 10,* 1–9.
Larson, C. L., Schaefer, H. S., Siegle, G. J., Jackson, C. A. B., & Anderle, M. J. (2006). Fear is fast in phobic individuals: Amygdala activation in response to fear-relevant stimuli. *Biological Psychiatry, 60,* 410.
Marshall, W. L., Gauthier, J., Christie, M. M., Currie, D. W., & Gordon, A. (1977). Flooding therapy: Effectiveness, stimulus characteristics, and the value of brief in vivo exposure. *Behaviour Research and Therapy, 15*(1), 79–87.
McNally, R. J. (2002). On nonassociative fear emergence. *Behaviour Research and Therapy, 40,* 169.
Meyerbroeker, K., & Emmelkamp, P. M. G. (2010). Virtual reality exposure therapy in anxiety disorders: A systematic review of process-and-outcome studies. *Depression and Anxiety, 27,* 933–944.
Michaliszyn, D., Marchand, A., Martel, M.-O., Gaucher, M. (2006). *Predicting treatment outcome for arachnophobia's virtual reality therapy through measures of fear.* Poster presented at the 11th annual cyber therapy conference 2006, Gatineau, June 13–15.
Michaliszyn, D. R., Marchand, A., Bouchard, S., Martel, M.-O., & Poirier-Bisson, J. (2010). A randomized control trial of in virtuto and in vivo exposure for spider phobia. *Cyber Psychology, Behavior and Social Networking, 13*(6), 689–695.
Mineka, S., & Thomas, C. (1999). Mechanisms of change in exposure therapy for anxiety disorders. In T. Dagleish & M. Powers (Eds.), *Handbook of cognition et emotion* (pp. 747–764). New York: Wiley.
Mineka, S., Mystkowski, J. L., Hladek, D., & Rodriguez, B. I. (1999). The effects of changing contexts on return of fear following exposure therapy for spider fear. *Journal of Consulting and Clinical Psychology, 67*(4), 599–604.
Mühlberger, A., Sperber, M., Wieser, M. J., & Pauli, P. (2008). A virtual reality behavior avoidance test (VR-BAT) for the assessment of spider phobia. *Journal of Cyber Therapy & Rehabilitation, 1*(2), 147–158.
Mulkens, S. A. N., de Jong, P. J., & Merckelbach, H. (1996). Disgust and spider phobia. *Journal of Abnormal Psychology, 105,* 464–468.
Mohlman, J., & Zinbarg, R. E. (2000). What kind of attention is necessary for fear reduction? An empirical test of the emotional processing model. *Behavior Therapy, 31,* 113–133.
Murris, P., & Merkelbach, H. (1996). A comparison of two spider fear questionnaires. *Journal of Behavioural Therapy and Experimental Psychiatry, 27*(3), 241–244.
Mystkowski, J., Craske, M. G., & Echiverri, A. M. (2002). Treatment context and return of fear in spider phobia. *Behavior Therapy, 33,* 399.

Mystkowski, J. L., Mineka, S., Vernon, L. L., & Zinbarg, R. E. (2003). Changes in caffeine states enhance return of fear in spider phobia. *Journal of Consulting and Clinical Psychology, 71*(2), 243–250.

Mystkowski, J. L., Craske, M. G., Echiverri, A. M., & Labus, J. S. (2006). Mental reinstatement of context and return of fear in spider-fearful participants. *Behavior Therapy, 37,* 49–60.

North, M. M., North, S. M., & Coble, J. R. (1996). *Virtual reality therapy. An innovative paradigm.* CO: IPI Press.

Opris, D., Pintea, S., Garcia-Palacios, A., Botella, C., Szamoskozi, S., & David, D. (2012). Virtual reality exposure therapy in anxiety disorders: A quantitative meta-analysis. *Depression and Anxiety, 29,* 85–93.

Öst, L. G. (1987). Age at onset in different phobias. *Journal of Abnormal Psychology, 96,* 223.

Öst, L. -G. (1997). Rapid treatment of specific phobias. In G. C. L. Davey (Ed.), *Phobias: A handbook of theory, research and treatment* (pp. 227–246). Chichester: Wiley.

Öst, L. G., Salkovskis, L. -G. P. M., & Hellström, K. (1991). One-session therapist directed exposure vs. self-exposure in the treatment of spider phobia. *Behavior Therapy, 22,* 4072

Öst, L.-G., Ferebee, I., & Furmark, T. (1997). One session group therapy of spider phobia: Direct versus indirect treatments. *Behaviour Research and Therapy, 35,* 721.

Otto, M. W., & Hofmann, S. G. (2010). *Avoiding treatment failures in the anxiety disorders.* New York: Springer.

Paquette, V., Lévesque, J., Mensour, B., Leroux, J. -M., Beaudoin, G., Bourgouin, P., & Beauregard, M. (2003). "Change the mind and you change the brain": Effects of cognitive-behavioral therapy on the neural correlates of spider phobia. *NeuroImage, 18,* 401–409.

Parrott, M., Bowman, D., & Ollendick, T. (2004). *An immersive virtual environment for the treatment of ophidiophobia.* Presentation at the 9th annual cyber therapy conference 2004.

Phillips, M. L., Drevets, W. C., Rauch, S. L., & Lane, R. (2003). Neurobiology of emotion perception II: Implications for major psychiatric disorders. *Biological Psychiatry, 54,* 515–528.

Powers, M. B., Smits, J. A. J., Leyro, T. M., & Otto, M. W. (2006). Translational research perspectives on maximizing the effectiveness of exposure therapy. In D. C. S. Richards & D. L. Lauterbach (Eds.), *Handbook of exposure therapies* (pp. 109–126). Burlington: Academic.

Rachman, S. J. (1966). Studies in desensitization: II. Flooding. *Behaviour Research and Therapy, 4,* 1–6.

Ressler, K. J., Rothbaum, B. O., Tannenbaum, L., Anderson, P., Graap, K., Zimand, E., et al. (2004). Cognitive enhancers an adjunct to psychotherapy: Use of D-Cycloserine in phobic individuals to facilitate extinction of fear. *Archives of General Psychiatry, 61*(11), 1136–1144.

Richards, D. C. S., Lauterbach, D., & Gloster, A. T. (2006). Description, mechanisms of action, and assessment. In D. C. S. Richards & D. L. Lauterbach (eds), *Handbook of exposure therapies* (pp. 1–28). Burlington: Academic.

Rowe, M. K., & Craske, M. G. (1998). Effects of varied-stimulus exposure training on fear reduction and return of fear. *Behaviour Research and Therapy, 36,* 719.

Schienle, A., Schäfer, A., Stark, R., & Vaitl, D. (2009). Long-term effects of cognitive behavior therapy on brain activation in spider phobia. *Psychiatry Research: Neuroimaging, 172,* 99172.

Silva, C., Bouchard, S., & Bélanger, C. (2011). Youths are more apprehensive and frightened than adults by a virtual environment used to treat arachnophobia. *Journal of Cybertherapy and Rehabilitation, 4*(2), 200–201.

Shiban, Y., Pauli, P., & Mühlberger, A. (2013). Effect of multiple context exposure on renewal in spider phobia. *Behaviour Research and Therapy, 51,* 68–74.

Smith, K. L., Kirkby, K. C., Montgomery, I. M., & Daniels, B. A. (1997) Computer-delivered modeling of exposure for spider phobia: Relevant versus irrelevant exposure. *Journal of Anxiety Disorders, 11*(5), 489–497.

Smiths, J. A. J., Telch, M. J., & Randall, P. K. (2002). An examination of the decline in fear and disgust during exposure-based treatment. *Behaviour Research and Therapy, 40,* 1243.

Stanney, K.M., Kennedy, R.S., & Kingdon, K. (2002). Virtual environment protocols. In K. M. Stanney (Ed.), *Handbook of virtual environments* (pp. 721–730). Boca Raton: CRC Press.

References

Stinson, F. S., Dawson, D. A., Chou, S. P., Smith, S., Goldstein, R. B., Ruan, W. J., & Grant, B. F. (2007). The epidemiology of DSM-IV specific phobia in the USA: Results from the National Epidemiologic Survey on Alcohol and Related Conditions. *Psychological Medicine, 37,* 1047.

St-Jacques, J., Bouchard, S., & Bélanger, C. (2006). *Does virtual reality motivates children to do exposure?* Oral presentation at the 11th annual cybertherapy conference, Gatineau (Québec), June 12.

Straube, T., Glauer, M., Dilger, S., Mentzel, H. -J., & Miltner, W. H. R. (2006). Effects of cognitive-beavioral therapy on brain activation in specific phobia. *NeuroImage, 29,* 125.

Szymanski, J., & O'Donohue, W. (1995). Fear of spiders questionnaire. *Journal Behavior Therapy and Experimental Psychiatry, 26*(1), 31–34.

Telch, M. J. (2004). Pushing the envelope on treatments for phobia. In M. Maj, H. S. Akiskal, J. J. López-Ibor, & A. Okasha (Eds.), *Phobias* (pp. 232–234). Chichester: Wiley.

Vansteenwegen, D., Vervliet, B., Hermans, D., Thewissen, R., & Eelen, P. (2007). Verbal, behavioural and physiological assessment of the generalization of exposure-based fear reduction in a spider-anxious population. *Behaviour Research and Therapy, 45*(2), 291–300.

Watts, F. N. (1986). Cognitive processing in phobias. *Behavioural Psychotherapy, 14,* 295.

Wiederhold, B. K. (1999). A comparison of imaginal exposure and virtual reality exposure for the treatment of fear of flying. (Doctoral dissertation, California School of Professional Psychology, 1999). *Dissertations Abstracts International.*

Wolitsky, K. B., Rellini, A. H., & Telch, M. J. (2005). *Investigating the mechanisms of change during exposure-based treatments for acrophobia.* Poster presentation at the meeting of Anxiety Disorder Association of America, Seattle.

Woody, S. R., McLean, C., & Klassen, T. (2005). Disgust as a motivator of avoidance of spiders. *Journal of Anxiety Disorders, 19,* 461–475.

World Health Organization. (1992). The ICD-10 classification of mental and behavioural disorders. Geneva: WHO.

Wrzesien, M., Alcañiz, M., Botella, C., Ortega, M., & Brotons, D.B. (2013). The therapeutic lamp: Treating small-animal phobias. *IEEE Computer Graphics and Applications, 33*(1), 80–86.

Chapter 6
Fear of Heights (Acrophobia): Efficacy and Lessons Learned from Psychophysiological Data

Stéphane Bouchard, Brenda K. Wiederhold and Jessie Bossé

6.1 Key Variables Involved in Acrophobia

Acrophobia, or the fear of heights, is a phobic anxiety disorder that falls under the category of specific (isolated) phobia in the International Classification of Diseases-10 (ICD-10; World Health Organization 1992) and is classified as a specific phobia in the *Diagnostic and Statistical Manual of Mental Disorders*, Fourth Edition (DSM-IV; APA 2000). It is characterized by an irrational fear of heights, resulting in the avoidance of such situations or enduring the situations with marked distress. Acrophobics avoid a large range of stimuli, from climbing ladders to walking stairwells, getting close to windows in high-rise buildings, crossing bridges, sitting in the balcony section at the theater, etc. Acrophobia is different from physiological height vertigo, with the former being related to excessive fear of falling despite objective risks and avoidance while physiological height vertigo is the whirling sensation and visual destabilization of posture caused when the distance between the observer and the closest stationary visible object becomes critically large (Brandt et al. 1980; Brandt 2003).

National epidemiological surveys conducted in the USA (Curtis et al. 1998; Stinson et al. 2007) estimated the lifetime prevalence rate of specific phobia of heights to be 5.3 %. This would make the phobia of heights the second most common specific phobia after animal phobias. However, a recent large-scale study on specific phobia prevalence in the Netherlands indicated that acrophobia had the highest lifetime prevalence of all specific phobias, with almost 5 % of the general population being affected by fear of heights (Depla et al. 2008). The point prevalence, as estimated with 1000 participants by Fredrickson et al. (1996) using DSM-IV criteria, is 7.5 %. The lifetime prevalence for fear of heights, including but not limited to pathological fear, could be as frequent as 20 % (Curtis et al. 1998). For some people, this fear is endured with marked distress, whereas for others the fear is so intense that height situations must be avoided altogether. In any case, to be considered a specific phobia, the level of distress or impairment must significantly interfere with the patient's functioning. It may severely restrict the patient's personal, professional, or social life. The specific phobia of heights often appears in the absence of any direct aversive conditioning episodes (Menzies 1997; Poulton et al. 2001), the age of onset varies across studies from mid-teens to mid-20s (Antony and Barlow 2002), and it affects almost equally both genders.

A better understanding of mechanisms underlying acrophobia's development is important. Researchers studying height phobia recently proposed that specific physiological and psychological biases may contribute to the development of such phobia (Coelho and Wallis 2010). More precisely, they discovered that specific factors related to posture and sensory cues processing were significantly more present in acrophobic subjects compared to non-acrophobic subjects. Hence, they proposed that the presence and interaction of the four following factors may predispose an individual to develop acrophobia: (1) visual field dependence, (2) poor postural control, (3) high space and motion discomfort, and finally (4) higher propensity to interpret bodily sensations as threatening. The field dependence characteristic in acrophobics implies that they tend to over-rely on visual cues to locate themselves in space and to adjust their physical posture accordingly. Since there are less motion cues at heights compared to ground level, subjects who rely on visual cues can struggle with locating and positioning themselves physically in such context. To compensate for the lack of visual cues at heights, subjects may increase subtly postural sway in order to create visual feedback. Having poor postural control, such an attempt will likely cause more instability. Added to this mix is a tendency to experience space and motion discomfort, which only makes matters worst. Finally, Coelho and Wallis (2010) explained that acrophobic subjects were more likely to interpret anxiety-related bodily sensations as threatening, which contribute to explain why they fear heights. Surprisingly, trait anxiety was not found to be a predictive factor in acrophobia, suggesting that it might be a nonspecific factor. Clinicians may find the above information useful when asked by their patients why they feel drawn by cliffs and avoid high places.

6.2 Description of Significant Efficacy Studies Using Non-VR Approaches

Among the efficacy studies, two outcome studies with large samples stand out as they have compared an active treatment to a waiting-list control condition. In 1985, Marshall found that standard (1.2 h) and prolonged (1.5–1.6 h) exposures were more effective than brief exposure (0.5 h) or no treatment at all. Also in 1985, Williams et al. replicated findings from an earlier study (Williams et al. 1984) with a mixed sample suggesting that exposure was effective, but that guided mastery was even more effective. They recruited 38 adults suffering from height phobia and ascertained severity by selecting only people who were unable to stand at the railing of a fifth floor balcony. Participants were randomly assigned to one of three conditions: (a) waiting-list control, (b) exposure, or (c) guided-mastery exposure. The treatment did not include any cognitive restructuring techniques and was delivered over two 90-min sessions. Guided mastery is an approach to exposure where the patient benefits from more guidance from the therapist than in straight *in vivo* exposure or desensitization as it was applied at the time. In guided mastery, the therapist initially accompanies the patient in the phobic situation and progressively becomes less and less involved in the patient's exposure exercise. The therapist also actively helps the patient perform more effective exposure exercises by modeling adaptive behaviors, using mid-steps in the exposure hierarchy, instructing the patient to focus on intermediate goals if the current goal appears too difficult, eliminating safety-seeking behavior, etc. In sum, the therapist takes a more active role during the exposure than simply rating subjective units of distress scale (SUDS) and waiting for the anxiety to decline before moving on to the next step in the hierarchy. This is an approach most cognitive-behavioral therapy (CBT) therapists would now adopt implicitly, probably with the exception of the modeling component. Results at posttreatment and follow-up revealed that simple *in vivo* exposure was more effective than no treatment. However, guided mastery was significantly more effective than exposure alone on all measures, including a behavior avoidance test and ratings of anxiety and self-efficacy. This study also revealed that perceived self-efficacy was an influential predictor of treatment outcome. Other studies have compared different methods for delivering exposure (e.g., Bourque and Ladouceur 1980) and, in sum, all confirmed the efficacy of exposure treatment (Öst 1997).

6.3 Description of the Studies Using VR Approaches to Treat Acrophobia

Acrophobia was targeted in the earliest outcome studies on virtual reality (VR) and remains extensively studied. Several articles describing case studies have been published for *in virtuo* exposure (Bouchard et al. 2003; Choi et al. 2001; Jang et al. 2002; Kuntze et al. 2003; North et al. 1996; Rothbaum et al. 1995b; Sik-Lányi et al. 2004; Sirbu et al. 2004; Vale et al. 2010; Whitney et al. 2005) and a few research centers are still in the development process of VR environments for heights (e.g., Sik-Lányi et al. 2004). All of these less controlled case studies report positive results, some with older participants (e.g., 61 years old in Choi et al. 2001; Jang et al. 2002) or younger ones (e.g., 19 years old in Rothbaum et al. 1995), with many series of single cases (Bouchard et al. 2003), with the inclusion of a no-treatment control period (Kuntze et al. 2003), with a one-session treatment lasting 3 h (Sirbu et al. 2004) or with the inclusion of a behavior avoidance test to measure outcome (North et al. 1996; see Fig. 6.1 for screenshots of VR environments).

In a thoroughly detailed paper illustrating a case of fear of heights and comorbid physiological problem, Whitney et al. (2005) report on the results of a patient suffering from acrophobia and physiological height vertigo caused by vestibular problems. The 37-year-old man showed no abnormalities of the vestibular system but was diagnosed by an otoneurologist with a mild disorder in maintaining his standing balance. He first received eight sessions of *in virtuo* exposure that significantly improved his acrophobia but did not help his space and motion discomforts.

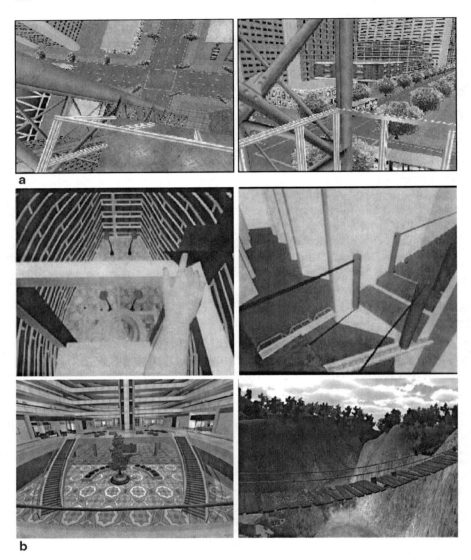

Fig. 6.1 Screenshots of various VR environments used to treat height phobia. **a** Screenshots from the environment used by Choi et al. (2001) and Jang et al. (2002) and developed by S. Kim at Hanyang University in Korea. **b** Images from North et al. (1996), and Rothbaum et al. (1995) environments, with screenshots from the revised versions underneath. © Copyright Virtually Better, Inc. All rights reserved. **c** Images from Bouchard et al. (2003) environments. **d** Images from Emmelkamp et al. (2002) environments. **e** Image from Emmelkamp et al. (2001) environment

His visual dependence to optic flow had not decreased, as he illustrates himself by reporting being able to help hang the Christmas lights on his neighbor's roof but still experiences feeling dizzy and imbalanced while doing so (p. 453). At post-VR treatment, he still had frequent dizzy spells, sensations of fogginess, nausea, etc. He

Fig. 6.1 (continued)

received eight additional sessions of vestibular physical therapy where he practiced *in vivo* exercises that challenged specifically his balance or that made him dizzy. This additional treatment had a significant impact on his postural sensitivity to optic flow and his space and motion discomfort, as measured with several objective and subjective measures. The vestibular therapy also had an impact on the residual phobia symptoms and the level of anxiety experienced in a behavior avoidance test. Although a controlled group trial is necessary before reaching any firm conclusion and no such study has ever been conducted with *in vivo* exposure, it highlights the importance of a thorough assessment and the usefulness of referring a patient to physical therapy if residual postural imbalance symptoms persist.

One of the early studies on the efficacy of *in virtuo* exposure was conducted by Ralph Lamson. The general outline of the study was presented in 1994, but almost no specific results were reported. In a later book, Lamson (1997) provided more details about the design of the study, which was supposed to involve four conditions, including a pharmacological treatment and a waiting list. However, very few additional results were presented, and only on the 32 adults (mean age 54 years old) who received the VR treatment. No data have been reported for the control conditions, leaving us with an uncontrolled trial. After a single *in virtuo* exposure session lasting 50 min and 30 additional minutes of discussions with their therapists, posttreatment results showed that 90 % of the participants were considered much improved since they reached their self-assigned goals. At the 3-month follow-up, 90 % were able to ascend a 15-story building riding in a glass elevator while standing near the glass and looking out and down. Case studies from the study are described in Lamson (1997), including results from physiological measures.

In the first controlled study, Rothbaum et al. (1995; see also Hodges et al. 1995) recruited 20 university students using a screening questionnaire and randomly assigned them to either *in virtuo* exposure or a waiting-list condition. Three participants dropped out from the study (two in the *in virtuo* exposure condition). Participants were exposed during seven weekly 35- to 45-min sessions in a VR environment depicting four outdoor balconies at varying heights (ground level, second floor at 6 ms, tenth floor at 30 m, and 20th floor at 60 m), three bridges suspended over water at varying heights (7, 50, and 80 m) and steadiness (the highest bridge is a rope bridge with wooden slats), and a glass elevator modeled after an actual elevator in the Atlanta Marriott Marquis convention hotel (a 49-story hotel; see Fig. 6.1). This early study used a Silicon Graphics™ computer and a Flight Helmet from Virtual Research™. The treatment protocol included a first session used to familiarize participants with VR equipment and subsequent sessions dedicated to *in virtuo* exposure. The therapist commented on patients' behaviors and improvements during the therapy sessions. Methodologically, it is important to note that seven of the ten participants who completed the treatment also exposed themselves *in vivo* on their own (i.e., it was not a prescribed homework) quite significantly between therapy sessions. Results showed that measures of fear of heights (see Fig. 6.2), anxiety, distress, and avoidance all improved significantly for the VR group but not the waiting-list control group. It is worthy to note that several participants experienced significant negative side effects induced by the immersion (see Chap. 3 for more on cybersickness), with one actually vomiting during an immersion.

Using a more affordable computer (by standards of the time, IBM™ Pentium pro 233 MHz), head-mounted display (HMD; I-Glass from IO Display™), and three-dof tracker, Emmelkamp et al. (2001) treated ten acrophobics in a within-group design with two sessions of *in virtuo* exposure followed by two sessions of *in vivo* exposure. Participants were not encouraged to conduct self-exposure exercises between sessions. The therapy sessions lasted about 60 min and were held twice a week. In both conditions, the gradual exposure technique was straightforward; no

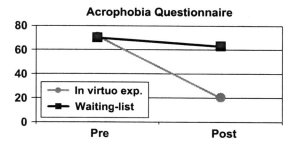

Fig. 6.2 Results from Rothbaum et al. (1995)

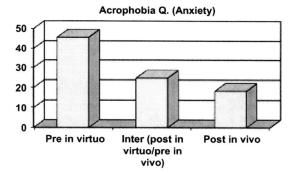

Fig. 6.3 Results from Emmelkamp et al. (2001)

cognitive restructuring, relaxation, or other treatment strategies were used. The two VR environments used had previously been tested with a few other acrophobic patients to gather their comments (Schuemie et al. 2000) and consist of a diving tower overlooking a swimming pool (see Fig. 6.1) and a tower building with a glass elevator. As is often the case with affordable HMDs, the user could see the floor and his physical body in addition to the virtual environment. Therefore, a piece of black cloth was placed over the HMD to make the experience more immersive, a trick that is also used by many other researchers and clinicians. The user was surrounded by a metal railing that could be physically grasped to provide more credibility to the VR experience. Results (see Fig. 6.3) revealed a statistically significant reduction in scores on the Acrophobia Questionnaire (Cohen 1977) and the Attitudes Towards Heights (Abelson and Curtis 1989). Further analyses also found that the addition of *in vivo* exposure after *in virtuo* exposure had a significant impact, but only on the anxiety subscale of the Acrophobia Questionnaire (Cohen 1977). These results suggest that 2 h of *in virtuo* exposure might be quite effective on some measures yet insufficient on others.

In a following study with a larger sample and a control condition, Emmelkamp et al. (2002) randomly assigned 33 adults to either an *in virtuo* or an *in vivo* exposure

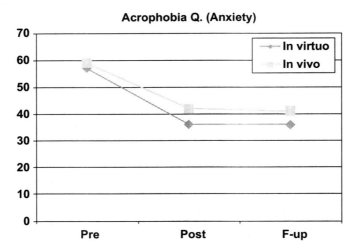

Fig. 6.4 Results from Emmelkamp et al. (2002)

treatment. Interestingly, the virtual environments used in the study were close replicas of the physical environment used for exposure. They created a virtual replica of an Amsterdam shopping center with four floors, escalators, and balustrades, and also a 50-ft fire escape and a 65-ft high roof garden on the top of a university building. At the time, this was the first randomized control trial to compare exactly the same situation *in vivo* and recreated *in virtuo*. This is an interesting methodological asset as it clearly restrains the difference between the two treatments to the fact that the therapy is delivered in VR or not. The study also includes a 6-month follow-up and a behavior avoidance test. The treatment lasted for three 1-h sessions held weekly. The exposure protocol and the computer were similar to Emmelkamp et al. (2001) but the VR equipment was slightly different. They used a Cybermind™ Visette Pro stereoscopic HMD and a Flock of Bird from Ascension™. The possibility of using stereoscopy in the HMD might have contributed to depth perception at short distance. This is much less relevant for stimuli that are located farther than 9 or 10 ms away, such as looking down from a balcony, as the brain uses cues other than stereopsis and eye convergence for depth perception, but it may help users assess distances when they approach the balustrade or the railing of the fire escape. The use of a six degree of freedom motion tracker also allows the user to physically walk closer to the edge of the roof or bend over the railing. With a three-dof tracker, forward motion could only be simulated. The clinical advantages of using these devices deserve to be tested, not because of the increased realism they could provide, but for their potential role in learning new mastery and counter-phobic behaviors. Looking at their results, the analyses revealed significant pre–post differences in both conditions on all subjective and objective measures. All gains remained stable at follow-up, even when excluding the participants who received additional *in vivo* exposure in the meantime. The authors did not find any significant difference in treatment efficacy between both conditions (see Fig. 6.4), either during the treatment or at follow-up. The very small effect sizes of the differences between both

6.3 Description of the Studies Using VR Approaches to Treat Acrophobia

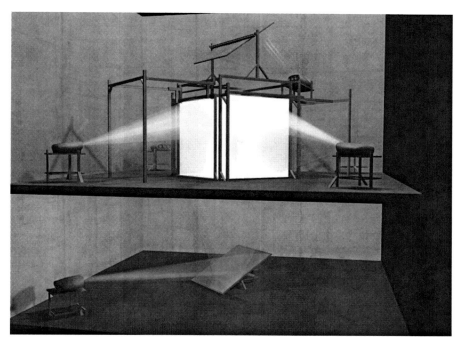

Fig. 6.5 Graphic representation of the six-wall (i.e., images are retro projected seamlessly on six walls) CAVE-Like system in operation at the Cyberpsychology Lab of the Université du Québec en Outaouais. Note: CAVE stands for C-Automatic Virtual Environment, and because it is a trademark, similar systems purchased from companies that do not own the trademark are referred to as CAVE-Like. Reproduced with permission by S. Bouchard

treatments suggest that any potential one would be marginal, if not trivial. This led Emmelkamp et al. (2002) to conclude that "there is now considerable evidence that VR exposure is an effective treatment" (p. 515).

A critical question commonly asked is how realistic a VR environment should feel. One way to address this question is to compare the results of immersions conducted using an HMD to those using the most immersive technology possible, the C-Automatic Virtual Environment (CAVE). A CAVE (or a CAVE-like system) consists of a very expensive and sophisticated system where images are projected on large walls (usually around 3 m × 3 m) and the use of lightweight glasses allows for the recreation of stereoscopic images (see Fig. 6.5 for an illustration of a six-wall CAVE-like system). The user can then stand up in the virtual environment, sees himself or herself in the virtual environment, and move around with a very strong sense of presence. Krijn et al. (2004) therefore compared the efficacy of treating acrophobics with *in virtuo* exposure when immersed in VR with an HMD or in a four-wall CAVE. A waiting-list control condition was also used. The hardware used in the HMD condition was the same as in the study by Emmelkamp et al. (2002). The VR environment used in both conditions included the three VR environments used by Emmelkamp et al. (2002) with an eight-floor virtual building in addition.

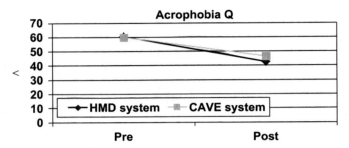

Fig. 6.6 Results for the comparative efficacy of a VR treatment delivered with less immersive HMD system and more immersive CAVE system. From Krijn et al. (2004)

The treatment consisted of three 1.5 h weekly sessions. To analyze the comparisons between the waiting list ($n=11$) and the *in virtuo* exposure treatment, the HMD and CAVE conditions were collapsed together ($n=17$). Statistical analyses revealed a highly significant condition by time (pre vs. post) interaction between both conditions on measures of anxiety, avoidance attitudes towards heights, and the behavior avoidance test. On the behavioral avoidance test (BAT), participants were able to climb twice as many stairs (i.e., on average up to the fourth floor) compared to participants in the control condition on a six-floor fire escape while looking at the ground over the railing. These results confirm with a control group the efficacy of *in virtuo* exposure reported in 2002. Participants in the waiting list were then reassigned to the HMD or the CAVE condition and treated. The final sample consisted of 14 participants in the HMD and 10 in the CAVE conditions. Statistical analyses revealed that the only statistical differences were in pre/post comparisons. Both treatments lead to significant improvements from pre- to posttreatment (see Fig. 6.6 for results on the Acrophobia Questionnaire). As shown by the effect sizes of the pre–post main effects, treatment had a very large impact on all measures, bringing the scores on the Acrophobia Questionnaire, for example, one standard deviation below the scores at pretreatment. Gains were maintained at follow-up. The most interesting finding of this study is the lack of any significant difference in efficacy between the HMD and the CAVE conditions (all effect sizes were trivial), even if participants in the CAVE condition felt significantly more present during all of their immersions. An important fact reported in this study is also the number of dropouts. A fairly high number of participants dropped out of *in virtuo* exposure therapy because they did not experience enough anxiety to conduct exposure ($n=3$ in the CAVE and $n=7$ in the HMD conditions). However, the participants appeared to be less severe in terms of phobia and general psychopathology than other studies. They also felt less present in the VR environment. These results question the role of presence in treatment outcome and also the need for expensive and highly immersive technology.

To explore further the differences in CAVE versus HMD technologies, Juan and Pérez (2009) also compared levels of presence and anxiety in 25 non-acrophobic subjects immersed in a virtual environment via a CAVE-like condition and an HMD condition. Participants were randomly assigned to immersions using both technologies in a counterbalanced order: (1) HMD immersion followed by CAVE immersion, or (2) CAVE immersion followed by HMD immersion. In order to enable users to move around and explore the virtual environment in the HMD condition, a GamePad and a three-dof tracker were used. In the CAVE condition, users were placed inside a four-wall immersive stereoscopic room. The virtual environment being viewed and the animations taking place within the immersion were the same in both conditions: a small room with office-like features and furniture (desks, filling cabinets, chairs, etc). Participants were subjected to three fear-inducing situations: (1) three blocks from the floor underneath the participant's feet dropped sequentially until only one block remained (the one on which the user was standing), (2) four blocks from the floor underneath the user's feet dropped sequentially, with the last block to fall being the one the user was standing on, and (3) four blocks from the floor underneath the user's feet dropped simultaneously, including the one the user was standing on, and the walls rose up in order to create the falling sensation (elevator effect). Results revealed that participants felt a significantly higher sense of presence when immersed in the CAVE condition compared to the HMD condition. Comparison between anxiety levels indicated that both the CAVE and HMD technologies induced anxiety in non-phobic participants. However, results also showed that immersion in the CAVE condition induced significantly more anxiety in participants when compared to the HMD condition. Taken altogether, Juan and Pérez's (2009) results replicated with non phobics results from Krijn et al. (2004) about the superiority of the CAVE system in evoking more anxiety and presence than HMDs. They explained this superiority in the three following ways: (1) users have an unrestricted field of view (FOV) in with CAVE technology, (2) the equipment being used in CAVE technology is more comfortable and allows users to move freely compared to the HMD technology, and (3) CAVE technology enables users to see parts of their own bodies while being immersed, which was found to be highly important according to participants. The role of presence and anxiety on treatment outcome is discussed in Chaps. 2 and 5 and elsewhere (Bouchard et al. 2012). To reinstate what was argued strongly by Rachman and others (e.g., Rachman 1990; Richard et al. 2006), the level of fear reached during an exposure session is not a good predictor of outcome. Enough anxiety must be present to confirm the limbic system is activated, but beyond a certain point what matters is not as much experiencing anxiety as developing new and convincing associations with lack of threat. In 2010, Juan and Perez used a similar methodology to compare HMD and augmented reality technology and found both methods to be as effective to induce presence and anxiety. Therefore, these results should not be surprising but they raise two important issues. First, extremely expensive systems such as CAVEs are not required for most patients and more affordable systems are probably sufficient. This makes CAVEs excellent tools for research but overpowered tools for therapy. Second, highly immersive systems such as CAVEs may still be useful when HMDs are not immersive enough to induce presence and anxiety.

In the most convincing acrophobia outcome study so far, Bullinger (2005) randomly assigned 213 adults to an *in virtuo* exposure condition (74 using a stereoscopic

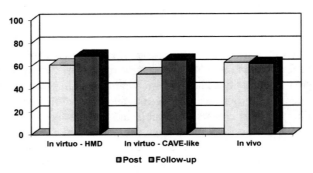

Fig. 6.7 Results from Bullinger et al. (2005)

V-8 HMD by Virtual Research™ and 40 using a CAVE-like system), an *in vivo* exposure control condition ($n=52$), and a waiting-list control condition ($n=47$). Just as Emmelkamp et al. (2002), the VR environment was a replica of the physical skyscraper used for *in vivo* exposure, which is an infrequent but interesting methodological control. They also controlled for the therapist factor, which nails down the differences in the manner in which exposure was provided. The manualized treatment protocol consisted of three sessions of exposure. Assessment included questionnaires, a behavior avoidance test (climb to the top of the bell tower of the Münster of Basel and look down), and physiological measures (heart rate, salivary cortisol, etc.). Results of questionnaire and behavior avoidance data showed that *in virtuo* exposure was as effective as in vivo exposure, which were both superior to the waiting list (results on the BAT are reported in Fig. 6.7). Physiological data have not yet been analyzed. The methodology of this study and the large sample size makes it quite unique and convincing. This study also replicates findings from Krijn et al. (2004) and did not find a statistically or clinically significant advantage of using the highly immersive CAVE-like setting compared to the much less expensive HMD technology in terms of treatment efficacy.

6.4 Available Software

A few VR environments are commercially available for the treatment of acrophobia and at least two more are available for free. The system originally used in the Rothbaum et al. (1995) study now works on Windows and with currently available HMDs and trackers. It is distributed by Virtually Better™ although it has evolved significantly in terms of visual realism. Figure 6.1 illustrates the virtual environments developed for the early outcome studies and more recent and realistic versions. The program allows the use of stereoscopy to increase the impression of realism and the quality of depth perception. The user physically stands on a wooden platform and can physically grab a railing (which is purposely loose and unsteady).

A sound amplifier and two bass shakers (a type of "speaker" allowing the user to feel the low-frequency bass) attached to the wooden base enhance the sensations felt when riding elevators. Atlanta's Marriott Marquis hotel glass elevator (49 stories, that can be stopped at anytime during the ascension) and the three bridges (a concrete one 7 m above the ground, a stone one 50 m above the ground, and a wooden one 80 m above the ground) were included in the original package. A third environment includes an elevator and a series of 19 balconies leading to small ledges that users are asked to walk out onto.

Previ offers a VR application that includes several situations relevant for people who are suffering from acrophobia, such as a high apartment building, riding a Ferris wheel, being in an outdoor lift, having to escape fire from a high building by a fireman ladder, etc.

Two additional software programs are available for free from the Université du Québec en Outaouais (UQO) Cyberpsychology Lab web site (w3.uqo.ca/cyberpsy, under Productions and Virtual Environments) and with NeuroVR (www.neurovr2.org). As noted in the chapter on arachnophobia, the advantage of getting free VR environments is not without its drawbacks, such as the lack of technical support and challenges in staying up to date with new versions of operating systems. The UQO environments have been developed using two different game engines that are barely functioning under the current version of Windows but still work fine under Windows XP. A first set of environments was developed by slightly modifying several scenarios (called maps in the gaming industry) used in the first-person shooter game Unreal Tournament: Game of the Year Edition™. Simply by removing the violent content and enabling the motion tracker, Bouchard et al. (2003; see Fig. 6.1 on the right) were able to access a dozen situations that could be used for *in virtuo* exposure. A second set of VR scenarios was created using the Max Payne™ game. In this case, the environments were created from scratch and included a glass elevator that can bring the user from the ground floor of a cafeteria up to the fifth floor, the back store of the cafeteria where the user can walk on a series of scaffolding and wooden footbridges, and a 15-story building where the user can take the elevator to any floor, walk outside on a narrow ledge and cross the street over to the other building on a wooden scaffold.

6.5 Relevant Findings from Studies Using VR Approaches

Based on the above studies, it seems VR is an effective alternative treatment for acrophobia, showing equal efficacy with in vivo treatment in controlled studies completed to date. Treatment usually lasts between three and four sessions and is conducted using affordable computer and VR equipment. Acrophobia is one of the rare mental disorders for which several studies used stereoscopic HMD. To the other extreme of the high-tech spectrum, two studies using million-dollar CAVE systems revealed that, in terms of treatment outcome, *in virtuo* exposure was just as effective when conducted with HMDs. Although fear and presence were higher in the CAVE system, past clinical research has documented that the level of fear experienced during exposure is not such a good predictor of treatment outcome (see Rachman 1990). The therapeutic content of most treatment packages was distilled and devoid of any CBT strategies that would blur the unique contribution of exposure (e.g., no cognitive restructuring was provided). Most of the large outcome trials used patients diagnosed with a specific phobia of heights and the sample size varies between adequate and impressive. Some researchers report data on participants that were not included in the study during the selection process and about dropout rates and VR-induced side effects. An interesting diversity of VR environments has been used, from glass elevators to balconies, cliffs, skyscrapers, and bridges. Two studies even used VR replicas of a physical environment. All in all, every study points to the same conclusion: *In virtuo* exposure is as effective as *in vivo*.

In terms of treatment mechanism, few studies on acrophobia have addressed the contribution of psychological factors. Huang et al. (2000) have attempted to correlate scores on the patient's visualization ability and anxiety. However, their small sample ($N=9$) was further divided into participants who were exposed *in virtuo* and *in vivo*, precluding the possibility of finding meaningful and significant correlations. Regenbrecht et al. (1998) developed a VR environment to study the relationship between anxiety and presence. They immersed a sample of 36 non-phobics using a monoscopic VR4 HMD and a six-dof Polhemus™ motion tracker. Their visually simple environment (no lighting techniques, no texturing, and a simple scene with the illusion of depth being induced by linear perspective, colors, and reference objects) consisted of a floor with several sections lowered 8 m below ground level and a few crossing bridges. They found a nonsignificant correlation between anxiety and presence ($r=0.25$) experienced during the immersion, but a regression controlling for fear-of-heights avoidance behavior led to a moderate but statistically significant effect of presence on anxiety. However, anxiety and presence levels were low to moderate, probably due to the poor quality (by current standards and in comparison with more recent studies) of their VR environment.

Although the vast majority of studies evaluating treatment efficacy in acrophobic subjects has mainly relied on exposure, a recent study by Krijn et al. (2007) examined the impact of adding a cognitive component to *in virtuo* exposure. More precisely, they compared the outcome of pure *in virtuo* exposure therapy to that of *in virtuo* exposure with an added cognitive component. During the cognitively enhanced segment of the experiment, subjects were instructed to think about neutral coping self-statements rather than anxiety-provoking thoughts (in an earlier phase of the experiment, subjects wrote down anxiety-provoking cognitions and replaced them with neutral ones). Results indicated that the addition of a cognitive component such as neutral self-statements to exposure-based therapy had no impact on treatment efficacy. Both treatments successfully reduced avoidance, anxiety, and negative cognitions linked to acrophobia.

Research on the psychophysiological side has been more fruitful. Wilhelm et al. (2005) were puzzled by the observation that several studies found that heart rate response during *in virtuo* immersion or exposure was minimal while electrodermal

6.5 Relevant Findings from Studies Using VR Approaches

response appears to always be strong. They brought forth Gray's psychophysiological theory (1975) of anxiety suggesting that the anxiety response is composed of two complementary reactions involving a behavioral activation (BA) system (which includes active avoidance) and a behavioral inhibition (BI) system (which includes passive avoidance). According to Fowles (1988), heart rate change expresses activity in the BA system and change in skin conductance expresses activity in the BI system. Since with three-dof VR systems approaching and avoiding stimuli is achieved by pressing a button instead of walking, it is not possible to physically perform substantial motor activation moving back and forth towards the feared stimuli. Wilhelm et al. (2005) predicted that these technical constraints in VR would cause an activation of the BI system but not the BA system. They immersed 20 non-phobic participants in an elevator ride (see images from Choi et al. 2001; Fig. 6.1) and monitored their heart rate and skin conductance. Both heart rate and skin conductance statistically increased as participants were going higher in the elevator ride. However, only the skin conductance was significantly higher in the high-anxiety group and in the Group by Time interaction. Analysis of the heart rate data revealed no significant differences or interactions between the high- and low-anxiety participants. This is intriguing since both skin conductance and heart rate were significantly different when phobic individuals were exposed *in vivo*. This led Wilhelm et al. (2005) to conclude that there may be a physiological difference between *in virtuo* and *in vivo* exposure. The weaker heart rate response may reflect a lack of activation of the BA system, a sign of a more passive exposure. If Wilhelm et al. (2005) are right, then an important limitation of some VR systems (at least those using three-dof trackers) may be the impossibility to engage in active motor approach and avoidance. Activating the BA system in addition to the BI system could lead to more powerful and permanent improvements. Interestingly, results of this study were replicated with a different methodology and sample by Bauman (2007). Further studies on this topic are clearly warranted given the potential application of this finding to improve treatment efficacy.

While we are discussing the psychophysiology involved in the treatment mechanism of exposure, it is timely to mention a study from the Atlanta group where VR was used to help decipher the contribution of neurophysiological factors involved in learning during exposure treatment. Studies on animals have linked glutamate (a neurotransmitter that mediates many synaptic transmissions, including for cognitive functions and learning), or more precisely the N-methyl-D-aspartate (NMDA) glutamate receptors in the amygdala, to the acquisition and extinction of conditioned fears. Based on these findings, Walker et al. (2002) successfully used D-Cyloserine, a broad-spectrum antibiotic that binds to a receptor on the NMDA protein and improves the ability of NMDA receptors to foster learning, to enhance extinction of fear in rats. Ressler et al. (2004) tested the enhancing effect of D-Cycloserine on exposure using the acrophobia virtual environment as a tool to standardize the exposure stimuli. As such, this is not exactly an outcome study on the efficacy of VR but a pilot study on the use of D-Cycloserine (for example, there is no control condition without *in virtuo* exposure). Participants were randomly and blindly assigned to either an *in virtuo* exposure combined with a pill placebo or to an *in virtuo* exposure combined with D-Cycloserine (two doses of 50 and 500 mg were used but participants were later collapsed given the absence of a dose–response relationship). Twenty-seven adults suffering from acrophobia were treated with two 35- to 45-min *in virtuo* exposure sessions with the "balcony" environment and the hardware previously used in other studies by Rothbaum's group. Medication or placebo was taken 2–4 h prior to the exposure session. The statistical analyses showed no difference between the two conditions during the first therapy session, supporting the contention that D-Cycloserine has no anxiolytic effect. As expected by the authors, participants receiving D-Cycloserine were significantly less anxious during the *second* therapy session and at the posttreatment immersion in the VR environment, as measured with subjective ratings and skin conductance. On every questionnaire data collected at mid-treatment, posttreatment, and 3-month follow-up, the analyses showed a clear superiority among participants who exposed themselves *in virtuo* under the influence of the learning-enhancing drug. Participants who received the medication also exposed themselves post therapy more often to height situations than those who received only exposure, suggesting that improvements observed in therapy were transposed in the physical world. This study revealed three interesting findings: (a) some drugs can enhance the (emotional) learning of new associations with non-threat, (b) glutamate receptors within the amygdala appear to play a role in exposure-based treatment of phobia, thus supporting the contribution of leaning mechanisms, and (c) VR can be used to standardize exposure in experimental research. This study stirred a significant amount of research on the use of D-Cycloserine and other enhancers of cognitive and emotional processing.

Smits et al. (2013) conducted another D-Cycloserine trial with people suffering from acrophobia which provides an interesting insight on the use of enhancers of fear extinction. Following two 30-min sessions of *in virtuo* exposure combined with either a placebo or 50 mg of D-Cycloserine, they discovered that functional exposure probably plays a role in the effectiveness of the treatment enhancer. More explicitly, compared to the placebo, the participants taking D-Cycloserine and whose exposure session concluded by a decrease in fear benefited more from the treatment than those whose fear was still elevated at the end of the exposure session.

As mentioned in Chap. 5, not all potential enhancers are effective (Meyerbroeker et al. 2012). But another group of researchers obtained interesting results on the impact of glucocorticoids (cortisol in humans) on extinction-based psychotherapy in people suffering from acrophobia (De Quervain et al. 2011). Since it has been well documented that glucocorticoids can greatly affect learning, memory, and the extinction process, the idea of using it during exposure-based therapy is an appealing one. To test the impact of cortisol on acrophobic subjects, De Quervain et al. (2011) recruited 40 height phobic patients to offer them *in virtuo* exposure and randomly assigned them to either an enhanced condition of 20 mg of cortisol or a control condition that received a placebo. Subjects in both conditions underwent three sessions of *in virtuo* exposure. The placebo or cortisol pills were administered 1 h before each therapy session. The VR was developed by the Virtual Reality Medical Center and consisted of many platforms connected together by bridges and elevators. Among other measures, the Acrophobia Questionnaire was administered at pretreatment, posttreatment (3–5 days after the last exposure sessions), and follow-up (1 month), as illustrated in Fig. 6.8. Results showed that acrophobics

6.5 Relevant Findings from Studies Using VR Approaches

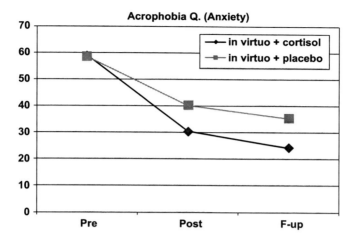

Fig. 6.8 Administering cortisol prior to *in virtuo* exposure enhances treatment efficacy (De Quervain et al. 2011)

receiving *in virtuo* exposure combined with cortisol showed greater fear reduction at posttreatment and follow-up, compared to subjects in the placebo condition. Participants receiving cortisol also had significantly lower anxiety levels (SUD) during the *in virtuo* exposure sessions and at posttreatment, compared to those taking the placebo. De Quervain et al. (2011) explained this facilitating effect of cortisol on the extinction of fear in two ways. Firstly, glucocorticoids lead to a reduction in memory retrieval, which during exposure therapy implies that the fearful memory is not being retrieved as patients are facing the aversive cues. Hence, the current experience is not being associated with the phobic memory, but rather with a somewhat less aversive experience. Secondly, glucocorticoids enhance consolidation of new information. Therefore, it is possible that the storage of the new corrective experience be enhanced as well. Taken altogether, these results point out the facilitating effects of cortisol on *in virtuo* exposure therapy. This conclusion offers a promising way of improving treatment efficacy. Along with studies reported in the chapter on spider phobia, these results are an illustration of how a better understanding of neurophysiological processes may help advance our clinical practice (McNally 2007).

Another very significant set of studies using VR and fear of heights tackles the factors that may explain why VR can induce anxiety (Meehan 2001; Zimmons 2004). These studies were conducted at the University of North Carolina at Chapel Hill, in the department of computer science, using a virtual environment adapted from previous work by Mel Slater and his team at University College London (Slater et al. 1995). These studies all use "the Pit room" in the hope of studying the feeling of presence. This virtual environment actually consists of two rooms: a training room and a pit room separated by a door (see Fig. 6.9). The training room contains furniture, tables, a curtain that moved as if caught in a gentle breeze (a physical fan is actually blowing air), music coming from a radio, etc. When opening the door into the adjacent room, the user enters a place where the floor is almost entirely open above the furnished apartment 6 m (19.68 ft) below. The hole is unguarded

Fig. 6.9 Image of "the Pit room" developed at the University of North Carolina at Chapel Hill. (Courtesy of the Effective Virtual Environments Project, Department of Computer Science, University of North Carolina at Chapel Hill).

and a 2-ft wide walkway borders to room and, in front of the entrance, comes a few feet over the pit like a diving board. Depending on the variables being tested, the virtual walkway could actually match with a physical 1.5-inch-thick wooden ledge and participants would wear slippers so they could physically feel that they are getting to the very edge of the pit. The 18 × 32 ft two-room VR environment actually fit the physical space within the research lab. Users are carrying a joystick and wearing a stereoscopic V8 HMD from Virtual Research™ and headphones transmitting three-dimensional (3D) spatialized sound while a six-dof infrared tracker

6.5 Relevant Findings from Studies Using VR Approaches

system follows the position of the head and the right hand. Participants also wear psychophysiological monitoring devices to record heart rate, skin conductance, and skin temperature. The task consists first of practicing walking in the training room, picking up and dropping objects (e.g., ball, books, blocks) in the training room, then entering the Pit Room, feeling the ledge (if any) of the walkway with their feet, and placing an object on the far side of the walkway or dropping objects on targets on the floor below. This environment aims to elicit fear in users while experimentally manipulating variables such as image quality, computer's latency, or usefulness of physical props like the wooden walkway. Several studies were conducted using "the Pit Room" environment and a few significant ones will be described below. These studies were designed mostly to study presence but, when it comes to physiological measures, unfortunately confounded presence with anxiety. In these experiments, the physiological measures used as a proxy for presence, and which are known to be reliable measures of anxiety such as heart rate, correlated significantly but poorly with self-report measures of presence (less than 0.30; Meehan et al. 2005), which is consistent with information presented in Chap. 2 on the relationship between anxiety and presence.

Meehan et al. (2002; see also Meehan et al. 2005) conducted three experiments with young adults who were not suffering from acrophobia. They consistently found across their experiments an increase in heart rate and skin conductance, and a decrease in skin temperature, when participants where in the Pit Room compared to the training room. This validates the potential of VR to induce anxiety in a height situation. Interestingly, an increase in both heart rate and skin conductance was found here, as opposed to the Wilhelm et al. (2005) study. Since Meehan et al. (2002) used a six-dof system, the participants could physically move towards or away from the pit. This may provide indirect support for Wilhelm et al. (2005) that active motor action may be needed to stimulate both the BA and BI systems.

When Meehan et al. (2002) immersed 10 participants on 12 consecutive occasions, the researchers found a decrease in users' impression that they were behaving as if they were in physical reality (they called this behavioral presence, as opposed to the feeling of presence) and in skin temperature, but only when comparing the second immersion to the first one. Albeit some drop in anxiety and the feeling of presence were noted, none were significant when: (a) further repeated immersions followed the second one, or (b) at any additional immersion for the subjective feeling of being there and on skin conductance. Heart rate was not measured in this experiment. Thus, there was no evidence that presence and anxiety generally diminish significantly over repeated immersion in the Pit Room, or at least not after the first orienting or novelty effect was over. This finding is clinically useful as it suggests that height environments could be used repeatedly and still induce anxiety.

In a second experiment, they immersed 52 non-phobic young adults twice in a counterbalanced repeated design with either the physical wooden ledge prop installed or not. They found a significant increase in heart rate, skin conductance, and the impression of behaving as if in the physical reality (behavioral presence) when the physical ledge was added in the Pit Room. However, moving into the Pit Room caused a significantly stronger increase in anxiety than the addition of the prop.

Surprisingly, feeling the wooden ledge led to an increase in presence that was not statistically significant. The impact of this finding for *in virtuo* exposure is that adding a prop increases anxiety and probably some elements of presence, but perceiving a threat appears to have a much stronger impact.

The third study was performed with 33 young adult participants who were not suffering from acrophobia in order to test the impact of the speed at which the graphic frame is updated (a variable affecting image quality). Four immersions were conducted in a repeated counterbalance order with 10, 15, 20, and 30 frames per second. At ten frames per seconds (FPS), participants were significantly losing their balance, which probably increased the perceived threat of having to stand near a 20-ft pit. When statistically controlling for the loss of balance, the researchers found a statistically significant increase in heart rate between 15 and 20 or 30 FPS. Again, moving from the training room to the Pit Room had a stronger impact on anxiety than improvements in the frame rate. The feeling of presence was statistically higher in the condition with the best frame rate (30 FPS) compared to the 10 FPS and the 15 FPS. But this statistical finding may not be very robust. A difference in presence was found only when analyzing the first immersion for each participant but not when performing more traditional analyses such as comparing all four immersions in within-subject analysis (Meehan 2001, p. 81 and 89). The impact on presence may therefore not be that strong. These results confirmed again that image quality may have an impact on anxiety, and on presence to some extent, but not as much as having to perform a task on the edge of an open pit.

Meehan et al. (2003, see also Meehan et al. 2005) used "the Pit Room" paradigm during a demonstration at a convention to test the impact of latency (the time it takes for an action to be visible in the HMD) with more than 60 participants. Two latencies were compared, the actual latency of the VR system (50 ms) and an increased latency (90 ms). It was hypothesized that longer latency would negatively impact presence, anxiety, and VR-induced side effects. As expected from previous experiments, the impact of moving from the training room to the Pit Room was significant for both the heart rate and skin conductance. Their hypotheses were confirmed, but only for change in heart rate after controlling statistically for nausea felt by the participants. No difference was found between the two latencies on presence. Finding a difference in anxiety but not on presence is unexpected but consistent with other studies from this research group where performing a task in the Pit Room seemed to lead to a ceiling effect on the measures of presence they used. Since presence was not measured at the time of transition from the training room to the Pit Room, it is impossible to know whether the anxiogenic effect of the task is responsible for the high level of presence. The previous studies also highlight the methodological importance for researchers to report data such as frame rate, latency, or the use of props in the experiments on anxiety and presence.

Another fascinating result from a study using "the Pit Room" paradigm comes from Zimmons and Panter (2003). In order to test the impact rendering image quality, they immersed 55 non-phobic college-age participants in one of five conditions: low texture resolution (128×128), high texture resolution (1024×1024), low-fidelity

6.5 Relevant Findings from Studies Using VR Approaches

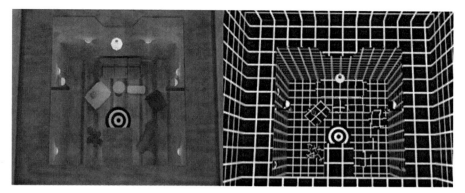

Fig. 6.10 Screenshots of two conditions used by Zimmons (2004) to study the impact of resolution and lighting properties on anxiety and presence. (Courtesy of the Effective Virtual Environments Project, Department of Computer Science, University of North Carolina at Chapel Hill). A view of the Pit Room from above in two of the five experimental conditions, the low-texture/high-lighting qualities and the black-and-white grid control condition

lighting quality (no shadows or illumination effects), high-fidelity lighting quality (with shadows, etc.), and a control condition with a simple black and white environment and a white grid for depth perspective. Results revealed no significant difference in heart rate and skin conductance during the immersions, and in presence post immersion, between any of the five conditions. What is most fascinating is the statistically significant increase in heart rate and skin conductance between the training room and the Pit Room for all conditions, *including* the black and white grid control condition. The Zimmons and Panter (2003) study demonstrates very effectively that differences in image quality "were overshadowed by a sense of personal danger" (p. 2). It strongly militates in favor of taking into account knowledge developed over the years in clinical setting and experimental psychopathology about what stimuli are processed as fear inducing when developing virtual environments, as opposed to insisting mostly on image quality or high-end technological refinements. A simple and plain black and white grid was sufficient to induce a fear-of-heights reaction in non-phobics! The impact of perceived threat of height stimuli appears to be a pretty resistant variable, over and above the use of props and technical sophistication (Figs. 6.10 and 6.11).

Beyond these studies, it is important to note that VR has now been used for years to treat acrophobia in a clinical setting. For example, at the Virtual Reality Medical Centers in San Diego, Palo Alto, and Los Angeles, CA, the success rate of VR exposure treatment for specific phobias is estimated at 92%. At these clinics, the treatment is set up much like many of the studies above (including a vibrating platform, a metal railing for the patient to grasp, and a fully immersive HMD). However, the nature of clinical treatment allows therapists to combine strict VR exposure protocols with other forms of therapy (e.g. CBT, relaxation, and physiological feedback) to improve the chances for successful treatment.

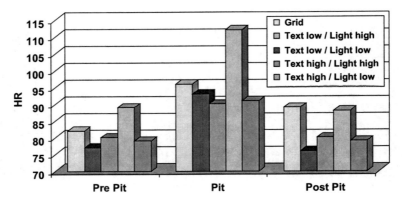

Fig. 6.11 Results from Zimmons (2004)'s study on image quality and its impact on anxiety and presence.

6.6 Conclusion

A few large randomized control trials conducted with people suffering from the specific phobia of heights are making a very strong case about the efficacy of *in virtuo* exposure. Studies from Emmelkamp's and the Bullinger's groups used a virtual replica of the environment used *in vivo* to compare both forms of exposure and Bullinger even included a waiting list. There was no evidence that conducting exposure in VR could be less effective than *in vivo*. Comparisons between very expensive/highly immersive VR systems with more affordable HMD systems revealed that both were equally effective. This may not mean that investing in hardware is not important however. First, most studies have been conducted with high-quality HMD and some even used stereoscopic HMDs. Second, most studies have used physical props to mix the physical and the VRs, such as railings, wooden ledges, etc. These devices may increase presence in some case, but it is uncertain if they significantly affect treatment outcome. Third, data based on psychophysiological measures revealed the possibility that allowing people to physically move toward or away from the feared stimuli may more fully elicit the anxiety reaction compared to the artificial motion used with three-dof trackers. Direct comparison between both three-dof-based systems and six-dof modes of locomotion remains to be performed, along with assessment of the impact it might have on treatment outcome. One significant advantage of using VR to treat fear of heights is that exposure can be easily conducted in the safety and confidentiality of the therapist's office. It may even be used with people suffering from some vestibular disorders. Most VR environments provide a variety of exposure contexts, such as balconies, bridges, elevators, cliffs, or skyscrapers. Such standardization of the exposure exercises attracts researchers who want to control as much parameters of the exposure as possible. An example can be found in experimental studies testing drugs that can be used to enhance the impact of exposure. D-Cycloserine and glucocorticoids seem likely candidates to facilitate emotional processing and extinction. Methodologically, several studies used BAT, which is a strong asset, and a few studies reported information about unwanted negative side effects induced by immersions in VR and dropout rates.

Psychophysiological measures revealed that several factors that play an important role in fostering the feeling of presence, such as image quality or the use of props, could be less powerful in eliciting fear and anxiety than the threat stimuli themselves. This may suggest to clinicians that including in the virtual environments key important cues triggering perceived threat plays an important role and that technological factors, albeit important, may be less so than initially thought. More research is definitely needed to understand why people react to virtual stimuli. Since users of VR will comment that they are not anxious when they are not present, the exact role played by the subjective feeling of presence still eludes use to some extent.

References

Abelson, J. L., & Curtis, G. C. (1989). Cardiac and neuroendocrine responses to exposure therapy in height phobics: Desynchrony with the "physiological response system". *Behaviour Research and Therapy, 27,* 556–561.
American Psychiatric Association: APA. (2000). *Diagnostic and statistical manual of mental disorders fourth edition text revision.* Washington, DC: American Psychiatric Association.
Antony, M. M., & Barlow, D. H. (2002). Specific phobias. In D. H. Barlow (Ed.), *Anxiety and its disorders* (2nd ed., pp. 380–417). New York: Guilford.
Bauman (2007). *Physiology during anxiety-provoking VR simulations.* Oral presentation at the 12th Annual CyberTherapy Conference 2007, Washington, DC, 11–14 June.
Bouchard, S., St-Jacques, J., Robillard, G., Côté, S., & Renaud, P. (2003). Efficacité de l'exposition en réalité virtuelle pour l'acrophobie: Une étude préliminaire. *Journal de Thérapie Comportementale et Cognitive, 13*(3), 107–112.
Bouchard, S., Robillard, G., Larouche, S., & Loranger, C. (2012). Description of a treatment manual for in virtuo exposure with specific phobia. In C. Eichenberg (Ed.) *Virtual reality in psychological, medical and pedagogical applications* (Chap. 4, pp. 82–108). Rijeka (Croatia): InTech.
Bourque, P., & Ladouceur, R. (1980). An investigation of various performance-based treatments with acrophobics. *Behavior Research & Therapy, 18,* 161–170.
Brandt, T. (2003). *Vertigo: Its multisensory syndromes* (2nd ed.). New York: Springer.
Brandt, T., Arnold, F., Bless, W., & Kapteyn, T. S. (1980). The mechanism of physiological height vertigo, I: Theoretical approach and psychophysics. *Acta Otolaryngologica, 89,* 513–523.
Bullinger, A. H. (2005). *Treating acrophobia in a virtual environment.* Oral presentation at the 10th Annual CyberTherapy Conference 2005, Basel (Switzerland), 6–10 June.
Choi, Y. H., Jang, D. P., Ku, J. H., Shin, M. B., & Kim, S. I. (2001). Short-term treatment of acrophobia with virtual reality therapy (VRT): A case report. *Cyberpsychology & Behavior, 4*(3), 349–354.
Coelho, C. M., & Wallis, G. (2010). Deconstructing acrophobia: physiological and psychological precursors to developing a fear of heights. *Depression and Anxiety, 27,* 864–870.
Cohen, D. C. (1977). Comparison of self-report and behavioral procedures for assessing acrophobia. *Behavior Therapy, 8,* 17–23.
Curtis, G. C., Magee, W. J., Eaton, W. W., Wittchen, H.-U., & Kessler, R. C. (1998). Specific fears and phobias: Epidemiology and classification. *British Journal of Psychiatry, 173,* 212–217.
De Quervain, D. J. F., Bentz, D., Michael, T., Bolt, O. C., Wiederhold, B. K., Margraf, J., & Wilhelm, F. H. (2011). Glucocorticoids enhance extinction-based psychotherapy. *Proceedings of the National Academy of Sciences, 108*(16), 6621–6625.

Depla, M. F. I. A., ten Have, M. L., van Balkom, A. J. L. M., & de Graaf, R. (2008). Specific fears and phobias in the general population: Results from the Netherlands Mental Health Survey and Incidence Study (NEMESIS). *Social Psychiatry and Psychiatric Epidemiology, 43,* 200.

Emmelkamp, P. M. G., Bruynzeel, M., Drost, L., & van der Mast, C. A. P. G. (2001). Virtual reality treatment in acrophobia: A comparison with exposure in vivo. *Cyberpsychology & Behavior, 4*(3), 335–340.

Emmelkamp, P. M. G., Krijn, M., Hulsbosch, L., de Vries, S., Schuemie, M. J., & van der Mast, C. A. P. G. (2002). Virtual reality treatment versus exposure in vivo: A comparative evaluation in acrophobia. *Behaviour Research and Therapy, 40*(5), 25–32.

Fowles, D. C. (1988). Psychophysiology and psychopathology: A motivational approach. *Psychophysiology, 25*(4), 373–391.

Fredrickson, M., Annas, P., Fischer, H., & Wik, G. (1996). Gender and age differences in the prevalence of specific fears and phobias. *Behaviour Research & Therapy, 26,* 241–244.

Gray, J. A. (1975). *Elements of a two-process theory of learning.* New York: Academic.

Hodges, L. F., Kooper, R., Rothbaum, B. O., Opdyke, D., de Graaff, J. J., Williford, J. S., & North, M. M. (1995). Virtual environments for treating the fear of heights. *Computer Innovative Technology for Computer Professionals, 28*(7), 27–34.

Huang, M. P., Himle, J., & Alessi, N. E. (2000). Vivid visualization in the experience of phobia in virtual environments: Preliminary results. *Cyberpsychology & Behavior, 3*(3), 321–326.

Jang, D. P., Ku, J. H., Choi, Y. H., Wiederhold, B. K., Nam, S. W., Kim, I. Y., & Kim, S. I. (2002). The development of virtual reality therapy (VRT) system for the treatment of acrophobia and therapeutic case. *IEEE Transactions on Information Technology and Medicine, 6*(3), 213–217.

Juan, M. C., & Pérez, D. (2009). Comparison of the levels of presence and anxiety in an acrophobic environment viewed via HMD or CAVE. *Presence, 18*(3), 232–248.

Juan, M. C., & Pérez, D. (2010). Using augmented and virtual reality for the development of acrophobic scenarios. Comparison of the levels of presence and anxiety. *Computers & Graphics, 34,* 756–766.

Krijn, M., Emmelkamp, P. M. G., Biemond, R., de Wilde de Ligny, C., Schuemie, M. J., & van der Mast, C. A. P. G. (2004). Treatment of acrophobia in virtual reality: The role of immersion and presence. *Behaviour Research and Therapy, 42,* 229–239.

Krijn, M., Emmelkamp, P. M. G., Ólafsson, R. P., Schuemie, M. J., & Van Der Mast, A. P. G. (2007). Do self-statements enhance the effectiveness of virtual reality exposure therapy? A comparative evaluation in acrophobia. *Cyberpsychology & Behavior, 10*(3), 362–370.

Kuntze, M. F., Störmer, R., Mager, R., Müller-Spahn, F., & Bullinger, A. (2003). Die behandlung der Höhenangst in einer virtuellen umgebung, *Nervenarzt, 74,* 428–435.

Lamson, R. J. (1997). *Virtual therapy.* Montreal: Polytechnic International Press.

Marshall, W. L. (1985). The effects of variable exposure in flooding therapy. *Behavior Therapy, 16,* 117–135.

McNally, R. J. (2007). Mechanisms of exposure therapy: How neuroscience can improve psychological treatments for anxiety disorders. *Clinical Psychology Review, 27*(6), 750–759.

Meehan, M. (2001). *Physiological reaction as an objective measure of presence in virtual environments.* Doctoral dissertation, University of North Carolina at Chapel Hill.

Meehan, M., Insko, B., Whitton, M. C., & Brooks, F. P. (2002). *Physiological measures of presence in stressful virtual environments.* Proceedings of the 29th Annual Conference on Computer graphics and interactive techniques, San Antonio, Texas, pp. 645–652.

Meehan, M., Razzaque, S., Whitton, M. C., & Brooks, F. P. (2003). *Effect of latency on presence in stressful virtual environments.* Proceedings of the IEEE Virtual Reality 2003.

Meehan, M., Razzaque, S., Insko, B., Whitton, M. C., & Brooks, F. P. (2005). Review of four studies on the use of physiological reaction as a measure of presence in stressful virtual environments. *Applied Psychophysiology and Biofeedback, 30*(3), 239–258.

Menzies, R. (1997). Height phobia. In G. C. L. Davey (Ed.), *Phobias: A handbook of theory, research and practice* (pp. 139–151), Chichester: Wiley.

Meyerbroeker, K., Powers, M. B., van Stegeren, A., & Emmelkamp, P. M. G. (2012). Does yohimbine hydrochloride facilitate fear extinction in virtual reality treatment of fear of flying? A randomized placebo-controlled trial. *Psychotherapy and Psychosomatics, 81*(1), 29–37.

North, M. M., North, S. M., & Coble, J. R. (1996). *Virtual reality therapy. An innovative paradigm.* Colorado Springs: IPI.

Öst, L.-G. (1997). Rapid treatment of specific phobias. In G. C. L. Davey (Ed.), *Phobias: A handbook of theory, research and treatment* (pp. 227–246). Chichester: Wiley.

Poulton, R., Waldie, K. E., Menzies, R. G., Craske, M. G., & Silva, P. A. (2001). Failure to overcome "innate" fear: A developmental test of the non-associative model of fear acquisition. *Behaviour Research and Therapy, 39,* 29–43.

Rachman, S. J. (1990). *Fear and courage* (2nd ed.). New York: Freeman.

Regenbrecht, H. T., Schubert, T. W., & Friedmann, F. (1998). Measuring the sense of presence and its relations to fear of heights in virtual environments. *International Journal of Human-Computer Interaction, 10*(3), 233–249.

Ressler, K.J., Rothbaum, B.O., Tannenbaum, L., Anderson, P., Graap, K., Zimand, E., Hodges, L., Davis, M. (2004). Cognitive enhancers as adjuncts to psychotherapy: Use of D-cycloserine in phobic individuals to facilitate extinction of fear. *Archives of General Psychiatry, 61*(11), 1136–1144.

Richards, D. C. S., Lauterbach, D., & Gloster, A. T. (2006). Description, mechanisms of action, and assessment. In D. C. S. Richards & D. L. Lauterbach (Eds.), *Handbook of exposure therapies* (pp. 1–28). Burlington: Academic.

Rothbaum, B. O., Hodges, L. F., Kooper, R., Opdyke, D., Williford, J. S., & North, M. (1995a). Effectiveness of computer-generated (virtual reality) graded exposure in the treatment of acrophobia. *American Journal of Psychiatry, 152,* 626–628.

Rothbaum, B. O., Hodges. L. F., Kooper. R., Opdyke. D., Williford, J. S., & North, M. (1995b). Virtual reality graded exposure in the treatment of acrophobia: A case report. *Behavior Therapy, 26,* 547–554.

Schuemie, M. J., Bruynzeel, M., Drost, L., Brinkman, M., de Haan, G., Emmelkamp, P. M. G., & van der Mast, C. A. P. G. (2000).Treatment of Acrophobia in VR: A pilot study. In F. Brockx & L. Pauwels (Eds.) Conference Proceedings Euromedia 2000, 8–10 May 2000, Antwerp Belgium, pp. 271–275.

Sik-Lányi, C., Laky, V., Tilinger, Á., Pataky, I., Simon, L., Kiss, B., et al. (2004). Developing multimedia software and virtual reality worlds and their use in rehabilitation and psychology. In M. Duplaga et al. (Eds.), *Transformation of health care with information technologies* (pp. 273–284). Amsterdam: IOS Press.

Sirbu, C., Ruscio, A. M., & Ollendick, T. H. (2004). *Virtual reality versus in vivo one session treatment for acrophobia.* Poster presented at the 38th Annual Convention of the Association for Advancement of Behavior Therapy, New Orleans, 18–21 November.

Slater, M., Usoh, M., & Steed, A. (1995). Taking steps: The influence of a walking technique on presence in virtual reality. *ACM Transactions Computer-Human Interactions, 2,* 201–219.

Smits, J.A.J., Rosenfield, D., Otto, M.W., Powers, M.B., Hofmann, S. G., Telch, M.J., Pollack, M.H., & Tart, C.D. (2013). D-cycloserine enhancement of fear extinction is specific to successful exposure sessions: Evidence from the treatment of height phobia. *Biological Psychiatry, 73*(11), 1054–1058.

Stinson, F. S., Dawson, D. A., Chou, S. P., Smith, S., Goldstein, R. B., Ruan, W. J., & Grant, B. F. (2007). The epidemiology of DSM-IV specific phobia in the USA: Results from the National Epidemiologic Survey on Alcohol and Related Conditions. *Psychological Medicine, 37,* 1047–1059.

Vale, H. M. C., Oliveira, C., Sena, D. C., & Porto, A. J. V. (2010). Construction of immersive multi-projection environments for treatment of phobia of heights. In P. Bartolo et al. (Eds.), *Innovative Developments in Design and Manufacturing* (pp. 619–624), London: CRC.

Walker, D.L., Ressler, K.J., Lu, K.-T., Davis, M. (2002). Facilitation of conditioned fear extinction by systemic administration or intra-amygdala infusions of D-cycloserine as assessed with fearpotentiated startle in rats. Journal of Neuroscience, *22*(6), 2343–2351.

Whitney, S. L., Jacob, R. G., Sparto, P. J., Olshansky, E. F., Detweiler-Shostak, G., Brown, E. L., & Furman, J. M. (2005). Acrophobia and pathological height vertigo: Indications for vestibular physical therapy? *Physical Therapy, 85*(5), 443–458.

Wilhelm, F. H., Pfaltz, M. C., Gross, J. J., Mauss, I. B., Kim S. I., & Wiederhold, B. K. (2005). Mechanisms of virtual reality exposure therapy: The role of the Behavioral activation and behavioural inhibition systems. *Applied Psychophysiology and Biofeedback, 30*(3), 271–284.

Williams, S. L., Dooseman, G., & Kleifeld, E. (1984). Comparative effectiveness of guided mastery and exposure treatments for intractable phobics. *Journal of Consulting and Clinical Psychology, 52,* 505–518.

Williams, S. L., Turner, S. M., & Peer, D. F. (1985). Guided mastery and performance desensitization treatments for severe acrophobia. *Journal of Consulting and Clinical Psychology, 53,* 237–247.

World Health Organization (1992). *The ICD-10 classification of mental and behavioural disorders.* Geneva: WHO.

Zimmons, P. M. (2004). *The influence of lighting quality on presence and task performance in virtual environments.* Doctoral dissertation, University of North Carolina at Chapel Hill.

Zimmons, P. M., & Panter, A. (2003). *The influence of rendering quality on presence and task performance in a virtual environment.* Proceedings of the IEEE Virtual Reality 2003.

Chapter 7
Claustrophobia: Efficacy and Treatment Protocols

Stéphane Bouchard, Brenda K. Wiederhold and Claudie Loranger

7.1 Key Variables Involved in the Phobia of Enclosed Spaces

Claustrophobia is the fear and avoidance of enclosed spaces. It is described as a specific phobia and falls under the general "situational subtype" in the *DSM-IV* (APA 2000) and corresponds to the "enclosed spaces" subtype of specific (isolated) phobia in International Classification of Diseases (ICD-10; WHO 1992). It is defined as a marked, persistent, excessive, or unreasonable fear that is cued by being, or anticipation of being, in an enclosed space. For the claustrophobic person, feeling trapped or being in a confined space should almost invariably provoke fear and discomfort if the phobia is mild or anxiety and panic attack if the phobia is more severe. The patient usually avoids the feared claustrophobic situations or else endures them with intense anxiety, discomfort, and a desire to escape. To qualify as a phobia, the severity of the avoidance, anxiety, or anticipation must interfere significantly with the person's life and the symptoms must have been present for at least 6 consecutive months. The anxiety, panic attacks, or avoidance must not be better accounted for by another mental disorder such as, for example, agoraphobia or posttraumatic stress disorder. Typical situations that trigger claustrophobic fears are small rooms, locked rooms, closets, tunnels, elevators, subway trains, airplanes, functional magnetic resonance imaging (fMRI) or computerized tomography (CT) scans, etc. Feared situations can also involve the mere subjective impression of being trapped, as in situations of physical restraint or in a crowded place. A potentially difficult case of differential diagnosis is between panic disorder with agoraphobia and claustrophobia. Although many agoraphobics will be afraid of being trapped: (a) their anxiety is essentially motivated by the fear of a panic attack, (b) they are also afraid of being in open places and other situations where help would not be available in case of a panic attack, and (c) in the case of panic disorder with agoraphobia the patient usually experiences at least some uncured and unexpected panic attacks.

Claustrophobia appears to be related to two main dimensions: the fear of suffocating and the fear of restriction (Rachman 1997; Rachman and Taylor 1993). A more detailed analysis by Febbraro and Clum (1995) revealed that claustrophobia is indeed not a unitary phenomenon, especially if one looks separately at anxiety, avoidance, and beliefs. Claustrophobic anxiety is induced in situations related to entrapment (due to physical or social constraints, such as being in a closet or in a crowded train) or to physical confinement (e.g., trying on clothes with a tight neck or being alone in a small, compact car). Claustrophobic avoidance relates either to crowds or to physical confinement, and dysfunctional beliefs tend to regroup under the categories of fear of losing control, fear of suffocating, or fear of being unable to escape. All these sources of anxiety, avoidance, and dysfunctional beliefs should become targets for cognitive behavioral therapy (CBT).

Early estimates of the lifetime prevalence of claustrophobia (e.g., Bourdon et al. 1988) were below 3% but more reliable ones (e.g., Curtis et al. 1998) based on the national comorbidity survey suggest a prevalence of 4.2% in the general population. Data derived from a large sample of the adult population in the USA indicate that 3.2% of their sample suffered from claustrophobia (Stinson et al. 2007). This makes claustrophobia the third most prevalent specific phobia. The point prevalence is estimated at 4% (Fredrickson et al. 1996), with twice as many women as men being affected. However, it appears that only a small proportion of people suffering from claustrophobia actually seek treatment (Rachman 1997).

7.2 Description of Significant Efficacy Studies Using Non-Virtual-Reality Approaches

Despite the high prevalence of claustrophobia, only a few randomized controlled trials have been published. However, the results from these outcome studies are very straightforward: CBT is effective. Öst et al. (1982) randomly assigned 34 adults to either *in vivo* exposure, applied relaxation, or a waiting list control condition. The treatment consisted of eight 1-h weekly sessions. Exposure was conducted using hierarchies that were specifically tailored to each patient. Analyses at posttreatment and at the 14-month follow-up revealed that participants in both treatment conditions were significantly more improved than the control condition. In another study, Booth and Rachman (1992) treated 48 participants with either *in vivo* exposure, interoceptive exposure (exposure to sensations experienced when anxious with such means as hyperventilating, spinning, or running in place), or cognitive restructuring and compared the efficacy of 3 h of these treatments to a wait-list control condition. To conduct *in vivo* exposure, they used a darkened $4 \times 2 \times 7$ foot filing cabinet. All treatments were more effective than no treatment and, in general, there were few differences between the active treatments. *In vivo* exposure was the most effective with statistically significant improvements on five out of six measures, followed by cognitive restructuring (three out of six measures) and interoceptive exposure, which was only effective on two out of six measures. *In vivo* exposure also appears to act faster, although the authors did not want to perform direct comparisons between the three active treatments.

In 2001, Öst et al. randomly assigned 46 adults to either 3 h of *in vivo* exposure delivered in one session, 5 h of *in vivo* exposure delivered over five sessions, 5 h of cognitive therapy without *in vivo* exposure delivered over five sessions, or a waiting list. Participants were assessed using a variety of self-report instruments, plus three behavior avoidance/approach tests (using an elevator, staying in a locked $1 \times 0.7 \times 2.3$-m room for 5 min and putting on a gas mask for up to 5 min). The *in vivo* exposure situations used for therapy varied from riding elevators or staying in very small locked rooms to taking an underground train. Results showed that all three active treatments were significantly more effective than the mere passage of time, both at posttreatment and at follow-up. No significant difference was found between the three active treatments at posttreatment and at follow-up. On average, patients were able to successfully complete the behavioral avoidance tests (BATs) and, for example, stay slightly more than 4 min in the small locked room at posttreatment and even longer at the follow-up.

Studies on the treatment of claustrophobia have also contributed to our understanding of treatment process. Issues about the treatment mechanisms of *in vivo* exposure have been addressed in Chap. 5 on spider phobia. Two additional studies deserve to be mentioned here. Kamphuis and Telch (2000) tested the effect of distraction versus threat reappraisal with 58 students afraid of enclosed spaces. During exposure, participants either: (a) focused on any available information relevant to their core dysfunctional belief (guided threat reappraisal); (b) listened to numbers and sounds and, depending on the sequence of numbers or sounds, pushed a button or performed arithmetical operations (cognitive load distraction); (c) tried to perform the distraction task and devote the remainder of their attention to threat reappraisal; or (d) just exposed themselves, without further instructions. *In vivo* exposure with guided threat reappraisal had the strongest impact on claustrophobia at posttreatment (i.e., after 30 min of exposure) and at the 2-week follow-up. The cognitive-load distraction task had a detrimental impact on exposure, and the effect of plain exposure (control condition) was better than exposure with distraction but less than exposure with guided reappraisal.

In order to test the impact of avoidance, or safety seeking behavior, Powers et al. (2004) recruited 72 claustrophobics and assessed the severity of their claustrophobia with two behavior avoidance/approach tests, one using a $183 \times 61 \times 53$-cm "coffin" (i.e., patients had to lay down) and one using a "closet" with the same cubic space (i.e., same dimensions but patients had to stand up). The experimental manipulation consisted of a standard exposure "alone" treatment, an exposure treatment that fostered avoidance behaviors (e.g., being able to open a window to access fresh air, unlock the cabinet, or communicate with the therapist), an exposure treatment that simply expressed the possibility of avoidance (e.g., patients were told they could use the same avoidance strategy as in the previous, but only as a last resource), a psychological placebo (relaxation), and a waiting list. Exposure consisted of being locked *in vivo* in the "coffin" for up to 5 min on six repeated occasions. Statistical analyses revealed that the simple perception of being able to avoid complete entrapment was sufficient to significantly hinder treatment success. At posttreatment, 94% of the participants in the exposure-only condition were clinically improved compared to 45% in both conditions where safety aids were used or simply made available, 25% in the placebo condition, and 0% in the waiting list. Results were maintained at follow-up and were similar on the "closet" behavior avoidance/approach test (a potential measure of generalization). Additional analyses also suggested that the deleterious effect of safety behaviors were not correlated with age, gender, or ethnicity.

Results from these two studies provide more examples of the importance of helping patients to disconfirm the association between claustrophobic stimuli and threat and to make sure patients do not engage in any form of avoidance or safety-seeking behaviors during exposure. There are no data available yet on the generalization of these findings from *in vivo* to *in virtuo* exposure, but until proven otherwise, clinicians would be wise to conduct their virtual reality (VR) exposure with these results in mind.

The current randomized controlled trials on the efficacy of *in vivo* exposure confirm that claustrophobia can be treated effectively within 3–8 h. The treatment usually consists of helping the patient confront physically confined environments (e.g., closet or elevator) that can elicit the impressions of suffocating, being unable to escape and losing control, or socially constraining situations (e.g., a large crowd in a shopping mall). It also appears to be a methodological standard in claustrophobia research to use a behavior avoidance/approach test, such as asking the patient to enter and remain in a dark, locked, and very tiny room.

7.3 Description of the Studies Using VR approaches to Treat Claustrophobia

In the late 1990s, Bullinger and his team in Switzerland developed a VR environment for claustrophobia and tested their pilot version with 13 nonphobic participants and 2 women suffering from claustrophobia to assess its impact on fear and VR-induced side effects (Bullinger et al. 1998). Participants were immersed in a VR environment consisting of a 2.8-m^2 room without windows or doors and with a movable front wall, allowing for the room to be shrunk to a tight 1.2 m^2. The hardware used was a Silicon Graphics™ workstation, a VR4 HMD from Virtual Research™, and a Flock of Bird 6dof motion tracker from Ascension™. The pilot study revealed that both physiological and subjective measures of anxiety or impairment were within normal ranges for the nonphobic controls and an increase in heart rate was observed for the two claustrophobic participants. Following their pilot assessment, an outcome study was designed. Unfortunately, only limited information is available on the results of the outcome study since they were only presented at a scientific conference (Bullinger et al. 1999) and have not yet been published. According to Bullinger et al. (1999), participants suffering from "claustrophobia without panic disturbances" were assigned to either an *in vivo* exposure condition

Fig. 7.1 Three screenshots of the VR environments used in Botella et al. (1999), the large room, the "magic room," and inside the elevator. Screenshots were actually taken in PC-based version of the software. Reproduced with permission from C. Botella

or an *in virtuo* exposure condition. A group of nonphobics also served as a control condition to document if the patient's scores fell within the range of the control sample after therapy. The treatment consisted of 12–45-min exposure sessions. It is reported that statistical analyses did not detect any significant differences between both forms of exposure at posttreatment and at follow-up. The VR environment has also been used with success in a pilot study testing if event-related potential can be used along with a head-mounted displayer (HMD) with people suffering from claustrophobia (Mager et al. 2001).

A case study by Botella et al. was published in 1998 that reports on a 43-year-old widow who was afraid of enclosed spaces (e.g., elevator, closed rooms) since childhood and was referred for an incapacitating fear of CT Scans. The virtual environment (VE) was run on a Silicon Graphics™ workstation with a FS5 HMD from Virtual Research™ and two 6dof Fastrack sensors from Polhemus™ that tracked the head and the hand. The treatment consisted of eight 35–45-min sessions delivered by two therapists well trained in CBT. Exposure followed a traditional habituation paradigm, where the therapist monitored Subjective Units of Distress Scale (SUDS) levels every 5 min and the patient had to interact with the VR environment long enough to let the anxiety decrease within the session. No formal cognitive restructuring or other CBT techniques were used. The software consisted of three VR environments (see Fig. 7.1): (a) a 2×5-m balcony, (b) a 4×5-m room with doors and a window that could be opened and closed (sounds coming from outside could be heard as well), and (c) a 3×3-m room without windows or furniture and where the entrance door could be locked from outside and the walls could be progressively and loudly closed in on the user until the available space is reduced to only 1 m² (in the treatment manual, this room is referred to as the "magic room"). Several questionnaires were used to assess treatment outcome (no behavior avoidance/approach test was used) and SUDS ratings during each therapy session were reported. The patient was treated successfully, although an actual CT scan had to be performed on her at the sixth session which, based on the SUDS ratings during the session, seemed to have a significant impact on treatment success. All self-report measures showed a progressive decrease in anxiety following each VR immersion, and treatment gains were maintained at 1-month follow-up. During *in virtuo* exposure, the patient reported several times that "the wall produces even more fear to me than the CT scan does" or "If I can do it here, I'll do it anywhere". Although this is only a case study, it suggests that VR alone, without the addition of any cognitive or behavioral techniques, could be used with success.

A second case study is reported by Botella et al. (1999) on the treatment of a 37-year-old female who suffered, according to *DSM-IV* criteria, from claustrophobia, storm phobia, and panic disorder with agoraphobia. Her fear of enclosed places had begun 12 years earlier when she felt trapped in the middle of a crowd that rushed in a shopping mall during a storm. Following this situation, she also developed a specific phobia of storms and, over a year, progressively avoided unknown places or shopping alone and had an unexpected panic attack during a vacation, to the point of developing panic disorder with agoraphobia. The same hardware as described above was used and the software was very much alike, except that the VR environment with the balcony was not used and a fourth VR environment was added. A 1 × 2-m virtual elevator was created (see Fig. 7.1), where the patient could open or close the elevator door, select a floor, and ride up or down. Two additional features of the virtual elevator are that one wall could close in on the user and the elevator could be stopped and locked between floors (accompanied with cracking sounds and flickering lights) as if there is a breakdown. The treatment was identical as in Botella et al. (1998) and will be detailed further in Sect. 7.5. A visual analysis of the data on self-monitoring of claustrophobic fear from the baseline through the entire duration of treatment and the 3-month follow-up revealed an important and progressive reduction in fear. Posttreatment and follow-up behavior avoidance/approach tests confirmed that treatment was a success, with the patient being able to stay 5 min in a locked closet (75 cm × 1 m × 2 m) without feeling any anxiety. Interestingly, the patient not only achieved improvement on the BAT and the measure of impairment but the treatment appeared to generalize to improvements in trait anxiety, anxiety sensitivity, and her fear of storms and avoidance of shopping alone. Results were maintained at the 3-month follow-up.

Two other uncontrolled cases studies were reported by Bouchard et al. (2003). Two female patients received a principal diagnosis of claustrophobia according to *DSM-IV* criteria and had no additional comorbid disorders. One participant was aged 62, had suffered from claustrophobia for over 20 years, and could not recall any specific trigger for her incapacitating fear. The second patient was 48 years old, suffered from extreme claustrophobia since her childhood, and recalled having been sequestrated several times before developing her phobia. The therapy was delivered by two interns who, at the time, did not have extended experience in CBT. The hardware consisted of a Windows™-based PC computer (866 MHz), an ATI™ Radeon 64 graphics card, an I-Glass HMD from IO-Display™, an Intertrax^2 3dof motion tracker from Intersense™, and a Microsoft™ joystick. Most of the dozen or so VR environments were created with minor edits made to the 3D first-person shooter game *Unreal Tournament: Game of the year* from Epic Games™. An additional VR environment was created from scratch using the *Unreal Tournament* game editor and consisted of a series of elevators, caves, tunnels, and mazes (see Fig. 7.2). Bouchard et al. (2003) treatment followed a standardized treatment manual and consisted in four 90-min weekly sessions. The first therapy session was used to present the treatment rationale, the role of avoidance, the principles

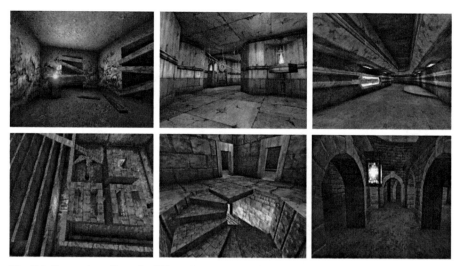

Fig. 7.2 Screenshots from the VR environments used in Bouchard et al. (2003). The three on the first row are minor adaptations from the *Unreal Tournament: Game of the year* game and the three on the second row are based on more complex modifications of the game. Reproduced with persmission from S. Bouchard

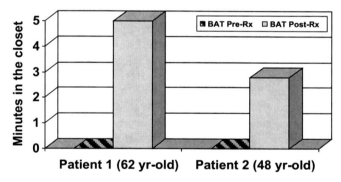

Fig. 7.3 Performance of two claustrophobics in a $41 \times 68 \times 205$ cm dark closet in Bouchard et al. (2003) study

guiding exposure, and to allow the patient to try VR in an environment devoid of claustrophobic cues. Handouts summarizing key information were given to patients to take home. The last 20 min of the fourth therapy session were devoted to relapse prevention. All remaining contacts with the therapist focused exclusively on *in virtuo* exposure (see Sect. 7.5 for more details). Results of the *in virtuo* exposure were very positive with these two patients, with both of them showing marked improvements in their performance on a behavior avoidance/approach test (a dark $41 \times 68 \times 205$-cm closet). At pretreatment, both patients barely entered the closet, and at posttreatment, one was able to stay in the closet for 5 min and the other stayed almost 3 min (see Fig. 7.3). These results mirror the outcome reported by Öst et al. (2001). Results on self-report measures show additional improvement between posttreatment and the 6-month follow-up.

Fig. 7.4 Screenshots of Riva's elevator (used by Wiederhold and Wiederhold 2000) and from inside the subway train. Reproduced with permission from G. Riva

A case study by Wiederhold and Wiederhold (2000) also reported successful treatment of claustrophobia using a VR software available for free on the web and developed by Giuseppe Riva consisting of a virtual elevator environment (see Fig. 7.4). A 75-year-old Caucasian female presented for treatment of severe claustrophobia. She had been referred to the clinic by her physician due to an impending MRI that was necessary for a medical condition. Because of comorbid medical conditions, she and her physician had agreed that she should try to undergo the MRI without the use of intravenous valium. The patient had a 40-year history of fear of elevators and other small, enclosed places. An initial history revealed no comorbid psychological disorders and a high level of motivation to overcome her claustrophobia. She was first taught diaphragmatic breathing to use as a coping mechanism during *in virtuo* exposure. Biofeedback-assisted relaxation training was practiced using peripheral skin temperature, heart rate, breathing rate, and skin conductance. It allowed her to differentiate between relaxation and physiological arousal and more efficiently master the relaxation exercises. She was also taught thought-stopping and distraction techniques. Despite the patient's severe claustrophobia, wearing the HMD caused no problem during sessions, an observation also noted by most therapists using VR with claustrophobics. Initial immersion consisted of familiarization with VR in an environment which would not cause anxiety—a virtual beach—but which would allow for practice in navigational abilities. During her first exposure to the virtual elevator scene, she walked forward and opened the door of the elevator, but did not initially want to go inside. She commented that it "looked very small." When asked for an SUDS rating she gave "80 out of 100," indicating a high level of arousal. After several minutes of facing the virtual elevator door and doing diaphragmatic breathing, she agreed to venture inside. She stood in the elevator briefly and then exited. The rest of the 20-min *in virtuo* exposure session was spent walking around the lobby, facing the elevator, entering the elevator, and closing the doors. Subsequent sessions included a combination of *in virtuo* exposure in the virtual elevator and *in vivo* exposure in a physical elevator located in the clinic. At

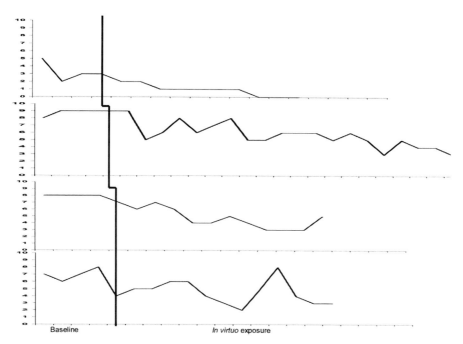

Fig. 7.5 Results of the multiple baselines across subjects from Botella et al. (2000). Scores represent daily self-monitoring of claustrophobic fears during baseline and therapy. The *vertical line* represents the beginning of the treatment

the end of seven therapy sessions, the patient was able to successfully stand in the clinic's elevator for a sustained period of 15 min with little or no anxiety. She was subsequently able to successfully complete her MRI without the use of medication.

The most rigorous outcome study on claustrophobia used a single-case design with multiple baselines across subjects (Botella et al. 2000). The four adults received a *DSM-IV* principal diagnosis of claustrophobia ($N=1$) or panic disorder with agoraphobia along with a significant fear and avoidance of enclosed spaces ($N=3$). Participants had suffered from claustrophobic fears for an average of 10 years. Hardware and software were similar to Botella et al. (1999). Participants in the study were given eight 35–45 min sessions of graded *in virtuo* exposure over a month. The therapists paid careful attention not to engage in cognitive or other behavioral techniques. Participants self-monitored the degree of their claustrophobic fear daily during each baseline period and during therapy (results are reported in Fig. 7.5). Self-report questionnaires and a behavioral avoidance/approach test were also completed at pre- and posttreatment and at a 3-month follow-up. As can be seen with the visual analysis of each case, the effect of treatment started to manifest progressively after the introduction of the treatment and was strong in most cases. Performance on the BAT was perfect in all four cases at posttreatment and 3-month follow-up, with participants being able to remain locked in a small and dark closet

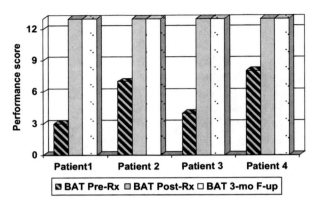

Fig. 7.6 Performance of four claustrophobic people in a 75 × 100 × 200-cm dark closet in the Botella et al. (2000) study. BAT scores range from 0 (refusing to enter the closet) to 13 (staying in the closet with the door locked for 5 min)

for 5 min. In addition, there was a decline in anxiety sensitivity, suggesting some generalization of the treatment gains to panic and agoraphobia symptoms (Fig. 7.6).

In 2008, Malbos et al. studied the effectiveness of a multiple component therapy involving VR for the treatment of claustrophobia. The first three sessions involved psychoeducation, relaxation initiation, cognitive restructuring, and homework assignments, while the fourth to the eighth sessions consisted of exposure to nine different VEs (with graded fear-provoking stimuli from one VE to the next). Six participants had to explore each VE in 50–55 min and were invited to enter enclosed spaces or to remain in narrow places as long as possible. Just like in some previous studies (e.g. Bouchard et al. 2003), the research team used an affordable level editor software (the Unreal Tournament game editor) to develop VEs which comprise houses, corridors, hallways, caverns, concrete channels, underground access, and elevators. Results of this uncontrolled study present a statistically significant improvement of patients from pre- to post-test on the Claustrophobia Questionnaire (suffocation and restriction scales), the Beck Depression Inventory, and the Life Quality Scale (Malbos et al. 2008). Moreover, gains were maintained after the therapy, with no significant differences being found between post-test and follow-up (after 6 months) ratings. In other words, results from this study support the idea that *in virtuo* exposure using a video game level editor can be an efficient tool in the treatment of claustrophobia.

In order to learn more about the effect of a consolidation experience, Dumoulin et al. (2008) assessed the addition of a brief "check on their improvement" on the efficacy of *in virtuo* exposure for claustrophobia. According to the authors, checking improvement is not an additional *in vivo* exposure exercise since participants were only asked to test how much progress they made in therapy; they did not have to push themselves as they would do during exposure or behavioral experiments. Participants were randomly assigned to two conditions: VR-only or VR plus a brief test of improvements. Participants received the same treatment in both conditions which consisted of seven weekly 90-min therapy sessions. *In virtuo* exposure was conducted with the elevator or the magic room environments sold by Previ™. The only difference between both groups is that a portion of each session (10 min) was devoted to "check on improvements" in the VR plus test condition, which was not the case for the VR-only condition. More specifically, in the check on improvements period, participants were asked to enter a closet, close or lock the door, and stay there as long as they wanted. Results indicate significant improvement on the suffocation and restriction subscales of the Claustrophobia Questionnaire for both groups with superior progress in the VR plus consolidation condition. A behavior avoidance test (getting inside a dark 22 × 31-in. closet, locking the door, and staying there alone for up to 5 min) also revealed better amelioration in the VR plus consolidation group. Dumoulin et al. (2008) results show that consolidation can be a useful addition to VR exposure. They suggest that small reality checks on improvements may increase self-efficacy to cope in the feared situation, which confirms the importance to test in real-life therapy progress and to add *in vivo* homework to *in virtuo* therapy.

7.4 Available Software

A few VR environments are available for the interested user. The early VR environment used by Bullinger et al. (1999) is not commercially available. The software used in the different studies by Botella and the Spanish research team have been adapted to the Windows™ PC platform and are now commercially available from Previ (http://www.previsl.com/ing). The claustrophobia package named "OpenOut" provides different levels of difficulty based on two rooms with several degrees of openness and an elevator with different options of functioning. The different VR environments have been described when detailing studies from Botella et al. (1998, 1999) and in Fig. 7.1. It may be important to note however that navigation in the VR environment is different from many other software programs used with anxiety disorders. The tracker follows head movement, but to walk in any direction, the user must use the mouse. Orientation of forward and backward motion is performed by rolling the mouse in the desired direction (an arrow is visible in the user's field of view) and pushing a button of the mouse to actually move. If patients have difficulty walking by moving the mouse, the therapist can do it for them.

A VE for claustrophobia was once commercially available from Fifth Dimensions Technologies' web site (www.5dt.com), but it is not sold anymore. The software contained VR environments for three phobias, namely fear of heights, enclosed spaces, and darkness. The claustrophobia module consisted of a series of passages with decreasing dimensions. When wearing a HMD and a 3dof tracker, the user could navigate with a joystick in the VR environment and control how quickly the passageways decreased in size (see Fig. 7.7). No studies have been reported on the use of this software with clinical populations.

Several VR environments can be downloaded for free either from Riva's web site (http://www.cybertherapy.info). Two of the four VEs developed by Giuseppe Riva in Milan for panic disorders with agoraphobia can be used for claustrophobia (an elevator and an underground subway, see Fig. 7.4). The elevator has the advantage

Fig.7.7 Screenshots from the VR environment from 5DT. (Reproduced with permission from 5DT)

of being crowded with virtual people and the therapist can add a substantial number of people to fill the elevator. Even if the virtual people are 3D sprites (i.e., flat 2d images that turn to always face the user) they are sufficient to induce anxiety. In the subway environment, the user has to go underground following a series of stairs, walk in a dark concrete corridor, get inside, and ride in the subway. The therapist can add more virtual people in the subway and some of them actually block access to the door.

The VEs developed by the Cyberpsychology Lab are available on the web (see w3.uqo.ca/cyberpsy, under Productions and Virtual Environments) and are mostly based on minor modifications made to the maps of the 3D first-person shooter game *Unreal Tournament: Game of the year* edition by Epic Games™. For nine environments, the only modification consists of removing violent (e.g., bombs, guns, ammunitions) or irrelevant (e.g., booby traps, teleporters) content. The options of the graphic user's interface were set to hide information only relevant to the game (e.g., the user's gun, number of ammunitions left, life packs) and the game was set to the practice level. This allows the user[1] to walk in deep and sinuous caverns, walk in tunnels, walk in dark basements, or dive under water. One additional environment was constructed with small edits to an existing map from the game in order to create a small maze while a second one was entirely built and designed as a complex underground maze with caverns, dead ends, endless corridors, elevators, and dark rooms.

Finally, other VR environments for claustrophobia have been developed in Brazil (Costa et al. 2002), Hungary (Sik Lanyi et al. 2004), and The Netherlands (Krijn et al. 2007).

---

[1] Note: It is only possible to install the VR environment if a legaly purchased copy of the game is installed on the user's computer.

7.5 Clinical Applications from Treatment Protocols Using *In Virtuo* Exposure

A thorough search of the literature did not reveal many outcome studies on VR and claustrophobia. Given that there are only a few studies available on *in virtuo* exposure for claustrophobia, we will take the opportunity in this chapter to provide more details about the actual treatment protocols used in standardized treatment manuals.

In the treatment manual developed and used in Canada at UQO (Bouchard et al. 2012), and upon which Bouchard et al. (2003) was based, VR immersions for *in virtuo* exposure lasted 20 min with 5 min breaks between each immersion. Immersions were planned for blocks of 20 min in order to avoid accommodation of the eyes due to the proximity of the optics in HMD, but therapists were allowed some flexibility in the duration of the immersion in order to clinically respect the flow of exposure and changes in anxiety. Individualized hierarchies were developed using the situations afforded by the various VR environments. Therapists then encouraged patients to enter the feared situations and confront their fears until anxiety decreased to baseline level. The therapist probed the patient every 5 min to rate SUDS, feeling of presence, and VR-induced side effects on "0" to "100" scales. Discussions were otherwise kept minimal during *in virtuo* exposure in order to minimize the risks of distraction or avoidance. Whenever necessary, the therapist would highlight the phobogenic aspect of a situation to increase its exposure potential. Therapists also voluntarily talked to the patient in terms that would foster presence, for example, by using active verbs that convey the impression that their actions are occurring in a physical environment (e.g., saying "walk towards the back of the room" rather than saying "push the right button of the mouse to go forward"), by referring to virtual stimuli as if they were physically real (e.g., "let's lock this heavy door" rather than "let's pretend the virtual door is locked"), and by using phrases that support or induce the illusion of realism (e.g., "this room is very small and dark, isn't it?"). It is important to observe signs of presence in therapy and to work on improving presence if it appears too low. Typical examples of phrases expressed by immersed patients that illustrate a strong presence are, for example, "It doesn't make me anxious if it is I who lock the door but I will panic 200 % if it is you who lock it", or "what really makes me anxious is that this door is in brick so I won't be able to break it once it is locked. It was much different with the wooden door because I would have been able to break it with a strong kick". Patients' behaviors during the immersion could also reveal signs of presence, such as when they physically bend down to enter into a cavern with a low ceiling. Reappraisals of the patient's performance during exposure were conducted in the 5-min breaks between immersions. These were occasions to reinforce the patient's ability to face his fears and to disconfirm dysfunctional expectations. Guided mastery strategies were used to support the patient's progress, eliminate avoidance behavior, vary and generalize adaptive behaviors, and individually adjust the hierarchy. After the completion of each therapy session, participants had to remain in the clinic's waiting room for 15 min to confirm they were not afflicted by VR side effects. In this regard, the Simulator

Sickness Questionnaire (Kennedy et al. 1993) is routinely completed before and after the therapy session. In clinical trials, patients did not have to practice any homework between sessions and were even asked not to expose themselves until the therapy was finished. But homework exercises could be performed between therapy sessions in clinical settings where stringent research criteria are not applied.

When *in virtuo* exposure was used at the Cyberpsychology Lab of UQO to conduct therapy in an outpatient practice (i.e., outside clinical trials), therapists often alternate with VEs developed by different companies in order to find one that suits the specific needs of each patient. For example, it is not unusual to use the virtual airplane developed for the fear of flying for claustrophobics. Combining *in virtuo* and *in vivo* exposure is also used in nonresearch outpatient practice. Interestingly, *in virtuo* exposure has been used by therapists who had a great deal of experience in CBT as well as by novice interns, and in every case learning to use VR was considered easy. Over the years working with claustrophobics in VR, there is a clinical impression in the UQO laboratory that some patients suffering from the specific phobia of enclosed spaces do not sufficiently benefit from VR because the available environments do not effectively and fully elicit all the cues feared by patients. The majority of VR environments allow confining patients in an enclosed space but they do not provide many opportunities for exposure to social constraints (except for Riva's environment developed for panic disorder with agoraphobia, all other virtual situations are devoid of people) or motor constraints (e.g., feeling tied to a chair or wearing clothes with a tight neck) and to fear of suffocating or losing control.

Botella and her group from Spain published a treatment manual for claustrophobia (Botella et al. 2002) that builds on their published outcome studies. As is often the case in the field of VR, the theory behind the treatment is rooted in Foa and Kozak (1986) and Lang (1977) fear structure theory. It implies that effective treatment must elicit the entire fear structure, with its physiological, meaning/cognitive, and response/behavioral components. The treatment manual followed the traditional style of most published manuals on CBT for anxiety disorders, with a detailed section on claustrophobia, its assessment, general treatment mechanisms, an overview of treatment strategies, and a session-by-session treatment plan. Therapeutic strategies described in this manual, which were broader than those used in Botella et al. (1998, 1999, 2000) outcome studies, included psychoeducation about claustrophobia, cognitive restructuring, *in virtuo* exposure, and *in vivo* exposure. The exposure components of the therapy were rather similar for *in virtuo* and *in vivo* exposure, with the development of a hierarchy, the use of SUDS during exposure, instances of repeated practice, and postexposure analyses of what happened. The first therapy session was based on a general introduction to CBT, anxiety, avoidance, and the description of a model explaining the patient's current problems. The second session focused on the development of the hierarchy and practicing how to navigate in VR with an immersion in a VR environment that is irrelevant to claustrophobia (e.g., a virtual beach). The third and following therapy sessions were devoted to exposure and other therapy techniques.

In Botella's clinic *in virtuo* exposure was presented to the patient as being similar to *in vivo* exposure, with the exception that this time the patient is inside the computer. The therapist reminded patients that VR allowed them to feel and experience what happens when coping with phobic stimuli. They helped patients get inside the VR experience, adapted the context of the immersion to patient's day-to-day life, and highlighted that the emotions felt by the patients were real even if they were triggered by virtual images.

Treatment protocol at the Virtual Reality Medical Center is similar to treatments described above (Wiederhold and Wiederhold 2005). Each patient undergoes an initial intake and evaluation session. On the first visit, a therapist takes a thorough history of the patient's problem. The therapist then proceeds to educate the patient about CBT techniques and gives a homework assignment that includes reading in the patient workbook Conquering Panic, Anxiety and Phobias and questionnaires to complete (Wiederhold 2003). During the next session, patients are taught breathing and relaxation skills and are allowed to become familiar with physiological monitoring instruments. All patients are encouraged to enter a relaxed state prior to VR exposure, performing 5 or more minutes of slow, diaphragmatic breathing. The therapist takes a baseline measure of the patient's physiology and assigns more homework, including practicing the relaxation and breathing skills. In the third session, the patient is allowed to enter a neutral VE to become familiar with the VR hardware and navigation in the VE. This session does not involve exposure to anxiety-inducing simulations. At this point, the therapist and patient have constructed a hierarchy of anxiety-inducing stimuli for exposure treatment. In the fourth session, this exposure begins. From this session until the completion of treatment (typically 8–10 sessions), the patient undergoes 20 min of VR exposure at a time. Each session begins with a baseline measure of physiology, followed by a 20-min exposure that climbs the hierarchy at the patient's own pace. The therapist then reviews the physiological reactions with the patient and the exposure progresses to the next level if a suitable decrease in anxiety has occurred.

An original aspect of *in virtuo* exposure as first conducted at the Virtual Reality Medical Center is their use of physiological feedback. Since they began treating specific phobias with VR exposure more than a decade ago, Wiederhold and Wiederhold (2000) have been using both subjective and objective measures to evaluate treatment outcome. These consist of the SUDS ratings and other self-report measures, therapist observation of patient behavior, and physiological monitoring (including heart rate, respiration rate, skin resistance, peripheral skin temperature, and brain wave activity) measured at baseline and during exposure for each treatment session. Based on SUDS and skin resistance (SR) measures (an updated version of this framework also includes heart rate variability; Wiederhold et al. 2002), Wiederhold and Wiederhold (2000) have shown that patients can be clustered into four categories that may indicate how effective VR treatment will be for them. Type 1 includes patients who show high SUDS and high SR arousal during VR immersion, meaning that they are highly phobic and are present enough in the virtual world to feel both subjective and physiological anxiety. These patients tend to become highly immersed in the VE, allowing them to progress rapidly through treatment. Type 2 patients are those who demonstrate high physiological arousal but report no subjective anxiety (a low score on SUDS). This person might be having some sort of mind–body disconnect; they feel they are not immersed in the VE though their physiology indicates otherwise. This might be due to an unwillingness to admit that an "animated world" is causing them anxiety, or it could be a lack of awareness of when they are physically aroused. People labeled Type 3 are those who experience no physiological arousal but report anxiety on the SUDS. In this case, patients may be unable to become immersed in the virtual world but do not want to admit this to their therapist. Finally, Type 4 consists of patients who are neither physiologically nor cognitively aroused upon exposure to the virtual world. This could be due to the patient being nonphobic, it could be someone who is simply not able to become immersed and is aware of this fact, or it might be a person who has become desensitized to the virtual stimuli through treatment and is now ready to attempt *in vivo* exposure.

Within this framework, Wiederhold and Wiederhold (2000) found that those patients who are never Type 1 are not typically able to achieve success through VR treatment. Both subjective and objective arousal appear to be necessary elements of successful treatment, since desensitization to anxiety-invoking stimuli requires initial arousal and then a decrease in that arousal within and across sessions. Awareness that some patients will not benefit from VR exposure treatment, and an objective means of measuring this probability, has contributed greatly to the understanding of the mechanisms behind VR treatment for many types of anxiety disorders.

7.6 Conclusion

Claustrophobia, the fear of being trapped in enclosed spaces, commonly manifests in the fear of riding in an elevator, but it can also be related to aviophobia, PTSD due to motor vehicle accidents, or fear of medical testing equipment, such as MRI. Empirically supported treatments for claustrophobia focused on *in vivo* exposure. A few VR environments have been developed and tested for this disorder. No randomized controlled trials have yet been published but case studies supported the general finding observed in other phobias that *in virtuo* exposure works well. Large outcome studies with control groups and an assessment of nonresponders and dropouts would be welcome.

Results on behavior avoidance/approach tests collected on the few patients that participated in the case studies showed marked improvements. Treatment lasted between four and 12 sessions. In most cases, the treatment was restricted to *in virtuo* exposure only with no cognitive restructuring or coping strategies (e.g., relaxation, breathing retraining, etc). The first studies were using complex and costly computers (i.e., Silicon Graphics computers using Sun technologies) but they have been replaced by affordable PC-based systems. In terms of software, most tackle physical confinement to an enclosed space. That may not be sufficient to address the complexity and variety of claustrophobic fears, most notably the fear of suffocating that is so prominent in claustrophobia, although no studies have looked at this hypothesis.

References

American Psychiatric Association (APA). (2000). *Diagnostic and statistical manual of mental disorders fourth edition text revision*. Washington, DC: American Psychiatric Association.

Bourdon, K. H., Boyd, J. H., Rae, D. S., & Burns, B. J. (1988). Gender differences in phobias: Results of a ECA community survey. *Journal of Anxiety Disorders, 2*, 227–241.

Booth, R., & Rachman, S. (1992). The reduction of claustrophobia—I. *Behaviour Research and Therapy, 30*(3), 207–221.

Botella, C., Baños, R. M., Perpiñá, C., Villa, H., Alcañiz, M., & Rey, A. (1998). Virtual reality treatment of claustrophobia: A case report. *Behaviour Research and Therapy, 36*, 239–246.

Botella, C., Villa, H., Baños, R., Perpiñá, C., & García-Palacios, A. (1999). The treatment of claustrophobia with virtual reality: Changes in other phobic behaviors not specifically treated. *Cyberpsychology and Behavior, 2*(2), 135–141.

Botella, C., Baños, R. M., Villa, H., Perpiñá, C., & García-Palacios, A. (2000). Virtual reality in the treatment of claustrophobic fear: a controlled, multiple-baseline design. *Behavior Therapy, 31*(3), 583–595.

Botella, C., Baños, R. M., & Perpiñá, C. (2002). *Claustrophobia: Virtual reality treatment manual*. Valencia: Promolibro.

Bouchard, S., St-Jacques, J., Côté, S., Robillard, G., & Renaud, P. (2003). Exemples de l'utilisation de la réalité virtuelle dans le traitement des phobies (using virtual reality in the treatment of phobias). *Revue Francophone de Clinique Comportementale et Cognitive, 8*(4), 5–12.

Bouchard, S., Robillard, G., Larouche, S., & Loranger, C. (2012). Description of a treatment manual for in virtuo exposure with specific phobia. In C. Eichenberg (Ed.), *Virtual reality in psychological, medical and pedagogical applications* (Ch. 4, pp. 82–108). Rijeka: InTech.

Bullinger, A. H., Roessler, A., & Mueller-Spahn, F. (1998). Three-dimensional virtual reality as a tool in cognitive-behavioral therapy of claustrophobic patients. *Cyberpsychology and Behavior, 1*(2), 139–145.

Bullinger, A. H., Bergner, J., Roessler, A., Estoppey, K. H., & Mueller-Spahn, F. (1999). *Virtual reality in claustrophobia and acrophobia*. Presentation at the Medecine Meets Virtual Reality, San Francisco, January 20–23.

Costa, R. M., de Carvalho, L. A., Drummond, R., Wauke, A. P., & de Sá Guimaraes, M. (2002). The UFRJ-UERJ group: Interdisciplinary virtual reality experiments in neuropsychiatry. *Cyberpsychology and Behavior, 5*(5), 423–465.

Curtis, G. C., Magee, W. J., Eaton, W. W., Wittchen, H.-U., & Kessler, R. C. (1998). Specific fears and phobias: Epidemiology and classification. *British Journal of Psychiatry, 173*, 212.

Dumoulin, S., Bouchard, S., Robillard, G., & Arsenault, J.-E. (2008). *"Reality tests" increase the efficacy of in virtuo exposure for claustrophobics*. Presentation at the CyberTherapy Conference, San Diego, June 23–25.

Febbraro, G. A. R., & Clum, G. A. (1995). A dimensional analysis of claustrophobia. *Journal of Psychopathology and Behavioral Assessment, 17*(4), 335–351.

Foa, E. B., & Kozak, M. J. (1986). Emotional processing of fear: Exposure to corrective information. *Psychological Bulletin, 99*, 20.

Fredrickson, M., Annas, P., Fischer, H., & Wik, G. (1996). Gender and age differences in the prevalence of specific fears and phobias. *Behaviour Research and Therapy, 26*, 241.

Kamphuis, J. H., & Telch, M. J. (2000). Effects of distraction and guided threat reappraisal on fear reduction during exposure-based treatments for specific fears. *Behaviour Research and Therapy, 38*, 1163.

Kennedy, R. S., Lane, N. E., Berbaum, K. S., & Lilienthal, M. G. (1993). Simulator sickness questionnaire: An enhanced method for quantifying simulator sickness. *International Journal of Aviation Psychology, 3*(3), 203–220.

Krijn, M., Emmelkamp, P. M. G., Olapsson, R. P., Bouwman, M., van Gerven, L. J., Spinhoven, P., Schuemie, M. J., & van der Mast, C. A. P. G. (2007). Fear of flying treatment methods: Virtual reality exposure vs cognitive behavioural therapy. *Aviation, Space, and Environmental Medicine, 78*, 121–128.

Lang, P. J. (1977). Imagery in therapy: An information processing analysis of fear. *Behavior Therapy, 8*, 862–886.

Malbos, E., Mestre, D. R., Note, I. D., & Gellato, C. (2008). Virtual reality in claustrophobia: Multiple components therapy involving game editor virtual environments exposure. *Cyberpsychology and Behavior, 11*(6), 695–697.

Mager, R., Bullinger, A. H., Mueller-Spahn, F., Kuntze, M. F., & Stoermer, R. (2001). Real-time monitoring of brain activity in patients with specific phobia during exposure therapy, employing a stereoscopic virtual environment. *Cyberpsychology and Behavior, 4*(4), 465–469.

Öst, L.-G., Johansson, J., & Jerrehalm, A. (1982). Individual response patterns and the effects of different behavioral methods in the treatment of claustrophobia. *Behaviour Research and Therapy, 20*(5), 445–460.

Öst, L.-G., Alm, T., Brandberg, M., & Breitholtz, E. (2001). One vs five sessions of exposure of cognitive therapy in the treatment of claustrophobia. *Behaviour Research and Therapy, 39*, 167.

Powers, M. B., Smits, A. J., Telch, M. J. (2004). Disentangling the effects of safety-behavior utilization and safety behaviour availability during exposure-based treatment: A placebo-controlled trial. *Journal of Consulting and Clinical Psychology, 72*(3), 448–454.

Rachman, S. J. (1997). Claustrophobia. In G. C. L. Davey (Ed.), *Phobias: A handbook of theory, research and treatment* (pp. 163–181). Chichester: Wiley.

Rachman, S., & Taylor, S. (1993). Analyses of claustrophobia. *Journal of Anxiety Disorders, 7*, 281–291.

Sik Lányi, C., Laky, V., Tilinger, A., Pataky, I., Simon, L., Kiss, M., Simon, V., Szabo, J., & Páll, A. (2004). Developing multimedia software and virtual reality worlds and their use in rehabilitation and psychology. In M. Duplaga et al. (Eds.), *Transformation of health care with information technologies* (pp. 273–284). Amsterdam: IOS Press.

Stinson, F. S., Dawson, D. A., Chou, S. P., Smith, S., Goldstein, R. B., Ruan, W. J., & Grant, B. F. (2007). The epidemiology of DSM-IV specific phobia in the USA: Results from the National Epidemiologic Survey on Alcohol and Related Conditions. *Psychological Medicine, 37*, 1047.

Wiederhold, B. K. (2003). *Conquering panic, anxiety, & phobias: Achieving success through virtual reality and cognitive behavioral therapy*. San Diego: Interactive Media Institute.

Wiederhold, B. K., & Wiederhold, M. D. (2000). Lessons learned from 600 virtual reality sessions. *Cyberpsychology and Behavior, 3*(3), 393–400.

Wiederhold, B. K., & Wiederhold, M. D. (2005). *Virtual reality therapy for anxiety disorders: Advances in evaluation and treatment*. Washington, DC: American Psychological Association.

Wiederhold, B. K., Jang, D. P., & Wiederhold, M. D. (2002). *Refining the physiometric profile in virtual reality treatment*. Proceedings of the VR and Mental Health Symposium, Medicine Meets Virtual Reality Conference, Newport Beach, CA.

World Health Organization. (1992). *The ICD-10 classification of mental and behavioural disorders*. Geneva: WHO.

Chapter 8
Panic Disorder, Agoraphobia, and Driving Phobia: Lessons Learned From Efficacy Studies

Cristina Botella, Azucena García-Palacios, Rosa Baños and Soledad Quero

8.1 Key Variables Involved in Panic Disorder, Agoraphobia, and Driving Phobia

The main feature of panic disorder (PD) is recurrent panic attacks. This is closely followed by concern over having additional panic attacks, worry about adverse physical or psychological implications of panic attacks, or a significant change in behavior that could take the form of avoidance of situations or activities which may increase the likelihood of having a panic attack. The avoidance syndrome usually accompanying recurrent panic attacks is called agoraphobia (*DSM*-IV-TR, APA 2000), and its presence or absence distinguishes three psychopathological disorders marked in the *Diagnostic and Statistical Manual of Mental Disorders,* Fourth Edition, Text Revision (*DSM*-IV-TR): panic disorder without agoraphobia (PD), panic disorder with agoraphobia (PDA), and agoraphobia without history of panic disorder (AG).

PD, PDA, and AG are among the most prevalent mental disorders in the general population. Significant epidemiological studies, such as the National Comorbidity Survey Replication (NCS-R), reported a 12-month prevalence of 2.7 % for PD and 0.8 % for AG (Kessler et al. 2005). These disorders occur more frequently in women than men (Magee et al. 1996; Goodwin et al. 2005); studies conducted in the USA and Europe established the average age of onset as 25 years (Eaton et al. 1994; Goodwin et al. 2005). Epidemiological findings are similar in several parts of the world (i.e., Horwath et al. 2002; Weissman et al. 1997), making PD a common psychological problem in many cultures.

PD is associated with significant psychiatric comorbidity, mainly with other anxiety disorders, depression, and substance abuse (i.e., Iketani et al. 2002; Magee et al. 1996; Zimmermann et al. 2003). Additionally, PDA is associated with significant impairment in important life areas such as social functioning, work activity, family, and leisure, leading to numerous adverse consequences that undermine patients' quality of life (Schmidt and Telch 1997; Wittchen and Jacobi 2005). For example, PDA sufferers attend medical centers seven times more frequently than the general population and present rates of work absenteeism twice as high as the general population.

The classification of PD, indeed of psychiatric classification in general, is under active review, due in part to the forthcoming publication of the *DSM-V* by the American Psychiatric Association. The work group for panic disorder, led by Michelle Craske, is studying the possible inclusion of several changes suggested by the latest scientific data. Discussion of these changes is beyond the scope of this chapter, but it bears mentioning that the proposals for the *DSM-V* emphasize the relevance of panic attacks as a syndrome that can appear in any psychopathology. This focus attempts to overcome the classical debate over prioritizing panic or agoraphobia by differentiating them into two diagnostic entities: (1) panic disorder and (2) agoraphobia (agoraphobia would not be classified a syndrome but rather a codable disorder). A review of the new proposal can be found on the *DSM-V* web page: www.dsm5.org.

Other proposals from respected researchers regarding the concept of panic disorders go beyond the *DSM-V*, notably one by Brown and Barlow (2009). These researchers propose a dimensional classification of emotional disorders (anxiety and mood disorders) attending to basic dimensions of temperament: (1) neuroticism/behavior inhibition and low positive affect/behavior activation that would be related to clinical features such as mood (depression, mania); (2) focus of anxiety (somatic anxiety, panic, intrusive thoughts, social evaluation, trauma); and (3) avoidance (interoceptive, behavioral, emotional, and cognitive avoidance). The differential expression of those dimensions would lead to diagnoses of varying anxiety and mood disorders. These authors emphasize the role of emotion regulation (that is, the ways in which individuals are influenced by the intensity, experience, and expression of emotions) in the phenomenology of anxiety and mood disorders, including panic disorder and phobias. This transdiagnostic approach opens the door to new areas of research aimed at reorganizing the assessment and treatment of emotional disorders. In fact, there is already a proposal for unified treatment programs for the emotional disorders regardless of specific diagnosis instead of the traditional cognitive-behavioral approach used thus far that focused on specific programs for specific disorders (Clark 2009; Ellard et al. 2010). There is increasing work in this area and descriptions of the strategies used from this transdiagnostic perspective (Boisseau et al. 2010) are consistent with recent dimensional classification proposals (Brown and Barlow 2009).

As one of the most studied anxiety disorders, there is agreement on which key features of PD are the most important in its assessment and treatment. The Consensus Development Conference on the Treatment of Panic Disorder, supported by the National Institute of Health (NIH 1991), set the standard for the assessment of PD that was later published (Shear and Maser 1994). This standard required assessments in the following areas: (1) diagnosis of PD using *DSM*-based structured interviews; (2) assessment of panic attacks using interviews, questionnaires, or daily self-records; (3) anticipatory anxiety, or apprehension about the possibility of suffering a panic attack; (4) phobic symptoms (behavioral and interoceptive avoidance); (5) severity and impairment; (6) comorbidity; (7) treatment response, remission, and relapse; and (8) follow-ups in order to obtain both short- and long-term efficacy data.

Driving phobia is classified among the specific phobias, which are identified by the *DSM-IV-TR* (APA 2000) as including persistent and excessive or unreasonable fear related to a specific object or situation as well as the subsequent avoidance of said object or situation. Driving phobia is considered "situational," and is one of five types of specific phobias that also includes animal, natural environment, blood–injection–injury, and others. Revisions to the *DSM-V* do not significantly affect the diagnostic criteria, with the possible exception of adding a criterion of duration; for the most part, the definition rewords and reorders criteria to increase consistency and improve ease of use and clinical utility (*DSM-IV-TR*).

Specific phobias have a high prevalence rate (12-month prevalence of 8.7%, NCS-R, Kessler et al. 2005) and can be very disabling for many people (Agras et al. 1969; Boyd et al. 1990; Magee et al. 1996). Furthermore, between 60 and 80% of people who suffer from phobias do not seek treatment (Agras et al. 1969; Boyd et al. 1990; Magee et al. 1996). This is one of the main social problems associated with specific phobias: As untreated mental health disorders become more severe, social and economic costs to society will increase (Kessler and Greenberg 2002; Kessler et al. 2008).

Driving phobia has not received as much attention from researchers as other specific phobias such as arachnophobia or claustrophobia, and recent noteworthy reviews have excluded mentioning its epidemiological and efficacy data (i.e., Barlow et al. 2007; McCabe et al. 2010). This is surprising, given that driving phobias might increase the risk of traffic accidents. Although there are no specific data pertaining to driving phobia, other studies have shown that, compared with nonphobic controls, individuals with height phobia experience an increased probability of serious injury resulting from falling from a ladder (Menzies and Clarke 1995). Based on this research, there is a strong possibility that driving phobia could increase traffic accidents or injuries resulting from such accidents. This is a significant problem, considering that the World Health Organization (WHO 2005) predicted that by 2020 traffic accidents will be the third leading cause of disability.

Furthermore, the likelihood of psychological pathologies arising from traffic accidents is significant. Mayou et al. (1993) found that 20% of accident survivors developed psychiatric symptoms; of them, 10% developed a mood disorder, 11% a posttraumatic stress disorder, and 20% a driving phobia.

Despite these worrisome data about PD, specific phobias, and driving phobia, current research supports the efficacy of cognitive-behavioral treatment (CBT) programs to treat these disorders. Some encouraging results are discussed below.

8.2 Description of Significant Efficacy Studies Using Nonvirtual Reality Approaches

The efficacy of CBT programs for the treatment of PDA has been widely demonstrated through several meta-analysis and literature reviews (Barlow 2002; Barlow et al. 2007; Gould et al. 1995; Margraf et al. 1993; Otto et al. 2000; Wolfe and Maser 1994). These treatment programs meet the criteria set by the Task Force on Promotion and Dissemination of Psychological Procedures (APA 1993, 1995) necessary to be considered well-established treatments for PDA (Barlow et al. 2007;

Barlow et al. 2000; Botella 2001; Chambless and Gillis 1993; Craske and Barlow 2008; Morisette et al. 2010).

The list of empirically validated treatments published by the American Psychological Association (Woody and Sanderson 1998) contains two CBT treatment programs for PDA: one designed by Barlow's team (Barlow and Cerny 1988; Barlow and Craske 1994) and one designed by Clark's team (Clark 1989; Salkovskis and Clark 1991). Both of these are multicomponent programs which include: (1) education about anxiety, panic and avoidance; (2) cognitive restructuring strategies to alter misinterpretations of bodily sensations; (3) exposure therapy to reduce behavioral and interoceptive avoidance; and (4) strategies (e.g., breathing training, relaxation) for the management of physiological symptoms. These programs achieve significant improvement in approximately 80 % of PDA sufferers and therapeutic gains are maintained in the long term (Barlow et al. 2007).

For specific phobias, the treatment of choice is in vivo exposure (Antony and Swinson 2000; McCabe et al. 2010). The list of empirically supported treatments (Woody and Sanderson 1998) includes two treatment manuals: one published by Marks in 1978, *Living with Fear*; and the more recent *Mastery of your Specific Phobia* published by Craske et al. in 1997 and reedited in 2006. Meta-analyses confirm that exposure therapy is superior to other treatments such as cognitive restructuring or progressive muscle relaxation (Wolitsky-Taylor et al. 2008). Since 1960, the research in the application of in vivo exposure has progressed into efficacious and efficient treatments such as the single session in vivo exposure program developed by Öst that can lead to clinically significant improvement in a wide variety of specific phobias (Zlomke and Davis 2008).

The scientific literature supports the positive results of such treatments, though there is room for improvement. One of researchers' and clinicians' main concerns is ensuring that these programs are available to all individuals in need. Unfortunately, there are still limitations on the availability of these treatments, such as the difficulties that mental health practitioners encounter in the practical application of empirically validated programs (Barlow et al. 1999), the fact that a percentage of PDA sufferers do not seek professional help (Bebbington et al. 2000), and patients' difficulties with acceptance and application of some therapeutic strategies in these programs.

One of the main elements of CBT for PDA and phobias is exposing patients to the object of their fear. Despite the efficacy of this strategy, it presents motivation and adherence problems (Choy et al. 2007). High dropout rates (approximately 20–25 %) occur when patients are informed about how the exposure therapy will proceed (García-Palacios et al. 2007; Marks 1978, 1992). A possible explanation for these high rejection and attrition rates is that patients consider the feared object or situation to be too threatening or aversive to confront (Choy et al. 2007). In addition to patients' concerns, some therapists may also have a negative view of exposure therapy, considering it inhumane and inconsistent with certain ethical considerations because it purposefully evokes distress in patients (Olatunji et al. 2009). Richard and Gloster (2007) conducted a survey among professional members of the Anxiety Disorders Association of America, and found that a significant number of clinicians were averse to providing exposure-based therapies.

Clearly, further research is necessary to improve CBT programs for PDA and phobias. One tactic that some researchers are employing, in order to focus on expanding the reach of CBT therapy while retaining its efficacy, is to investigate the use of new technologies in mental health treatment. There is increasing interest in exploring the utility of Information and Communication Technologies (ITCs) for the assessment and treatment of mental disorders. One of the technological innovations that is providing promising efficacy data is virtual reality (VR). In the following section, we review the work done in exploring the utility of VR in the treatment of PDA and one of the specific phobias, driving phobia.

8.3 Description of Studies Using VR Approaches to Treat Panic Disorder and Driving Phobia

8.3.1 VR in the Treatment of Panic Disorder and Agoraphobia

VR is a technology that allows the simulation of different real-life situations in a tridimensional, computer-generated environment in which the user can interact with the environment as if it were the real world. VR has potential as an exposure technique for the treatment of anxiety disorders because VR and real objects have similar characteristics, which create the illusion that the user is immersed and engaged with objects in the real world. For phobic individuals, the virtual environment can elicit an anxiety response similar to one from a real phobic situation (Moore et al. 2002).

VR can be used to maximize the benefits of in vivo exposure or as an alternative for those individuals who do not find in vivo exposure acceptable. There are an increasing number of studies that support the use of VR as an effective tool in the treatment of several anxiety disorders including specific phobias and PDA (see meta-analyses by Parsons and Rizzo (2008) and Powers and Emmelkamp (2008)). The main advantage of using VR environments in this context is the high degree of control exercised by the therapist over the feared objects or situations. This control may encourage patients to begin exposure treatment, as it can prevent the occurrence of unpredictable events which sometimes occur in in vivo treatments. Furthermore, in contrast to in vivo situations, VR allows for an accurate gradation of the exposure to the feared object or situation by permitting therapists to progressively add feared cues to the computer-generated environment. Furthermore, a specific exposure task can be repeated as often as necessary without real-life limitations. This advantage facilitates "overlearning," one of the processes that increases the efficacy of exposure (Marks 1978). VR also offers a more confidential setting than in vivo exposure; patient exposure to multiple environments takes place within the discreet confines of the therapist's office. Finally, an important component in the treatment of PDA is exposure to bodily sensations (interoceptive exposure (IE); as described later in this chapter, VR is a promising method for delivering this component.

In summary, VR can be useful in delivering exposure that simultaneously increases the acceptability of exposure therapy. In fact, in Richard and Gloster's survey, VR exposure therapy was viewed as more acceptable, helpful, and ethical than traditional exposure-based therapies by therapists (Richard and Gloster 2007). Using Delphi methodology, Norcross et al. (2002) reported that VR was rated third out of 38 interventions predicted to increase in use over the next 10 years. Finally, another recent study exploring 271 therapists' perceptions of VR in psychotherapy found that they perceived the benefits as outweighing the costs. The highest rated benefit was the ability to expose the patient to stimuli that would otherwise be difficult to access, followed by the ability for therapists and patients to have more control over the stimuli, and, thirdly, by the potential of VR therapy to reduce patients' feelings of embarrassment. The highest rated cost was the monetary expense of VR, with following concerns being potential technical difficulties and potential required training (Segal et al. 2010).

Clinically significant VR environments for PDA are currently being constructed (Vincelli et al. 2000 and Botella et al. 2004). For example, Moore et al. (2002), presented VR agoraphobic scenarios and reported data demonstrating that the VR environment activated the anxiety response in a nonclinical sample. However, in order to build clinically significant VR environments for PDA, certain aspects must be taken into account. Firstly, it is necessary to have a thorough understanding of the psychopathology of the specific disorder being addressed (e.g., the relevance of fear to restriction and asphyxia in claustrophobia, the role of a fear of bodily sensations in PD). At the same time, it is important to deeply understand the therapeutic technique to be used (e.g., exposure therapy) and the various strategies used to deliver exposure therapy for each specific disorder. Additionally, VR environments must be designed to be meaningful from an emotional perspective in order to achieve a high degree of sense of presence and reality judgment (Baños et al. 2000). With exposure techniques, an important parameter to be considered is time. VR scenarios have to allow the patient to stay in the situation as long as is needed for their anxiety to decrease, and this time varies from one patient to another. VR environments have to be flexible about the duration of each task (such as a bus trip). Additionally, they must be flexible enough to build meaningful exposure hierarchies adapted for each patient. To accomplish this, enough situations must be simulated so that the several modulators can be used. All of these issues have guided researchers' design and development choices for VR environments for treating PDA.

Similar to VR's use in exposure therapy, some preliminary studies offer descriptions and noncontrolled data on the use of VR to treat panic and agoraphobic avoidance in nonclinical populations. One of these studies showed a reduction in negative attitudes toward agoraphobic situations in a nonclinical sample after being exposed to a VR environment (North et al. 1996). However, this virtual environment did not include some of the most characteristic situations that comprise the agoraphobic cluster (e.g., crowds, public transportation, or shopping centers); therefore, it is not possible to claim that the VR environment was clinically significant for treating PDA.

8.3 Description of Studies Using VR Approaches to Treat Panic Disorder

Several works address the use of VR and PDA with clinical populations. Jang et al. 2000 published a noncontrolled study with seven PDA patients. However, they used just one virtual scenario (a traffic jam in a tunnel) and the scenario was not able to provoke an anxiety response in many participants. Because the limited VR environment was not suitable for the treatment of PDA, no strong conclusions could be made.

Botella et al. (1999) applied a VR program to the treatment of claustrophobia in a patient with a PDA diagnosis. Although VR exposure was restricted to claustrophobic situations, therapeutic gains generalized to other agoraphobic behaviors that were not specifically treated. After these positive results, this team designed a VR environment specifically for PDA (Botella et al. 2004) and tested its preliminary efficacy and acceptability in a case study. The study demonstrated both short- and long-term (12-month follow-up) positive outcomes and acceptability of the application of VR exposure.

There are two controlled studies exploring the efficacy of VR exposure in the treatment of PDA. Vincelli et al. (2003) compared the efficacy of a standard CBT program with both a control group and a multicomponent CBT program that included the use of VR The treatment protocol, Experiential-Cognitive Therapy (ECT), included eight sessions and several booster sessions. Session 1 was devoted to CBT-structured education about the disorder, an introduction to the VR environment, and establishment of the VR hierarchy. Homework included keeping a record of panic attacks that would continue through the end of treatment. Session 2 included a cognitive assessment informed by graded exposure to the virtual environments and an introduction to and scheduling of in vivo self-exposure. Homework was in vivo self-exposure. Session 3 began cognitive restructuring through graded exposure to VR environments; further in vivo self-exposure was assigned as homework. Session 4 included graded VR exposure and face-to-face cognitive restructuring with in vivo self-exposure as homework. In session 5, IE was introduced and conducted through VR. Homework included in vivo IE. Sessions 6 and 7 were devoted to IE in VR and face-to-face cognitive restructuring including in vivo IE as homework. Session 8 was dedicated to relapse prevention and cognitive restructuring. Booster sessions were planned as needed to review and reinforce patients' tasks.

The Virtual Environment for Panic Disorder (VEPD) was designed by Riva's team and developed using the VRT 5.6 toolkit. It runs on a standard PC with Pentium IV/Celeron/Athlon 1.2 GHz, 64 MB of RAM, graphic card with 32 MB of VRam, and uses Windows 95/98/2000/NT/XP. The VR hardware used was a head-mounted display (Glasstron PLM-A35 by Sony), a motion gyroscopic tracker (InterTrax 30), and a joystick.

The VR environment includes four scenarios: an elevator where the user becomes familiar with the VR environment and VR devices; a supermarket where the user can shop for, pick up, and pay for objects at the cash register; a subway; and a large public square containing a church, buildings and a bar (see Fig. 8.1).

The therapist can set the duration of the virtual experience and the number of virtual individuals in each scenario (from none to a crowd).

Fig. 8.1 Image of Virtual Environment for Panic Disorders. (VEPD, Vincelli et al. 2003). Reproduced with permission from G. Riva.

Twelve patients were randomly assigned to the three experimental conditions. Patients were excluded if they suffered from psychosis, bipolar disorder, strong suicidal tendencies, or physical illness. The measures for assessing treatment efficacy included the *Beck Depression Inventory* (BDI; Beck et al. 1961) for measuring depression, the *State Trait Anxiety Inventory* (Spielberger et al. 1970) for measuring anxiety; the *Agoraphobic Cognition Questionnaire* (Chambless et al. 1984) for assessing agoraphobic cognitions; the *Fear Questionnaire* (FQ; Marks and Mathews 1979) for measuring phobic symptoms, and an individually reported panic diary for assessing panic attack frequency. After the treatment, both treatment groups reported significantly reduced numbers of panic attacks (see Fig. 8.2) and lower levels of depression, as well as reduced state and trait anxiety. There were no differences in the results of the two treatment conditions, indicating that the program including VR was as effective as the traditional CBT program. Furthermore, none of the participants in the VR condition experienced any nausea or ill effects due to the simulator.

This study presented some methodological limitations. The sample size was small and it is not clear how much improvement in the VR group could be attributed to VR exposure or to in vivo exposure, since participants assigned to that experimental condition received instructions to practice in vivo exposure between sessions. A noteworthy finding was that VR produced the same results as CBT but required 33% fewer sessions (the VR group received eight sessions, whereas the CBT group received 14 sessions).

8.3 Description of Studies Using VR Approaches to Treat Panic Disorder

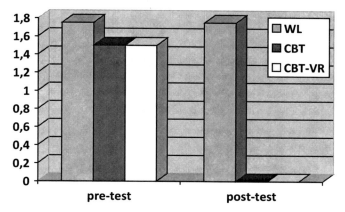

Fig. 8.2 Weekly panic attack frequency from pretest to posttest. (Vincelli et al. 2003) *WL*: Waiting list; *CBT*: Traditional cognitive behavioral treatment; *CBT-VR*: cognitive behavioral treatment including VR exposure

The other controlled study was conducted by Botella et al. (2007) within the framework of an EU project (VEPSY-Updated, IST-2000–25323). These authors compared a control group with both the efficacy of a traditional CBT multicomponent program including in vivo exposure (IVE) and the efficacy of a multicomponent program that included VR for the delivery of situational and IE (VRE). The treatment program included the most important components of the empirically supported CBT programs for PDA: the Clark's cognitive component (Salkovskis and Clark 1991) and the Barlow's interoceptive and situational exposure component (Barlow and Craske 1994). The treatment included three modules delivered in nine weekly, 1-h sessions: (1) education about anxiety and PDA, cognitive restructuring, and breathing training (two sessions); (2) exposure to internal and external stimuli (IVE or VRE; six sessions); and (3) relapse prevention (one session). The difference between the two treatment conditions was the exposure component, which was delivered in vivo in the IVE group and in a computer-generated environment in the VRE group.

The hardware included a Pentium III (1000 KHZ, 256 MB of RAM and CD-ROM drive) and an AGP graphics card, 64 MB, with support for OpenGL and with support for a 60 Hz rest frequency at 640×480 resolution. The patients' visual device was a V6 (*Virtual Research*) head-mounted display by Virtual Research; and the therapists' visual device was a 17" monitor. A tracker device (InterTrax 2) was used. The patients' navigation and interaction device was a mouse, while the therapists' interaction device was a keyboard. Finally, the patients' audio device was a V6 headphone set and the therapists' audio device was a standard headphone set. The software ran on Microsoft Windows (95, 98, ME, 2000 or NT 4.0, with Service Pack 6).

The VR program was named "Panic-Agoraphobia" and it included six virtual environments (see Fig. 8.3):

The training room: This scenario includes objects on a table with which the user can interact in different ways. The aim of this scenario is to introduce patients to

Fig. 8.3 Images of VR environment for the treatment of PDA and therapy setting. (Botella et al. 2007). Reproduced with permission from C. Botella.

the virtual world and to allow them to practice engaging with objects and moving around within it.

The room: This scenario portrays a living room containing objects including a phone and answering machine. The patients can interact with the virtual objects, read magazines, and listen to a radio on which sales at a shopping center are announced. The patients can also listen to messages on the answering machine from a friend asking him/her to do some errands (each subsequent message increases the difficulty of the errand). The patient can leave the room and take an elevator up or down, or to ultimately leave the building. The therapist can adjust the number of people in the elevator (from zero to four people). If there are people in the elevator, there is an option wherein two people have a conversation pertaining to agoraphobia. Therapists also have the option to stop the elevator to simulate a breakdown and to encourage people in the elevator to talk about the breakdown; patients have the additional option of pushing the elevator's emergency alarm button.

The subway: The main objective of this scenario is to expose the patient to the use of public transportation. The situation begins in the underground station, where the patient waits for a train to arrive, then enters the car. The number of passengers can be changed to reflect minimum, medium, or maximum levels. The duration of the trip between two stations is controlled by the therapist who can adjust the speed of the train or stop it completely whenever necessary. The patient also has the option to disembark and reboard the train at any of the nine stations.

The bus: This scenario is similar to the subway but instead simulates a public bus.

The shopping mall: The mall has two levels: a books and music level (first floor) and, via an escalator, a supermarket level (second floor). In this scenario, several elements can be modified to increase the situation's level of difficulty: (1) the number of people present; (2) the aisles can be blocked with people, preventing the patient from easily moving around the environment; (3) once the patient is in the cashier line, a problem with a credit card can increase the patient's wait.

The tunnel: This scenario is a dark tunnel designed to simulate a situation in which panic attacks can be triggered by the difficulty of escaping or finding an exit. This scenario also provides IE: given that the absence of external stimuli (due to the tunnel's darkness) redirects the patients' attention to their bodily sensations even more so than in the other virtual scenarios.

8.3 Description of Studies Using VR Approaches to Treat Panic Disorder

Table 8.1 summarizes the characteristics of each scenario, the anxiety modulators that can be introduced, and some of the target agoraphobic behaviors that can be addressed.

In each scenario, exposure to external and interoceptive stimuli can be conducted simultaneously. Bodily sensations that can not only be prompted by the scenarios but also separately simulated are: (1) heart palpitations and breathing difficulties with three levels of intensity (mild, moderate, and accelerated) and (2) visual effects (e.g., tunnel vision, blurred vision, and double vision). The activation of these sensations in a controlled environment allowed for the application of interoceptive and situational exposure simultaneously, whereas in the traditional program interoceptive and situational exposure is conducted separately. For example, in a traditional CBT program, the therapist requires the patient to climb and descend stairs in order to incur palpitations and to expose the patient to the bodily sensations of anxiety without the presence of the actual anxiety-producing stressor, an intervention known as IE. In a different session, the patient executes an IVE task in a shopping mall (situational exposure). In Botella's program, while the patient is being exposed to a virtual shopping mall, the computer program can provoke palpitations in the patient through sound effects of a heart beating, combining situational and IE simultaneously.

The difficulty of each scenario can be graded using modulators which allow for the establishment of flexible virtual exposure hierarchies (e.g., number of people present, duration of the trips, difficulties such as a problem with a credit card at the shopping mall, the elevator suddenly stopping between two floors, etc.). This ability increases the likelihood of obtaining significant exposure hierarchies for each patient, and allows for progressive and controlled exposure to the feared situations, which is a significant challenge in exposure therapy. Also, each action in the VR can be repeated as many times as needed with as much time as needed for each patient.

Thirty-seven participants took place in the controlled study trial. Inclusion criteria for the participants were: to be 18 years of age or older; to meet *DSM-IV* (APA 2000) criteria for the diagnosis of panic disorder with or without agoraphobia (PDA) as principal diagnosis; and, in the case of those patients already taking medication for PDA, to not increase or modify the kind of medication taken during the study. Criteria excluding patient participation included psychosis, severe organic illness, or substance abuse or dependence.

Several measures were used to test the efficacy of the treatment program. Using the *Fear and Avoidance Scales* (adapted from Mark and Mathews 1979), patients rated fear and avoidance related to three target behaviors that they sought to overcome by the end of the treatment. The *Panic Disorder Severity Scale* (PDSS; Shear et al. 1992) assesses important features of panic disorder and agoraphobia, such as panic frequency, distress caused by the PA, severity of anticipatory anxiety, situational avoidance, interoceptive avoidance, and social and work impairment. Other tools measuring anxiety and depression included the *Anxiety Sensitivity Index* (ASI; Reiss et al. 1986), the *Agoraphobia Subscale (FQ-Ag) of the Fear Questionnaire* (FQ; Marks and Mathews 1979), and the BDI (Beck et al. 1961). The *Maladjustment Scale* (MS; Echeburúa et al. 2000) assesses the level of impairment that the

Table 8.1 Summary of virtual environments. (Botella et al. 2004)

Virtual scenario	Actions	Anxiety modulators	Exposure Situations	Interoceptive
Room	Answering machine on/off Radio on/off Reading magazines Leave the room Take the elevator	Messages in answering machine Announcements about sales in the radio *Number of people* Nobody Two people Four people *Conversations* About sales in the shopping mall About the elevator breakdown *Breakdown* The elevator stops Light on/off	Anticipatory anxiety Being alone at home Leave home alone Take the elevator	*Breathing and heart rate* Mild Moderate Accelerated *Visual effects* Tunnel vision Blurred vision Double vision
Subway	Subway/bus starts Requesting a stop Passengers entering/exiting (max. four people)	*Number of people in the station* Zero Low presence level Moderate presence level High presence level *Number of people in the subway* Only seated people Low presence level (standing) Moderate presence level (standing) High presence level (standing)	Using public transportation: Subway Train Bus Being in crowded places Being far from home	
Bus		*Trip length*: Short (3 stops) Long (8 stops) *Number of people inside the bus* Only seated people Low presence level (standing) Moderate presence level (standing) High presence level (standing)		
Tunnel	Walking through a tunnel	Distance from the exit	Being in an enclosed space	

8.3 Description of Studies Using VR Approaches to Treat Panic Disorder

Table 8.1 (continued)

Virtual scenario	Actions	Anxiety modulators	Exposure Situations	Interoceptive
Shopping mall	Interact with objects Books CDs Food (milk, cookies) Pay the cashier Use escalator	*Number of people*: Low presence level Moderate presence level High presence level Very high presence level *Difficult situations*: Aisles blocked Problem with credit card	Go shopping Being in crowded places Being in line Being in narrow spaces Going to unknown places Using escalators	

patient's reported problem causes in different life areas, while the *Clinician Global Impression* (CGI, adapted from Guy 1976) therapist to assess the global severity of the patient's distress. In addition, an instrument to assess patient satisfaction with the treatment was included following Borkovec and Nau (1972).

Results indicated that the improvement achieved by the program that included virtual exposure was superior to a control group and similar to results achieved using in vivo exposure. The improvement was significant in most variables related to PDA, as measured by key instruments: anxiety sensitivity, panic attack frequency, interoceptive and situational avoidance, impairment, and depression. The outcomes achieved at posttreatment were maintained at 12-month follow-up. Patients reported satisfaction with treatment in both treatment conditions. This study was included in the meta-analysis carried out by Powers and Emmelkamp (2008) that explored the efficacy of VR in the treatment of anxiety disorders.

In summary, the empirical evidence supports the efficacy of VR exposure in the treatment of PDA at short- and long-term.

8.3.2 VR in the Treatment of Driving Phobia

There are some preliminary results in the literature about the efficacy of VR exposure in the treatment of driving phobia from a case study, a case series study, a multiple baseline across-subject design, and an open trial (Wald 2004; Wald and Taylor 2001; Walshe et al. 2003).

Wald and Taylor (2001) conducted a pilot study using a single-case design including a 7-day baseline followed by three treatment sessions. Driving phobia symptoms decreased from pretest to posttest and outcomes were maintained at 7-month follow-up assessment. Wald (2004) presented efficacy data from a multiple baseline across-subjects design that included five participants who followed a VR exposure treatment with eight weekly sessions. There were significant reductions in fear and avoidance symptoms in three out of five participants that were maintained at 1-year follow-up, as measured by self-monitoring (in a driving diary) and interviews (*SCID-IV,* First et al. 1996; *Driving History Interview,* Ehlers 1990). However, VR exposure did not result in an increase in actual driving frequency for any of the participants. Given these limited results, the author concluded that VR exposure might be most useful as a preparatory intervention or as an adjunct for IVE rather than as a stand-alone intervention. Immersion VR was used in these studies using a driving simulator (driVRI, Imago Systems Inc 1996) that incorporated sound effects and visual display IO i-glasses 640×480 with an Intersense Intertrax 2 that provided a 360-degree horizontal field of view. The VR environment included six scenarios: residential route, rural route, highway with bridge route, highway merging route, urban intersections route, and urban industrial route.

Walshe et al. (2003) conducted an open trial investigating the effectiveness of the combination of two technologies involving computer-generated environments: a driving game (game reality, GR) and an immersive VR driving environment (Hanyang University Driving Phobia Environment). Fourteen subjects who met *DSM-IV* criteria for specific phobia after a motor vehicle accident participated in the study. Patients who experienced "immersion" in one of the driving simulations entered a CBT program with a maximum of 12 1-h sessions involving graded exposure tasks in the driving environments. In addition to the exposure component, the program included self-monitoring, cognitive reappraisal, physiological feedback, and diaphragmatic breathing. Measures included physiological responsivity, subjective ratings of distress, severity of fear of driving, posttraumatic stress, depression, and achievement of target behaviors. Findings at posttreatment supported the utility of VR and computer games in the treatment of driving phobia even when comorbid conditions such as posttraumatic stress disorder and depression were present.

Studies on the use of VR exposure therapy are still contradictory and preliminary. The open trial by Walshe et al. (2003) offers promising findings. However, the study by Wald (2004) offers very limited results regarding the use of VR in the treatment of driving phobia. The literature on IVE therapy for driving phobia is also very scarce (Townend and Grant 2006) and there are no available controlled studies with a group design. The literature on the use of exposure therapy for specific phobias offers strong evidence for its efficacy. Controlled studies exploring the efficacy of exposure therapy in driving phobia are needed in order to investigate if this phobia has a differential response to exposure therapy.

8.4 Available Software

The virtual environments for PDA described in this chapter include:

VEPD designed by Riva's team and developed using the VRT 5.6 toolkit. It was used in the Vincelli et al. (2003) study. The software, originally developed using Superscape, is now available for free download as part of the NeuroVR 2 suite: http://www.neurovr2.org.

The VR environment used in the Botella et al. (2007) study is called Panic-Agoraphobia. The software was designed by Botella's team and can be obtained at PREVI SL: www.previsl.com.

8.5 Relevant Findings from Studies Using VR Approaches

The efficacy studies exploring the utility of VR exposure in the treatment of PDA revealed that a multicomponent CBT treatment that includes a VR program to deliver VR exposure is superior to a control group and as efficacious as a traditional multicomponent CBT program that includes in vivo exposure. Significantly, therapeutic outcomes were maintained at 12-month follow-up. Furthermore, participants showed a high level of satisfaction with the VR exposure component (Vincelli et al. 2003; Botella et al. 2007). These findings are strong, but must be reproduced. As far as the mechanisms of change in the field of VR for PDA, there are no studies exploring this topic. There is some research pertaining to this issue in the field of phobias (i.e., Côté and Bouchard 2009), as described in other chapters of this book. As for PDA, there is only one study which aims to distinguish IE in the traditional CBT programs from that in VR-based programs. As described in the previous section, the VR program designed by Botella's team included the ability to deliver interoceptive VR exposure simultaneously with situational virtual exposure. However, in the first study the focus was on efficacy (Botella et al. 2007), the VR condition did not use virtual interoceptive exposure (VRIE) alone; situational exposure was accompanied by both traditional IE and VRIE.

In traditional CBT treatments, IE and behavioral exposure are usually conducted separately. In some sessions, patients are exposed to bodily sensations by means of exercises (e.g., climbing stairs to evoke palpitations). In other sessions, patients are exposed to agoraphobic environments such as malls, public transportation, etc. In the Botella et al. (2007) study, while the patients were exposed to virtual agoraphobic situations (e.g., virtual mall), they were also exposed to heightened bodily sensations by means of VRIE (e.g., blurred vision simulated through visual effects) or by means of IE exercises (e.g., hyperventilation triggered through exposure to the virtual mall).

Pérez-Ara et al. (2010) explored the differential efficacy of VRIE in order to clarify the effects of using VRIE versus traditional methods for IE. Twenty-nine PDA sufferers were randomly assigned to two experimental conditions: (1) VRIE Simultaneous Condition (VRIE-sim) and (2) Interoceptive Exposure Traditional Condition (IET). All participants received the treatment program that included VR exposure designed by Botella's team, as described in the former section. However, participants in the VRIE-sim condition were simultaneously exposed to visual and audio effects (fast heartbeat, panting, blurred vision, double vision) and agoraphobic virtual scenarios (for approximately 50 min). In contrast, participants in the IET condition were first exposed to the agoraphobic virtual scenarios (for approximately

Fig. 8.4 Individual performing IE (blowing through a straw to induce dizziness). Reproduced with permission from C. Botella.

25 min), and then the IE was conducted in a traditional way, by eliciting bodily sensations with physical exercises such as hyperventilation or spinning (for approximately 25 min; see Fig. 8.4). At posttest, the treatment conditions were equally effective at reducing relevant variables related to PDA as measured by the ASI and the PDSS. Outcomes were maintained and even improved at 3-month follow-up assessment. The authors concluded that these findings supported both the efficacy of VR exposure in the treatment of PDA and the efficacy of IE in the absence of anxiety control techniques in the treatment of PDA (Bitran et al. 2008; Craske et al. 1997). The authors also discussed the advantages of using IE and situational exposure simultaneously and emphasized that this form of delivery is more ecological (e.g., experiencing accelerated breathing while entering a mall). Another advantage is that VRIE can also be helpful when trying to evoke sensations such as blurred vision, which are difficult to provoke with traditional IE exercises. Finally, it is possible to combine VR exposure to agoraphobic virtual situations with traditional IE (e.g., a patient experiencing the virtual mall can be asked to hyperventilate).

With regard to driving phobia, the efficacy studies are scarce and compromised by methodological shortcomings; moreover, they do not address mechanisms of change or other related issues. As previously mentioned, it would be insightful to conduct controlled efficacy studies and studies about the mechanisms of change.

In conclusion, we would like to encourage researchers to carry out both studies that further examine the positive outcomes found in the use of VR exposure in PDA treatment as well as studies focusing on mechanisms of change in this field. It is also necessary to determine the differential efficacy of VR exposure for panic versus agoraphobia (as most participants in the studies described herein suffered from PDA).

As for driving phobia, as previously mentioned, surprisingly few related efficacy studies have been conducted thus far. This is a significant oversight, given the increasing number of motor vehicle accidents resulting in psychological consequences (Mayou et al. 1993). It is imperative that controlled studies be conducted that explore the efficacy of exposure therapy in treating this phobia. VR might be effective at delivering exposure therapy for driving fears. VR environments for driving would be useful not only for helping individuals suffering from this phobia, but could also prove useful for strengthening driving technique and preventing accidents in the general population. This is a very important field of intervention given the increase in road traffic accidents affecting a large number of individuals and involving high social and financial costs.

8.6 Conclusions

ICTs can help improve the delivery of CBT treatments. Data support the efficacy of VR exposure in the treatment of anxiety disorders, including PDA (Powers and Emmelkamp 2008). Furthermore, data support good acceptance of VR by both patients and therapists (Garcia-Palacios et al. 2007; Segal et al. 2010).

These data are promising and encourage researchers to continue exploring the use of ICTs in the treatment of anxiety disorders. Many people suffering anxiety disorders never seek help, or do so only after years of suffering, largely due to treatment expenses or limited access to assistance (e.g., the lack of well-trained professionals, long waiting lists, or living in rural areas; i.e., Clark 1999; King and Poulos 1998). To the benefit of such people, a new method of delivering psychological treatment has emerged that merges CBT with Internet technology (Anderson 2009). In these approaches, patients usually work through a self-administered guide adapted for the Internet, and can use this guide whenever they choose and at their own pace. This alternative method, which utilizes Internet-based, self-administered interventions, has been proven to be both low cost and effective at treating anxiety disorders (i.e., Botella et al. 2010c; Botella et al. 2004). Systematic reviews of the literature on evidence-based CBT treatments delivered online demonstrate that these approaches are indeed effective (e.g., Anderson 2009; Cuijpers et al. 2008; Spek et al. 2007). These online programs have several advantages. For example, they can reduce contact time between patients and therapists; hence, patients who would not otherwise be able to receive treatment can do so. In general, these technological approaches can help disseminate evidence-based treatments more widely (Bauer et al. 2005; Caspar 2004; Rochlen et al. 2004).

Independent researchers have been investigating PDA treatments from this Internet-delivered CBT perspective (Carlbring et al. 2005; Carlbring et al. 2006; Carlbring et al. 2003; Carlbring et al. 2001; Kiropoulos et al. 2008; Klein et al. 2006; Richards et al. 2006). Overall results obtained by various research groups offer similar, promising results; however, potential possible problems still need to be addressed, such as the amount of guidance provided by the therapist to the patients and attrition rates (Anderson 2009).

In conclusion, a new era is beginning in the field of psychological treatments, in which therapists can employ evidence-based CBT programs delivered via ICT technologies. VR exposure has already proven to be efficacious for certain treatments, and the Internet has likewise proven effective at delivering CBT treatments (at least to some patients). Other strategies, such as augmented reality (AR), are beginning to be used to treat specific phobias (Botella et al. 2010b); other new technologies such as mobile games have demonstrated their usefulness in facilitating exposure therapy in treating specific phobia (Botella et al. 2010a). Considering the difficulties that exposure therapy presents for some patients, VR, AR, and other ICT approaches have great potential to improve existing psychological treatments. Both VR exposure therapy (Garcia-Palacios et al. 2007; Richard and Gloster 2007) and AR therapy (Botella et al. 2010b) have already been deemed more acceptable to users than traditional exposure-based therapies. Considering the thousands of people that need intervention and the difficulty of disseminating evidence-based treatment programs, the Internet holds great promise for improving treatment delivery. Therefore, continued research in this area is imperative. ICTs are already being employed in the service of patients and therapists, and they are poised to continue to develop and improve significantly in the coming years.

References

Agras, S., Sylvester, D., & Oliveau, D. (1969). The epidemiology of common fears and phobia. *Comprehensive Psychiatry, 10*, 151–156.
American Psychological Association (Task force on Promotion and Dissemination of Psychological Procedures) (1993). *A report to the Division 12 board of the American Psychological Association*. Available from the Division 12 of the American Psychological Association, 750, First street, NE, Washington, DC 20002–4242, USA.
American Psychological Association (Task force on Psychological Intervention Guidelines). (1995). *Template for developing guidelines: Interventions for mental disorders and psychological aspects of physical disorders*. Washington, DC: American Psychological Association.
American Psychiatric Association. (2000). *Diagnostical and statistical manual of mental disorders DSM-IV-TR (4th edn., rev.)*. Washington, DC: American Psychological Association.
Andersson, G. (2009). Using the Internet to provide cognitive behaviour therapy. *Behaviour Research and Therapy, 47*, 175–180.
Antony, M. M., & Swinson, R. P. (2000). *Phobic disorders and panic in adults: A guide to assessment and treatment*. Washington, DC: American Psychological Association.
Baños, R. M., Botella, C., García-Palacios, A., Villa, H., Perpiñá, C., & Alcañiz, M. (2000). Presence and reality judgment in virtual environments: A unitary construct? *Cyberpsychology and Behavior, 3*, 327–335.
Barlow, D. H. (2002). *Anxiety and its disorders: The nature and treatment of anxiety and panic* (2nd ed.). New York: Guilford.
Barlow, D. H., & Cerny, J. A. (1988). *Psychological treatment of panic*. Nueva York: Guilford.
Barlow, D. H., & Craske, M. (1994). *Mastery of your anxiety and panic-II*. San Antonio: The Psichological Corporation.
Barlow, D. H., Levitt, J. T., & Bufka. (1999). The dissemination of empirically supported treatments: A view to the future. *Behaviour Research and Therapy, 37*, S47–S62.
Barlow, D. H., Gorman, J. M., Shear, M. K., & Woods, S. W. (2000). Cognitive behavioral therapy, imipramine, or their combination for panic disorder: A randomized controlled trial. *Journal of the American Medical Association, 19*, 2529–2536.
Barlow, D. H., Allen, L. B., & Basden, S. L. (2007). Psychological treatments for panic disorders, phobias, and generalizad anxiety disorders. In P. E. Nathan & J. M. Gorman (Eds.), *A guide to treatments that work* (3rd ed., pp. 351–394). New York: Oxford University Press.
Bauer, S., Golkaramnay, V., & Kordy, H. (2005). E-Mental-Health: The use of new technologies in psychosocial care. *Psychotherapeut, 50*, 7–15.

References

Bebbington, P. E., Brugha, T. S., Meltzer, H., Jenkins, R., Ceresa, C., Farrell, M., & Lewis, G. (2000). Neurotic disorders and the receipt of psychiatric treatment. *Psychological Medicine, 30,* 1369–1376.

Beck, A. T., Ward, C. H., Mendelson, M., Mock, J., & Erbaugh, J. (1961). An inventory for measuring depression. *Archives of General Psychiatry, 4,* 561–571.

Bitran, S., Morissette, S. B., Spiegel, D. A., & Barlow, D. H. (2008). A pilot study of sensation-focused intensive treatment for panic disorder with moderate to severe agoraphobia: preliminary outcome and benchmarking data. *Behavior Modification, 32,* 196–214.

Boisseau, C. L., Farchione, T. J., Fairholme, C. P., Ellard, K. K., & Barlow, D. H. (2010). The development of the unified protocol for the transdiagnostic treatment of emotional disorders: A case study. *Cognitive and Behavioral Practice, 17,* 102–113.

Borkovec, T. D., & Nau, S. D. (1972). Credibility of analogue therapy rationales. *Journal of Behaviour Therapy and Experimental Psychiatry, 3,* 257–260.

Botella, C. (2001). Tratamientos psicológicos eficaces para el trastorno de pánico. *Psicothema, 13,* 465–478.

Botella, C., Villa, H., Baños, R. M., Perpiñá, C., & García-Palacios, A. (1999). The treatment of claustrophobia with virtual reality: Changes in other phobic behaviours not specifically treated. *Cyberpsychology and Behavior, 2,* 131–141.

Botella, C., Villa, H., García-Palacios, A., Baños, R. M., Perpiñá, C., & Alcañiz, M. (2004). Clinically significant virtual environments for the treatment of panic disorder and agoraphobia. *Cyberpsychology & Behavior, 7,* 527–535.

Botella, C., Villa, H., García-Palacios, A., Baños, R. M., Quero, S., Alcañiz, M., & Riva, G. (2007). Virtual reality exposure in the treatment of panic disorder and agoraphobia: A controlled study. *Clinical Psychology and Psychotherapy, 14,* 164–175.

Botella, C., Breton-Lopez, J., Quero, S., Baños, R. M., García-Palacios, A., Zaragoza, I., & Alcaniz, M. (2010a). Treating cockroach phobia using a serious game on a mobile phone and augmented reality exposure: A single case study. *Computers in Human Behavior, 26,* 217–227.

Botella, C., Breton-Lopez, J., Quero, S., Baños, R. M., & Garcia-Palacios, A. (2010b). Treating cockroach phobia with augmented reality. *Behavior Therapy, 41,* 401–413.

Botella, C., Gallego, M. J., Garcia-Palacios, A., Guillen, V., Baños, R. M., Quero, S., & Alcañiz, M. (2010c) An internet-based self-help treatment for fear of public speaking: A controlled trial. *Cyberpsychology Behavior, and Social Networking.* doi:10.1089/cyber.2009.0224.

Boyd, J. H., Rae, D. S., Thompson, J. W., Burns, B. J., Bourdon, K., Locke, B. Z., et al. (1990). Phobia: Prevalence and risk factors. *Social Psychiatry and Psychiatric Epidemiology, 25,* 314–323.

Brown, T. A., & Barlow, D. H. (2009). A proposal for a dimensional classification system based on the shared features of the DSM-IV anxiety and mood disorders: Implications for assessment and treatment. *Psychological Assessment, 21,* 256–271.

Carlbring, P., Westling, B. E., Ljungstrand, P., Ekselius, L., & Andersson, G. (2001). Treatment of panic disorder via the Internet: A randomized trial of a self-help program. *Behavior Therapy, 32,* 751–764.

Carlbring, P., Ekselius, L., & Andersson, G. (2003). Treatment of panic disorder via the Internet: A randomized trial of CBT vs. applied relaxation. *Journal of Behavior Therapy and Experimental Psychiatry, 34,* 129–140.

Carlbring, P., Nilsson-Ihrfelt, E., Waara, J., Kollenstam, C., Buhman, M., Kaldo, V., et al. (2005). Treatment of panic disorder: Live therapy vs self-help via Internet. *Behaviour Research and Therapy, 43,* 1321–1333.

Carlbring, P., Bohman, S., Brunt, S., Buhman, M., Westling, B. E., Ekselius, L., et al. (2006). Remote treatment of panic disorder: A randomized trial of internet-based cognitive behavioural therapy supplemented with telephone calls. *American Journal of Psychiatry, 163,* 21.

Caspar, F. (2004). Technological developments and applications in clinical psychology and psychotherapy: Introduction. *Journal of Clinical Psychology, 60,* 221–238.

Chambless, D., & Gillis, M. M. (1993). Cognitive therapy of anxiety disorders. *Journal of Consulting and Clinical Psychology, 61*(2), 248–260.

Chambless, D. L., Caputo, G. C., Bright, P., & Gallagher, R. (1984). Assessment of "fear of fear" in agoraphobics: The body sensations questionnaire and the agoraphobic cognitions questionnaire. *Journal of Consulting and Clinical Psychology, 52,* 1090–1097.
Choy, Y., Fyer, A. J., & Lipsitz, J. D. (2007). Treatment of specific phobia in adults. *Clinical Psychology Review, 27,* 266–286.
Clark, D. M. (1989). Anxiety states: Panic and generalized anxiety. In K. Hawton, P. Salkovskis, J. Kirk & D. M. Clark (Eds.), *Cognitive Behaviour Therapy for Psychiatric Problems.* Oxford: Oxford University Press.
Clark, D. M. (1999). Anxiety disorders: Why they persist and how to treat them. *Behaviour Research and Therapy, 37,* S5–S7.
Clark, D. M. (2009). Cognitive behavioral treatment for anxiety and depression: Possibilities and limitations of a transdiagnostic perspective. *Cognitive Behaviour Therapy, 38,* 29–34.
Côté, S., & Bouchard, S. (2009). Cognitive mechanisms underlying virtual reality exposure. *Cyberpsychology and Behavior, 12,* 121–129.
Craske, M. G., & Barlow, D. H. (2008). Panic disorder and agoraphobia. In D. H. Barlow (Ed.), *Clinical handbook of psychological disorders: A step-by-step treatment manual* (4th ed., pp. 1–64). New York: Guilford.
Craske, M. G., Rowe, M., Lewin, M., & Noriega-Dimitri, R. (1997). Interoceptive exposure versus breathing retraining within cognitive-behavioral treatment for panic disorder with agoraphobia. *British Journal of Clinical Psychology, 36,* 85–99.
Cuijpers, P., van Straten, A.-M., & Andersson, G. (2008). Internet-administered cognitive behavior therapy for health problems: A systematic review. *Journal of Behavioral Medicine, 31,* 169–177.
Eaton, W. W., Kessler, R. C., Wittchen, H. U., & Magee, W. J. (1994). Panic and panic disorder in the United States. *American Journal of Psychiatry, 41,* 413–420.
Echeburúa, E., Corral, P., & Fernández-Montalvo, J. (2000). Escala de inadaptación (EI): Propiedades psicométricas en contextos clínicos. *Análisis y Modificación de Conducta, 107*(26), 325–338.
Ehlers, A. (1990). *Driving history interview and driving concerns questionnaire.* Unpublished tests.
Ellard, K. K., Fairholme, C. P., Boisseau, C. L., Farchione, T. J., & Barlow, D. H. (2010). Unified protocol for the treatment of the transdiagnostic treatment of emotional disorders: Protocol development and initial outcome data. *Cognitive and Behavioral Practice, 17,* 88–101.
First, M. B., Spitzer, R. L., Gibbon, M., & Williams, J. B. W. (1996). *Structured clinical interview for DSM-IV Axis I disorders—Patient edition (SCID-I/P, Version 2.0).* New York: Biometrics Research Department, New York State Psychiatric Institute.
García-Palacios, A., Botella, C., Hoffman, H., & Fabregat, S. (2007). Comparing acceptance and refusal rates of virtual reality exposure vs. in vivo exposure by patients with specific phobias. *Cyberpsychology and Behavior, 10,* 722–724.
Goodwin, R. D., Faravelli, C., Rosi, S., Cosci, F., Truglia, E., de Graaf, R., & Wittchen, H. U. (2005). The epidemiology of panic disorder and agoraphobia in Europe. *European Neuropsychopharmacology, 15,* 435–443.
Gould, R. A., Otto, M. W., & Pollack, M. H. (1995). A meta-analysis of treatment outcome for PD. *Clinical Psychology Review, 15,* 819–844.
Guy, W. (1976). *ECDEU. Assessment manual for psychopharmacology revised.* NIMH Publ. DHEW Publ. No (Adm), pp. 76–338.
Horwath, E., Cohen, R. S., & Weissman, M. M. (2002). Epidemiology of depressive and anxiety disorders. In M. T. Tsuang & M. Tohen (Eds.), *Textbook in psychiatric epidemiology* (2nd ed.). New York: Wiley-Liss.
Iketani, T., Kiriike, N., Stein, M. B., Nagao, K., Nagata, T., Minamikawa, N., Shidao, A., & Fukuhara, H. (2002). Relationship between perfectionism, personality disorders and agoraphobia in patients with panic disorder. *Acta Psychiatrica Scandinavica, 106,* 171–178.
Jang, D. P., Ku, J. H., Shin, M. B., Choi, Y. H., & Kim, S. I. (2000). Objective validation of the effectiveness of virtual reality psychotherapy. *Cyberpsychology and Behavior, 3,* 369–374.

Kessler, R. C., & Greenberg, P. E. (2002). The economic burden of anxiety and stress disorders. In L. D. Kennet, D. Charney, J. T. Coyle, & C. H. Nemeroff (Eds.), *Neuropsychopharmacology: The fifth generation of progress* (pp. 981–991). Philadelphia: Lippincott Williams & Wilkins.

Kessler, R. C., Chiu, W. T., Demler, O., & Walters, E. E. (2005). Prevalence, severity, and comorbidity of 12-month DSM-IV disorders in the national comorbidity survey replication. *Archives of General Psychiatry, 62,* 617–627.

Kessler, R. C., Heeringa, S., Lakoma, M. D., Petukhova, M., Rupp, A. E., Schoenbaum, M., et al. (2008). Individual and societal effects of mental disorders on earnings in the United States: Results from the national comorbidity survey replication. *American Journal of Psychiatry, 165,* 703–711.

King, S. A., & Poulos, S. T. (1998). Using the Internet to treat generalizad social phobia and avoidant personality disorder. *Cyberpsychology and Behavior, 1,* 29–36.

Kiropoulos, L. A., Klein, B., Austin, D. W., Gilson, K., Pier, C., Mitchell, J., et al. (2008). Is Internet-based CBT for panic disorder and agoraphobia as effective as face-to-face CBT? *Journal of Anxiety Disorders, 22,* 1273–1284.

Klein, B., Richards, J. C., & Austin, D. W. (2006). Efficacy of internet therapy for panic disorder. *Journal of Behavior Therapy and Experimental Psychiatry, 37,* 213–238.

Magee, W. J., Eaton, W. W., Wittchen, H. U., McGonagle, K. A., & Kessler, R. C. (1996). Agoraphobia, simple phobia, and social phobia in the national comorbidity survey. *Archives of General Psychiatry, 53,* 159–168.

Margraf, J., Barlow, D. H., Clark, D. M., & Telch, M. J. (1993). Psychological treatment of panic: Work in progress on outcome, active ingredients, and follow-up. *Behaviour Research and Therapy, 31,* 1–8.

Marks, I. M. (1978). Behavioral psychotherapy of adult neurosis. In S. L. Gardfield & A. E. Bergin (Eds.), *Handbook of psychotherapy and behaviour change* (pp. 493–598). New York: Wiley.

Marks, I. M. (1992). Tratamiento de exposición en la agorafobia y el pánico. In E. Echeburúa (Ed.), *Avances en el tratamiento psicológico de los trastornos de ansiedad* (pp. 35–55). Madrid: Pirámide.

Marks, I. M., & Mathews, A. M. (1979). Brief standard self-rating for phobic patients. *Behaviour Research and Therapy, 17,* 263–267.

Mayou, R., Bryant, B., & Duthie, R. (1993). Psychiatric consequences of road traffic accidents. *British Medical Journal, 307,* 647–651.

McCabe, R. E., Ashbaugh, A. R., & Antony, M. M. (2010). Specific and social phobia. In M. M. Antony & D. H. Barlow (Eds.), *Assessment and treatment planning for psychological disorders*. New York: Guilford.

Menzies, R. G., & Clarke, J. C. (1995). The etiology of acrophobia and its relationship to severity and individual response patterns. *Behaviour Research and Therapy, 33,* 795–803.

Moore, K., Wiederhold, B. K., Wiederhold, M. D., & Riva, G. (2002). The Impact of the Internet, multimedia and virtual reality on behavior and society. *Cyberpsychology and Behavior, 5*(3), 197–202.

Morisette, S. B., Bitran, S., & Barlow, D. H. (2010). Panic disorder and agoraphobia. In M. M. Antony & D. H. Barlow (Eds.), *Assessment and treatment planning for psychological disorders*. New York: Guilford.

Norcross, J., Hedges, M., & Prochaska, J. (2002). The face of 2010: A Delphi poll on the future of psychotherapy. *Professional Psychology: Research and Practice, 33,* 316–322.

North, M. M., North, S. M., & Coble, J. R. (1996). Effectiveness of virtual environment desensitization in the treatment of agoraphobia. *Presence, Teleoperators and Virtual Environments, 5*(4), 346–352.

Olatunji, B. O., Deacon, B. J., & Abramowitz, J. S. (2009). The cruelest cure? Ethical issues in the implementation of exposure-based treatments. *Cognitive and Behavioral Practice, 16,* 172–180.

Otto, M. W., Pollack, M. H., & Maki, K. M. (2000). Empirically supported treatments for panic disorder: Costs, benefits, and stepped care. *Journal of Consulting and Clinical Psychology, 68*(4), 556–563.

Parsons, T. D., & Rizzo, A. A. (2008). Affective outcomes of virtual reality exposure therapy for anxiety and specific phobias: A meta-analysis. *Journal of Behavior Therapy and Experimental Psychiatry, 39,* 250–261.

Pérez-Ara, M. A., Quero, S., Botella, C., Baños, R., Andreu-Mateu, S., Garcia-Palacios, A., & Breton-Lopez, J. (2010). Virtual reality interoceptive exposure for the treatment of panic disorder and agoraphobia. *Studies in Health Psychology and Informatics, 154,* 77–81.

Powers, M. B., & Emmelkamp, P. (2008). Virtual reality exposure therapy for anxiety disorders: A meta-analysis. *Journal of Anxiety Disorders, 22,* 561–564.

Reiss, S., Peterson, R., Gursky, D. M., & McNally, R. J. (1986). Anxiety sensitivity, anxiety frequency and the prediction of fearfulness. *Behaviour Research and Therapy, 24,* 1–8.

Richard, D. C. S., & Gloster, A. T. (2007). Exposure therapy has a public relations problem: A dearth of litigation amid a wealth of concern. In D. C. S. Richard & D. Lauterbach (Eds.), *Comprehensive handbook of the exposure therapies* (pp. 409–425). New York: Academic Press.

Richards, J. C., Klein, B., & Austin, D. W. (2006). Internet CBT for panic disorder: Does the inclusion of stress management improve end-state functioning? *Clinical Psychologist, 10,* 2–15.

Rochlen, A. B., Zack, J. S., & Speyer (2004). Online therapy: Review of relevant definitions, debates, and current empirical support. *Journal of Clinical Psychology, 60,* 269–283.

Salkovskis, P. M., & Clark, D. M. (1991). Cognitive treatment of panic disorder. *Journal of Cognitive Psychotherapy, 3,* 215–226.

Schmidt, N. B., & Telch, M. J. (1997). Non-psychiatric medical comorbidity, health perceptions, and treatment outcome in patients with panic disorder. *Health Psychology, 16,* 114–122.

Segal, R., Bathia, M., & Drapeau, M. (2010). Therapists' perception of benefits and costs of using virtual reality treatments. *Cyberpsychology, Behavior and Social Networking, 14,* 1–6.

Shear, M. K., & Maser, J. D. (1994). Standardized assessment for panic disorder research. A conference report. *Archives of General Psychiatry, 51,* 346–354.

Shear, M. K., Sholomskas, D., & Cloitre, M. (1992). *The panic disorder severity scale.* Department of Psychiatry, University of Pittsburgh, Pittsburg, Pennsylvania.

Spek, V., Cuijpers, P., Nyklicek, I., Riper, H., Keyzer, J., & Pop, V. (2007). Internet-based cognitive behaviour therapy for symptoms of depression and anxiety: A meta-analysis. *Psychological Medicine, 37,* 319–328.

Spielberger, C. D., Gorsuch, R. L., & Lushene, R. (1970). *Manual for the state-trait anxiety inventory.* Palo Alto: Consulting Psychologists Press (TEA, 1988).

Townend, M., & Grant, A. (2006). Integrating science, practice and reflexivity-cognitive therapy with driving phobia. *Journal of Psychiatric and Mental Health Nursing, 13,* 554–561.

Vincelli, F., Choi, Y. H., Molinari, E., Wiederhold, B. K., & Riva, G. (2000). Experiential cognitive therapy for the treatment of panic disorder with agoraphobia: Definition of a clinical protocol. *Cyberpsychology and Behavior, 3,* 375–385.

Vincelli, F., Anolli, L., Bouchard, S., Wiederhold, B. K., Zurloni, V., & Riva, G. (2003). Experiential cognitive therapy in the treatment of panic disorder with agoraphobia: A controlled study. *Cyberpsychology and Behavior, 6,* 321–328.

Wald, J. (2004). Efficacy of virtual reality exposure therapy for driving phobia: A multiple baseline across-subjects design. *Behavior Therapy, 35,* 621–635.

Wald, J., & Taylor, S. (2001). Efficacy of virtual reality exposure therapy to treat driving phobia: A case report. *Journal of Behaviour Therapy and Experimental Psychiatry, 31,* 249–257.

Walshe, D. G., Lewis, E. J., Kim, S. I., O'Sullivan, K., & Wiederhold, B. K. (2003). Exploring the use of computer games and virtual reality in exposure therapy for fear of driving following a motor vehicle accident. *Cyberpsychology and Behavior, 6,* 329–334.

Weissman, M. M., Bland, R. C., Canino, G. J., Faravelli, C., Greenwald, S., Hwu, H. G., et al. (1997). The cross-national epidemiology of panic disorder. *Archives of General Psychiatry, 54,* 305–309.

Wittchen, H. U., & Jacobi, F. (2005). Size and burden of mental disorders in Europe: A critical review and appraisal of 27 studies. *European Neuropsychopharmacology, 15,* 357–376.

Wolfe, B. E., & Maser, J. D. (Eds.). (1994). *Treatment of panic disorder: A consensus development conference.* Washington, DC: American Psychiatric Association.

Wolitsky-Taylor, K. B., Horowitz, J. D., Powers, M. B., & Telch, M. J. (2008). Psychological approaches in the treatment of specific phobias: A meta-analysis. *Clinical Psychology Review, 28*, 1021–1037.

Woody, S. R., & Sanderson, W. C. (1998). Manuals for empirically supported treatments: 1998 update. *The Clinical Psychologist, 51*, 17–21.

World Health Organization (WHO). (2005). Road traffic injuries. http://www.who.int/violence_injury_prevention/road_traffic/en/. Accessed 1 April 2012.

Zimmermann, P., Wittchen, H. U., Hofler, M., Pfister, H., Kessler, R. C., & Lieb, R. (2003). Primary anxiety disorders and the development of subsequent alcohol use disorders: A 4-year community study of adolescents and young adults. *Psychological Medicine, 33*, 1211–1222.

Zlomke, K., & Davis, T. E. (2008). One-session treatment of specific phobias: A detailed description and review of treatment efficacy. *Behavior Therapy, 39*, 207–223.

Chapter 9
Social Anxiety Disorder: Efficacy and Virtual Humans

Stéphane Bouchard, Jessie Bossé, Claudie Loranger and Évelyne Klinger

9.1 Key Variables Involved in Social Phobia

According to the *Diagnostic and Statistical Manual of Mental Disorders*, 4th Edition, Text Revision (*DSM*-IV-TR; APA 2000) and the International Classification of Diseases (ICD)-10 (WHO 1992), the excessive, unreasonable, and persistent fear of social situations and social interactions is known as social phobia or social anxiety disorder (SAD). Individuals suffering from SAD dread social interactions because they fear scrutiny or negative judgment from others. Hence, interaction with other people can automatically bring on feelings of self-consciousness, judgment, evaluation, and inferiority and can lead to feelings of inadequacy, embarrassment, humiliation, and depression (Légeron and Tanneau 1998; Pélissolo and Lépine 1996). A diagnosis is appropriate only when the avoidance, fear, or anxiety related to the anticipation of a social interaction interferes significantly with one's everyday life. The *DSM*-IV-TR classification distinguishes two forms of social anxiety disorder: a generalized and a specific form. When anticipatory anxiety, worry, indecision, depression, embarrassment, feelings of inferiority, and self-blame are involved across most life situations, a generalized form of SAD is usually at work (André and Légeron 1995). Conversely, the specific form of SAD is present when fear is related to a single performance situation (e.g. speaking in public) or multiple performance situations, but not related to social interaction situations. According to Clark and Beck (2011), there is an important debate on the validity of the generalized versus specific distinction in social phobia. Since *DSM*-IV-TR criteria are ambiguous, researchers tend to employ different definitions of the specific social phobia subtype. Thus, it sometimes makes it difficult to compare results from different researchers. Another fundamental problem with social phobia subtypes is that this mental disorder seems to lie on a continuum of severity with no clear-cut boundaries (Clark and Beck 2011). A hierarchical classification of social anxiety has also been proposed (Holt et al. 1992), with four domains of fear: performance anxiety (speaking in public), intimacy anxiety (establishing contacts, small talk), assertiveness anxiety (protecting one's interests, point of views, being respected), and observation anxiety (acting while being under scrutiny). It is very likely that the next version of the *DSM* will limit subtyping to "performance only" to distinguish people who are struggling with the full features of SAD from those whose fears are limited to public speaking or playing in concerts.

According to the National Comorbidity Survey (NCS) and the National Comorbidity Survey Replication (NCS-R; Kessler et al. 1994, 2005a, b), the 12-month and lifetime prevalence of SAD could be as high as 8 and 13%, respectively. This disease, which is one of the most frequently occurring mental disorders, has an age onset that varies between 15 and 20 and is about equally distributed in women and men (11% among males and 15% among females according to the NCS). This disorder is often accompanied by significant social disabilities and exposes the subject to severe complications such as depression, suicide, alcoholism, etc. (Kessler et al. 1998). In an epidemiological survey conducted in the USA by Grant et al. (2005), lifetime prevalence of SAD was associated with lifetime prevalence of personality disorders (55.4%), mood disorders (56.3%), other anxiety disorders (54.1%), and alcohol use disorders (48.2%). Such findings indicate the necessity of thorough clinical assessments, since comorbidity seems to be very common in social phobic patients. Furthermore, Wang et al. (2005) studied mental health-care services usage among the NCS-R sample. Results indicated that <25% of respondents diagnosed with SAD sought help from any mental health-care services in the last 12-month period prior to assessment.

People with SAD usually experience significant emotional distress accompanied by physiological manifestations that may include intense fear, racing heart, blushing, excessive sweating, dry throat and mouth, trembling, difficulty swallowing and muscle twitches, particularly in the face and neck areas. In addition, individuals suffering from SAD display an array of cognitive biases (Clark 2001; Clark and Wells 1995). More precisely, social phobics are known to make more negative and threatening interpretations of ambiguous social situations, have unrealistic expectations about how they should perform during social interactions (expectations of perfection), discount positive cues, and fail to recognize positive outcomes during interpersonal interactions. Social phobics are also known to overly focus on themselves and to closely monitor their inner processes (self-focused attention) during social interactions, which in return increase anxiety levels. In order to cope with the anxiety generated by such cognitive biases, social phobics will develop what is known as safety behaviors; they consist of subtle behaviors carried out in order to avoid or decrease the risk of negative evaluation on behalf of others (e.g., contracting muscles to reduce shaking; Clark 2001; Clark and Wells 1995).

Studies in the field of neurobiology are providing an interesting support to our understanding of SAD and the underlying mechanisms involved in the disorder. It has been found that when evaluating social stimuli, individuals suffering from SAD show an exaggerated amygdala response, a part of the brain involved in emotional regulation, threat detection, and activation of the fear response (Furmark 2009). There is also evidence that activation of frontocortical regions involved in top-down inhibitory processes is compromised in social phobics, which prevents proper regulation of the overactive amygdala during social situations. In that same direction, Liao et al. (2010) found an increased interconnectivity between the hyperactive amygdala and the hypoactive orbitofrontal cortex in social phobics, which may contribute to the emotional dysregulation commonly seen in social phobics. However, the prefrontal inhibitory control hypothesis elicits controversy, as conflicting results have been found. Recent studies have found an increased activation of prefrontal brain areas (medial prefrontal cortex and dorsolateral prefrontal cortex), which could possibly indicate social phobics' efforts to control their emotions or that self-focused thoughts are at play (Brühl et al. 2011). Most interesting, however, is to observe neurophysiological changes occurring after receiving cognitive-behavior therapy (CBT), as shown for example, by Goldin et al. (2013). Further studies are needed in order to better understand the mechanisms involved in the limbic system and the role of frontocortical brain areas in SAD.

9.2 Description of Significant Efficacy Studies Using Non-Virtual-Reality Approaches

Research has shown that two forms of treatment may well be of value in SAD: drugs (Liebowitz et al. 1992) and CBT (Mersch 1994). A few studies have directly compared the efficacy of CBT and pharmacotherapy for SAD and are suggesting that CBT is superior or at least clearly not inferior (Canton et al. 2012; Clark et al. 2003; Rodebaugh et al. 2004).

CBT is among the treatments of choice for SAD (Canton et al. 2012; Heimberg et al. 1995; Servant 2002). Indeed, it is the most well-researched class of psychosocial treatment for SAD and meta-analyses show that all forms of CBT seem likely to provide some benefit for adults (Canton et al. 2012; Rodebaugh et al. 2004; Clark et al. 2006; Stangier et al. 2011). In addition, researches generally present large effect sizes for this treatment (Butler et al. 2006), with success rates up to 70 or 80 % (Clark et al. 2006; Stangier et al. 2011). CBT is considered to structure its treatment strategies around three different mechanisms, depending on the model privileged by researchers (Barlow and Lehman 1996): (a) through a regular and prolonged confrontation of the subject to anxiety-producing social situations (i.e., classical exposure model based in extinction), (b) through a modification of the subject's thoughts and of her/his assessments of social situations (cognitive therapy using exposure as an opportunity to build confidence in alternative and more functional beliefs), and (c) through the learning of more efficient relational behaviors (assertiveness therapy).

Exposure to anxious social situations seems essential for effective treatment of SAD in order to correct patients' maladaptive interpretations, beliefs, and behaviors (Clark 2001; Clark and Beck 2011; Légeron and Tanneau 1998). Thus, it is a key ingredient of most CBT treatments, despite differences in ways to apply it under classical extinction models or more cognitive and neo-conditioning model of building new associations with lack of threat (see Chap. 5 for more information on models of exposure). Traditionally, exposure to social situations is done either *in vivo* or in imagination. The latter is often carried out when a confrontation to real situations is difficult to achieve, with the major drawback of reproducing imperfectly the situations. Initiating a conversation, introducing oneself to a stranger, making a telephone call, making a speech, eating in public, making errors purposefully during a speech, and behaving ridiculously are typical examples of exposure for SAD (Abramowitz et al. 2011; Heimberg and Becker 2002).

More recently, a few research teams have empirically evaluated the impact of different CBT components to treat SAD. For example, in 2011, Stangier et al. compared CBT to interpersonal psychotherapy. One hundred and six patients diagnosed with SAD were randomly assigned to one of the two treatment conditions or a waiting list. The CBT was derived from Clark and Wells' (1995) model of SAD. For patients in treatment both conditions, treatment consisted of up to 16 weekly sessions. All SAD measures at posttreatment indicated that both treatments were superior to the wait-list. However, results at posttreatment and at the 1-year follow-up revealed that CBT was statistically superior to interpersonal psychotherapy. On the whole, these findings illustrate the efficacy of CBT (see Acarturk et al. 2009 for other examples).

As mentioned in Chap. 5, how exposure is conducted might however influence treatment success. In 2009, Rapee et al. randomly assigned 195 adults suffering from SAD to three different treatment conditions: standard CBT, "enhanced" CBT, or stress management training (nonspecific treatment control condition). Their standard or basic CBT program included cognitive restructuring, *in vivo* exposure and assertiveness or general social skills training (toward the end of the treatment). In the enhanced CBT condition, sessions also covered cognitive restructuring and *in vivo* exposure, but with an overlap between both techniques, with exposure being conducted in a more cognitive style of evidence-gathering or hypothesis testing instead of relying on a simple extinction paradigm. Moreover, the enhanced CBT included additional strategies like the identification and refutation of the individuals' broader or underlying beliefs, elimination of safety behaviors and subtle avoidance, realistic appraisal, performance feedback, and attention retraining. Finally, the control condition in the study, stress management, essentially focused on relaxation, problem-solving, time management, and healthy lifestyle habits. For the three conditions, treatment was delivered in a group format (of approximately six participants) of 2-h sessions across 12 weeks. As hypothesized, the authors found that the enhanced treatment was overall superior to the basic CBT, although basic CBT was efficacious and generally superior to nonspecific stress management training (Rapee et al. 2009). Even if this study lacks follow-up and therapy was delivered in a group format, it reveals two points that are relevant for this book. First, anxiety disorders presented in Chap. 8 and above involve treatments that are more complex than specific phobias. Not only avoidance and neutralization behaviors must be controlled and eliminated during exposure but also the way exposure is presented and integrated with other treatment components matters. Second, there are ways to increase the efficacy of exposure. This issue will be addressed in more detail in this chapter.

9.3 Description of Studies Using Virtual Reality to Treat Social Anxiety Disorder

Advances in the field of virtual reality (VR) offer the exciting possibility of creating sufficiently realistic virtual humans or avatars (i.e., a virtual representation of a person) and use them as therapeutic tools in the treatment of SAD. Such possibility has not gone unnoticed, as many researchers are already studying the option of integrating computer-generated humans in psychotherapy. At first, researchers investigated the efficacy of VR in the treatment of the specific anxiety subtype of SAD, more precisely the fear of public speaking (Harris et al. 2002; North et al. 1998). As this chapter will illustrate, the use of virtual human was progressively extended from exposure for people suffering from fear of public speaking, to targeting fear of public speaking in people suffering from SAD, to finally addressing the full feature of SAD with various situations more complex to reproduce than a conference room or an auditorium full of people.

North et al. were the first to publish a study for people diagnosed with the specific phobia of public speaking. They compared eight people receiving *in virtuo*[1] exposure to eight people in a control condition (North et al. 1998). Patients in the active treatment condition were exposed to a VR public scene, a virtual lecture theatre with a large audience, and guided to manage their phobias. Participants in the control condition were exposed to a trivial VR scene and were advised by the experimenters to manage their fear and expose themselves on their own, without any systematic treatment program. The treatment was carried out through five weekly sessions, each lasting between 10 and 20 min. A variety of outcome measures were used, from questionnaires (i.e., Attitude Towards Public Speaking Questionnaire and Subjective Units of Discomfort, SUD) to objective measures such as heart rate. A series of paired t tests indicated that the six participants who completed the *in virtuo* exposure treatment showed significant improvement after 5 weeks of treatment (see Fig. 9.1), while no meaningful changes were noticed in the control condition. Based on these analyses, the authors concluded that exposure in VR was successful to reduce fear of public speaking.

From the same research team, Harris et al. (2002) selected 14 university students whose Personal Report of Confidence as a Speaker (PRCS; Paul 1966) scores were > 16 and assigned them to two conditions: *in virtuo* exposure treatment or waiting list. The treatment group was exposed to a virtual auditorium scene. The treatment was delivered by a therapist in four weekly sessions, each lasting 12–15 min. Assessment measures included four self-report inventories, SUD during *in virtuo* exposure and physiological measures of heart rate during speaking tasks. Results of *in virtuo* exposure indicated that the treatment sessions were associated with significant reductions in public speaking anxiety in university students in most measures, and almost significant difference not in the only measure addressing SAD

---

[1] *In virtuo* is a termed coined by Tisseau to refer to "in virtual reality," which is an expression consistent with others such as *in vivo* to describe exposure "in real life." It should be privileged over "virtual exposure" or "virtual therapy," because the exposure and the therapy are real, not virtual.

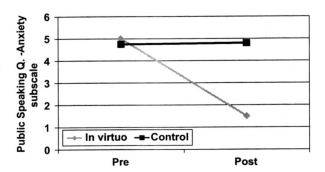

Fig. 9.1 Illustration of the results from North et al. (1998) comparing *in virtuo* exposure and a no intervention control condition on one of their measures of fear of public speaking

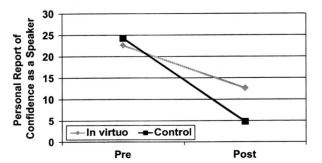

Fig. 9.2 Illustration of the results from Harris et al. (2002) comparing *in virtuo* exposure and a waiting-list control condition on the PCRS

(the Liebowitz Social Anxiety Scale, LSAS; Liebowitz 1987). When compared to the waiting list, the only significant difference at posttreatment was on the PRCS (See Fig. 9.2).

In order to compare *in virtuo* exposure to another active treatment, and focus on apprehension instead of anxiety or avoidance, Heuett and Heuett (2011) recruited 80 students from a general public speaking course and assigned them to a one-session immersion in VR, one-session visualization exercise, or a no-intervention condition. As in the case of North et al. (1998) study, only a series of *t* tests were performed to compare pre–post scores within the in three experimental conditions. Their results show improvements in the *in virtuo* exposure condition in willingness to communicate, self-perceived communication competence and apprehension to communicate. For those in the visualization condition, results were similar except for a lack of improvement in self-perceived communication competence. No change was observed in the no-intervention condition. This study is not describing a treatment per se, but professionals training people to master their public speaking skills and reduce their level of social anxiety when communicating in public had until now the only options of either practicing in groups or use visualization.

In exploring alternative technologies to conduct exposure, Lister et al. (2010) tested a stereoscopic (3D) television. They randomly assigned 15 participants to either four sessions of exposure in front of a virtual audience, or a waiting list. The treatment consisted of waiting 2 min for a virtual audience to pay attention to the

9.3 Description of Studies Using Virtual Reality to Treat Social Anxiety Disorder

Fig. 9.3 Screenshots of virtual environments developed by Virtually Better Inc.: A small meeting room used in early studies on fear of public speaking (*left*), and a more recent version of a virtual classroom (*right*). © Copyright Virtually Better, Inc. All rights reserved

patient, followed by the patient reading a book to the audience for a few minutes. Paired *t* test revealed improvements in the active intervention on the state anxiety measure and negative self-statements during public speaking, and no change in positive self-statements or on the general measure of social anxiety. Although the treatment intervention could exploit much more the potential of exposure, these results suggest that less immersive technologies could be used with people suffering from fear of public speaking.

So far, this chapter has presented only small trials. These were all pioneer work that paved the way for more robust studies and revealed that fear of something as complex to reliably reproduce such as a virtual audience could be triggered and conquered with synthetic stimuli. The first randomized clinical trial on *in virtuo* exposure for public speaking anxiety was realized by a group from Israel (Safir et al. 2012; Wallach et al. 2009). A total of 88 participants completed a study where they were randomly assigned to CBT with exposure *in virtuo*, CBT with exposure in imagination, or a wait-list control condition. Both treatment conditions included 12 individual 1-h sessions administered following a standardized protocol. They also shared the same cognitive treatment components, such as presentation of the cognitive model of SAD, identification of automatic thoughts or thinking errors, and cognitive restructuring. As for the behavioral treatment components, they included the rational for graded in-session exposure. A VFX3D head-mounted display (HMD; from Interactive Imaging Systems Inc.) and virtual environments designed by Virtually Better Inc. (see Fig. 9.3) were used to conduct *in virtuo* exposure. Statistically significant results for the majority of self-rating questionnaires allowed the authors to conclude that both treatments were effective treatments for public speaking anxiety. CBT combined with conducting exposure *in virtuo* or *in imago* was superior to the waiting list, no differences were found between the two methods of delivering exposure, and results were maintained at the 1-year follow-up (Safir et al. 2012; see Fig. 9.4). Results were assessed with a variety of instruments pertaining to the fear of public speaking, and also to SAD, notably with the use of the LSAS. Most interestingly, twice as many participants dropped out from the

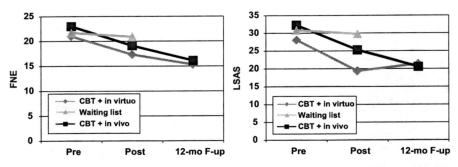

Fig. 9.4 Results from Wallach et al. (2009) and Safir et al. (2012) on the Fear of Negative Evaluation questionnaire and the fear subscale of the LSAS when comparing CBT with exposure *in virtuo*, *in vivo* and a waiting list

condition where exposure was delivered in imagination (15 participants) compared to VR (6 participants). Hence, Wallach et al. (2009) suggested that using *in virtuo* exposure may be more attractive to people suffering from public-speaking anxiety.

When looking at the efficacy of a combined treatment, some may criticize that is it hard to draw conclusions about the role of VR because the treatment protocol did not rest on pure exposure only. First, both treatments in the Wallace et al. study (2009) differ only in the format of exposure and, as documented by Heuett and Heuett (2011), imaginal exposure is often used as an option to conduct exposure. But most of all, SAD is a more complex anxiety disorder to treat than specific phobias addressed in Chaps. 4–7 of this book. For SAD, pure exposure only is hardly used outside of experimental settings. CBT naturally integrates a variety of techniques and our confidence in the strength of *in virtuo* exposure to convey change in patients is based in both research from specific phobias and pioneering studies on fear of public speaking.

The above studies were conducted with people who were significantly afraid of speaking in public, but it is unclear to what extent their condition was severe enough to warrant the diagnosis of SAD. To address this claim, a US group led by Anderson (Anderson et al. 2003, 2005, 2013; Price and Anderson 2012) conducted a large randomized control trial with people reliably diagnosed with SAD. The VR hardware and software were from Virtually Better and similar to what were used by Wallach et al. (2009). *In virtuo* exposure consisted essentially in talking to virtual audiences of various sizes, it was done in previous studies on fear of public speaking. Exposure was integrated as part of a more complete CBT manual for public speaking anxiety and SAD. The first control condition in this study was an active CBT treatment where exposure was delivered in groups. Both treatments lasted eight sessions, were delivered by trained therapists, and participants performed in about the same amount of exposure. Treatment integrity was assessed and confirmed, and the assessment battery was thorough and included a behavior avoidance test. The second control condition was a waiting list. Results at posttreatment and at the 12-month follow-up were very strong and extended results from Wallach et al. (2009) to a population of SAD sufferers. Both active treatments led to statistically

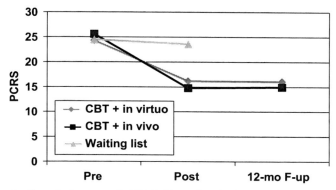

Fig. 9.5 Results from Anderson et al. (2013) illustrating the impact of CBT combined with *in virtuo* exposure, *in vivo* exposure, or a waiting list on the PCRS for people suffering from SAD treated for their fear of public speaking

significant improvement, superiors to the waiting list, and without any significant difference between the two (see Fig. 9.5). There was no difference in either process measures regarding the two treatments. Outcome expectancies were positive, working alliance was high, compliance between session homework was similar, and treatment satisfaction was high.

Interestingly, complementary analyses revealed that expectations about treatment efficacy predict improvement (Price and Anderson 2012). In both forms of exposure, treatment was more effective for participants who had higher outcome expectancies. The contribution of the feeling of presence (see Chap. 2 for more information on presence) was also assessed (Price et al. 2011), with a few more SAD patients combined to the Anderson et al. (2013) study. Presence and anxiety were assessed at each *in virtuo* exposure session and the PRCS was used to predict pre- to posttreatment improvements. The analyses revealed two pieces of important and complementary information. When measured globally, presence was related to the level of anxiety experienced during the therapy sessions but not treatment outcome. A second profile emerges when presence is examined at the level of sub-factors. Assessment of the realism of the virtual stimuli was related to in-session anxiety but not treatment outcome, whereas involvement (keeping attention focused to virtual stimuli and not paying attention to incongruent information) was the only factor associated with treatment outcome. Spatial presence, or the illusion of being *in* the virtual environment (i.e., somewhere else than the therapist's office), did not predict in-session anxiety nor treatment success. These findings have interesting implications for the role of presence and are consistent with idea of perceptual illusion described in Chap. 2. The place illusion has a significant "wow" factor when users are immersed in VR and it may be an important target when developing games, attractions, or artistic installations. But what matters for eliciting anxiety is rather that key threatening ingredients be present. Although exposure must elicit some anxiety to lead to emotional learning and the development of sound associations with lack of threat, the level of anxiety experienced during exposure is a poor predictor of treatment success (Clark 2001; Rachman 1990). What should matter is essentially processing threat-related information to develop new mental representations with lack of threat.

As it became possible to create virtual humans that are more subtle, realistic, and can be integrated in more complex environments, researchers and clinicians developed treatment protocols that address the broad spectrum of social situations and interactions (e.g., Klinger et al. 2005; Robillard et al. 2010). A research laboratory specialized in virtual humans in Switzerland developed and tested complex social scenarios for SAD and *in virtuo* exposure, using probably for the first time virtual humans that were entirely computer generated (Riquier et al. 2005; Herbelin et al. 2005). In 2006, Grillon et al. published their findings. They conducted a study with eight adults diagnosed with SAD in order to measure the effectiveness of CBT with *in virtuo* exposure, and also to assess its flexibility as a treatment adjunct and gain some insight into the treatment processes of *in virtuo* exposure. Their treatment protocol is different from previous researches since their CBT treatment was delivered in a group format for one session (that included giving a speech) combined by immersions in eight individual sessions using VR. The authors suggest this combination allowed patients to practice skills learnt in individual sessions in a real social situation, realize while seeing others that "things can change," share difficulties with people living similar problems, and encourage each other in their progress (Grillon et al. 2006). As for *in virtuo* exposure, several virtual scenes were developed: public speaking situations or interacting with virtual characters of both genders in locations such as an office, a cafeteria, or a bar. The virtual characters had prerecorded sentences that could be triggered when needed. They also had different facial expressions and could stare at the user. Every week, patients would be given a theme to prepare and practice a speech that they would have to pronounce in front of the virtual characters. In order to increase the level of anxiety between each session, the virtual scenes were always different and the themes would get more personal. The immersion in VR was modified every week to fit patients' needs according to their subjective levels of anxiety. For example, people who did not feel enough anxious during the last sessions of *in virtuo* exposure were asked to recite a poem or sing, or tolerate being stared at by others in the bar. The immersion was performed using a HMD and, before and after each exposure session, patients were immersed in a 3-min test scene where an eye-tracking system was used to document eye contact with the virtual characters. Results were examined only qualitatively, due to sample size. Out of eight participants, six showed improvements on most of the measures, including the LSAS. As for the eye-tracking test, it suggests that pretreatment patients tended to avoid looking at the virtual humans, especially the face. However, after treatment, eye contact behavior changed for most patients, with a reduction in eye contact avoidance.

These findings are in line with previous studies showing that people suffering from SAD react emotionally to synthetic humans, although not only when performing in front of a virtual crow but also when interacting directly with computer-generated people. A smaller pilot study was also reported from another group that used interactions with virtual humans in a bank to treat during eight CBT

Fig. 9.6 Screenshots of virtual environments for SAD developed by Klinger et al. (2002) and used by Klinger et al. (2005) for assertiveness situations (*left*) or intimate social gathering (*right*). (Screenshots courtesy of Évelyne Klinger)

sessions a person suffering from SAD (Moussaoui et al. 2010). They reported good improvements in the patient, including on the LSAS.

A more robust clinical trial was conducted in France by Klinger et al. (2005), which was built around four virtual environments that dealt with performance, intimacy, scrutiny, and assertiveness. The sample consisted of 36 participants diagnosed with SAD assigned to either CBT with *in virtuo* exposure or group CBT with *in vivo* exposure. Participants were allocated to each group according to practical constraints such as the ability to use computers and maintain homogeneity on significant criteria (gender, age, severity of SAD, etc.). Both treatments lasted as 12 weekly sessions and were delivered according to a manual. More precisely, participants in the CBT with *in virtuo* exposure condition attended 45-min individual sessions with exposure exercises lasting 20 min or less, while patients in the group-CBT with *in vivo* exposure condition met for 2 h in groups of approximately eight persons. Their exposure exercises were done in session and focused on various social concerns (i.e., not only speaking in public). Each virtual environment depicts a specific story board and was used for two consecutive sessions. With the help of the therapist, the patient learned adapted cognitions and behaviors in order to reduce anxiety in the corresponding real situations. For example, in the "assertiveness" environment, patients had to practice protecting their interests and to be respected in a shoe store were employees would try repeatedly to sell them shoes (see Fig. 9.6). In order to learn how to establish contact with neighbors or friends and to have small talk, participants were immersed in the "intimacy" environment presenting an apartment with guests. To address observation anxiety, a "scrutiny" environment was designed with many people looking at the patient in a coffee shop. Finally, as in previous studies on fear of public speaking, participants had to give a speech in a meeting room in the "performance" environment. All virtual environments were displayed on a large monitor screen. Results showed statistically and clinically significant improvement in both conditions (see Fig. 9.7). The effect sizes comparing the efficacy of both forms of exposure revealed that the differences between the

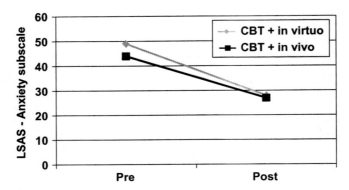

Fig. 9.7 Illustration of trivial differences in efficacy when comparing CBT for SAD with all exposure exercises conducted *in virtuo* or *in vivo* by Klinger et al. (2005)

two treatments were trivial (Klinger et al. 2005) and a sample size between 300 and 3000 participants would be required to detect a statistically significant difference (which, if significant would favor *in virtuo* exposure).

Following the collaborations established during the Klinger et al. (2005) study, a full randomized control trial for SAD was conducted in Canada (Bouchard et al. 2011; Robillard et al. 2010). In this study, 54 adults receiving a diagnosis of SAD were randomly assigned to CBT with traditional *in vivo* exposure, CBT with *in virtuo* exposure, and a waiting list. Participants in the active treatment conditions received 16 individual sessions of therapy with exposure sessions (only either *in vivo* or *in virtuo*) conducted every week. The virtual environments were varied and those created by Klinger (see Klinger et al. 2005) were used, as well as those for fear of public speaking developed by Virtually Better Inc., or the job interview developed by Virtually Better Inc. for stuttering. All *in virtuo* exposure exercises were conducted in immersions using an eMagin z800 3D Visor and its built-in motion tracker. Treatment integrity was maintained by reliance on a treatment manual adapted from Clark (2001) and assessment included anxiety scales and self-report questionnaires (e.g. LSAS, SAD Scale, Fear of Negative Evaluation, Beck Depression Inventory II) and a Behavior Avoidance Test. Cortisol samples were also collected for a portion of the sample. Two sets of analyses were performed: (a) classical statistical inferences tests to find differences between the two active treatments and (b) noninferiority tests to document with statistical tests the lack of difference between the two active treatments. Results with the final sample and the follow-up data (Bouchard et al. 2011) confirmed that both treatments were more effective than the no-treatment condition and as effective to each other. This finding is already interesting, but raises the question as to why bother with VR if it is not more effective than traditional CBT. There are at least two answers to this important question. First, Bouchard et al. (2011) also documented the efforts required by therapists to conduct the exposure sessions. And there they found important advantages of conducting exposure *in virtuo*. *In virtuo* exposure exercises were significantly less cumbersome and costly to conduct than *in vivo* ones, in terms of having access to relevant stimuli to induce ridicule, duration, preparation, worries about confidentiality, costs

9.4 Relevant Findings from Studies Using VR Approaches

Fig. 9.8 Screenshots of virtual environments where people suffering from SAD could perform intense exposure exercises, while signing to the waitress when being stared at in a restaurant (*left*) or while making jokes with a stranger at the urinals (*right*). Reproduced with permission from S. Bouchard

of gathering staff members to attend at public speaking exercises. Second, *in virtuo* exposure may become more effective than *in vivo* if clinicians were trying to take advantages of all the possibilities afforded by VR instead of trying to replicate what is done *in vivo*. Therapists using VR with SAD patients are starting only now to include findings from Bandura et al. (1982) and ask patients to do *in virtuo* things they may not dare do *in vivo* but would clearly disconfirm their fears (e.g., say inappropriate comments to a waitress in a restaurant while every customer is looking, see Fig. 9.8).

Since VR is a promising avenue for the treatment of SAD, researchers and clinicians could benefit from learning from research on virtual humans. Only a few examples of studies relevant for the treatment of SAD will be presented given the richness of investigations in the field of virtual humans.

9.4 Relevant Findings from Studies Using VR Approaches

Several studies on virtual humans have been conducted in London and Barcelona by a team lead by Mel Slater. One study that deserves mentions for its potentially interesting implication was published by Pertaub et al. (2001, 2002; Slater 2006c). They examined whether different types of virtual audiences would influence the speaker's emotional response. In their experiment, participants who were not suffering from SAD were divided into three groups, each group having to give a 5-min presentation to a different type of virtual audience: group 1 gave a speech to a static or neutral audience, group 2 gave a speech to a positive audience, and group 3 gave a speech to a negative audience. In each condition, the virtual humans were continuously animated. In the positive and negative conditions, avatars gazed at and turned their heads to visually follow the speaker, showed different facial expressions at varying levels of intensity, displayed different short behavioral animations (e.g., nodding and maintaining eye contact in the positive condition; yawning, walking out of the room; and putting their feet on the table in the negative condition), and verbally reacted to the speaker. The neutral audience remained static and did not look in the direction of the participant giving the speech. As expected, results indicated a significantly greater anxiety response among subjects in the negative audience condition (as measure by PRCS) compared to both the positive and the neutral condition. What is most intriguing is the result reported in Pertaub et al. (2001) on participant's satisfaction toward their performance. Participants were significantly less satisfied with their performance in both the positive and negative audience compared to the neutral audience. These results were hard to interpret when examined from the angle of perceived threat, as performance with the positive audience should not be frightening and given results on the PCRS. However, this result fits very well with what is observed clinically with SAD patients. One important element in the model of SAD presented in the introduction to this chapter is self-focused attention. It describes a process where people engaged in socially stressful interactions may focus more on how bad they feel than how the audience is actually reacting. Pertaub et al. (2001, 2002) participants were not diagnosed with SAD, but self-focus attention might very well explain why they were dissatisfied with their performance in both situations where the audience reacted to their speech. The role of self-focused attention in *in virtuo* exposure certainly deserves more attention and this study raises interesting questions about it.

In a similar fashion, it has been found that socially anxious subjects, when compared with nonsocially anxious subjects, show an increase in heart rate when immersed in a socially relevant virtual environment (Slater et al. 2006b). These results were obtained in an experiment using a computer-assisted virtual environment CAVE-like setting to immerse participants in a virtual bar scenario where virtual characters would interact with them. Measures showed that socially anxious subjects were more stressed throughout the bar scenario immersion. Results also showed an increase in heart rate in some subjects when avatars approached and spoke to them.

VR has also allowed researchers to learn more about SAD itself by providing ecologically valid environments to conduct various experiments. In order to test the vigilance-avoidance hypothesis (which proposes that hypervigilance to the feared stimuli is followed by its avoidance) with socially anxious people, Mühlberger et al. (2008) measured participants' visual attention in virtual social situations. According to their scores on the Social Phobia and Anxiety Inventory, participants were divided by a median-split into low and high socially anxious groups. The immersion with a V6 HMD took with a place in a virtual elevator where doors would open at 60 floors to present persons and objects during 6 s. Three different trial conditions were presented in a pseudorandomized order to the participants: (a) an angry person with a happy person; (b) a happy person with an object (a rack shelf); and (c) an angry person with an object (a rack shelf). With recordings of horizontal eye movements, initial attention (between 500 and 1000 ms after the doors opened) and sustained attention (between 1500 and 4500 ms after presentation of the virtual persons and the object) were compared. Results indicated that highly socially anxious individuals initially avoid looking at faces, especially the angry faces (Mühlberger et al. 2008). Thus, this study could not confirm the vigilance-avoidance hypothesis. Another example of the different possibilities that VR offers to study SAD is presented in a study by Vrijsen et al. (2010). The aim of this research was to compare the evaluation of mimicry by socially anxious and nonanxious women. In various social situations, people tend mimic or change their behavior to match that of the person they are interacting with. Research has shown that this unintentional behavior makes the mimicker more likeable. However, the authors hypothesized it would not be the case with socially anxious individuals. Participants were immersed twice in a virtual environment with a virtual human giving a short speech (about 140 s). Two different virtual characters were presented in a counterbalance order across participants: character A mimicked the participant, while character B mimicked the movements of the previous participant's trial. The virtual character's mimicry was based on the participant's head position recorded by a sensor on the HMD and was presented with a 4-second delay. As expected, mimicry positively affected the evaluation of the person one was interacting with, but this effect was absent in socially anxious individuals (Vrijsen et al. 2010).

These two studies thus show it is possible to conduct quality research with people suffering from SAD with the help of VR. Moreover, virtual environments add possibilities that would not exist otherwise. Whether it is to assure that the context of the experiment is ecologically valid or to properly standardize a protocol, VR seems to be a promising tool in fundamental research as well. There is a growing body of evidence suggesting that humans tend to react very similarly to virtual humans as they do with actual humans, including when it comes to social concepts biases such as skin tone bias (Rossen et al. 2008), social facilitation effects (Park and Catrambone 2007), respect of interpersonal distance (Bailenson et al. 2003), or even when replicating the well-known obedience experiment of Stanley Milgram (Slater et al. 2006a), just to name a few.

While some researchers have been studying the social aspect of the human–avatar interaction, others have been concentrating on the fine-tuning of realism levels in virtual humans in order to generate a more human-like feeling among human subjects interacting with avatars. For example, Garau et al. (2003) studied the impact of visual and behavioral realism with the help of a CAVE-like system and HMD to support the virtual interaction between dyads of human subjects impersonating avatars (Garau et al. 2003). More precisely, visual and behavioral realism were manipulated in order to examine their impact on the perceived quality of communication. The behavioral realism component was studied through eye movements or gaze. This component was manipulated in order to create two types of gaze: a random gaze, where eyes randomly moved, and an inferred gaze, where gaze was sustained more while listening than while talking. The experimental design consisted of a between-group two-by-two factor design, the two factors being low avatar realism and high avatar realism, with each factor being paired with a random gaze and an inferred gaze. Participants were matched in groups of two with same-sex partners and were randomly assigned to one of the four experimental conditions. In each dyad, one

Fig. 9.9 Graphical illustration from Garau et al. (2003) of the effect of inconsistency between visual realism of avatars and their eye-gaze behaviors

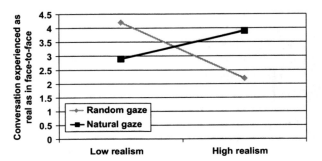

subject experienced the shared virtual environment through a HMD while the other could experience it with the help of a CAVE-like system. Participants from each dyad had the same avatar. The avatar in the low realism condition consisted of a genderless avatar looking somewhat like a matchstick character, while the avatar in the high realism condition consisted of either a male or a female avatar with human-like facial features. Subjects had the task of negotiating with one another in order to reach a mutually acceptable solution to a problem. After the experimental trial ended, participants answered questionnaires assessing perceived quality of communication and copresence. Results confirmed the presence of an interaction between avatar type and gaze type for how much the communication was perceived as if occurring in face to face (see Fig. 9.9) and copresence. As expected, the more realistic avatar displaying natural inferred gaze produced higher ratings of perceived quality of communication and copresence than random eye-gaze behavior. Actually, the random eye-gaze behavior is associated with even less natural communication and copresence than the unrealistic avatar. Results are also very informative when looking at the low realism avatar. Emitting natural inferred-gaze behaviors was associated with negative ratings in perceived quality of communication and copresence. The unrealistic avatar conveyed a more naturalistic feel and copresence when its eye-gaze behavior was unnatural and random, as opposed to natural inferred-gaze behaviors. To paraphrase the authors, consistency between the visual appearance of synthetic humans and their behavior seems to be necessary; low fidelity appearance demands low fidelity behavior, and correspondingly higher fidelity appearance demands a more realistic behavior model (p. 6). These results are in line with previous findings suggesting that higher image realism leads to heightened expectations of behavioral realism in users.

Because virtual humans are not yet replicating reliably human appearance and behaviors, much can be learned from the field of robotics when it comes to designing humanoid robots or virtual humans. Findings from fundamental research in that field could serve in improving a virtual human's aesthetic component in order to make the experience more pleasing for individuals undergoing VR-assisted therapy, for example. A popular concept in the field of robotics that deserves mention when it comes to designing virtual humans is the uncanny valley phenomenon. The uncanny valley is a term that was first used to describe human raters' sudden drop in

9.4 Relevant Findings from Studies Using VR Approaches

appreciation levels regarding avatars or humanoid robots as they became more human-like or more realistic (Mori 1970). More precisely, Mori explained that higher levels of realism in humanoid robots contributed to a better appreciation of the robot on behalf of human raters because of the familiarity of it. However, Mori warned that there is a specific point along the line where increasing realism of humanoid robots creates uneasiness and negative appreciation in human raters; the robot very closely resembles a realistic human's physique, but is not quite as realistic as an actual human. At that specific moment, raters' appreciation of the robot dramatically drops: it is what is referred in graphical displays as the uncanny valley. Some empirical research has been conducted in order to further study this phenomenon and to verify its validity as well as to eventually provide plausible explanations. Results are more nuanced than the initial theory suggested.

An example of such studies comes from Japanese researchers Seyama and Nagayama (2007). Their uncertainty in the phenomenon's validity arose from the following observation: some characters in graphic films (e.g., dolls, cartoons) are very unrealistic but still elicit pleasant reactions in observers, while some real humans elicit unpleasant reactions among other humans despite the fact that they are genuine. Hence, they conducted an experiment in which they manipulated the degree of realism of human faces while raters had to evaluate levels of pleasantness or unpleasantness in regard to images of faces randomly morphing from artificial to realistic. Their results indicated that the synchronous augmentation in degree of realism was associated with an augmentation in raters' positive appreciation of the faces. Contrary to Mori's theory, there was no drop in appreciations at any levels of augmented realism, suggesting that they was actually no uncanny valley phenomenon emerging. In a second experiment, Seyama and Nagayama (2007) evaluated raters' appreciation of faces while their eyes and head were asynchronously morphed. Conversely to their first experiment, faces now simultaneously possessed realistic and unrealistic features (e.g., 100 % real human eyes matched with 0 % real human head), which created mismatches in degrees of realism. Results indicated the presence of the uncanny valley when eyes and head showed the highest mismatch in degrees of realism, suggesting that such a mismatch may be a necessary condition for the emergence of the phenomenon. Finally, authors evaluated the respective contribution of realism and abnormality in morphing faces on raters' appreciation. Results indicated that users preferred abnormally big eyes on an unrealistic human face rather than abnormally big eyes on a realistic human face, suggesting that the abnormal characteristic of stimuli is a crucial element in the emergence of the uncanny valley. Hence, authors concluded that mismatches in degrees of realism taken alone cannot fully explain the uncanny phenomenon: the abnormal aspect of the stimuli also plays a crucial role in the occurrence of the phenomenon.

Another experiment looking to better understand the uncanny hypothesis evaluated participants' subjective ratings of robot and human video clips (MacDorman 2006). More precisely, MacDorman tested whether or not the drop in raters' appreciation was in fact due to variations in the robot's human likeliness. Raters had to evaluate robot and human videos on three different scales: a mechanical to human-like scale, a strange to familiar scale and a not eerie to extremely eerie scale. Results revealed that robots rated in a similar fashion on the mechanical to human-like scale had significantly different scores on the two other scales, indicating that a robot's human likeliness is not the only factor responsible for perceived familiarity, strangeness, and eeriness. Such findings provide insightful information on the nature of the uncanny phenomenon, since they indicate that variables other than human likeliness are at play and could be manipulated in order to avoid specific drop in users' appreciation of robots or human-like figures. In that same direction, a researcher from the University of Texas studied whether or not realism was a defining factor and further explored the possibility to escape the uncanny phenomenon by tuning the images of humanoid robots in order to make them more attractive (Hanson 2006). In a first control experiment, Hanson (2006) exposed subjects to images of a robot slowly morphing into a human without trying to tune those images to make them attractive. The uncanny dip was reproduced. In a second experimental trial, he exposed subjects to the same morphing images, but adjusted those images aesthetically in order to make them more attractive. Surprisingly, the tuned images consistently received low scores of eeriness and high scores of appeal independently of their levels of realism, indicating that observers' ratings are at least in part decoupled from realism. The uncanny valley was thus eliminated from the first to the second experimental trial. This suggests that at any given level of realism, it is possible to finely tune the humanoid robot's appearance in order to make it look more attractive and aesthetically pleasing, making degrees of realism irrelevant. Hanson's results clearly support those of others (e.g., MacDorman 2006; Seyama and Nagayama 2007) demonstrated the preponderance of the aesthetic component over realism and indicate that the formerly known as inevitable uncanny valley might in fact only be related to dysmorphia and eeriness.

9.5 Conclusion

SAD is an anxiety disorder that is real, common, and treatable effectively. Overall, research on SAD has supported major conclusions about the efficacy of *in virtuo* exposure. Using synthetic humans and immersion in VR to conduct exposure is effective for fear of public speaking and it is also effective for the full syndrome of SAD (Meyerbröker and Emmelkamp 2010; Opris et al. 2012). Many small studies are pointing in this direction and a few randomized control trials are providing convincing evidences (e.g., Anderson et al. 2013; Bouchard et al. 2011; Wallach et al. 2009). Further research is now needed to bring the level of investigation up to what is done in CBT in general and presented in the introduction of this chapter. For example, research could look at refining exposure protocols, exploit more creatively the potential of virtual situations, compare *in virtuo* exposure and pharmacotherapy, study the impact VR-based treatment on comorbid disorders (especially if VR environments include stimuli relevant to the comorbid disorder such as alcohol, for example), and document therapists reluctance to accompany their patients or model behaviors when engaging in exposure to ridicule situations.

9.5 Conclusion

Much research is going on in the field of virtual humans. As the power of computer and graphics cars are improving, we can foresee the days when virtual humans will possess visual and behavioral qualities that currently are only possible in 3D films that are not rendered in real time (see the end of Chap. 11 for more on the creation of virtual environments). The first virtual environments designed for fear of public speaking used human actors who were filmed and inserted in the virtual environment, behind a podium, a table, or in an auditorium. But, it is not possible to use virtual humans that are entirely synthetic. The next steps are to include real-time integration of speech recognition and artificial intelligence into affordable computers systems. In the meantime, *in virtuo* scenarios can already provide contexts to perform exposure to situations that are more powerful and unexploited, such as taking to risk of exposing personal attributes that are perceived as inadequate or not meeting social norms and expectancies (Moscovitch 2009). However, cultural issues may still matter when dealing with virtual human interactions and their physical context (Gorini et al. 2009). This has not been studied much, and in the meantime simple "cheat" are used in therapy. For example, it is possible to tell a patient from a non-western culture that he or she is visiting friends or colleagues in North America or Europe. But because social behaviors are implicitly regulated by cultural context, clinical research in the field remains essential.

Social psychology research with virtual humans is one of the most fascinating fields of study these days. The emerging conclusion so far is that findings from classical studies are replicated *in virtuo* what is observed *in vivo*. This must be because of the illusion of nonmediation (see Chap. 2). It is a necessary step in scientific inquiries, and in the near future VR will occupy a greater role in our toolkit to experiment on and understand social interactions and SAD. Recent developments in the field include using virtual human as coach for people going through emotionally challenging situations, or to supervise doctors performing interviews and differential diagnosis. But contrary to specific phobias, where lack of realism in the behaviors of insects (see Chap. 5) or of airplanes (see Chap. 4) were not so detrimental to the impact of the immersion, in the case of virtual humans we may face a new challenge. As virtual humans become more realistic, expectations of user's of virtual environments may be raising and small inconsistencies between their appearance and behavior may disrupt the magic of VR.

On the practical side, conducting exposure *in virtuo* seems to be more efficient for therapists. They have less work to do to prepared and conduct their exposure sessions. They have more control over the (virtual) people involved in the social interaction. They do not have to get away from their office to conduct and supervise the exposure session. And they can do things in VR they would not dare doing in vivo.

As a closing argument, let us not forget that technology is just a tool to implement effective CBT techniques, and therefore therapists should focus on exposing people with SAD to situations that are dreaded by systematically collected evidence that fear is unfounded.

References

Abramowitz, J. S., Deacon, B. J., & Whiteside, S. P. H. (2011). *Exposure therapy for anxiety: Principles and practice*. New York: Guilford.

Acarturk, C., Cuijpers, P., van Straten, A., & de Graaf, R. (2009). Psychological treatment of social anxiety disorder: A meta-analysis. *Psychological Medicine, 39*(2), 241–254.

American Psychiatric Association (APA). (2000). *Diagnostic and statistical manual of mental disorders fourth edition text revision*. Washington: American Psychiatric Association.

Anderson, P., Rothbaum, B. O., & Hodges, L. F. (2003). Virtual reality in the treatment of social anxiety: Two case reports. *Cognitive and Behavioral Practice, 10,* 240–247.

Anderson, P. L., Zimand, E., Hodges, L. F., & Rothbaum, B. O. (2005). Cognitive behavioral therapy for public-speaking anxiety using virtual reality for exposure. *Depression and Anxiety, 22*(3), 156–158.

Anderson, P., Price, M., Edwards, S. M., Obasaju, M. A., Schmertz, S. K., Ziman, E., et al. (2013). Virtual reality exposure therapy for social anxiety disorder: A randomized controlled trial. *Journal of Consulting and Clinical Psychology, 81*(5), 751–760.

André, C., & Légeron, P. (1995). La phobie sociale: Approche clinique et thérapeutique. *Encephale, 21*(1), 1–13.

Bailenson, J.N., Blascovich, J., Beall, A.C., & Loomis, J.M. (2003). Interpersonal distance in immersive virtual environments. *Personality and Social Psychology Bulletin, 29* (7), 819–833.

Bandura, A., Reese, L., & Adam, N.E. (1982). Microanalysis of action and fear arousal as a function of differential levels of perceived self-efficacy. *Journal of Personality and Social Psychology, 43* (1), 5–21.

Barlow, D. H., & Lehman, C. L. (1996). Advances in the psychosocial treatment of anxiety disorders: Implications for national health care. *Archives of General Psychiatry, 53*(8), 727–735.

Bouchard, S., Dumoulin, S., Robillard, G., Guitard, T., Klinger, É., Forget, H., & Roucaut, F.-X. (2011). A randomized control trial for the use of in virtuo exposure in the treatment of social phobia: Final results. *Journal of Cybertherapy and Rehabilitation,* 4(2), 197–199.

Brühl, A. B., Rufer, M., Delsignore, A., Kaffenberger, T., Jäncke, L., & Herwig, U. (2011). Neural correlates of altered general emotion processing in social anxiety disorder. *Brain Research, 1378,* 72–83.

Butler, A. C., Chapman, J. E., Forman, E. M., & Beck, A. T. (2006). The empirical status of cognitive-behavioral therapy: A review of meta-analyses. *Clinical Psychology Review, 26*(1), 17–31.

Canton, J., Scott, K.M., & Glue, P. (2012). Optimal treatment of social phobia: Systematic review and meta-analysis. *Neuropsychiatric Disease and Treatment, 8,* 203–215.

Clark, D.M. (2001). A cognitive perspective on social phobia. In W. Ray Crozier & L.E. Alden (Eds.): *International handbook of social anxiety: Concepts, research and interventions relating to the self and shyness* (ch. 18, pp. 405–430). New YorK: Wiley.

Clark, D. M., & Beck, A. T. (2011). *Cognitive therapy of anxiety disorders: Science and Practice*. New York: Guilford Press.

Clark, D. M., & Wells, A. (1995). A cognitive model of social phobia. In R. Heimberg, M. Liebowitz, D. A. Hope & F. R. Schneier (Eds.), *Social phobia: Diagnosis, assessment, and treatment* (pp. 69–93). New York: Guilford.

Clark, D.M., Ehlers, A., McManus, F., Hackmann, A., Fennell, M., Campbell, H., et al. (2003). Cognitive therapy vs fluoxetine in generalized social phobia: a randomized placebo-controlled trial. *Journal of Consulting and Clinical Psychology, 71* (6), 1058–1067.

Clark, D. M., Ehlers, A., Hackmann, A., McManus, F., Fennell, M., Grey, N., Waddington, L., & Wild, J. (2006). Cognitive therapy versus exposure and applied relaxation in social phobia: A randomized controlled trial. *Journal of Consulting and Clinical Psychology, 74*(3), 568–578.

Furmark, T. (2009). Neurobiological aspects of social anxiety disorder. *Israel Journal of Psychiatry & Related Sciences, 46*(1), 5–12.

Garau, M., Slater, M., Vinayagamoorthy, V., Brogni, A., Steed, A., & Sasse, M. A. (2003). The impact of avatar realism and eye gaze control on perceived quality of communication in a shared

References

immersive virtual environment. Proceedings of the SIG-CHI on human factors in computing systems, Fort-Lauderdale, Florida.

Goldin, P. R., Ziv, M., Jazaieri, H., Hahn, K., Heimberg, R., & Gross, J. J. (2013). Impact of cognitive behavioral therapy. *JAMA Psychiatry, 70*(10), 1048–1056.

Gorini, A., Mosso, J. L., Mosso, D., Pineda, E., Ruíz, N. L., Ramíez, M., Morales, J. L., & Riva, G. (2009). Emotional response to virtual reality exposure across different cultures: The role of the attribution process. *Cyberpsychology and Behavior, 12*(6), 699–705.

Grant, B. F., Hasin, D. S., Blanco, C., Stinson, F. S., Chou, P., Goldstein, R. B., et al. (2005). The epidemiology of social anxiety disorder in the United States: Results from the National Epidemiologic Survey on alcohol and related conditions. *Journal of Clinical Psychiatry, 66*(11), 1351–1361.

Grillon, H., Riquier, F., Herbelin, B., & Thalmann, D. (2006). Virtual reality as therapeutic tool in the confines of social anxiety disorder treatment. *International Journal of Disability and Human Development, 5*(3), 243–250.

Hanson, D. (2006). *Exploring the aesthetic range for humanoid robots*. Proceedings of the ICCS/CogSci-2006 Symposium, towards social mechanisms of android science, Vancouver, BC.

Harris, S. R., Kemmerling, R. L., & North, M. M. (2002). Brief virtual reality therapy for public speaking anxiety. *Cyberpsychology and Behavior, 5*(6), 543–550.

Heimberg, R. G., & Becker, R. E. (2002). *Cognitive-behavioral group therapy for social phobia: Basic mechanisms and clinical strategies*. New York: Guilford.

Heimberg, R. G., Liebowitz, M. R., Hope, D. A., & Schneier, F. R. (1995). *Social phobia: Diagnosis, Assessment and Treatment*. New York: Guilford.

Herbelin, B., Ponder, M., & Thalmann, D. (2005). Building exposure: Synergy of interaction and naration through the social channel. *Presence, 14*(2), 234–246.

Heuett, B. L., & Heuett, K. B. (2011). Virtual reality therapy: A means of reducing public speaking anxiety. *International Journal of Humanities and Social Science, 1*(16), 1–6.

Holt, C. S., Heimberg, R. G., Hope, D., & Liebowitz, M. (1992). Situational domains of social phobia. *Journal of Anxiety Disorders, 6*, 63–77.

Kessler, R. C., McGonagle, K. A., Zhao, S., Nelson, C. B., Hughes, M., Eshleman, S., et al. (1994). Lifetime and 12-month prevalence of DSM-III-R psychiatric disorders in the United States. Results from the National Comorbidity Survey. *Archives of General Psychiatry, 51*(1), 8–19.

Kessler, R. C., Stein, M. B., & Berglund, P. (1998). Social phobia subtypes in the National Comorbidity Survey. *The American Journal of Psychiatry, 155*(5), 613–619.

Kessler, R. C., Berglund, P., Demler, O., Jin, R., & Walters, E. E. (2005a). Lifetime prevalence and age-of-onset distributions of DSM-IV disorders in the National Comorbidity Survey Replication. *Archives of General Psychiatry, 62*, 593–602.

Kessler, R. C., Chiu, W. T., Demler, O., & Walters, E. E. (2005b). Prevalence, severity and co-morbidity of 12-month DSM-IV disorders in the National Comorbidity Survey Replication. *Archives of General Psychiatry, 62*, 617–627.

Klinger, E., Chemin, I. & Légeron, P. (2002). *Issues in the design of virtual environments for the treatment of social phobia*. Presented at the VRMHR2002. Lausanne, Switzerland.

Klinger, E., Bouchard, S., Légeron, P., Roy, S., Lauer, F., Chemin, I., et al. (2005). Virtual reality therapy versus cognitive behavior therapy for social phobia: A preliminary controlled study. *Cyberpsychology and Behavior, 8*(1), 76–88.

Légeron, P., & Tanneau, E. (1998). Thérapie comportementale et cognitive de groupe de la phobie sociale. *Journal de Thérapie Comportementale et Cognitive, 8*(3), 84–94.

Liao, W., Qiu, C., Gentili, C., Walter, M., Pan, Z., Ding, J., Zhang, W., Gong, Q., & Chen, H. (2010). Altered effective connectivity network of the amygdala in social anxiety disorder: A resting-state fMRI study. *PLoS One, 5*(12), 1–9.

Liebowitz, M. R. (1987). Social phobia. *Modern Problems of Pharmacopsychiatry, 22*, 141–173.

Liebowitz, M. R., Schneier, F., Campeas, R., Hollander, E., Hatterer, J., Fyer, A., et al. (1992). Phenelzine vs atenolol in social phobia: A placebo-controlled comparison. *Archives of General Psychiatry, 49*(4), 290–300.

Lister, H. A., Piercey, D., & Joordens, C. (2010). Effectiveness of 3-D video virtual reality for the treatment of fear of public speaking. *Journal of CyberTherapy and Rehabilitation, 3*(4), 375–381.

MacDorman, K. F. (2006). Subjective ratings of robot video clips for human likeliness, familiarity and eeriness: An exploration of the Uncanny Valley. Proceedings of the ICCS/CogSci-2006 Symposium, Towards social mechanisms of android science, Vancouver, BC.

Mersch, P. P. (1994). *The behavioral and cognitive therapy for social phobia.* Groningen: proefschrift.

Meyerbröker, K., & Emmelkamp, P. M. G. (2010). Virtual reality exposure therapy in anxiety disorders: A systematic review of process-and-outcome studies. *Depression and Anxiety, 27,* 933–944.

Moscovitch, D. A. (2009). What is the core fear in social phobia? A new model to facilitate individualized case conceptualization and treatment. *Cognitive and Behavioral Practice, Cognitive and Behavioral Practice, 16*(2), 123–134.

Mori, M. (1970). Bukimi no tani (the uncanny valley). *Energy, 7,* 33–35.

Moussaoui, A., Pruski, A., Bendiouis, Y. S., & Cherki, B. (2010). Régulation des émotions dans le cadre d'une thérapie par réalité virtuelle: Étude d'un cas de phobie sociale. 1er Congrès International de Thérapie cognitivo-comportementale, Constantine, June.

Mühlberger, A., Wieser, M. J., & Pauli, P. (2008). Visual attention during virtual social situations depends on social anxiety. *Cyberpsychology and Behavior, 11*(4), 425–430.

North, M. M., North, S. M., & Coble, J. R. (1998). Virtual reality therapy: An effective treatment for the fear of public speaking. *International Journal of Virtual Reality, 3*(2), 2–6.

Opris, D., Pintea, S., Garcia-Palacios, A., Botella, C., Szamosközi, S., & David, D. (2012). Virtual reality exposure therapy in anxiety disorders: A quantitative meta-analysis. *Depression and Anxiety, 29,* 85–93.

Park, S., & Catrambone, R. (2007). Social facilitation effects of virtual humans. *Human Factors, 49*(6), 1054–1060.

Paul, G. (1966). *Insight vs. desensitization in psychotherapy.* Stanford: Stanford University Press.

Pélissolo, A., & Lépine, J. P. (1996). Phobies sociales. *Revue du Praticien, 350,* 19–22.

Pertaub, D. P., Slater, M., & Barker, C. (2001). An experiment on fear of public speaking in virtual reality. In J. Westwood (Ed.), *Medicine meets virtual reality 2001* (pp. 372–378). Amsterdam: IOS Press.

Pertaub, D. P., Slater, M., & Barker, C. (2002). An experiment on public speaking anxiety in response to three different types of virtual audience. *Presence, 11*(1), 68–78.

Price, M., & Anderson, P. L. (2012). Outcome expectancy as a predictor of treatment response in cognitive behavioral therapy for public speaking fears within social anxiety disorder. *Psychotherapy, 49*(2), 173–179.

Price, M., Metha, N., Tone, E. B., & Anderson, P. L. (2011). Does engagement with exposure yield better outcomes? Components of presence as a predictor of treatment response for virtual reality exposure therapy for social phobia. *Journal of Anxiety Disorders, 25,* 763–770.

Rachman, S. J. (1990). *Fear and courage* (2nd ed., 405 p.). San Francisco: Freeman.

Rapee, R. M., Gaston, J. E., & Abbott, M. J. (2009). Testing the efficacy of theoretically derived improvements in the treatment of social phobia. *Journal of Consulting and Clinical Psychology, 77*(2), 317–327.

Riquier, F., Herbelin, B., & Chevalley, F. (2005). *Thérapies par réalité virtuelle dans le traitement et l'évaluation clinique de la phobie sociale.* Paper presented at the 11th Congrès de l'Association Francophone de Formation et de Recherche en Thérapie Comportementale et Cognitive. June 2005, Aix-les-Bains.

Robillard, G., Bouchard, S., Dumoulin, S., Guitard, T., & Klinger, E. (2010). Using virtual humans to alleviate social anxiety: Preliminary report from a comparative outcome study. *Studies in Health Technology and Informatics, 154,* 57–60.

Rodebaugh, T. L., Holaway, R. M., & Heimberg, R. G. (2004). The treatment of social anxiety disorder. *Clinical Psychology Review, 24*(7), 883–908.

Rossen, B., Johnsen, K., Deladisma, A., Lind, S., & Lok, B. (2008). Virtual humans elicit skin-tone bias consistent with real-world skin-tone biases. In H. Prendinger, J. Lester, and M. Ishizuka (Eds.), *Intelligent virtual agents 2008: Lecture notes in artificial intelligence.* Springer-Verlag Berlin

Safir, M. P., Wallach, H. S., & Bar-Zvi, M. (2012). Virtual reality cognitive-behavior therapy for public speaking anxiety: One-year follow up. *Behavior Modification, 36*(2), 235–246.

Servant, D. (2002). *Soigner les phobies sociales.* Paris: Masson Collection Pratiques en Psychothérapie.

Seyama, J., & Nagayama, R. S. (2007). The Uncanny valley: Effect of realism on the impression of artificial human faces. *Presence, 16*(4), 337–351.

Slater, M., Antley, A., Davidson, A., Swapp, D., Guger, C., Barker, C., Pistrang, N., & Sanchez-Vives, M. V. (2006a). A virtual reprise of the Stanley Milgram obedience experiment. *PLoS One, 1*(1), e39. doi:10.1371/journal.pone.0000039.

Slater, M., Guger, C., Edlinger, G., Leeb, R., Pfurtscheller, G., Antley, A., Garau, M., Brogni, A., & Friedman, D. (2006b). Analysis of physiological responses to a social situation in an immersive virtual environment. *Presence, 15*(5), 553–569.

Slater, M., Pertaub, D.-P., Barker, C., & Clark, D. M. (2006c). An experimental study on fear of public speaking using a virtual environment. *CyberPsychology and Behavior, 9*(5), 627–633.

Stangier, U., Schramm, E., Heidenreich, T., Berger, M., & Clark, D. (2011). Cognitive therapy vs international psychotherapy in social anxiety disorder. *Archives of General Psychiatry, 68*(7), 692–700.

Vrijsen, J. N., Lange, W.-G., Dotsch, R., Wigboldus, D. H. J., & Rinck, M. (2010). How do socially anxious women evaluate mimicry? A virtual reality study. *Cognition and Emotion, 24*(5), 840–847.

Wallach, H. S., Safir, M., & Bar-Zvi, M. (2009). Virtual reality cognitive behavior therapy for public speaking anxiety: A randomized clinical trial. *Behavior Modification, 33,* 314–333.

Wang, P. S., Lane, M., Olfson, M., Pincus, H. A., Wells, K. B., & Kessler, R. C. (2005). Twelve-month use of mental health services in the United States. Results from the National Comorbidity Survey Replication. *Archives of General Psychiatry, 62,* 629–640.

World Health Organization. (1992). *The ICD-10 classification of mental and behavioural disorders.* Geneva: WHO.

Chapter 10
Virtual Reality for Posttraumatic Stress Disorder

Brenda K. Wiederhold and Mark D. Wiederhold

Exposure to an incident in which an individual encounters severe physical harm or a life-threatening occurrence can leave a person with repercussions of psychological distress. Such an event becomes a mechanism for an individual's psychological defenses to cope with a traumatic event, which will affect 60.7% of men and 51.2% of women at least once in their lifetime (National Center for PTSD 2009). The lifetime prevalence of posttraumatic stress disorder (PTSD), a heterogeneous disorder that may occur following a traumatic event and that may include symptoms of anxiety, arousal, dissociation, and flashbacks, is 6.8%—about 1 out of every 15 Americans (National Center for PTSD 2009). At-risk individuals often experience symptoms of PTSD within 3 months of a trauma (American Psychiatric Association 2000). The distress caused by the symptoms of PTSD can lead to depression and even suicide if left untreated.

Virtual reality (VR) holds the potential to make a tremendous impact on health care with its diverse capabilities, especially the ability to mold itself to fit an individual's therapeutic needs. In a VR environment for PTSD, a patient is transported into a setting similar to an experience where an anxiety-causing event occurred. The process slowly and systematically consolidates the fragmented memories and allows for emotional processing to occur and desensitization to be achieved. Though other treatment methods for PTSD exist (e.g., medication, psychotherapy, *in vivo* (real-life) exposure therapy, imaginal exposure therapy), VR therapy may work more quickly and be more effective in alleviating symptoms and preventing relapse. Studies including diverse populations have shown VR therapy to enhance traditional cognitive behavioral treatments of PTSD in the majority of studies, reporting a success rate of 66–90% (Wiederhold and Wiederhold 2008b).

VR has helped to treat individuals who have developed PTSD after motor vehicle accidents, due to natural disasters (such as earthquakes), post deployment in combat and peace-keeping missions, and after being affected by terrorism such as the attacks of September 11th. In addition to alleviating individuals' PTSD symptoms, VR provides those who have used VR therapy with learned coping skills, which gives the patients the necessary techniques to handle future psychological issues.

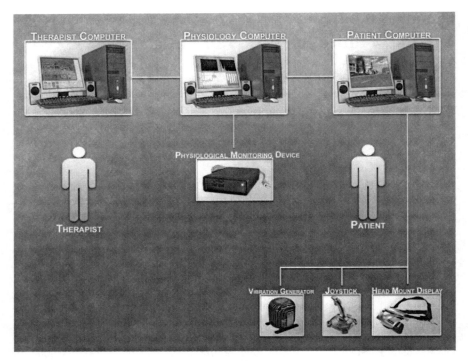

Fig. 10.1 The Virtual Reality Medical Center PTSD computer setup

While each creator of virtual environments as therapy aids for treatment of PTSD has his or her own computer system setup, certain components are standard (see, for example, description of the system in Croatia in the Prevention of PTSD section of this chapter). The Virtual Reality Medical Center (VRMC) VR PTSD system provides a good example of a comprehensive system. Its hardware consists of the VR client system, VR controller, monitor, cordless keyboard/mouse, cordless joystick controller, speaker/headset/microphone, vibration generator, and head-mounted display (HMD). The physiological system consists of a laptop and a physiological monitoring device and sensors. The VR client system displays the visual and auditory environments to the patient through a HMD equipped with headphones. The VR controller houses the control panel and menu that the therapist manipulates to add arousing elements such as combat events and background sounds. The diagram (Fig. 10.1) depicts the hardware configuration for the VR PTSD system.

A real-time physiological device that records vital signs monitors patients. The physiological device, currently I-330-C2 Plus from J&J Engineering, monitors and records up to 12 channels of physiological activity. Four channels are for surface electromyography (sEMG)/electroencephalography (EEG) or electrocardiography (ECG) with the remaining channels dedicated to temperature, heart rate (HR), respiration, and skin resistance. The measurement of the physiological arousal, such as respiration rate, skin conductance, peripheral temperature, and HR, will allow clinicians to monitor sympathetic nervous system arousal and parasympathetic nervous system response and to modify interventions in real time based on the patient's arousal levels.

The HMD, currently eMagin Z800 3DVisor, provides an immersive three-dimensional (3D) experience to the patient. Its two high-contrast SVGA 3D OLED microdisplays deliver fluid full-motion video in more than 16.7 million colors. The built-in head tracking system has a set of three compasses and provides 360-degree head movement tracking, which allows the patient's perspective to shift to match the scene displayed as he/she navigates through the virtual environment.

The system includes a variety of combat-related scenarios to control exposure variables. Therapists control the degree of exposure with each of the scenarios and increase or decrease the level of stimuli with each scenario. In these scenarios, patients will reexperience certain situations like a convoy ambush, the screaming of patients in pain, the littered streets in Iraqi villages, citizen interaction, and pre-deployment at the battalion camp. The hardware and software setup is a turnkey solution with intuitive interfaces to the patient and therapist to allow efficient treatments. VRMC systems such as these are currently used in Veteran's Administration (VA) hospitals and other medical institutions throughout the USA and also in Iraq, Poland, and Croatia.

10.1 The Need for PTSD Treatment

With an estimated 5.2 million Americans suffering from symptoms of PTSD, the need for improved mental health-care treatment is imperative (Wiederhold and Wiederhold 2008b). Such events as the World Trade Center attacks, earthquakes, motor vehicle accidents, physical or sexual abuse, and exposure to combat can traumatize an individual. After repeated deployments, post-deployment combat veterans are one of the highest at-risk populations for PTSD. With improving health-care treatments (specifically during the war on Iraq), soldiers with severe injuries have a higher probability of survival, leaving injured soldiers with mental and physical ailments. At this time, we are unable to predict who will develop PTSD among individuals who experience a traumatic event (e.g., serious injury, threat of death).

10.2 Current Treatments for PTSD

Three clusters of symptoms characterize PTSD: reexperiencing of the trauma, avoidance of thoughts or acts that symbolize the trauma as well as emotional numbing, and hyperarousal symptoms. Due to the variety of symptoms, PTSD is often treated with a combination of anxiety-reducing medications, antidepressants, support from friends and family, and cognitive-behavioral therapy (CBT) involving exposure (Barlow 1988). As reviewed in Harvey et al. (2003), CBT has proven safe and effective. In a study of 91 terrorist bomb attack survivors in Ireland with PTSD, therapists (Gillespie et al. 2002) achieved an impressive effect size of 2.47 posttreatment on the Posttraumatic Diagnostic Scale (PDS; Foa et al. 1997). The eight-session protocol included imaginal and *in vivo* exposure and reducing unhelpful behavioral and cognitive strategies. The therapists intentionally structured "reliving" aspects of therapy to facilitate reappraisals of the experience. Although limited by the absence of a control group and follow up, a randomized controlled trial (RCT) replicated a large effect size (Ehlers et al. 2003). For CBT versus controls, this RCT produced an effect size of Cohen's $d=1.34$ for the PDS and 1.24 for the Clinician Administered PTSD Scale (CAPS) at 3 months and $d=1.01$ for the PDS and 0.74 for the CAPS at 9 months.

CBT encourages discussion of the sentinel event and one's reactions to it while in a safe therapeutic environment. A CBT-based therapy known as exposure therapy, recently found by the Institute of Medicine to have the most evidence of efficacy of all reviewed PTSD treatments (IOM 2008), directly confronts the internal arousal of the patient.

However, traditional treatments do not have an acceptable recovery rate. Many patients undergoing such treatments will still meet the criteria for PTSD at the end of an adequate treatment trial (Hamner et al. 2004). A meta-analysis of studies employing various treatments for PTSD showed that just 44 % of those who begin treatment that employs traditional techniques would be classified as improved at the end of the treatment period (Bradley et al. 2005).

10.3 VR Treatment for PTSD

VR has made substantial advancements in the field of anxiety disorders such as PTSD, improving and enhancing treatment efficacy for PTSD in the survivors of several types of trauma. Using emotional processing theory, VR exposure therapy creates a safe, virtual environment with the ability to allow patients to "relive" their experiences in a thorough and efficient method by slowly exposing them to the exact or similar events that cause anxiety. In some protocols, the therapist first teaches patients coping skills and patients can then use those skills while exposed to the traumatic events in VR. Patients can move through the traumatic scenarios at their own pace and experience the corresponding emotional responses.

Research has shown that the possibility of "retraumatizing" an individual by exposing them to the same scenario that originally caused PTSD should not be a cause for concern (Ballenger et al. 2000). Before the use of VR, the most effective treatment, yielding the highest percentage of improvement among PTSD patients, was imaginal exposure therapy, using the imagination as the sole means for exposure. Although imaginal therapy is effective, many patients fail to engage emotionally or visualize their experience well enough to elicit an adequate emotional response that facilitates effective treatment (Kosslyn et al. 1984; Jaycox et al. 1998; Van Etten and Taylor 1998). A recent study in 118 civilian trauma survivors with PTSD suggests that the most effective non-VR treatment may be a blend of imaginal and *in vivo* exposure, in combination with cognitive restructuring (Bryant et al. 2008). VR-augmented treatment works by more effectively engaging the patient in experiencing reminders of the trauma (Difede and Hoffman 2002), improving results for patients who are unable or unwilling to visualize effectively a traumatic event during imaginal therapy.

Because of its immersive essence, VR has the ability to surmount the shortcomings of imaginal therapy. VR provides external, visual, and auditory stimuli for the patient, thus eliminating the need for intense imaginal skills. VR overcomes limitations of *in vivo* therapy by allowing a patient to interact with anxiety-inducing scenarios in the safety and confidentiality of the therapy room. Patients can exert initial control over the session, empowered with the ability to administer the level of anxiety they are willing to experience during their therapy. The patient and therapist work together to determine treatment duration and intensity, thus ensuring the best possible outcome. In addition, the patient can complete multiple exposures during a single therapy session, reducing costs and increasing efficiency.

The VRMC treatment protocol is multifaceted, drawing from principles of cognitive behavioral and experiential therapies. In contrast to flooding-type exposure therapy, which attempts to extinguish conditioned reactions, this approach trains patients to control their physical arousal and attentional focus in order to tolerate exposure to a wide range of cues. VRMC researchers discovered this modified VR exposure approach through their groundbreaking work to treat fear of flying (Wiederhold and Wiederhold 2000, 2004a; Wiederhold et al. 2001a). Because the emphasis on personal control and skill development makes this therapy attractive to patients, VRMC researchers are conducting studies to show that this approach will be optimal for those suffering from acute or early chronic combat PTSD, will better generalize to a wide range of symptoms and situations, and will have the highest likelihood of long-term benefit.

VRMC therapists are currently conducting stress inoculation training (SIT; see Prevention of PTSD section later in this chapter for details), PTSD treatment, rehabilitation therapy, and pain distraction techniques for the US military, resulting in a program that provides a continuum of care for troops (Wiederhold and Wiederhold 2008a). Systems are in place in country, in partner countries, and in the USA (Fig. 10.2).

10.4 VR Treatment for War Veterans

Many studies have shown VR to enhance traditional therapy approaches for PTSD, including an initial case study using VR therapy to treat PTSD in Vietnam veterans in 1999 (Rothbaum et al. 1999). A recent study predicted a lifetime PTSD occurrence of 18.7% in Vietnam veterans, with 9.1% suffering from PTSD 11 and 12 years after the war; current PTSD was associated with moderate impairment (Dohrenwend et al. 2006). Using VR therapy to project virtual environments in-

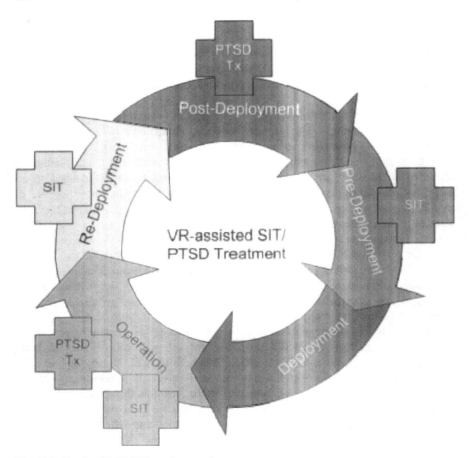

Fig. 10.2 Combat PTSD/SIT continuum of care

cluding a helicopter and jungle terrain, patients experienced a 34% decrease in clinician-rated PTSD symptoms and a 45% decrease in self-ratings (Rothbaum et al. 2001). According to the 2004 study by Hoge et al., the number of soldiers at risk for mental disorders 3–4 months post deployment increased from 9 to 11–17% for those who have returned from Iraq. A later study based on a Department of Defense screening showed that 20.3–42.4% of Iraq veterans require mental health treatment (Milliken et al. 2007).

New research on VR treatment for veterans of the war in Iraq and Afghanistan who suffer from PTSD is producing promising results. In a program funded by the Office of Naval Research, VRMC completed the first randomized controlled clinical trial using VR-enhanced exposure therapy with physiological monitoring and feedback (biofeedback) to treat troops at Balboa Naval Hospital and Camp Pendleton Marine Base in Southern California (McLay et al. 2011). Creating a virtual environment emulating, for example, Baghdad as a clinical therapy aid, which includes

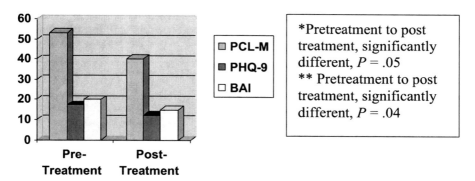

Fig. 10.3 Results of pretreatment and posttreatment PCL-M*, Patient Health Questionnaire (*PHQ*-9)**, and Beck Anxiety Inventory (*BAI*) assessments ($n=12$). (Wood et al. 2009)

auditory enhancements (e.g., sounds of a Baghdad market, battlefields, sounds of military vehicles burning, helicopters thundering overhead, explosions, Arabic prayers from a temple), has the ability to trigger emotions and levels of anxiety high enough to produce the necessary results needed for a successful treatment. Based on interviews with a population of Marine and Navy personnel recently diagnosed with combat-related PTSD, researchers found that the aforementioned stimuli were some of the most prominent memories veterans associate with recurring, intrusive thoughts (Spira et al. 2006). A study conducted by Wood et al. (2008) showed that after VR therapy for Iraqi war veterans, 100% of participants reduced their PTSD Checklist–Military (PCL-M) scores and nearly two-thirds of participants no longer met the criteria for PTSD after treatment. In the treatment, patients view a virtual world on a portable computer or with a HMD, easily transported and using minimal amounts of space (see Available Software section at the end of this chapter).

An analysis of the estimated training cost for enlisted hospital corpsmen illustrated the savings that accrue from the 75% effectiveness rate achieved thus far with VR exposure therapy (VRET) for PTSD (Wood et al. 2009) versus the 44% effectiveness rate for treatment as usual (Bradley et al. 2005; Fig. 10.3; Table 10.1).

Because of the intense nature of the VR treatment, the lead psychologist and a staff psychiatrist monitor troops' mental status during every visit for suicide risk. On-call personnel are available to address any problems troops experience during treatment and all patients are given a "survival plan" at the onset of treatment.

Other researchers have been testing virtual environments created by other groups to facilitate VR exposure therapy for war veterans. After six sessions of VRET, an Army infantryman with combat-related PTSD reduced his PCL score from 58—above the 50 cutoff for PTSD—to 29, well below the PTSD cutoff (Reger and Gahm 2008). The virtual scenarios included a Humvee and an Iraqi city street scene, created by the University of Southern California, Institute of Creative Technologies (USC–ICT). In USC–ICT's own test of its system (see Available Software) at Naval Medical Center San Diego and Camp Pendleton, 16 of 20 completers no longer met PCL criteria for PTSD posttreatment (Rizzo et al. 2009).

Table 10.1 Estimated training cost (ETC) savings due to VRET at Naval Medical Center San Diego and Naval Hospital Camp Pendleton versus treatment as usual (TAU) for combat-related PTSD ($n=12$) and ETC savings for 5 clinical psychologists to treat 200 warriors with VRGET. (Adapted from Wood et al. 2009)

ETC for 12 VRET participants	ETC savings with TAU with 44% treatment effectiveness	ETC savings with VRET with 75% treatment effectiveness	ETC savings: VRET vs. TAU	ETC savings of VRET vs. TAU minus cost of clinical psychologist (i.e., US$ 21,600)	ETC savings of VRET vs. TAU minus cost of clinical psychologist (i.e., US$ 21,600) for 5 clinical psychologists to treat 200 warriors per year
US$ 439,000	US$ 193,160	US$ 329,250	US$ 136,090	*US$ 114,490*	*US$ 1,908,167*

Gamito et al. (2009) reported test results of a guerilla war environment (see Available Software) with ambush, mortar blasting, and waiting for injured rescue scenarios in five Portuguese combat survivors with long-term (30 years) PTSD. The protocol consisted of five sessions of therapy with three exposures each session. With the exception of a reduction in obsessive thoughts as evidenced by the Symptoms Checklist–Revised (SCL-90R), results were not statistically significant. The latest study by Gamito (2010, in press) of ten veterans showed significant reductions in depression and anxiety but not in CAPS scores. These results will inform the refinement of the protocol for these long-term survivors of PTSD.

10.5 VR Treatment for Motor Vehicle Accidents

VR has been extremely helpful in treating patients who suffer from PTSD due to a motor vehicle accident (MVA), which is one of the most frequent causes for PTSD. According to a study by Norris (1992), 23.4% of Americans will be involved in a MVA at some point within their lifetimes. The presence of PTSD at least 30 days post MVA is approximately 25–33% (Bryant et al. 2000; Harvey and Bryant 1998; Ursano et al. 1999). PTSD related to MVAs affects approximately 2.5–7 million people in the USA (Blanchard and Hickling 2004).

In an early study by VRMC, eight patients used virtual driving scenarios in residential areas and on freeways, producing an 88% treatment success rate (Wiederhold et al. 2001b). In a 2003 study (Walshe et al. 2003), immersed patients ($n=7$) who completed the exposure program showed significant posttreatment reductions on all measures of subjective units of distress (SUDS) and for rating scales to measure fear of driving (Fear of Driving Inventory or FDA), PTSD (CAPS), heart rate (HR), and depression (Hamilton Depression Scale or HAM-D) (Fig. 10.4; Table 10.2).

10.5 VR Treatment for Motor Vehicle Accidents

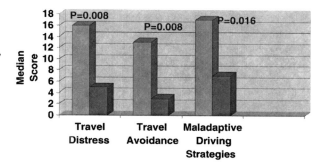

Fig. 10.4 Median scores of treated group on FDI subscales. *Light grey bars*, pretreatment; *dark grey bars*, posttreatment. (Walshe et al. 2003)

VRMC has treated 72 patients with a 90% success rate using VR exposure in combination with physiological monitoring and feedback protocols as part of an established CBT procedure (B. Wiederhold, personal communication, 12 Sept 2009).

A CBT-based therapy is most effective to treat the whole MVA patient, who often has at least one other diagnosis such as chronic pain, anxiety, or depression (Beck and Coffey 2007). The CBT with exposure model created by Blanchard and Hickling (2004) consists of 8–12 sessions, with a mode of 10 sessions, and results achieved using this model are in the 76–88% success range (Beck and Coffey 2007).

The advantage of VR, in those patients who can achieve immersion (easily tested in the first session), is that the treatment may be successful in a shorter time frame than traditional therapy. The essential ingredients for immersion in a driving scenario include projection of images onto a large screen, viewing the scene through a windscreen, using car seats for both driver and passenger, and increasing vibration sense through use of subwoofers (Walshe et al. 2005). In this study, 10 of 11 (91%) of the driving phobic participants met the criteria for immersion/presence, defined as subjective rating by the participant that the environment "feels real," together with an increase in SUDS ratings of >3 and/or an increase of HR of >15 beats per minute.

Skills can easily transfer from the virtual world into the real world, enabling patients to handle everyday driving scenarios that the patients thought were impossible before treatment. Patients who use VR in combination with traditional CBT show improvements on self-report questionnaires, SUDS, and physiological measures of

Table 10.2 Median and interquartile (IQR) scores of treated group on therapy outcome measures. (Walshe et al. 2003)

	Pretreatment		Posttreatment		P
	Median	IQR	Median	IQR	
SUDS ($n=7$)	6	4–7	0.5	0.5–1.5	0.008
FDI ($n=7$)	43	36–55	16	10–19	0.008
CAPS ($n=7$)	21	15–33	9	2–15	0.008
HR ($n=7$)	20	13–27	7	4–7	0.008
HAM-D ($n=6$)	10	4–15.25	3	2–6.75	0.031

Fig. 10.5 World Trade Center virtual environment

arousal. At least 70% of 200 patients completing a videogame-based VR exposure therapy protocol will declare themselves nonphobic after treatment (Walshe 2008).

10.6 VR in Other Situations that Trigger PTSD

VR applications have been successfully used in treating PTSD related to the 9/11 terrorist attacks, public vehicle terrorist bomb attacks, and earthquakes. VRET for survivors of the 9/11 terrorist attacks consists of replicating the attacks on the World Trade Center in a virtual environment (Difede et al. 2007). In a 14-session VR-enhanced treatment ($n=9$) compared to a waitlist control ($n=8$), analysis of variance (ANOVA) showed a significant interaction of time by the group ($P < 0.01$) with a large effect size of 1.53. Compared to controls, the VR group showed significantly greater posttreatment decline in CAPS (Difede et al. 2006; Fig. 10.5).

In Israel, researchers have begun using a virtual environment called BusWorld to provide VR therapy for terrorist bus bombing victims (Josman et al. 2006). In its initial design, the BusWorld graded the severity of the trauma experience in a VR world from stage 1 (views of a public bus stop with usual sounds of voices and traffic) to stage 12 (view of the bus exploding, flames, bus and body parts scattered, screaming voices, and emergency vehicle sirens). In a later iteration, the intensity levels were graded 1 through 4. Level 1 is a quiet street scene. In level 2, a bus appears and approaches the bus stop. At level 3, the bus pulls up to the stop, explodes (without sound effects), and burns, with smoke and shattered glass in the street. Level 4 adds the sound effects to the level 3 scenario, adding police sirens and flashing lights as well as people screaming and crying. A subsequent test of the immersive qualities of the environment in 30 asymptomatic volunteers showed a statistically significant difference between the mean SUDS of the four programmed intensity levels. In several planned paired comparisons, there were also significant

Fig. 10.6 BusWorld. (Josman et al. 2008)

increases in SUDS as the exposure progressed from level 1 to level 2 ($Z=-3.2$, $P<0.01$), from level 2 to level 4 ($Z=-3.6$, $P<0.001$), and from level 3 to level 4 ($Z=-3.9$, $P<0.001$; Josman et al. 2008; Fig. 10.6).

Clinicians have used other VR applications to deal with the aftereffects of natural disasters. In a 2003 study by Basoglu et al., survivors of the devastating earthquake in Turkey were exposed to an experimental treatment using VR to simulate earthquake tremors. Earthquake survivors were given one session of exposure to simulate earthquake tremors. Assessments were pre- and post session and at 2, 4, 8, and 12 weeks posttreatment. All measures showed significant improvement at all assessments. Eight patients were markedly and two slightly improved at follow up.

Another study in Greece utilized the same technologies to simulate earthquakes, in which 209 participants experienced a 78% improvement after one session and 89% improved after two sessions (Tarnanas and Manos 2004). Researchers randomized the Greek children to one of two conditions: behaviorally realistic avatars with unfamiliar faces or with faces of classmates. Children were then led by avatars through a SIT scenario on how to escape from their classroom in case of an earthquake. The researchers found that avatars with familiar faces were superior in generating emotion-focused variables such as fear-related coping abilities.

10.7 Prevention of PTSD

Research on the effectiveness of SIT to prevent PTSD is an emerging interest, with large-scale clinical trials yet to be conducted. For example, a 2009 study by Arnetz et al. using SIT with rookie police officers ($n=18$) yielded promising results. One year after a 10-week imagery and resilience skills training course, significant results were achieved in indicators such as less HR reactivity and better police performance compared to controls when tested in a live simulation.

Virtual reality stress inoculation training (VR-SIT) is a technique using a VR technology to prepare individuals for potential highly stressful situations in an effort to diminish their negative reactions to stress in a more realistic setting. This method is now being used to train and aid deployed military personnel prior to exposure to high levels of stress in hopes of lowering post-exposure PTSD rates and allowing better skill performance during exposure.

VRMC researchers have studied lessons learned from the Tactical Decision-Making Under Stress (TADMUS) project, sponsored by the Office of Naval Research, which resulted from the mistaken shooting down by the US Navy of a commercial Iranian airliner. VRMC staff has constructed a comparison chart that contrasts the lessons learned from the TADMUS study with lessons learned from investigators' clinical "lessons learned" using VR in combination with physiological monitoring and feedback to treat patients over the past 13 years (Table 10.3).

Dr. Mark Wiederhold served as Principal Investigator for phase I and phase II studies funded by a Defense Advanced Research Projects Agency (DARPA) grant. The purpose was to conduct SIT for combat medics to practice skills in a VR world, with stressors added, prior to deployment to Iraq. In the phase I study, combat and medical skills using war zone and evacuation images improved overall performance skills (Wiederhold and Wiederhold 2004b). In the phase II study, the investigators trained medics in tactical and medical training for Iraq and the skills developed through training in a virtual world transferred over to a real-world setting (Wiederhold and Wiederhold 2006a). Details of these studies follow.

Phase I results indicated that those trained in a VR simulation while having stressors added (being shot at while tending to the wounded) were able to perform skills more effectively in the test phase of the study as compared to those trained in a "sterile" VR environment (no one shooting at them while tending to the wounded). Those receiving SIT were able to develop divided attention skills and learned to moderate physiological responses to the stress while staying focused on the task. Those not receiving SIT were pulled off the task and experienced much more physiological arousal during the test phase (being shot at), which caused mistakes to be made ("patients died").

In the phase II DARPA study, researchers monitored physiology in real time to provide an objective measure of arousal state. Using an off-the-shelf video game, investigators assessed two training groups. One group was trained while having a stressor applied (having to return enemy fire while treating wounded patients). Another group was trained while having no real stressor (only treating the patients but not having to return enemy fire). Researchers then tested both groups in a novel simulation environment. As one might expect, those trained with stress were able to perform better in the new test environment than those who were trained without high stress. In addition, subjectively, individuals were unaware when they were becoming too physiologically aroused and perhaps not in the optimum training state. Investigators were also able to see changes in HR, brain wave activity, and skin conductance that correlated with peak performance.

One group trained on the virtual shoot house via laptop computer for 10 min before entering the shoot house. A control group was monitored over four runs in the real-world shoot house without any virtual training. Then the groups' performances were compared. The result showed that 10 min on the laptop produced the same result as 4 runs and 1 h in the real-world shoot house. Essentially, investigators saw that virtual training could reduce real-world training by 75% in terms of training sessions.

Table 10.3 Lessons learned from TADMUS and VRMC CBT: a comparison. (Wiederhold et al. 2006)

	TADMUS	VRMC
	Stress exposure training	Cognitive behavioral therapy
Education	Information provision	Patient education
Skill building	Skill acquisition and practice	Physiological feedback and training
Cognitive schema	Confidence-building application and practice	Cognitive coping techniques, desensitization in virtual reality then *in vivo* (real-life)
Degree of exposure	Over-learn	Over-learn
Training generalization	Training generalizes to real-life missions	Therapy generalizes to real-life situations
Content generalization	Skills generalize to novel tasks and novel stressors	Other phobias not specifically trained show improvement
Method of exposure	Gradual increase in stressors results in skill building	Gradual exposure is important
VR advantages	Virtual reality simulations crucial in allowing for a gradual increase in stressors	Virtual reality simulations allow for over-learning and gradual exposure to more and more intense situations
Internal belief	A sense of control and mastery occurs	Self-efficacy and a sense of mastery occurs
Ongoing support	Refresher sessions provide maintenance of skills	Booster sessions provide maintenance of skills
Pace of exposure	Initial exposure to high-demand/high-stress conditions does not result in skill development and generalization	Flooding does not result in development of skills
Order of exposure	Develop basic physiological control strategies first to control stress/reduce attention allocated to emotions	Teach physiological control first
Quality of exposure	Absolute fidelity is not necessary or desirable	Virtual reality simulations better than real video
Lessons learned	*Take-home message*: "an effective method for reducing anxiety and enhancing performance in stressful environments. The results of this analysis should clearly encourage further application and research"	*Take-home message*: CBT reduces anxiety, results in higher levels of functioning, and increases quality of life

In a different part of the study, a VR group completed a weapons search of a house about 2 min faster than the group without VR training. Additionally, the non-VR group, for all trials, located and cleared rooms successfully but two exercises resulted in teams clearing rooms multiple times (93% accuracy). The VR group, for all trials, located and cleared rooms successfully with no rooms cleared multiple times (100% accuracy).

Fig. 10.7 Medical professional immersed in B-HIVE. (Stetz et al. 2006)

Currently, Dr. Brenda K. Wiederhold serves as a consultant on a study originally funded by a Telemedicine and Advanced Technologies Research Center (TATRC) grant and conducted by the US Army Aeromedical Research Lab (USAARL). The VRMC also developed customized VR software for the study with an en route medical evacuation emphasis (MEDEVAC scenarios) and provided physiological monitoring systems and system support for the study. Initial VR-SIT training and data collection began at Ft. Rucker, Alabama, in April 2006 (Stetz et al. 2006). USAARL embedded the system components into the Battlefield Highly Immersive Virtual Environment (B-HIVE) with the intention of validating the VR-SIT approach in a population of flight medics (Fig. 10.7).

The objective of this study was to evaluate the utility of VR-SIT to inoculate (e.g., habituate, harden, protect) against harmful stress and help maintain or increase the performance of soldiers undergoing rigorous field-relevant medical training. Expected findings were that medics training with VR scenarios and receiving coping training would show less stress levels, with time, than those that did not get this opportunity. Further, it was predicted that this approach would not only improve soldiers' performance on real tasks but also increase their stress resilience and prevent chronic psychological decompensation (e.g., PTSD). Participants were matched as closely as possible based on factors thought to affect VR-SIT efficacy such as gender, age, prior gaming experience, and deployment history. Each participant was then assigned to one of the groups as defined below:

Group 0 ($n=9$) did not undergo any VR nor coping training (CT); only vital signs were measured.
Group 1 ($n=18$) had two (or four) VR game play sessions but no CT.
Group 2 ($n=18$) had two (or four) CT sessions but no VR sessions.
Group 3 ($n=18$) had VR-SIT (VR+CT) training during two (or four) sessions of game play.

Investigators measured the stress of each participant using various psychological, biochemical, and physical metrics. Preliminary findings with a sample of 25 medics suggested that those who learned coping techniques during the VR training exhibited lower levels of stress than the rest (Stetz 2007; Stetz et al. 2007). Results showed that hostility levels were higher in the VR-only group than the rest. The VR-CT group showed higher levels of sensation seeking, an important first step in examining how VR-induced stress combined with relaxation training can be used to create psychological inoculation against combat stress (Stetz et al. 2008). In a follow-up study to test military personnel acceptability of such stress-management techniques (Stetz et al. 2009), preference for the type of VR relaxation experience varied but half ($n=29$) of the sample considered practicing these techniques after the study.

SIT is used to build up a tolerance to stressful situations as well as to increase the ability to effectively manage physiological, psychological, and emotional responses to stressful stimuli. By understanding the state of the student during training, the simulated training can then be modified to add or subtract stressors as would be most appropriate to the situation (Wiederhold et al. 2006). This type of training has been utilized in many different ways, which are illustrated in the following studies.

In Greece, where earthquakes are common, therapists taught Down syndrome children how to react during a simulated earthquake, with an 87% success rate in the panic control treatment group (PCT) versus 33% in the control group (Tarnanas and Manos 2001). These results were maintained at 3-month follow up, with 85% in the PCT group panic free versus 30% in a waitlist condition. A two-button input device and head tracker were used for navigating the virtual classroom and the child sat on a vibrating platform designed to mimic the earth's movements. A 12-week protocol began with creation of the child's "ideal self" as an avatar. The treatment provided ways to overcome panic and anxiety in the face of a simulated earthquake. To engage the child emotionally, anxiety showed up in the avatar's body, and the child's actions worked to change that body toward the "ideal self" image as coping skills were acquired.

Two studies of workplace stress in a virtual environment with 60 healthy participants and 60 patients with work-related stress disorders showed that a VR group test had psychometric properties comparable to its derivative individual scenarios (Tarnanas et al. 2003). The virtual environment consisted of the interior of an office and included hostile situations. In the first test, patients differed from controls on the number of trials to attain a given category but not on the overall pattern of response (Pearson's $r=0.44$, $P=0.001$). The second test asked participants to search four rooms in search of a specific task that was deliberately not included, randomly assigned them to a group or individual condition in "yoked" pairs, and asked the pairs to complete the collaborative coping skills test. A repeated-measures ANOVA confirmed a significant effect of healthy coping skills versus work-related stress ($df=1.24$; $F=80.4$; $P<0.001$).

In Croatia, where large peacekeeping operations have been in place for years, researchers are studying the use of SIT. A recent presentation (Popovic et al. 2009) described four subsystems of physiology-driven adaptive VR stimulation: stimuli generator, emotional state estimator, adaptive controller, and graphical interface. The stimuli generator receives signals from the controller; such signals are compared to a stimuli database to resolve them into stimuli. The emotional state estimator reads the participant's emotional state from acquired physiological signals in the form of, for example, arousal values. The adaptive controller contains the decision-making logic based on a reference database and the accumulated data from the participant. The therapist or trainer uses the graphical interface to override the adaptive controller's decisions as needed.

10.8 Discussion

Because a VR environment can be adapted and modified to any specific situation, condition, or event, this technology has the capacity to cross international borders and language barriers. For example, the use of mobile narratives on a smart phone may improve the mood and the state of the soldier when a specific therapeutic protocol is combined with the treatment (Riva et al. 2008). With further adaptations and research, the possibilities for VR therapy are seemingly endless, possessing the potential to become a cross-cultural technology improving the mental health of both war veterans and civilian populations suffering from PTSD worldwide. VR has made a significant impact on behavioral health care, permeating the field with its multiple effective functions. VR is an embodied technology with potential far wider than the simple reproduction of real worlds. Superior graphics tested in development by objective measures of physiological arousal can produce, enhance, and maximize cognitive interaction. By designing meaningful embodied activities, VR can facilitate cognitive modeling and change.

10.9 Available Software

Hanyang University, Seoul, Korea; contact Sun I. Kim, Professor and Director, Department of Biomedical Engineering, +82 (2) 2290 8280, sunkim@hanyang.ac.kr (Fig. 10.8).

Universidade Lusófona de Humanidades e Tecnologias: contact Pedro Gamito, pedro.gamito@sapo.pt, pedro.gamito@gmail.com.

A guerrilla war world was created to treat war veterans who developed PTSD during the Portuguese African colonies wars in the 1960s–1970s. The patients go on patrol through a jungle trail "picada," where, from time to time, they suffer an ambush and/or a mortar mine explosion. Every time casualties occur, they need to wait close to the victim for rescue by helicopter (Fig. 10.9).

One potential outcome of an MVA is an anxiety disorder such as fear of driving or even PTSD. To treat patients with such disorders, a virtual highway was developed. In this world, it is possible to increase or decrease cues such as traffic, horns, horizon confinement, etc. (Fig. 10.10).

University of Southern California, Institute for Creative Technologies, 13274 Fiji Way, Marina del Rey, CA 90292, (310) 574–5700, http://ict.usc.edu/contact.

10.9 Available Software

Fig. 10.8 MVA PTSD scenario (Source: Wiederhold and Wiederhold 2006b)

Fig. 10.9 Guerilla war PTSD scenario. (reproduced with permission from P. Gamito)

Fig. 10.10 MVA PTSD scenario (Source: Saraiva et al. 2007)

The Virtual Iraq application and the Virtual Afghanistan scenario consist of a series of virtual scenarios including Middle-Eastern-themed city and desert road environments. In addition to the visual stimuli presented in the VR HMD, directional 3D audio, and vibrotactile and olfactory stimuli of relevance can be delivered. A therapist via a separate clinical interface while in full audio contact can control the presentation of additive, combat-relevant stimuli in the VR scenarios with the patient (Figs. 10.11 and 10.12).

The Virtual Reality Medical Center, 9565 Waples Street, Suite 200, San Diego, CA 92121, (858) 642–0267, mwiederhold@vrphobia.com.

Fig. 10.11 Iraq/Afghanistan war scenarios

Fig. 10.12 Clinician interface

Fig. 10.13 Iraq War PTSD treatment system

Fig. 10.14 Iraq War PTSD scenes

The virtual world, which can be viewed on a laptop computer or with a HMD, features a market, a battlefield (with a car, helicopter, Humvee, and explosions), a battalion aid station, and houses. Three computers are used to deliver treatment: (1) one on which the therapist can track where the patient is located in the virtual environment and can, with a simple click, trigger events to occur based on the state of the patient; (2) another on which the virtual world is displayed (and observed by the patient if wearing the HMD is too overwhelming at the beginning of treatment); and (3) a computer on which the patient's physiological functions are monitored and feedback is projected. The environment is composed of sights and sounds, such as Arabic prayer from a temple, helicopters thundering overhead, distant explosions, vehicles burning, terrorists running while firing guns, and the voices of Iraqi civilians (see Figs. 10.13 and 10.14).

References

American Psychiatric Association. (2000). *Diagnostic and statistical manual of mental disorders* (4th ed., DSM-IV, text revision). Washington, DC: American Psychiatric Association.

Arnetz, B. B., Nevedal, D. C., Lumley, M. A., Backman, L., & Lublin, A. (2009). Trauma resilience training for police: Psychophysiological and performance effects. *J Police Crim Psych, 24*, 1–9.

Ballenger, J. C., Davidson, J. R., Lecrubier, Y., Nutt, D. J., Foa, E. B., Kessler, R. C., McFarlane, A. C., & Shalev, A. Y. (2000). Consensus statement on posttraumatic stress disorder from the international consensus group on depression and anxiety. *Journal of Clinical Psychiatry, 61*(Suppl 5), 60–66.

Barlow, D. H. (1988). *Anxiety and its disorders: The nature and treatment of anxiety and panic.* New York: Guilford.

Basoglu, M., Livanou, M., & Salcıoglu, E. (2003). A single session with an earthquake simulator for traumatic stress in earthquake survivors. *The American journal of psychiatry, 160*, 788–790.

Beck, J. G., & Coffey, S. F. (2007). Assessment and treatment of PTSD after a motor vehicle collision: Empirical findings and clinical observations. *Professional Psychology: Research and Practice, 38*(6), 629–639.

Blanchard, E. B., & Hickling, E. J. (2004). *After the crash. 2.* Washington, DC: American Psychological Association.

Bradley, R., Greene, J., Russ, E., Dutra, L., & Westen, D. (2005). A multidimensional meta-analysis of psychotherapy for PTSD. *American Journal of Psychiatry, 162*(2), 214–227.

Bryant, R. A., Harvey, A. G., Guthrie, R. M., & Moulds, M. L. (2000). A prospective study of psychophysiological arousal, acute stress disorder, and posttraumatic stress disorder. *Journal of Abnormal Psychology, 109*, 341–344.

Bryant, R. A., Moulds, M. L., Guthrie, R. M., Dang, S. T., Mastrodomenico, J., Nixon, R. D. V., Felmingham, K. L., Hopwood, S., & Creamer, M. (2008). A randomized controlled trial of exposure therapy and cognitive restructuring for posttraumatic stress disorder. *Journal of Consulting and Clinical Psychology, 76*(4), 695–703.

Difede, J., & Hoffman, H. G. (2002). Virtual reality exposure therapy for World Trade Center posttraumatic stress disorder: A case report. *Cyberpsychology and Behavior, 5*(6), 529–536.

Difede, J., Cukor, J., Patt, I., Giosan, C., & Hoffman, H. (2006). The application of virtual reality to the treatment of PTSD following the WTC attack. *Annals of the New York Academy of Sciences, 1071*, 500–501.

Difede, J., Cukor, J., Jayasinghe, N., Patt, I., Jedel, S., Speilman, L., Giosan, C., & Hoffman, H. G. (2007). Virtual reality exposure therapy for the treatment of posttraumatic stress disorder following September 11, 2001. *Journal of Clinical Psychiatry, 68*(11), 1639–1647.

Dohrenwend, B. P., Turner, J. B., Turse, N. A., Adams, B. G., Koenen, K. C., & Marshall, R. (2006). The psychological risks of Vietnam for U.S. veterans: A revisit with new data and methods. *Science, 313*(5789), 979–982.

Ehlers, A., Clark, D. M., Hackmann, A., McManus, F., Fennell, M., Herbert, C., & Mayou, R. (2003). A randomized controlled trial of cognitive therapy, a self-help booklet, and repeated assessments as early interventions for posttraumatic stress disorder. *Archives of General Psychiatry, 60*, 1024–1032.

Foa, E. B., Cashman, L., Jaycox, L., & Perry, K. J. (1997). The validation of a self-report measure of posttraumatic stress disorder: The posttraumatic diagnostic scale. *Psychological Assessment, 9*, 445–451.

Gamito, P., Oliveira, J., Rosa, P., Morais, D., Duarte, N., Oliveira, S., & Saraiva, T.(2010). PTSD elderly war veterans: A clinical controlled pilot study. *Cyberpsychology Cyberpsychology, Behavior, and Social Networking, 13* (1), 43–48. doi:10.1089/cyber.2009.0237.

Gamito, P., Oliveira, J., Morais, D., Oliveira, S., Duarte, N., Saraiva, T., Pombal, M., & Rosa, P. (2009). Virtual reality therapy controlled study for war veterans with PTSD. Preliminary results. In B. K. Wiederhold & G. Riva (Eds.), *Annual review of cybertherapy and telemedicine 2009: Advanced technologies in the behavioral, social and neurosciences* (pp. 165–171). San Diego: Interactive Media Institute.

Gillespie, K., Duffy, M., Hackmann, A., & Clark, D. M. (2002). Community based cognitive therapy in treatment of post-traumatic stress disorder following the Omagh bomb. *Behaviour Research and Therapy, 40*, 345–357.

Hamner, M. B., Robert, S., & Frueh, B. C. (2004). Treatment resistant posttraumatic stress disorder: Strategies for intervention. *CNS Spectrums, 9*(10), 740–752.

Harvey, A. G., & Bryant, R. A. (1998). The relationship between acute stress disorder and posttraumatic stress disorder: A prospective evaluation of motor vehicle accident survivors. *Journal of Consulting and Clinical Psychology, 66*, 507–512.

Harvey, A. G., Bryant, R. A., & Tarrier, N. (2003). Cognitive behaviour therapy for posttraumatic stress disorder. *Clinical Psychology Review, 23*, 501–522.

Hoge, C. W., Castro, C. A., Messer, S. C., McGurk, D., Cotting, D. I., & Koffman, R. L. (2004). Combat duty in Iraq and Afghanistan, mental health problems, and barriers to care. *The New England Journal of Medicine, 351*(1), 13–22.

Institute of Medicine (IOM). (2008). *Treatment of posttraumatic stress disorder: An assessment of the evidence*. Washington, DC: The National Academies Press.

Jaycox, L. H., Foa, E. B., & Morral, A. R. (1998). Influence of emotional engagement and habituation on exposure therapy for PTSD. *Journal of Consulting and Clinical Psychology, 66*, 185–192.

Josman, N., Somer, E., Reisberg, A., Weiss, P. L., Garcia-Palacios, A., & Hoffman, H. (2006). BusWorld: Desigining a virtual environment for post-traumatic stress disorder in Israel: A protocol. *Cyberpsychology and Behavior, 9*(2), 241–244.

Josman, N., Reisberg, A., Weiss, P. L., Garcia-Palacios, A., & Hoffman, H. G. (2008). BusWorld: An analog pilot test of a virtual environment designed to treat posttraumatic stress disorder originating from a terrorist suicide bomb attack. *Cyberpsychology and Behavior, 11*(6), 775–777.

References

Kosslyn, S. M., Brunn, J., Cave, K. R., & Walach, R. W. (1984). Individual differences in mental imagery ability: A computational analysis. *Cognition, 18*(1-3), 195–243.

McLay, R. N., Wood, D. P., Webb-Murphy, J. A., Spira, J. L., Wiederhold, M. D., Pyne, J. M., & Wiederhold, B. K. (2011). A randomized, controlled trial of virtual reality-graded exposure therapy for post-traumatic stress disorder in active duty service members with combat-related post-traumatic stress disorder. *Cyberpsychology, Behavior & Social Networking, 14*(4), 223–229.

Milliken, C. S., Auchterlonie, J. L., & Hoge, C. W. (2007). Longitudinal assessment of mental health problems among active and reserve component soldiers returning from the Iraq war. *Journal of American Medical Association, 298*(18), 2141–2148.

National Center for PTSD. (2009). Epidemiological Facts about PTSD. http://ncptsd.va.gov/ncmain/ncdocs/fact_shts/fs_epidemiological.html. Accessed 15 Sept 2009.

Norris, F. H. (1992). Epidemiology of trauma: Frequency and impact of potentially traumatic events on different demographic groups. *Journal of Consulting and Clinical Psychology, 60*, 409–418.

Popovic, S., Horvat, M., Kukolja, D., Dropuljić, B., & Ćosić, K. (2009). Stress inoculation training supported by physiology-driven adaptive virtual reality stimulation. In B. K. Wiederhold & G. Riva (Eds.), *Annual review of cybertherapy and telemedicine 2009: Advanced technologies in the behavioral, social and neurosciences* (pp. 61–65). San Diego: Interactive Media Institute.

Reger, G. M., & Gahm, G. A. (2008). Virtual reality exposure therapy for active duty soldiers. *Journal of Clinical Psychology, 64*(8), 940–946.

Riva, G., Gorini, A., Grassi, A., & Villani, D. (2008). Mobile narratives for combating battlefield stress: Rationale, preliminary research and protocol. In B. K. Wiederhold (Ed.), *Lowering suicide risk in returning troops* (NATO science for peace and security series E: Human and societal dynamics) (Vol. 42, pp. 113–128). Amsterdam: IOS Press.

Rizzo, A. A., Difede, J., Rothbaum, B. O., Johnston, S., McLay, R. N., Reger, G., Gahm, G., Parsons, T., Graap, K., & Pair, J. (2009). VR PTSD exposure therapy results with active duty OIF/OEF combatants. *Studies in Health Technology and Informatics, 142*, 277–282.

Rothbaum, B. O., Hodges, L., Alarcon, R., Ready, D., Shahar, F., Graap, K., Pair, J., Hebert, P., Gotz, D., Wills, B., & Baltzell, D. (1999). Virtual reality exposure therapy for PTSD Vietnam veterans: A case study. *Journal of Traumatic Stress, 12*(2), 263–271.

Rothbaum, B. O., Hodges, L., Ready, D., Graap, K., & Alarcon, R. (2001). Virtual reality exposure therapy for Vietnam veterans with posttraumatic stress disorder. *Journal of Clinical Psychiatry, 62*(8), 617–622.

Saraiva, T., Gamito, P., Oliveira, J., Morais, D., Pombal, M., Gamito, L., & Anastácio, M. (2007). The use of VR exposure in the treatment of motor vehicle PTSD: A case report. In B. K. Wiederhold, G. Riva, & S. Bouchard (Eds.), *Annual review of cybertherapy and telemedicine* (Vol. 5, pp. 199–205). San Diego: Interactive Media Institute.

Spira, J. L., Pyne, J. M., & Wiederhold, B. K. (2006). Experiential methods in the treatment of PTSD. In C. R. Figley & W. K. Nash (Eds.), *For those who bore the battle: Combat stress injury theory, research and management*. New York: Routledge.

Stetz, M. C. (2007). *Flight medic's virtual reality training to enhance performance under combat stress*. Presented at Medicine Meets Virtual Reality 15, Long Beach, California.

Stetz, M. C., Wildzunas, R. M., Wiederhold, B. K., Stetz, T. A., & Hunt, M. P. (2006). *The usefulness of virtual reality stress inoculation training for military medical females: A pilot study*. Presented at the CyberTherapy 11 conference, Gatineau, Canada.

Stetz, M. C., Long, C. P., Schober, W. V., Cardillo, C. G., & Wildzunas, R. M. (2007). Stress assessment and management while medics take care of the VR wounded. In B. K. Wiederhold, G. Riva, & S. Bouchard (Eds.), *Annual review of cybertherapy and telemedicine* (Vol. 5, pp. 165–171). San Diego: Interactive Media Institute.

Stetz, M. C., Long, C. P., Wiederhold, B. K., & Turner, D. D. (2008). Combat scenarios and relaxation training to harden medics against stress. *Journal of CyberTherapy and Rehabilitation, 1*(3), 239–246.

Stetz, M. C., Bouchard, S., Wiederhold, B. K., Riva, G., & Folen, R. A. (2009). The responsiveness of stress management techniques by military personnel. In B. K. Wiederhold & G. Riva (Eds.), *Annual review of cybertherapy and telemedicine 2009: Advanced technologies in the behavioral, social and neurosciences* (pp. 126–128). San Diego: Interactive Media Institute.

Tarnanas, I., & Manos, G. (2001). Using virtual reality to teach special populations how to cope in crisis: The case of a virtual earthquake. *Studies in Health Technology and Informatics, 81*, 495–501.

Tarnanas, I., & Manos, G. (2004). A clinical protocol for the development of a virtual reality behavioral training in disaster exposure and relief. In B. K. Wiederhold, S. Bouchard, & G. Riva (Eds.), *Annual review of cybertherapy and telemedicine* (Vol. 2, pp. 78–84). San Diego: Interactive Media Institute.

Tarnanas, I., Tsoukalas, I., & Strogiannidou, A. (2003). Virtual reality as a psychosocial coping environment. In B. K. Wiederhold & G. Riva (Eds.), *Annual review of cybertherapy and telemedicine* (Vol. 1, pp. 77–82). San Diego: Interactive Media Institute.

Ursano, R. J., Fullerton, C. S., Epstein, R. S., Crowley, B., Kao, T., Vance, K., Craig, K. J., Dougall, A. L., & Baum, A. (1999). Acute and chronic posttraumatic stress disorder in motor vehicle accident victims. *American Journal of Psychiatry, 156*, 589–595.

Van Etten, M. L., & Taylor, S. (1998). Comparative efficacy of treatments for PTSD: A meta-analysis. *Clinical Psychology and Psychotherapy, 5*(3), 126–145.

Walshe, D. G. (2008). *Lessons learned from treating 200 motor vehicle accident victims with videogames.* Presented at the CyberTherapy 13th conference, San Diego, California.

Walshe, D. G., Lewis, E. J., Kim, S. I., O'Sullivan, K., & Wiederhold, B. K. (2003). Exploring the use of computer games and virtual reality in exposure therapy for fear of driving following a motor vehicle accident. *Cyberpsychology and Behavior, 6*(3), 329–334.

Walshe, D., Lewis, E., O'Sullivan, K., & Kim, S. I. (2005). Virtually driving: Are the driving environments "real enough" for exposure therapy with accident victims? An explorative study. *Cyberpsychology and Behavior, 8*(6), 532–537.

Wiederhold, B. K., & Wiederhold, M. D. (2000). Lessons learned from 600 virtual reality sessions. *Cyberpsychology and Behavior, 3*(3), 393–400.

Wiederhold, B. K., & Wiederhold, M. D. (2004a). *Virtual reality therapy for anxiety disorders.* New York: American Psychological Association Press.

Wiederhold, B. K., & Wiederhold, M. D. (2004b). *Training combat medics using VR.* Presented at the CyberTherapy 9th conference, San Diego, CA.

Wiederhold, M. D., & Wiederhold, B. K. (2006a). *Virtual reality training transfer: A DARWARS study. Physiological monitoring during simulation training and testing.* San Diego: The Virtual Reality Medical Center.

Wiederhold, B. K., & Wiederhold, M. D. (2006b). Communication and experience in clinical psychology and neurorehabilitation: the use of virtual reality driving simulators. In G. Riva, M. T. Anguera, B. K. Wiederhold, & F. Mantovani (Eds.), *From communication to presence: Cognition, emotions and culture towards the ultimate communicative experience. Festschrift in Honor of Luigi Anolli* (pp. 267–280). Amsterdam: IOS Press.

Wiederhold, B. K., & Wiederhold, M. D. (2008a). Virtual reality as an adjunct for training and treatment. In B. K. Wiederhold (Ed.), *Lowering suicide risk in returning troops.* (NATO science for peace and security series E: Human and societal dynamics) (Vol. 42, pp. 184–200). Amsterdam: IOS Press.

Wiederhold, B. K., & Wiederhold, M. D. (2008b). Virtual reality for posttraumatic stress disorder and stress inoculation training. *Journal of CyberTherapy & Rehabilitation, 1*(1), 23–35.

Wiederhold, B. K., Gevirtz, R., & Spira, J. L. (2001a). Virtual reality exposure therapy vs. imagery desensitization therapy in the treatment of flying phobia. In G. Riva & C. Galimberti (Eds.), *Towards cyberpsychology: Mind cognition and society in the Internet age* (pp. 253–272). Amsterdam: IOS Press.

Wiederhold, B. K., Jang, D., Kim, S., & Wiederhold, M. D. (2001b). *Using advanced technologies to treat fear of driving.* Presented at the 9th Annual Medicine Meets Virtual Reality conference, Newport Beach, California.

Wiederhold, B. K., Bullinger, A. H., & Wiederhold, M. D. (2006). Advanced technologies in military medicine. In M. J. Roy (Ed.), *Novel approaches to the diagnosis and treatment of posttraumatic stress disorder* (pp. 148–160). Amsterdam: IOS Press.

Wood, D. P., Murphy, J. A., Center, K. B., Russ, C., McLay, R. N., Reeves, D., Pyne, J., Shilling, R., Hagan, J., & Wiederhold, B. K. (2008). Combat related posttraumatic stress disorder: A multiple case report using virtual reality graded exposure therapy with physiological monitoring. *Studies in. Health Technologies and Informatics, 132,* 556–561.

Wood, D. P., Murphy, J., McLay, R., Koffman, R., Spira, J., Obrecht, R. E., Pyne, J., & Wiederhold, B. K. (2009). Cost effectiveness of virtual reality graded exposure therapy with physiological monitoring for the treatment of combat related post traumatic stress disorder. In B. K. Wiederhold & G. Riva (Eds.), *Annual review of cybertherapy and telemedicine 2009. Advanced technologies in the behavioral, social and neurosciences* (pp. 220–226). San Diego: Interactive Media Institute.

Chapter 11
Generalized Anxiety Disorder and Obsessive–Compulsive Disorder: Efficacy and the Development of Virtual Environments

Tanya Guitard, Mylène Laforest and Stéphane Bouchard

11.1 Key Variables Involved in Generalized Anxiety Disorder (GAD) and Obsessive–Compulsive Disorder (OCD)

11.1.1 Generalized Anxiety Disorder

Generalized anxiety disorder (GAD) is the last anxiety disorder to have been included in the *Diagnostic and Statistical Manuel* (*DSM*). It made its appearance in the *DSM-III,* published in 1980. It is therefore no surprise that criteria for this disorder have evolved considerably over the years. However, through every edition of the *DSM,* GAD's main characteristic has always been the presence of excessive anxiety or worry. Worry in GAD must concern at least a few activities or events and be present during a minimum of 6 months. It is accompanied by difficulty controlling the worry which, in turn, can be associated with the following symptoms: relentlessness or feeling keyed up or on edge, being easily fatigued, difficulty concentrating or mind going blank, irritability, muscle tension, and sleep disturbance (APA 2000).

Worry is undoubtedly the main characteristic of GAD. It can be defined as "a thought process that is concerned with future events where there is uncertainty about the outcome, the future being thought about is a negative one, and this is accompanied by feelings of anxiety" (Macleod et al. 1991). Actually, it is important for clinicians to be aware that the general anxiety experienced by people suffering from GAD is the consequence of worry (Dugas et al. 1998b; Newman et al. 2013). Therefore, the target for the treatment of GAD should not be the general and pervasive anxiety but rather excessive and incontrollable worry. GAD is typically a chronic condition and patients often wait a considerable number of years before seeking treatment. This could be explained by the fact that the onset is often early in life and quite subtle, therefore leaving people to think that their worry is normal or part of their personality rather than a disorder (Kessler 2004). Consequently, the prevalence of GAD is quite significant. Based on the estimates from the National Comorbidity Survey (NCS; Kessler et al. 2005), lifetime prevalence is estimated at

5.7%, with the rate slightly higher in women (7.1%) compared to men (4.2%). The *DSM-IV-TR* (APA 2000) reported lifetime prevalence at 5% and 12-month prevalence at 3%.

11.1.2 Obsessive–Compulsive Disorder

Obsessive–compulsive disorder (OCD) is the fear of a thought, image, or impulse that provokes discomfort usually relieved by a mental or a behavioral ritual. This chronic and invalidating mental disorder is characterized, according to the *DSM-IV* (APA 2000), by recurrent obsessions and/or compulsions that interfere considerably with daily functioning. Obsessions are persistent ideas, thoughts, impulses, or images that are experienced as intrusive and inappropriate and cause marked anxiety or distress. Compulsions are described as repetitive behaviors (e.g., hand washing, ordering, checking), or mental acts (e.g., praying, counting, repeating words silently), that the person feels driven to perform in response to an obsession or according to rules that must be applied rigidly. The behaviors or mental acts are aimed at preventing or reducing distress or preventing some dreaded event or situation, even though they are not connected in a realistic way with what they are designed to neutralize or prevent or are clearly excessive. As mentioned, the obsessions or compulsions cause marked distress, are time consuming (take more than 1 h a day), or significantly interfere with the person's normal routine, occupational (or academic) functioning, or usual activities or relationships. The definition of OCD specifies that obsessions are not simply excessive worries about real-life problems, as it would be the case in GAD. The obsessive thoughts are egodystonic (i.e., in conflict with the person's ego and values) and can be classified into different subtypes, such as contamination, aggressive, sexual, hoarding, religious, symmetry/order, and somatic. As for compulsions, they usually appear in the form of washing/cleaning, checking, repeating, counting, ordering, and hoarding. OCD sufferers usually recognize that the obsessions and compulsions are excessive or unreasonable for most of the time during the episode. However, the person will be considered to have "poor insight" if he or she does not distinguish the irrationality of their fear.

Even though the diagnosis of OCD does not imply that the person presents both obsessions and compulsions, a field trial conducted by Foa and Kozak (1995) suggests that the vast majority (more than 90%) of OCD sufferers manifest both obsessions and behavioral compulsions. Interestingly, when mental rituals were included as compulsions, only 2% of the sample reported obsessions only. Thus, effective treatment should allow addressing both obsessions and compulsions.

According to the National Comorbidity Survey (Kessler et al. 2005), its lifetime prevalence is estimated at 2.3%, affecting more women (3.1%) than men (1.6%). OCD is one of the most debilitating anxiety disorders, severely interrupting social and occupational functioning (Leon et al. 1995), and linked to a fourfold risk of unemployment (Koran et al. 1996). This can be explained by the fact that OCD sufferers spend most of their time obsessing, completing their rituals, and avoiding situations related to the obsessive fears. Before 1960, OCD was considered a rare and untreatable condition (Abramowitz et al. 2001), which is not the case nowadays, as we will see in the next few sections.

11.1.3 Theoretical Models of GAD

There are many theoretical models explaining the central concepts of GAD. Among those, most frequently studied are the ones from Wells (1995), Borkovec et al. (2004), and Dugas et al. (1998b). For the purpose of this chapter, we will briefly describe the three with special attention to Dugas' model as it combines most key features of the others and has received strong empirical support.

Wells' metacognitive model bases its theory on the distinction of two types of worry, type 1 and type 2. Type 1 worry refers "to worrying about external events and noncognitive internal events such as physical symptoms" (Wells and Carter 1999). It is used by people suffering from GAD as a coping process in response to a situation or event that is viewed as potentially threatening (Wells 2004). It can be summarized as a way to propose answers to the "What if?" questions that people suffering from GAD are constantly asking themselves, in turn acting as the initiator for more of those anxiety-generating questions. As for type 2 worry, the term "meta-worry" is often used to describe the action of worrying about one's worry (Wells 1995). For example, a person who fears worrying will impact her condition to the point of going crazy is experiencing type 2 worry as described in Wells' conceptualization. According to the author, the latter type of worrying constitutes the core of pathological worry and GAD as it contributes in maintaining and even augmenting worry (Wells and Carter 1999; Wells 2004).

Alternatively, the theory by Borkovec et al. (2004) has for central premise cognitive avoidance in GAD. This theoretical model stipulates that worry in GAD is the first and foremost thought content as opposed to imagery. This refers to the idea that worry comes as verbal/linguistic activity and acts as a way to avoid imagery that is deemed too catastrophic to even imagine (Borkovec and Inz 1990; Borkovec and Lyonfields 1993; Freeston et al. 1996). This model highlights the role of worry as an avoidance strategy.

Finally, Dugas et al. (1998b) proposed a conceptual model of GAD that includes some elements of the previous models. It is based on the interaction between the following concepts: positive beliefs about worry, poor problem orientation, cognitive avoidance, and intolerance to uncertainty. Among these four components, intolerance to uncertainty is considered the key feature driving the perception of threat among GAD patients.

According to this model, intolerance of uncertainty contributes to developing and maintaining the pathological worry involved in GAD (Dugas et al. 2005). This component may be defined as "a dispositional characteristic that results from a set of negative beliefs about uncertainty and its implications" (Dugas and Robichaud 2007). In other words, it refers to the tendency to interpret uncertain or unexpected events or situations as necessarily stressful and leading to a negative outcome. Therefore, uncertainty is avoided as much as possible. Worrying becomes an attempt to find reassurance and avoid uncertainty. Furthermore, intolerance of uncertainty would also be responsible for the tendency in GAD to "live in the future" and resort to more "What if?" questions, which, in turn, exacerbate the worry (Dugas et al. 1998a).

Although worry can be found in order anxiety disorders, such as OCD, one of the difference lies in the worry themes. First of all, worry in GAD tends to be more oriented towards the future than in other disorders (Dugas et al. 1998a). Moreover, worry themes are egosyntonic in the case of GAD, meaning that worry themes are experienced as acceptable by the person, whereas people suffering from OCD consider their intrusive thoughts as horrible and something they should avoid thinking about.

11.1.4 Theoretical Models of OCD

As for GAD, there are several theoretical models of OCD. For the purpose of this chapter, we will focus solely on the CBT, seeing as it has proven itself to be the most effective treatment approach. Mowrer's (1960) was the first to propose a behavioral perspective according to which a person could learn fear and avoidance behavior through the pairing of a neutral stimulus with an event that causes distress. This theory suggests that once fear is acquired, escape or avoidance patterns (i.e., compulsions) develop to reduce fear and are maintained by the negative reinforcement of fear reduction (Franklin and Foa 2007). Forty years or so later, Salkovskis (1985) proposed an inflated responsibility model according to which obsessional thinking originates in the unwanted and unacceptable intrusive thoughts, images, and impulses that are perceived as having an important implication for the OCD sufferer's current concerns (interpreted as implying high personal responsibility and significance). Salkovskis (1996) went on to propose dysfunctional assumptions related to the theme of responsibility such as, beliefs about responsibility, thought–action fusion beliefs, thought control beliefs, and neutralization beliefs. Rachman (1997) also suggested that obsessions were caused by catastrophic interpretations of thoughts, images, and impulses. Later, the leading experts in the fields of OCD joined forces under the name of the Obsessive Compulsive Cognitions Work Group (1997), refined our understanding of what is perceived as threatening by OCD patients, and described multiple belief domains such as inflated responsibility, overimportance of thoughts, overestimation of threat, importance of controlling thoughts, intolerance to uncertainty, and perfectionism. In 2004, Clark (2004) integrated the different sources of information to propose a cognitive-behavioral explanation to OCD. This theory suggests that, even though the majority of people have intrusive thoughts, OCD sufferers believe that it is unacceptable to entertain such thoughts because they threaten the person's value system. The person also feels responsible for preventing the intrusive thoughts from actually happening and causing harm. Unfortunately, deliberate efforts to control, suppress, or neutralize are unproductive and facilitate a rebound effect where the intrusions come back. Moreover, an additional cognitive process enters in to play, which is people's threatening interpretation of the meaning and consequences of failing to adequately control their intrusive thoughts.

11.2 Description of Significant Efficacy Studies using Non-Virtual-Reality Approaches

11.2.1 Empirical Support for GAD Treatment

Earlier treatments for GAD mostly consisted of applied relaxation and other behavioral techniques in order to reduce hyperarousal (see Gould et al. 2004). However, using only those approaches left the cognitive side of GAD untreated and missed the role of worry and intolerance to uncertainty, which explains the limited success of the early treatments and the development of more complete CBT procedures in recent studies (Leahy 2004). To this date, many studies have shown noteworthy results while using CBT in the treatment of GAD. For example, a team of researchers have developed and studied a treatment plan based on the theoretical model proposed by Dugas et al. (1998b). Two randomized controlled trials using this treatment plan have given satisfying results for CBT in the treatment of GAD.

In the first study by Ladouceur et al. (2000), 26 subjects with primary GAD were randomly assigned to either a delayed treatment control condition or a 16-week treatment condition. The therapy consisted of an explanation of treatment rationale, awareness training (i.e., being able to recognize worry), and correction of erroneous beliefs about worry, negative problem-orientation training, and cognitive exposure. The treatment presented in this study also proposed an innovative feature—distinguishing two types of worry, worry about current problems, and worry about hypothetical and improbable situations (Dugas and Robichaud 2007). This classification of worries differs from Wells' types of worry as it refers to the situations provoking the anxiety rather than the process in which it is experienced. Participants were assessed using a structured clinical interview (Anxiety Disorders Interview Schedule, ADIS-IV; Brown et al. 1994) and self-report measures at pretreatment, posttreatment, 6-, and 12-month follow-up. Results from this study proved to be quite encouraging, with 77% of subjects receiving the treatment no longer meeting criteria for GAD at posttest (see Fig. 11.1). Gains were maintained at both follow-up periods.

Another study based on the same theoretical model was conducted with GAD patients using a similar treatment in a group format (Dugas et al. 2003). The final sample consisted of 48 subjects, all with a primary diagnosis of GAD. They were randomly assigned to either a group treatment or a waiting-list control condition. Therapy sessions were held in groups of four to six participants and based on the same components described in the Ladouceur et al. study (2000), the only difference being that 2-hour sessions were held weekly for a period of 14 weeks. A measure was added at the 24-month follow-up in order to further evaluate the long-term effects of this therapy. The clinical significance of change was assessed using the ADIS-IV and revealed interesting results with the following percentages of subjects no longer meeting GAD criteria: 60% at posttreatment, 88% at 6-month follow-up, 83% at 12-month follow-up, and 95% at 24-month follow-up. These findings were replicated by an independent group, which obtained even larger success rates (van der Heiden et al. 2012).

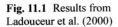

Fig. 11.1 Results from Ladouceur et al. (2000)

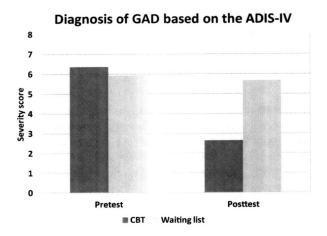

11.2.2 Empirical Support for OCD Treatment

Meyer (1966) demonstrated the effectiveness of two behavioral techniques in the treatment of OCD, coining the term exposure (E: confront feared stimuli) and response prevention (RP: restrain from carrying out rituals following exposure). Since his initial study, many investigations of this treatment have been demonstrated by numerous controlled studies conducted in various centers, different countries, and throughout a large population of patients (Abramowitz et al. 2001; Bouvard and Kaiser 2006). One of the classical outcome studies documenting its effectiveness was conducted by Lindsay et al. (1997) who found, after randomly assigning 18 participants to either ERP or anxiety management for 15 h of therapy over a period of 3 weeks, a significant reduction in obsessive–compulsive symptoms following ERP and no change in the control group. The authors concluded that the symptomatic change was associated to the specific behavioral techniques. A classical controlled treatment outcome study aiming to evaluate the efficacy of CBT for OCD was conducted by van Oppen et al. (1995) who compared the effects of cognitive therapy to those of exposure with response prevention. Seventy-one patients who met criteria for OCD according to the *DSM-III-R* were randomly assigned to either a cognitive therapy treatment based on cognitive therapy for depression and anxiety disorders (Beck 1976; Beck et al. 1985; Salkovskis 1985) or a self-controlled exposure with response prevention, both treatments lasting a total of 16 sessions of approximately 45 min. Patients' symptom change was measured by commonly used OCD measures. Results showed that both treatment conditions led to statistically, as well as clinically, significant improvement, thus both having a similar impact on OCD symptoms (see Fig. 11.2). This was replicated a few years later by Cottraux et al. (2001) with 65 OCD patients.

Another interesting study to mention is the one by Freeston et al. (1997) demonstrating the efficacy of a cognitive–behavioral treatment with 29 purely obsessional OCD sufferers (i.e, without any compulsions). Participants were randomly assigned

11.2 Description of Significant Efficacy Studies

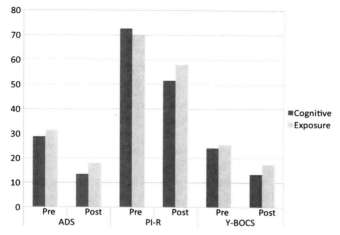

Fig. 11.2 Results from van Oppen et al. (1995)

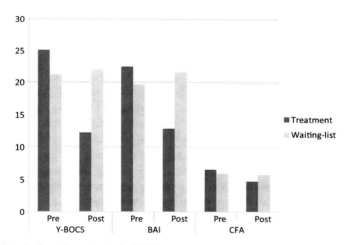

Fig. 11.3 Results from Freeston et al. (1997)

to a CBT group who received an average of 40.5 h of treatment or to a waiting-list group. Results demonstrated significant improvements in the treatment group compared with the waiting-list group (see Fig. 11.3). At post treatment, 67% of those who received treatment showed clinically significant change on the Yale–Brown Obsessive Compulsive Scale (Y-BOCS). This study shows not only the efficacy of CBT for OCD but also its effectiveness in the treatment of the resistant type of OCD with only obsessional ruminations (see Abramowitz et al. 2001 or Bouvard and Kaiser 2006 for more thorough reviews).

11.3 Description of Studies using VR with People Suffering from GAD and OCD

11.3.1 Empirical Status of VR Applications for GAD

Contrary to other anxiety disorders, research on VR for GAD and OCD is still at a very early stage. This is one of the reasons why these two disorders are addressed together in this book. Also, it is a good opportunity to illustrate, later in this chapter, how virtual environments (VEs) are developed and validated.

One of the key challenges faced by developers of VE for GAD is the wide variety of topics that can trigger and fuel the worries. It is therefore not surprising that the first effort targeted the control of anxiety in general. A research project lead by the Italian researcher Giuseppe Riva led to four publications addressing different aspects of one pilot clinical trial (Gorini et al. 2010; Gorini and Riva 2008; Repetto et al. 2013; Pallavicini et al. 2009).

They integrated VR as a means of fostering relaxation and anxiety management in the treatment of GAD. Practice of relaxation exercises at home was facilitated by the use of a mobile phone that could replay the VR session. This system was compared to a waiting-list control group and a group receiving the same treatment but with the VE coupled with a biofeedback that influenced the content of the VE. In both treatment conditions, VR was experienced, during sessions, using a head-mounted display (HMD). From session one to six, participants explored a virtual tropical island wearing a Vuzix HMD and were asked to relax in various calming locations on the island. Relaxation was supported by an audio narrative guiding the patients. Sessions seven and eight integrated stressful content in the form of preselected words or images related to personal stressors and patients had to practice their relaxation skills to cope with anxiety. A variation of the same treatment was offered to another group where elements of the VE were modified according to the heart rate of the participant. For example, decreases in heart rate could impact the intensity of a campfire, movements of the waves on the water, the flow of a waterfall, and of the size of the stressful stimuli presented during session seven and eight. Twenty-five participants suffering from GAD were assigned randomly to either the basic VR condition, the VR condition combined with biofeedback, or a waiting list.

The main outcome measure was Beck Anxiety Inventory and statistical analyses confirmed a significant reduction in pre- to post scores only in both groups of participants receiving an active treatment. The sample size was unfortunately too small to conduct parametric analyses and robustly compare the relative efficacy of each treatment. The first results of this VR application pave the way for other studies with larger considerable samples and treatment targeting core dysfunctional processes such as intolerance to uncertainty and techniques such as exposure to catastrophic scenarios.

It is interesting to explore further the use of mobile phones as a supplement for conducting homework. In this study, the mobile phone application was not immersive, but new technologies are now being tested where an iPhone can be used to generate complex VE that are displayed in a HMD and exploration of the environment is possible through the use of a game pad (e.g., Bouchard et al. 2012). In the study led by the Italian group, mobile phone technology was assessed qualitatively by interviews with patients at the end of their treatment. Although results should be interpreted with caution, a large majority of patients (91 %) reported being very satisfied with the use of a mobile phone as a tool to consolidate their relaxation techniques at home.

11.3.2 Empirical Status of VR Applications for OCD

Despite the fact that many studies have documented the effectiveness of computer-based assessment and treatment for OCD patients (Baer and Greist 1997; Baer et al. 1987, 1988; Herman and Koran 1998; Roca-Bennasar et al. 1991), research pertaining to the applications of VR to OCD treatment is lacking and for the most part still at an early stage of investigation.

The group of VR pioneers in Atlanta led by Max North reported as early as 1999, the case of a female student treated for compulsive checking and obsessional doubt (Wiederhold and Wiederhold 2005, p. 115). During eight weekly sessions, she was immersed for 10–15 min in a VE depicting a room with school material that she had to place in a virtual bag, exit the virtual room, and learn to tolerate her doubts. The intervention seemed to have been useful as the student reported being able to go back to her classes without being overwhelmed by obsessive thoughts. This interesting uncontrolled case study was not followed by further formal investigation for more than 10 years.

A group of researchers led by Sun Kim in Korea then launched a project attempting to validate whether VEs could be used with people suffering with obsessions and compulsions related to checking. Validating the potential of VR to induce anxiety in this population is important before launching full-scale clinical trials. Although *in virtuo* exposure can induce anxiety and be efficient to treat phobics, the perception of threat may be more difficult to trigger. What are the real consequences and patient's actual responsibilities if a virtual stove is left on and starts a virtual fire in a virtual house? Can a person suffering from OCD become anxious in touching a dirty yet virtual toilet that objectively cannot transmit any disease? Is it possible to make a person suffering from checking rituals care about a messy virtual desk that does not belong to them?

In an attempt to address this question, Kim et al. (2012a) asked 24 adults not suffering from OCD to arrange and put in order a messy a virtual desk under three conditions: without any time limit, within a total of 35 operations, or within 70 s. Participants performed the task under each of the three conditions, on a different day, in an order that was randomly assigned. The experiment was conducted using a desktop computer. Anxiety was assessed using 0–100 subjective units of discomfort at a pre-experimental baseline, when seeing the messy desk, during the task, and post experiment. Results revealed that anxiety was significantly increased only in the condition where there was a time constraint and habituation was observed as the experiment was repeated over time. Their study illustrates the need to find a task that is less dependent on time pressure and more on emotional content that would trigger reactions on OCD patients.

The same group conducted another experiment (Kim et al. 2010), this time with a sample of 30 OCD patients and 27 control participants. Participants were immersed in VR using a HMD in two VEs, an office and a house. The interactions with the VE were more complex and relevant to OCD than in the 2012 study. Users immersed *in virtuo* could operate light switches, windows, doors, gas stove, water faucet, etc. The assessment was also more elaborated, including the frequency of checking behavior, gazing time during checking an object (i.e., how long they looked at it), length of the trajectory traveled during the immersion, and time spent performing checking behaviors, etc. Users were requested to practice moving in the VE and perform the various actions possible in the office and the home (e.g., turning on and off the gas stove). After a distraction phase where users had to pick up virtual objects that are unrelated to the main tasks (e.g., picking up an umbrella), they were asked to check everything before leaving and go to the elevator at the end of the corridor.

As hypothesized, people diagnosed with OCD significantly differed from the control participants, performing more checking behaviors, spending more time gazing at the virtual stimuli during checking behavior, "walking" more in the VE, and spending more time checking. These positive results led the authors to conclude that VR could be used to assess checking behaviors in people suffering from OCD. It also documents that it is possible to elicit disruptive checking behaviors in an immersion in VR, opening the possibility to use VR in an exposure-based treatment.

The previously described study did not focus on anxiety but on the comparison of behaviors between people suffering from OCD and non-OCD control participants. Kim et al. (2008) improved our knowledge on the potential of VR this time by comparing self-reported levels of anxiety before and after performing checking behaviors *in virtuo*. The sample consisted in 33 people diagnosed with OCD and 30 controls not suffering from OCD. The immersion, using a HMD, was only in the virtual home. Results revealed significant differences in anxiety between the two groups before checking and a significant reduction in anxiety after checking behaviors are done. The statistical interaction was on the verge of being statistically significant and, if probably only one or two more additional participants have been included, would have revealed a larger decrease in anxiety in the clinical sample. Also, people suffering from OCD spent significantly more time checking than those in the control condition. Results like this are interesting because they mimic what is observed in clinical practice. People suffering from OCD check for longer periods of time objects like locked doors or gas valve and burners; before checking, they are more anxious than people not suffering from OCD and checking actually reduces their discomfort.

The Koran researchers further refined their methodology in a study comparing subtypes of OCD patients (Kim et al. 2012b). This time, they focused on checking

Fig. 11.4 Screenshots of the male section of the dirty public toilet tested by Laforest and Bouchard (2013) for people suffering from the contamination subtype of OCD. Reproduced with permission from S. Bouchard

behaviors instead of anxiety and compared the response of 22 people diagnosed with OCD and featuring mostly checking as their main symptoms, 17 people diagnosed with OCD and reporting no checking behaviors, and 31 healthy controls. As in the previous study, participants were immersed with a HMD in the virtual home and the immersion followed the three phases of training, distraction, and checking. As expected, they found significant differences in the three groups. In terms of checking time, OCD patients with a checking subtype spend more time checking than both the OCD controls and the healthy controls. The length of the trajectory "walked" in the VE by the checkers was also significantly longer then the healthy controls.

This series of studies illustrates well that checking in situations that are virtual can specifically elicit the expected response in people suffering from OCD. But does this extend to other subtypes of OCD? Laforest and Bouchard (2013) compared the anxiety experienced by people diagnosed with OCD of the contamination subtype to healthy controls. They measured their heart rate and self-reported anxiety before and after an immersion in a dirty public toilet (see Fig. 11.4). The immersion was conducted in a six-wall immersive cube where users have the impression of being totally visually immersed in the VE. Participants experienced an immersion in a clean control environment and in the disgusting public bathroom. Results revealed a significantly larger increase in anxiety on the clinical sample, both in terms of heart rate and state anxiety. This VE was also used in a pilot study using a single-case design (Laforest and Bouchard 2013). Statistical results of the time-series analyses based on daily assessment of the severity of obsessions and compulsions confirmed that the treatment was effective for two of the three participants. Cardenas-Lopez et al. (2010, unpublished data) have also created VEs for the treatment of OCD. These environments were developed in order to trigger obsessive fears such as contamination, disorder, and symmetry. Their ongoing study will attempt to treat OCD participants with a complete treatment protocol (psychoeducation, breathing training, cognitive restructuring, and exposure) while using VR scenarios such as a public bathroom, a bus, and a restaurant.

11.4 Development of a VE

The validation studies presented in this chapter illustrate the early steps taken by researchers before conducting large and costly control trials. This brings the opportunity to document even earlier steps and look under the hood at the how VEs are developed.

There are many ways of going about when developing a VE, some more structured than others. An optimal framework used to guide this tedious process would be following the Virtual Environment Development Structure (VEDS; Wilson 1997; Wilson et al. 1996). The current version (see Wilson et al. 2002) has six key stages, these being preparation, analysis, specification, building, implementation, and evaluation, each stage having specific tasks. Even though this method is rigorous, complete, and recommended, researchers do not always have the luxury of time to follow it. Because this chapter provides only an overview of what is involved in developing an environment, we will not go in as much details and illustrate only key points. Examples illustrating different developmental stages will be pulled from current research in GAD and OCD.

11.4.1 Needs and Goals

The first step is to evaluate the need of the research or clinical field. What is it in the current state of practice that cannot be done or is sufficiently challenging to do? It is helpful to determine what has been done and what is possible through the application of VR. This step basically includes that researchers find a way to incorporate VR into the task they want to accomplish. Evidently, knowledge about the domain and attributes of the VE are necessary at this stage. Usually, professionals who have a sound clinical experience in their field should be able to assess the needs of the expected end users and foresee what VR scenarios they would like to use in their treatment plan. However, unless the mental health professional has some experience with VR or the development of VEs, it is important to involve people with technical expertise in VR, such as engineers, computer programmers, game developers, etc., who could provide insights on what is technologically feasible and at what cost.

Clarifying the goals for the task that will be performed *in virtuo* is imperative since VR can serve many purposes, such as an assessment tool (i.e., is the patient meeting diagnosis criteria according to the task?), a treatment tool (i.e., for *in virtuo* exposure or relaxation), to provoke an emotion or thought (e.g., recreate a mood or a context that offers cues to the patient in order to elicit anxiety), or even be a distractor (e.g., from acute pain).

11.4.2 Scenario Development

Following needs and goal clarification, the researchers must then create a scenario, which is the specific content of the VE that will allow to accomplish the goals .

This can be done by only one person, but ideally it should be done in a scenario development meeting, grouping people with clinical expertise, and at least a few people with technical expertise. The concept is to brainstorm different possibilities that will result in the writing of a detailed scenario that will be used by 3D artists for initial modelization and by programmers. We cannot stress enough the importance of detailing explicitly what is expected by the creators. Ultimately, many people will work on the project and what may be obvious and assumed by clinicians may not be for computer programmers. As an example for OCD, how dirty should a virtual toilet be to please therapists without being overly disgusting? This can be answered by gathering images from Internet or camera shots to serve as references. This brainstorming brings the developers to think about the critical components that must be included in the environment while taking into consideration key aspects of the disorder. And as discussed in Chap. 2 on presence, realism of the stimuli may not be as important as incorporating the key features that are conveying the perception of threat (or disgust, in the case of some phobias) in the target population. In the case of a contamination OCD, it was discussed during the scenario development meeting that the immersion should elicit both obsessions and compulsions related to disgust in patients in order to be effective, and ideally, the task would include patients touching things in the VE in order to feel contaminated. Examples brought up during the meeting were a dirty public bathroom or a friend's bathroom without soap, towel, toilet paper, or hand sanitizer. For obsessions and compulsions related to doubt, the anxiety-provoking stimuli (e.g., image of naked people, words such as death or AIDS, or a picture provided by the patient) should be visible only for either less than a second or when in the peripheral field of view. Therefore, the user would have the impression they saw what they are afraid of without actually seeing it.

This phase in the process of development brings about decisions such as how VR will play a role for the particular disorder, which peripheral will be used (e.g., 3- or 6-dof tracker, haptic device), what will be available in terms of technical support, etc. To sum up, this phase of development provides information, ideas, and a set of requirements on which to base conceptual design (Wilson et al. 2002).

This task is necessary in the development of VEs for any disorders but can prove to be more complicated, as is the case with GAD. The fear of uncertainty that plague the life of people suffering from GAD does not translate well into specific stimuli to create in 3D. For the creation of GAD environments, it was decided in the scenario development meeting to create an alternative to cognitive exposure in GAD with the help of a few standardized catastrophic scenarios containing recurrent themes and moods found in scenarios used by GAD patients during treatment. As illustrated in Fig. 11.5, one of these VEs is an emergency room where the user feels helplessly uncertain about several events occurring around him, such as sick and strange people, doctors discussing information about the user's health, a doctor announcing bad news to a patient, a mother crying at her infant's bed, etc. The potential of using standardized scenarios to induce anxiety in patients suffering from GAD was preliminary tested in an experimental study where GAD patients were exposed in imagination to scenarios designed at the scenario development meeting (Guitard et al. 2011). Compared to a neutral scenario, exposure to a personalized catastrophic

Fig. 11.5 Screenshot of the emergency room developed for GAD. Reproduced with permission from S. Bouchard

scenario or a standardized catastrophic scenario both lead to similar statistically significant increase in anxiety and negative affect. These findings gave confidence in the potential of VEs to be used for cognitive exposure with people suffering from GAD (and recent preliminary findings are confirming these expectations).

11.4.3 Modelization

The goal of the next step, the modelization of the synthetic stimuli, is to represent the real world by molding various 3D polygon shapes. Depending on the complexity of the task at hand, modelization can be done by a graphic artist, alone, or a team. Frequently used computer programs in the case of modelization are 3DS Max, Softimage, Maya, Cinema 4D, Blender, and Sketchup. The objects can be reproduced in the environment in two different ways, high realism or stylized; the process to achieving both being similar. First, the graphic artist can search for an accurate reference of the object. The reference can be real (e.g., a real bathroom) or a reproduction (e.g., manual drawing of a bathroom). Once a convenient reference is found, the graphic artist will find the dimensions of the object and apply it to a polygon shape to mold it into its desired form.

For example, in the case of the bathroom setting for OCD, a real bathroom in a university setting was measured. Its dimensions were then applied to a square shape (see Fig. 11.6). The graphic artist then continued building onto this framework while using the same process to modelize other objects pertinent to the situation (see Fig. 11.7), such as sinks and toilets, in order to recreate piece by piece the entire bathroom.

11.4 Development of a VE

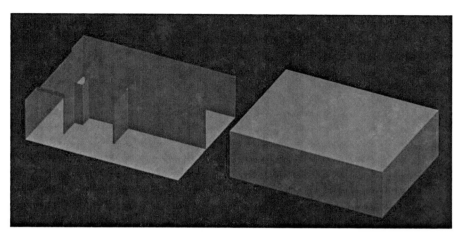

Fig. 11.6 Illustration of the initial model of the public toilet displayed in Fig. 11.4, from a square shape to the division between male and female sections. Reproduced with permission from S. Bouchard

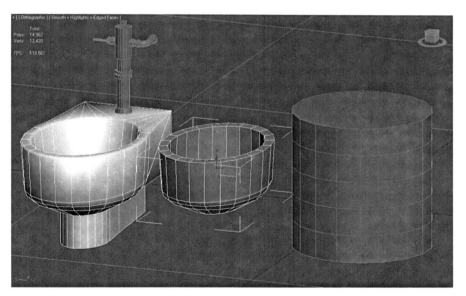

Fig. 11.7 Illustration of the process of modelizing a high-realism toilet from a polygon shape. Reproduced with permission from S. Bouchard

While some want to reproduce reality as it is, it is also possible to modelize objects while changing their real appearance to give them a particular style. For example, one could decide to create a 3D toilet that looks futuristic (see Fig. 11.8). As mentioned, the same process is followed as for high-realism objects. The difference rests in the final "look and feel" of the object.

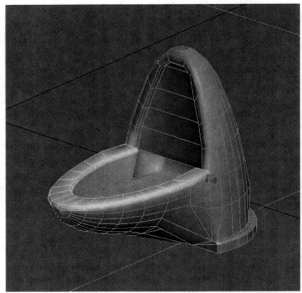

Fig. 11.8 Illustration of a stylized toilet bowl constructed in 3DS Max, with both polygons and textures visible. Reproduced with permission from S. Bouchard

11.4.4 Texturing

Once the numerous shapes and objects of the VE are created in the modelization process, providing us with a base to build upon, texturing becomes the main focus of the graphic artists. Texturing can be described as the process of adding an image on the set of polygons making a shape in order to create the appearance of the objects. This step is time consuming as it requires research and meticulous work.

The images used in the texturing process can be found on internet sites that specialize in sharing different textures or can be created by simply taking a picture of the representation needed (e.g., skin, flooring, cardboard, etc.). Once the image is found, it next needs to be modified so the texture can be added on the surface of the object being shaped. For this step, numerous software packages are available. Among the most frequently used are Adobe Photoshop, Filter Forge (a plug-in for Adobe Photoshop that allows the creation of one's own textures), GNU Image Manipulation Program (GIMP), and other computer-aided design software. Fig. 11.9 illustrates the creation of a virtual person based on actual pictures.

Objects or characters requiring animation are also animated at this stage. Animation can be done manually by the graphic artist. In this case, polygons or bones are manipulated and articulated to reproduce the movements. This is a tedious work requiring much talent and good observation skills. But it will make the difference between a virtual character that walks like a robot or a real person. Another option is to use motion capture devices that tracks and records several target points on an actor's body. Complex movements could appear very fluent and realistic, creating amazingly realistic effects. However, using this technology is still very costly,

11.4 Development of a VE

Fig. 11.9 Illustrations of texturing, starting with many reference pictures for the skin and clothing texture (see the front face picture *left*), the unwrap texture file (*center*, note the eyeballs and the face) with all the information required by the computer to texture the polygon-shaped skeleton of a virtual human, and the final product displayed in the 3D modeling software. Reproduced with permission from S. Bouchard.

requires a team of qualified staff, and generates files that need a lot of touch-up work by a graphic artist. In addition, the transition between each animation file requires work to ensure there are no visual glitches. In the end, both approaches to animation are very time consuming.

Another action taken at the end of this phase of the development process is adding light sources, shadows, and reflections in the environment. Generating the lightmaps could be done using 3D graphic software or by using scripting which is used to create the immersion (see the following section) and hence requires both programming and artistic skills. Once the light sources and how they are handled by the computer are decided, the next step is its creation. Generating the lightmaps is a long and intense computational operation performed by the computer, where all the visual information is computed, put together, and organized in a way that will be recognized and manipulated by the software performing the immersion.

Other final steps of the creation of the content of the VE involve creating sounds and stimuli for other senses (e.g., smell, haptic), if any. These stimuli are created once all the visual stimuli have been completed because they will be influenced by the visual scene (e.g., coughing sounds will vary depending on the gender of the virtual character, its movements, its distance from the user, and sounds from other events occurring in the environment).

11.4.5 Scripting

This next step requires a different set of skills and is usually completed by a person with experience in programming. Scripting represents the task of putting together and giving life to the virtual stimuli. All the objects created are programmed to behave in a certain way, with special attention to the type of movement required and their temporal sequence. Scripting is done with the software that will produce the actual immersion and hence decisions made at this point are influenced by the options and constraints imposed by the software. Frequently used software for scripting includes: Microsoft Visual Studio, Eclipse, Adobe Flash, Notepad++, Blender, Virtools, Vizard, Unity, and Unreal engine, in addition to many others. This task benefits greatly from a detailed scenario, as described in the previous pages, to make sure computer programmers deliver what was imagined during the scenario development meeting, including specification of the animations, real-time sequence, and the release mechanisms for the animations. All objects created during modeling and scripting need to be exported in the format recognized by the software that will be used for scripting. The process of putting all the 3D stimuli together into a final look, called rendering, differs significantly in VR and in cinema. In a movie, the final 3D scenes are rendered only once and every person who watches them will see the same thing. In VE, rendering must be computed continuously in real time because the content changes constantly based on the user's perspective and behavior. In order to avoid delays and lags in the VE, developers must reduce the information that requires real-time computing and optimize their environments. This explains why the quality of most VEs is not comparable to what is done in the movie industry. Other elements that need to be scripted include, for example, rules for detecting and handling collisions (e.g., can the user walk through an object and what will happen if there is a collision?), applications of physical properties to objects (e.g., will a ball bounce if dropped and how), and artificial intelligence. When programming, each movement, whether it be by a virtual person or object, must be calculated on a sequence. For example, for the emergency room created for GAD exposure, it was decided the full sequence will be activated in a linear mode following a pre-programmed order. For instance, in all cases, the doctor will come out of a room 2 min after the immersion began, followed by the reaction of one patient at 2:30 min. This means that no actions can be added, taken out, or even modified in the sequence once the environment has been created. Although this procedure can prove inflexible at times, it comes with a major advantage when the VE is used in a research context since it provides standardization as well when the goal is to create an ambiance or mood in the environment. Conversely, another option would be to launch animation by pressing specific keys on the keyboard. This option retained a virtual apartment also developed for GAD, where different clicks could launch animation such as a group of street bums throwing a rock at the window of the user's apartment or a phone message saying "Honey, I am at the hospital". While this method could be most practical in a clinical setting, it can also prove to be quite a challenge if too many animations are launched by different keys, opening the door for programming glitches and, most of all, difficulty and errors in using the program with patients. Developers must find the right balance between flexibility, usability, and ergonomy.

11.4.6 Evaluation

The evaluation of the VE constitutes the last step of the creation in the model proposed by Wilson et al. (2002). However, we feel that although a thorough evaluation is mandatory at the end of the process, it seems important that some form of assessment of the product also occurs on an ongoing basis throughout the construction of the environment. For example, although there was a progression of insalubrities from the first toilet stall to the last one, the first version of the dirty public toilet was considered too difficult to face by members of the scenario development meeting team. Lower difficulty levels were therefore created, leading to a VE that is more suitable to the OCD populations. Beta testing is also important. End users will often use the VE in ways that were not expected by programmers. They should also test the robustness of the program before starting their study. The final evaluation step is quite important and takes place when the product is thought to be ready. At this point, the VE is running and the first evaluation is often done by the computer programmer, to assess whether or not the environment is working without technical problems. The researcher will be brought in once all known technical problems are resolved and will then give feedback on the following basis: general appearance, user experience, and animations. Firstly, the evaluation of the general appearance is conducted to assess the presence of each key features of the scenario in the environment. As for user experience, this part of the evaluation aims at confirming that the VE is user friendly (i.e., created in an optimal way to make its use is as easy as possible). Examples of this range from ensuring that movements are not blocked by certain objects of the environment to confirming that the interactions with the virtual surroundings are appropriate (i.e., not being able to go through walls). Finally, animations deserve a considerable part of the evaluation process. The main objective is to assess whether or not the different actions are recognized for what they are meant to be. For instance, in the hospital waiting room, at some point, a woman cries because she is given bad news by the doctor. In this case, the attention will be focused on the capacity to recognize her physical cues as crying. After all this process, the VE is now ready to be put back in the hands of researchers and clinicians to conduct empirical validation and clinical trials.

11.5 Conclusion

Our knowledge on the efficacy of using VR in the treatment of GAD and OCD is still in its infancy. There is only one line of research so far with publications on GAD and it is for helping patients use VE to learn relaxation skills. Results are interesting and innovative in documenting the use of mobile phone to perform homework at home. The next step is to develop treatment protocols that will integrate immersions in VR in treatments targeting the core dysfunctional mechanisms maintaining GAD. As for OCD, the field is not ready to cumulate replication studies as it is the case with fear of flying or spider phobia. But there is already enough empirical data confirming that it is possible to elicit reactions in people suffering from OCD although the feared consequences are virtual and concern virtual behaviors that were conducted in VEs. Understanding the mechanisms involved in fear reactions and exposure processes mentioned in Chap. 5 on spider phobia and the literature on presence presented in Chap. 2, this does not come as a surprise.

Nevertheless, it had to be empirically documented. This line of research should be continued. But it is clearly time to develop and test treatment protocols for GAD and OCD. After a few more pilot studies to appraise how to exploit VR at its fullest, researchers should compare CBT using *in virtuo* exposure with gold-standard CBT protocols. Also, it is essential not to try replicating *in virtuo* with what is already done in vivo or in imagination, but to push the possibilities further and do *in virtuo* things patients and therapists would not dare doing in vivo (e.g., asking an OCD patient to grab a wedding ring dropped in the bottom of a dirty and overflowing toilet in a public washroom).

Using VR to conduct exposure with people suffering from GAD and OCD has several assets. It precludes the use of imaginal exposure, offers significant control over the exposure situations, facilitates varying the context of exposure, is more attractive for both patients and therapists, standardizes the exposure paradigm, and requires less efforts for therapists. At present time, VEs are being created in various part of part of the world with the aim of conducting these randomized control trials.

Observing the early stage of development of VR applications for GAD and OCD created the opportunity to document how VEs are developed. There is no recipe for success and models could be followed to create a useful treatment tool. But the sequence described in this chapter allows the reader to appraise the amount of work behind the development process. It also helps new researchers in the field to plan ahead and adjust their expectations when it comes to creating their own VEs. Finally, it illustrates how this field is combining the multidisciplinary input from clinical expertise, artistic creation of 3D (and other) stimuli, and from computer programming.

References

Abramowitz, J., Brigidi, B., & Roche, K. (2001). Cognitive-behavioral therapy for obsessive-compulsive disorder: A review of the treatment literature. *Research on Social Work Practice, 11*(3), 357–372.

American Psychiatric Association. (2000). *Diagnostic and statistical manual of mental disorders* (4th ed., text revised). Washington, DC: American Psychiatric Association.

Baer, L., & Greist, J. H. (1997). An interactive computer-administered self-assessment and self-help program for behavior therapy. *Journal of Clinical Psychiatry, 58*(Suppl. 12), 23–28.

Baer, L., Minichiello, W. E., & Jenike, M. A. (1987). Use of a portable-computer program in behavioral treatment of obsessive-compulsive disorder. *American Journal of Psychiatry, 144*, 1101.

Baer, L., Minichiello, W. E., Jenike, M. A., & Holland, A. (1988). Use of a portable computer program to assist behavioral treatment in a case of obsessive compulsive disorder. *Journal of Behavioral Therapy and Experimental Psychiatry, 19*, 237.

Beck, A. T. (1976). *Cognitive therapy and the emotional disorder*. New York: International Universities Press.

Beck, A. T., Emery, G., & Greenberg, R. L. (1985). *Anxiety disorders and phobias: A cognitive perspective*. New York: Basic Books.

Borkovec, T. D., & Inz, J. (1990). The nature of worry in generalized anxiety disorder: A predominance of thought activity. *Behaviour Research and Therapy, 28*, 153.

References

Borkovec, T. D., & Lyonfield, J. D. (1993). Worry: Thought suppression of emotional processing. In H. W. Khrone (Ed.), *Attention and avoidance: Strategies in coping with aversiveness*. Ohio: Hogrefe & Huber.

Borkovec, T. D., Alcaine, O. M., & Behar, E. (2004). Avoidance theory of worry and generalized anxiety disorder. In: R. G. Heimberg, C. L. Turk, & D. S. Mennin (Eds.), *Generalized anxiety disorder*. New York: Guilford.

Bouchard, S., Robillard, G., Larouche, S., & Loranger, C. (2012). Description of a treatment manual for in virtuo exposure with specific phobia. In C. Eichenberg (Ed.), *Virtual reality in psychological, medical and pedagogical applications* (Chap. 4, pp. 82–108). Rijeka: InTech.

Bouvard, M., & Kaiser, B. (2006). Cognitive-behavioral interventions for OCD. *Clinical Neuropsychiatry, 3*(6), 364–371.

Brown, T. A., Di Nardo, P. A., & Barlow, D. H. (1994). *Anxiety disorders interview schedule for DSM-IV*. Albany: Graywind.

Cardenas-Lopez, G., Munoz, S., & Oviedo, P. (2010). Clinical virtual environments for OCD treatment. *Journal of Cybertherapy & Rehabilitation, 3*, 189–190. Abstracts from the 15th annual cyberpsychology & cybertherapy conference, Seoul, Korea.

Clark, D. A. (2004). *Cognitive-behavioral therapy for OCD*. New York: Guilford.

Cottraux, J., Note, I., Yao, S. N., Lafont, S., Note, B., Mollard, E., et al. (2001). A randomized controlled trial of cognitive therapy versus intensive behavior therapy in obsessive compulsive disorder. *Psychotherapy and Psychosomatics, 70*(6), 288–297.

Dugas, M. J., & Robichaud, M. (2007). *Cognitive-behavioral treatment for generalized anxiety disorder*. New York: Routledge.

Dugas, M. J., Freeston, M. H., Ladouceur, R., Rhéaume, J., Provencher, M., & Boisvert, J.-M. (1998a). Worry themes in primary GAD, secondary GAD and other anxiety disorders. *Journal of Anxiety Disorders, 12*, 253–261.

Dugas, M. J., Gagnon, F., Ladouceur, R., & Freeston, M. H. (1998b). Generalized anxiety disorder: A preliminary test of a conceptual model. *Behaviour Research and Therapy, 36*, 215–226.

Dugas, M. J., Ladouceur, R., Léger, É., Freeston, M. H., Langlois, F., Provencher, M. D., & Boisvert, J.-M. (2003). Group cognitive-behavioral therapy for generalized anxiety disorder: Treatment outcome and long-term follow-up. *Journal of Consulting and Clinical Psychology, 71*, 821–825.

Dugas, M. J., Marchand, A., & Ladouceur, R. (2005). Further validation of a cognitive-behavioral model of generalized anxiety disorder: Diagnostic and symptom specificity. *Anxiety Disorders, 19*, 329–343.

Foa, E. B., & Kozak, M. J. (1995). DSM-IV field trial: Obsessive-compulsive disorder. *American Journal of Psychiatry, 152*, 90–96.

Franklin, M. E., & Foa, E. B. (2007). Cognitive-behavioral treatment of obsessive-compulsive disorder. In P. E. Nathan & J. M. Gorman, (Eds.), *A Guide to treatments that work* (3rd ed.). New York: Oxford University Press.

Freeston, M. H., Dugas, M. J., & Ladouceur, R. (1996). Thoughts, images, worry, and anxiety. *Cognitive Therapy and Research, 20*, 265–273.

Freeston, M. H., Ladouceur, R., Gagnon, F., Thibodeau, N., Rheaume, J., Letarte, H., & Bujold, A. (1997). Cognitive-behavioral treatment of obsessive thoughts: A controlled study. *Journal of Consulting and Clinical Psychology, 65*, 405–413.

Gorini, A., & Riva, G. (2008). The potential of virtual reality as anxiety management tool: a randomized controlled study in a sample of patients affected by generalized anxiety disorder. *Trials, 9*. doi:10.1186/1745-6215-9-25.

Gorini, A., Pallavicini, F., Algeri, D., Repetto, C., Gaggioli, A., & Riva, G. (2010). Virtual reality in the treatment of generalized anxiety disorder. *Studies in Health Technology and Informatics, 154*, 39–43.

Gould, R. A., Safren, S. A., O'Neill Washington, D., & Otto, M. W. (2004). A meta-analytic review of cognitive-behavioral treatments. In R. G. Heimberg, C. L. Turk, & D. S. Mennin (Eds.), *Generalized anxiety disorder*. New York: Guilford.

Guitard, T., Bouchard, S., & Bélanger, C. (2011). *Exposure to standardized catastrophic scenarios with patients suffering from GAD.* Poster presented at the 45th Annual Convention of the Association for Behavioral and Cognitive Therapy, Toronto, Nov 10–13.

Herman, S., & Koran, L. M. (1998). In vivo measurement of obsessive-compulsive disorder symptoms using palmtop computers. *Computers in Human Behavior, 14,* 449–462.

Kessler, R. C., Walters, E. E., & Wittchen, H.-U. (2004). Epidemiology. In R. G. Heimberg, C. L. Turk, & D. S. Mennin (Eds.), *Generalized anxiety disorder.* New York: Guilford.

Kessler, R. C., Berglund, P., Demler, O., Jin, R., Merikangas, K. R., & Walters, E. E. (2005). Lifetime prevalence and age-of-onset distributions of DSM-IV disorders in the National Comorbidity Survey Replication. *Archives of General Psychiatry, 62*(6), 593–602.

Kim, K., Kim, C.-H., Cha, K. R., Park, J., Han, K., Kim, Y. K., et al. (2008). Anxiety provocation and measurement using virtual reality in patients with obsessive-compulsive disorder. *Cyberpsychology and Behavior, 11*(6), 637–641.

Kim, K., Kim, C.-H., Cha, K. R., Park, J., Rosenthal, M. Z., Kim, J.-J., Han, K., et al. (2010). Development of a computer-based behavioral assessment of checking behavior in obsessive-compulsive disorder. *Comprehensive Psychiatry, 51,* 86–93.

Kim, K., Roh, D., Kim, C. H., Cha, K. R., Rosenthal, M. Z., & Kim, S. I. (2012a). Comparison of checking behavior in adults with or without checking symptoms of obsessive-compulsive disorder using a novel computer-based measure. *Computer Methods and Programs in Medicine, 108,* 434–441.

Kim, K., Roh, D., Kim, S. I., & Kim, C. H. (2012b). Provoked arrangement symptoms in obsessive-compulsive disorder using a virtual environment: A preliminary report. *Computers in Biology and Medicine, 42,* 422–427.

Koran, L. M., Thienemann, M. L., & Davenport, R. (1996). Quality of life for patients with obsessive compulsive disorder. *American Journal of Psychiatry, 153,* 783–788.

Ladouceur, R., Dugas, M. J., Freeston, M. H., Léger, É., Gagnon, F., & Thibodeau, N. (2000). Efficacy of a cognitive-behavioral treatment for generalized anxiety disorder: Evaluation in a controlled clinical trial. *Journal of Consulting and Clinical Psychology, 68,* 957–964.

Laforest, M., & Bouchard, S. (2013). *Validation and efficacy of a "contaminated" virtual environment in inducing anxiety and treating OCD.* Oral presentation at the 47th annual convention of the association for behavioral and cognitive therapy, Nashville (TN), Nov 21–24.

Leahy, R. L. (2004). Cognitive-behavioral therapy. In R. G. Heimberg, C. L. Turk, & D. S. Mennin (Eds.), *Generalized anxiety disorder.* New York: Guilford.

Leon, A. C., Portera, L., & Weissman, M. M. (1995). The social costs of anxiety disorders. *British Journal of Psychiatry, 166*(Suppl. 27), 19–22.

Lindsay, M., Crino, R., & Andrews, G. (1997). Controlled trials of exposure and response prevention in obsessive-compulsive disorder. *British Journal of Psychiatry, 171,* 135–139.

Macleod, A. K., Williams, J. M. G., & Bekerian, D. A. (1991). Worry is reasonable: The role of explanations in pessimism about future personal events. *Journal of Abnormal Psychology, 100,* 478–486.

Meyer, V. (1966). Modification of expectations in cases with obsessional rituals. *Behaviour Research and Therapy, 4,* 273–280.

Mowrer, O. H. (1960). *Learning theory and behavior.* New York: Wiley.

Newman, M. G., Llera, S. J., Erickson, T. M., Przeworski, A., & Castonguay, L. G. (2013). Worry and generalized anxiety disorder: A review and theoretical synthesis of evidence on nature, etiology, mechanisms, and treatment. *Annual Review of Clinical Psychology, 9,* 275–297.

Obsessive Compulsive Cognitions Working Group. (1997). Cognitive assessment of obsessive-compulsive disorder. *Behaviour Research and Therapy, 35,* 667–681.

Pallavicini, F., Algeri, D., Repetto, C., Gorini, A., & Riva, G. (2009). Biofeedback, virtual reality and mobile phones in the treatment of generalized anxiety disorder (GAD): A phase-2 controlled clinical trial. *Journal of Cybertherapy & Rehabilitation, 2,* 315–327.

Rachman, S. A. (1997). A cognitive theory of obsessions. *Behaviour Research and Therapy, 35,* 793–802.

References

Repetto, C., Gaggioli, A., Pallavicini, F., Cipresso, P., Raspelli, S., & Riva, G. (2013). Virtual reality and mobile phones in the treatment of generalized anxiety disorders: A phase-2 clinical trial. *Personal and Ubiquitous Computing, 17*(2), 253–260.

Roca-Bennasar, M., Garcia-Mas, A., Llaneras, N., & Blat, J. (1991). Kraepelin: An expert system for the diagnosis of obsessive-compulsive disorder. *European Psychiatry, 6,* 171–175.

Salkovskis, P. M. (1985). Obsessional-compulsive problems: A cognitive-behavioural analysis. *Behaviour Research and Therapy, 23,* 571–583.

Salkovskis, P. M. (1996). Cognitive-behavioral approaches to the understanding of obsessional problems. In R. Rapee (Ed.), *Current controversies in the anxiety disorders* (pp. 103–133). New York: Guilford.

Van der Heiden, C., Muris, P., & van der Molen, H. T. (2012). Randomized control trial on the effectiveness of metacognitive therapy and intolerance-of-uncertainty therapy for generalized anxiety disorder. *Behaviour Research and Therapy, 50*(2), 100–109.

van Oppen, de Haan, van Balkom, Spinhoven, Hoogduin, & van Dyck. (1995). Cognitive therapy and exposure in vivo in the treatment of obsessive compulsive disorder. *Behavior Research and Therapy, 33*(4), 379–390.

Wells, A. (1995). Meta-cognition and worry: A cognitive model of generalized anxiety disorder. *Behavioural and Cognitive Psychotherapy, 23,* 301–320.

Wells, A. (2004). A cognitive model of GAD. In R. G. Heimberg, C. L. Turk, & D. S. Mennin (Eds.), *Generalized anxiety disorder.* New York: Guilford.

Wells, A., & Carter, K. (1999). Preliminary tests of a cognitive model of generalized anxiety disorder. *Behaviour Research and Therapy, 37,* 585–594.

Wiederhold, B. K., & Wiederhold, M. D. (2005). *Virtual reality therapy for anxiety disorders. Advances in evaluation and treatment.* Washington, DC: American Psychological Association.

Wilson, J. R. (1997). Virtual environments and ergonomics: Needs and opportunities. *Ergonomics, 40*(10), 1057–1077. (London: Taylor & Francis).

Wilson, J. R., Cobb, S. V. G., D'Cruz, M. D., & Eastgate, R. M. (1996). *Virtual reality for industrial application: opportunities and limitations.* Nottingham: Nottingham University press.

Wilson, J. R., Eastgate, R. M., & D'Cruz, M. (2002). Structured development of virtual environments. In K. M. Stanney (Ed.), *Handbook of virtual environments. design, implementation, and applications.* New Jersey: Laurence Erlbaum.

Part III
Conclusions

Chapter 12
A Case Example of a Virtual Reality Clinic

Brenda K. Wiederhold and Mark D. Wiederhold

In the 1990s, there were no journals dedicated to virtual reality (VR) and psychology, no clinics, no conferences, no training programs, and very few technologies. And yet a handful of forward-thinking clinicians, researchers, and entrepreneurs have created a lasting footprint. The area is now cohesive and features a Medline journal, a magazine, a conference, an association, VR clinics, and clinician continuing education and training programs. The technologies have increased, contracted, changed, been refined, and evolved.

What is presented in this chapter is a model, a brief case study, similar in style to those presented in Harvard Business Review, of one VR clinic's process of creation and continued offerings.

12.1 Conducting Treatment in a VR Clinic

Virtual Reality Medical Center (VRMC) opened its first VR clinic in California in 1997.

Prior to opening the clinic, our approach to patient care involved using either imaginal exposure (in combination with physiological monitoring and feedback) or in vivo (real life) exposure to treat our patients with anxiety disorders. The ability to perform the exposure session in the virtual setting, allowing a combination of senses to be stimulated (visual, auditory, tactile), while still allowing for the monitoring of the patient's physiology, allowed therapy to progress more efficiently, often more rapidly and in most cases more effectively. It allowed the session to be more individually tailored and did not depend on the patient's ability to visualize well, which for imaginal therapy was essential. It also allowed the patient to "push the envelope" in a safe way, since suspension of disbelief (the individual felt "present" or "immersed") was achieved and was elicited. This necessary therapeutic component provided a setting whereby emotions could be accessed and processed to move towards changing cognitions and desensitization.

The first systems available in the 1990s were bulky and finicky, and the graphics were very cartoonish. However, the key components to cue anxiety and arousal were present, and paired with the correct clinical protocols, physiological monitoring, and feedback, the therapy worked. Not only did it work but also it worked well, and the dropout rates were dramatically reduced! As time has progressed and newer and more realistic graphics have become attainable, the need for good clinical skills still remains the most important aspect of practice. One of the key components that continues to bring success during therapy is when the therapist, programmer, and end user (patient or trainee) work together to build an environment containing the correct cues for eliciting the arousal or the correct scenario needed to learn a skill set. The triad is both necessary and powerful. The therapist does not wish to learn how to program or to spend their time with the computer. The computer is a tool and should not detract from the therapeutic alliance between patient and therapist. Working to meet this goal, successful programmers will create a few keystrokes that the therapist can easily master while remaining committed and focused on the patient during the therapy session. The VR and physiology should serve as only a backdrop.

Trolling through auto junkyards, airplane salvage yards, and videogame and toy stores for the right real-world objects to augment the virtual experience, the clinic set up various theme rooms: The flying treatment room contained airlines seats, allowing the patient to sit on the back row and buckle their seatbelt; the driving room featured a car seat, brake and gas pedal, and steering wheel; the public speaking room, a lectern, and microphone; and the heights room, an elevator box with a small fan simulating wind blowing on the patient's face as the elevator climbs higher and higher. With a primary interest on keeping costs low and providing the potential for more wide-scale adoption by the broader health-care community, platforms have also evolved to include full-wall screens, Xbox, PlayStation, iPads, iPhones, Android, and internet-based software.

12.2 The Workbook

As patients continue to be our greatest teachers, we often learn the most important clinical interventions and treatment protocols. When we first began, we provided a workbook to each patient to use during the therapy process. Most patients felt the workbook was too cumbersome and overwhelming, and many parts were unrelated to the therapy. This was our impetus for writing our own workbook, with input from our patients. The workbook was made manageable and focused on the short-term protocol using VR, physiology, and cognitive-behavioral therapy. It provided patients with an easy-to-use resource, with reproducible worksheets so that they could become more active participants in their own health and well-being. It also encouraged us to write an additional book for patients so they could easily find real-world places to "test" their new skills mastered in VR. Our main goal: to allow patients to achieve self-efficacy, self-confidence, and mastery so that they leave knowing they have the skills to deal with real-world situations, not only relating to their initial presenting difficulty but also to translate these new skills into dealing with other problems or stresses that may occur in life. We are always accessible if patients should need a refresher course or a booster session, but in most cases, patients have reported that they are able to transfer the skills they have learned to deal with other areas of their lives. Providing a careful, systematic approach for exposure, after having taught the patient a set of skills which they can then practice in the VR setting, has led to short-term gains in the majority of patients treated, and has led to long-term sustainability when patients are contacted, even after a 3-year lapse since the last treatment session. This level of empowerment is exciting and achievable for most of our patients!

Since the first one-room clinic in 1997, VRMC has expanded its offerings in the USA, Europe, and most recently into Asia, but has always remained grounded in its guiding principle: VR is only a tool to assist the therapist in providing more effective treatment to the patient. The technology does not take the place of good clinical skills or clinical judgment. In our case, it serves mostly as an adjunct to cognitive-behavioral therapy techniques or to stress inoculation training techniques, depending on whether we are training personnel to perform in stressful situations (first responders, medical personnel, police officers, military personnel, students, etc.) or teaching patients to overcome anxiety in previously anxiety-provoking scenarios. There are many similarities between training and therapy, and in some cases the lessons may apply to education in general. Teaching a patient "abdominal breathing" and "cognitive skills" and teaching a trainee "combat breathing" and "urban warfare skills" share many important similarities. We are working on several new models of care delivery that look at the continuum of patient abilities, range of experience, and individual coping mechanisms. Continued individualization of the therapy session while preserving the key components of the CBT foundation is key to creating an effective model that will survive the evolution of medical care.

12.3 Training

As interest continues to grow in the use of VR therapy for patient care, the need to train clinicians in this new approach becomes more important. There are three components for success: a broad knowledge and familiarity with CBT, comfort with computer-based and technology-supplemented practice, and knowledge of basic human physiological responses to stress and relaxation. Our affiliated 501c3 nonprofit, the Interactive Media Institute, has been certified by the American Psychological Association to provide continuing education and training for psychologists and other mental health professionals wishing to learn this new skill to add to their clinical offerings.

12.4 The Future

It is clear that the appropriate use of advanced technology can greatly improve mental health-care delivery and clinical outcomes. Previous barriers continue to be eliminated as cost, simplicity, and ease of use dramatically increase the availability of these tools. Overall, our approach has been patient centric, and as such we have consistently achieved successful results with both analytic and therapeutic outcomes. There are additional challenges however. The evolution of the current health-care system will demand strict adherence to patient privacy, security of medical records, and adherence to ethical policies, cognizance of new Federal regulations, and synergy with new requirements of payors. While this new universe of requirements may appear daunting to those who wish to add technology tools to their individual or group practice, we and others are making free resources available to all who seek inquiry, support, and guidance. Please visit www.vrphobia.eu or www.interactivemediainstitute.com to begin the quest for knowledge.

Chapter 13
Conclusions: The Present and the Future of Virtual Reality in the Treatment of Anxiety Disorders

Giuseppe Riva and Claudia Repetto

13.1 How to Treat Anxiety Disorders

In this book, we described anxiety as a human emotion that requires a complex cognitive system to be experienced (Damasio et al. 2000). When anxiety is directed to a specific event, increases in intensity and its activation is episodic, then we refer to this emotion calling it fear. Fear is easily recognizable even in animals, and has a strong evolutionary basis, since it triggers escape behaviours in the case of danger, and allows for survival. Anxiety and fear, however, share the same emotional features to the extent that they can be accounted for as two sides of the same coin; moreover, depending on the range of their intensity, they may be considered normal emotional reactions to the context, or the core symptom of many psychiatric diseases. The former, thus, are adaptive emotions that belong to the experience of each human being; the latter are maladaptive since they prevent people from conducting a normal life.

We will refer to the second situation as anxiety disorders, and they include the different disturbances addressed in the book: specific phobias (fear of flying, fear of spiders, fear of heights, etc), panic disorders with or without agoraphobia, social phobia, posttraumatic stress disorder, generalized anxiety disorder and obsessive–compulsive disorder. These disorders are very common among worldwide populations (Michael et al. 2007; Pull 2008) and strongly impact on personal and occupational life: usual activities such as taking a plane, travelling in the subway, meeting friends and colleagues, or staying in crowded places become very stressful to the extent that, if symptoms are not treated, may lead people to avoid the feared situation. Avoidance behaviours, as time progresses, tend to worsen and then they start a vicious circle: in terms of conditioning paradigms, avoidance behaviours serve as negative reinforcements, since they stop the occurrence of an aversive symptom (anxiety); but, on the other hand, at the same time, they contribute to maintain the link between conditioned stimulus and unconditioned stimulus, and then prevent the extinction phenomenon.

Many different kinds of treatment for anxiety disorders are now available: behavioural treatments, cognitive psychotherapy, medication and biofeedback are among the most common used. Different research studies investigating the effectiveness of the different treatments have demonstrated that exposure-based therapies are more suitable and effective than others (Asukai et al. 2010; Barlow et al. 2005; Craske and Barlow 2007; Deacon and Abramowitz 2004; Emmelkamp 2003; Franklin and Foa 2007; Landon and Barlow 2004; Olatunji et al. 2010; Rothbaum and Schwartz 2002).

Exposure is a process in which the patient is progressively exposed to the feared stimulus or the situation that provokes anxiety. Exposure alone, without relaxation training, is documented to be effective in treating a number of anxiety disorders and phobias, such as panic disorder with agoraphobia (Craske and Barlow 2007), social phobia (Heimberg et al. 1990) and obsessive–compulsive disorder (Franklin and Foa 2007). However, one of the most influential exposure techniques is the procedure of systematic desensitization developed by Wolpe (Wolpe 1958), in which exposure is applied during relaxation, an emotional and physiological state considered incompatible with anxiety and fear (Hazlett-Stevens and Craske 2008). In these protocols, the patient learns to manage anxiety symptoms by replacing emotional maladaptive activation with relaxation and, having the opportunity to monitor his thoughts and beliefs with the therapist, while experiencing anxiety, and learning to downsize his cognitive attributions. This process, repeated over time, helps people to face their fears and break the vicious circle of avoidance.

Traditionally, exposure may be achieved in two manners: in vivo, with direct contact to the stimulus, or by imagery (in the person's imagination). However, despite its effectiveness, both types of exposure presents some limitations: some patients report difficulties when asked to imagine the feared situation, because of poor abilities in creating mental images and in getting inside a specific situation; furthermore, emotions have been shown to modulate visual imagery and perception (Borst and Kosslyn 2010), and in particular fear seems to impair visualization of detailed scenes, making the mental reconstruction of the stimulus to some extent biased and inaccurate; in vivo exposure, in contrast, bypasses this limitation but poses other critical issues. First of all, many patients are rather unwilling to expose themselves to the real situations, since it is conceived as too frightening; second, the real situation is not fully under the control of the therapist; third, it requires a high effort in terms of money and time expenditure, since usually the therapist and the patient must meet each other outside the therapist's office to work together on the stimulus target.

For these reasons, the book introduced a novel tool to treat anxiety symptoms that overcomes most of these limitations: virtual reality (VR).

13.2 VR Exposure Treatments: A New Way of Dealing with Anxiety Disorders

As we have seen many times during the book, a VR system is a combination of technological devices that allows users in creating, exploring and interacting with 3D environments. This capability is made possible by the use of input tools (trackers, gloves, mice) that send to the computer the position and the movement of the user in real time, graphic rendering that changes the environment coherently with the information acquired, and output devices (visual, aural and haptic) that return to the user feedback of the interaction. The integration of these devices gives the user the opportunity to be immersed in the environment and to experience the sense of *presence* in a computer-generated world. As discussed in Chap. 2, presence is defined as "sense of being there" (Steuer 1992) or as "the feeling of being in a world that exists outside the self" (Riva et al. 2011b; Waterworth et al. 2010).

Thanks to these features, VR has been considered a useful tool to carry out exposure-based programs that better fit the needs of the patients (Botella et al. 2007). In effect, virtual reality exposure treatments (VRET) present several advantages when compared to traditional treatments carried out by both in vivo and imagination techniques (Wiederhold and WIederhold 2008). Many of the problems encountered with in vivo exposure are easily bypassed by the use of VRET: first of all, it is completely controllable by the therapist, who can grade the intensity of the stimulus following the personal needs of each patient and eventually stop the session in the case of excessive emotional activation (which is, indeed, extremely rare). In this way, the patient feels less uncomfortable about the treatment and his/her motivation increases. Furthermore, a portion of a more complex event can be selected and repeated, in order to practise exactly the critical stimulus instead of wasting time with all other concomitant aspects (Wiederhold et al. 2002).

Compared to imagination, VRET offers the possibility to visualize a realistic environment and to interact with it, making the experience more immersive and thus increasing the personal involvement. This will result in a more effective treatment, in terms of number of sessions needed to obtain improvements, and therefore of costs incurred.

There are also some caveats in the use of VRET that have to be taken into account. First of all, some VR users report symptoms of sickness that target different areas (visual, vestibular, central nervous system, musculoskeletal). The risk of this "cyber sickness" could be decreased by a gradual introduction to virtual environments (VE), but in people prone to this kind of symptoms it may be difficult to overcome symptoms. Furthermore, there are some medical conditions that represent significant contraindications for the use or VR, such as migraine headache and seizure disorder. Finally, attention should be paid when using VR with patients affected by psychosis or personality disorders, since they may be predisposed to becoming confused by real versus virtual worlds.

The main problem with the use of VRET is related to practical issues: up-to-date, VR technology is not yet widespread among private clinicians, and therefore a small amount of patients worldwide have had the opportunity to undergo this kind of treatment.

Even taking into account this consideration, in recent years there is an increasing interest in evaluating the capabilities of this tool, and many researchers have investigated the effects of VRET on reduction of symptoms of anxiety disorders and specific phobias. A number of qualitative reviews of VRET research studies have pointed out that VRET has good potential in the treatment of specific phobias

(Botella et al. 2004; Glantz and Rizzo 2003; Hodges et al. 2001; Krijn et al. 2004; Pull 2005; Wiederhold and Wiederhold 2003), since it produces better outcomes than imaginal exposure, and it is as effective as in vivo exposure, but being pragmatically a much more attractive alternative.

Recently, even more powerful statistical analyses, such as quantitative metaanalyses, have been conducted on studies reporting VRET treatments. Parson and Rizzo (Parsons and Rizzo 2008) have collected data from 21 articles who have evaluated anxiety and/or phobia before and after VRET. The results revealed that VRET has a statistically large effect on all affective domains, and thus it is a relevant approach to reduce anxiety-related symptoms. Similarly, Powers and Emmelkamp (Powers and Emmelkamp 2008) provide effect size estimates for VR treatment in comparison to in vivo exposure and other control conditions. They found a predictable larger effect of VRET compared to the control conditions; but more interestingly, VRET outperformed in vivo exposure.

Another line of research investigated the cognitive mechanisms underlying VRET and their weight in reducing symptoms (Côté and Bouchard 2005). The effectiveness of traditional cognitive-behavioural treatments is usually justified following three major explanations: the information processing model, the perceived self-efficacy model (PSE) and the cognitive/dysfunctional beliefs model. Even if all the three mechanisms are involved in VRET, the PSE and the change in dysfunctional beliefs are the best predictors of good outcome, and then are strictly required also when the stimuli are virtual in nature (Cotè and Bouchard 2009).

Table 13.1 summarizes the most recent studies (past 5 years) that examined the effects of VRET for reducing anxiety disorders and phobias (Beck et al. 2007; Botella et al. 2007, 2010; Cornwell et al. 2011; Difede et al. 2007; Freedman et al. 2010; Gamito et al. 2010; Gerardi et al. 2008; Krijn et al. 2007a, b; Malbos et al. 2008; McLay et al. 2010, 2011; Perez-Ara et al. 2010; Price and Anderson 2012; Price et al. 2011; Ready et al. 2010; Reger and Gahm 2008; Rizzo et al. 2009; Robillard et al. 2010; St-Jacques et al. 2010; Tortella-Feliu et al. 2011; Wallach et al. 2009, 2011; Wood et al. 2009).

13.3 From VR to InterReality

As shown by the most recent meta-analysis (Opris et al. 2012), that included most of the studies reported in Table 13.1, on one side VRET does far better than the waitlist control and has good stability of results over time, similar to that of the classical evidence-based treatments. On the other side, the posttreatment results show similar efficacy between the behavioural and the cognitive behavioural interventions incorporating a VR exposure component and the classical evidence-based interventions, with no VR exposure component.

In other words, even if VRET demonstrated good capabilities in the treatment of anxiety disorders, there is still room for improvement. But how may we improve VRET?

13.3 From VR to InterReality

Table 13.1 Summary of the most recent studies (past 5 years) that examined the effects of VRET for reducing anxiety disorders and phobias

First author and year of publication	Type of disorder	Samples	Experimental design	Condition(s)	Follow-up	Short-term outcome
Krijn et al. (2007b)	Acrophobia	26	Randomized crossover	VRET VRET+self statements	At 6-month follow-up, most gains during treatment were not fully retained	VRET effectiveness not influenced by the addition of self-statements
Botella (2007)	Arachnophobia	12	Open clinical trial	VRET	Therapeutic gains were maintained at the 3-month follow-up	Improvement in all clinical measures at posttreatment
St-Jacques (2010)	Arachnophobia	31(children)	Between subjects design	IVE IVE+VRET	–	The use of virtual reality did not increase motivation towards psychotherapy
Pérez-Ara et al. (2010)	Panic disorder and agoraphobia	29	Between subjects design	VR interoceptive Exposure Simultaneous condition Interoceptive Exposure Traditional Condition	Results maintained or even improved at 3-month follow-up	Both treatment conditions significantly reduced the main clinical variables at posttreatment
Malbos (2008)	Claustrophobia	6	Open clinical trial	VRET	Gains maintained at 3-month follow-up	Significant reduction in fear towards the enclosed space and quality of life improvement

Table 13.1 (continued)

First author and year of publication	Type of disorder	Samples	Experimental design	Condition(s)	Follow-up	Short-term outcome
Krijn et al. (2007a)	Fear of flying	86	Between subjects design	VRET Bibliotherapy (BIB) CBT	–	Treatment with VRET or CBT was more effective than BIB. No statistically significant difference between VRET and CB
Tortella-Feliu (2011)	Fear of flying	60	Randomized between subject design	VRET CAE-T CAE-S	Gains maintained at 1-Yr follow-up	Results indicate that the three interventions were effective in reducing fear of flying; furthermore, there were no significant differences between them in any of the outcome measure
Beck (2007)	PTSD	6	Open clinical trial	VRET	–	Significant reductions in post-trauma symptoms involving re-experiencing, avoidance and emotional numbing
Botella (2010)	PTSD	10	Randomized between subject design	CB CB+VRET		CBT+VRET was as effective as CBT
Difede (2007)	PTSD	21	Randomized between subject design	VRET WL		VRET group showed a significant decline in PTSD scores compared with the WL group
Freedman (2010)	PTSD	1	Case study	EI+VRET	Gains maintained at 6-month follow-up	Large posttreatment reductions in PTSD symptoms
Gamito (2010)	PTSD	10	Randomized between subject design	VRET EI WL		Decrease on PTSD as well as on psychopathological symptoms in the VRET group when compared to EI and WL groups
Gerardi (2008)	PTSD	1	Case study	VRET		Improvement in PTSD symptoms
Mc Lay et al. (2010)	PTSD	10	Open clinical trial	VRET IVE+EI		VR-based and traditional therapy were found to be safe and effective in the combat theatre

13.3 From VR to InterReality

Table 13.1 (continued)

First author and year of publication	Type of disorder	Samples	Experimental design	Condition(s)	Follow-up	Short-term outcome
Mc Lay et al. (2011)	PTSD	10	Randomized between subject design	VRET TAU		Seven of ten participants improved by 30% or greater while in VRET, whereas only one of the nine returning participants in TAU showed similar improvement
Ready (2010)	PTSD	9	Randomized between subject design	VRET Present-centred therapy		No significant differences emerged between treatments
Reger (2008)	PTSD	1	Case study	VRET		Self-reported PTSD symptoms and psychological distress were reduced at posttreatment relative to pretreatment reports
Rizzo (2009)	PTSD	20	Open clinical trial	Mixed clinical protocol including VRET, IVE, EI		16 patients no longer meet diagnostic criteria for PTSD at post treatment
Wood (2009)	PTSD	12	Open clinical trial	VRET		The VRET participants' clinical levels of PTSD and depression significantly reduced
Wallach (2009)	Fear of public speaking	88	Randomized between subject design	VRET CBT WL		VRET and CBT were significantly more effective than WL in anxiety reduction, but twice as many participants dropped out from CBT than from VRET
Wallach (2011)	Fear of public speaking	78	Randomized between subject design	VRET CBT WL		VRET and CT proved to be equally effective to CBT in reducing public speaking anxiety relative to a control group, with minimal differential effects between them. Therefore, employing either one may be satisfactory and sufficient

Table 13.1 (continued)

First author and year of publication	Type of disorder	Samples	Experimental design	Condition(s)	Follow-up	Short-term outcome
Robillard (2010)	Social anxiety	45	Randomized between subject design	VRET+IVE IVE WL		Significant reduction of anxiety on all questionnaires as well as statistically significant interactions between both treatment groups and the waiting list
Cornwell (2011)	Social anxiety	32	Open clinical trial	VRET		The VR environment is sufficiently realistic to provoke fear and anxiety in individuals highly vulnerable to socially threatening situations
Price (2011)	Social anxiety	41	Randomized between subject design	VRET WL		Results suggest that total presence and realness subscale scores were related to in-session peak fear ratings. However, only scores on the involvement subscale significantly predicted treatment response
Price (2012)	Social anxiety	67	Randomized between subject design	VRET CT CBT (EGT) WL		There were was no evidence for a difference in this effect across VRE and CBT. This is the first empirical study to show that early outcome expectancy is related to treatment response for a virtual reality-based treatment for social anxiety

CAE-S self-administered computer-aided exposure, *CAE-T* computer-aided exposure with a therapist's assistance throughout exposure sessions, *CBT* cognitive behavioural therapy, *CT* cognitive therapy, *EI* imaginal exposure, *IVE* in vivo exposure, *TAU* treatment as usual, *VRET* virtual reality exposure therapy, *WL* waiting list

13.3 From VR to InterReality

As underlined by Riva and colleagues (Riva 2009a; Riva et al. 2010b), in VRET the virtual experience is a distinct realm, separate from the emotions and behaviours experienced by the patient in the real world: The behaviour of the patient in VR has no direct effects on the real life experience; the emotions and problems experienced by the patient in the real world are not directly addressed in the VR exposure.

To overcome this limitation, the "InterReality" (IR) paradigm extends the clinical setting to a hybrid environment, bridging the physical and virtual world (Riva 2009a). By bridging virtual experiences—fully controlled by the therapist, used to learn coping skills and emotional regulation—with real experiences—that allow both the identification of any critical stressors and the assessment of what has been learned—using advanced technologies allows "IR" to offer a comprehensive clinical experience. The idea of a stricter link between real and virtual worlds is not new: The use of "augmented reality" or "mixed reality" technology blends virtual objects seamlessly into views of the real world. Nevertheless, all the previous attempts of connecting virtual and real worlds tried to remove the boundaries between. The main outcome is a blurred experience that is neither virtual nor real. Apparently, working in a blurred world, in which boundaries are not always clear, is more a problem than an advantage: The lack of boundaries calls for new concepts of self, identity and community that have to be learned, managed and shared. More, it does not allow us to exploit the specific advantages that virtual and real world afford us. For instance, virtual worlds are designed to augment humans and provide them with the capability to manipulate information in ways that are not normally possible in the real world. But in blurred worlds, the level of augmentation is constrained by the features of the task/context in which the user is involved.

The main goal of IR is the connection between virtual and real worlds without removing the boundaries that defines them.

The interconnections between the virtual and real world is bidirectional:

- *behaviour in the real world influences the VE*. For example, if emotional regulation is poor during the day, then some exercises in the VE are unlocked in order to train this ability.
- *behaviour in the virtual world influences the real life*. For example, if I participate in a virtual support group I can interact with other participants during the day via SMS.

The link between the virtual and real world is made possible by the following technologies:

- *3D individual and/or shared virtual worlds (3DWs)*: They are immersive (in the therapist's office) or nonimmersive (at home) environments inhabited by motional avatars, representing other users. The immersivity is produced by Providing immersive output devices (head-mounted display, force feedback robotic arms, etc.) and a system of head/body tracking to guarantee the exact correspondence and coordination of users' movements with the feedback of the environment. The user can interact with others, socialize and participate in individual and group activities.

- *Personal biomonitoring system (from the real to the virtual world)*: It is made up of bio and activity sensors that monitor the emotional status of the patient and coherently modify the VE. This link may be achieved in real time or not.
- *Personal digital assistance (PDA) and/or mobile phones (from the virtual to the real world)*: These devices offer the opportunity to always be connected with the virtual world where the user can receive warnings and feedback, perform homework assignments and meet other users in the context of social networks.

Compared to traditional cognitive behavioural therapy, IR presents some interesting specific characteristics of the patient; moreover, in the context of IR, the patient is engaged in activities and processes that focus on relational changes and self-efficacy as well; finally, IR, merging virtual and real worlds, gives the opportunity to address during the training the emotions and fears experienced in real life. Tables 13.2 and 13.3 summarize the clinical areas in which IR can improve the standard treatment for both patient and therapist, respectively.

Furthermore, from a clinical standpoint, IR offers some innovations to current VR protocols as well: objective and quantitative assessment of symptoms using biosensors; provision of warnings and motivating feedback to improve compliance and long-term outcome. The limitations of this approach parallel the ones of VR. The most evident limitation is related to the availability of the equipment: all the technological needs increases dramatically the costs of the intervention and makes the protocol less likely to be applicable by private clinicians; the contribution of the patient in the management of the sessions outside the therapist's office require a good level of familiarity with technology, and could prevent some patients from being included in the protocol.

To date, there is a lack of clinical trials assessing the usability and the effectiveness of the IR paradigm in the literature. Some pioneering applications of the technologies involved in IR protocols have been undertaken in the field of mental health, but never assembled together in the way aforementioned.

Recently, the capabilities of mobile phones as a tool for responding to a variety of clinical needs have been investigated (Preziosa et al. 2009). The interest demonstrated towards this device is motivated by its wide diffusion: The level of mobile phone penetration has rapidly increased in the past decades, to the extent that a large portion of the population in Europe and the USA owns at least one mobile phone. Furthermore, the advanced technology now available allows mobile phones to combine the use of traditional phones, such as calling someone, to the broader communication capabilities, supporting 3D graphics, pictures, musical sounds and software programs.

Authors presented two studies based on the use of the mobile phones for anxiety management. In the first experiment, a Stress Inoculation Training to reduce exam stress has been applied: The results demonstrated that the combination of video and audio narratives administered via UMTS induced more relaxation compared to the other experimental conditions (either only video or only narratives administered with alternative means, such as CD and Mp3 readers). In the second study, relaxation abilities were successfully trained in a sample of stressed patients by

Table 13.2 Advantages of the INTERSTRESS approach (patient)

Advantages of the INTERSTRESS approach (patient)	
Acceptance	- Through the *virtual worlds* patients will meet both the critical situation and the relaxation area and they will learn to face stressful events. In particular in the first area, users will be exposed to specific stressful situations and they will be helped in developing specific strategies, for avoiding and/or coping with them. While in the other one they will enjoy a very relaxing environment and will learn some basic relaxation procedures guided by a narrative voice. - Through daily review of recorded critical situations first experienced with the therapist in the clinical session. - Through participation in the *social virtual world* on specific days, under the therapist's guidance, patients will share their stressful experiences and they will learn news strategies to cope with them. - Through the *virtual experiences*, patients will acquire stressors-focused strategies and will perform coping exercises to relieve stress.
Coping skills	- Learning new coping skills (for example relaxation techniques) within the *virtual worlds*. - PDA/Smartphone will be used as training/simulation devices to facilitate the real-world transfer of the knowledge acquired in the virtual world. - By pressing a button users will signal and recognize their actual emotional state (for emotional awareness). - Learning through the other's behavior in the *social virtual world* and using them in the real world. - Users will improve their coping skills within the stress related *virtual experiences*.
Emotional regulation	- Through frequent experiencing of stressful situations in different safe environments within the *virtual worlds*. - Through mobile phone with an assistant that will intervene when patients show difficulties in real life displayed by biofeedback and recorded markers. - Through social support within the *social virtual world* and outside it through the social links created in the virtual worlds. - In the stress related *virtual experiences,* acquiring stressors-focused strategies and new emotion-focused coping strategies which can be used in the real world.
Cognitive restructuring	- Getting information needed to succeed with daily tips and expert ideas in the stress related. - Through therapist support and restructuring during patients' exploration of the stress related virtual experiences. - Through community shared experiences.

mobile narratives experienced on mobile phones. The outcome of this research, taken together with other experimental studies on mobile phones suggest that this technology is promising in the treatment of anxiety disorders, since it offers the opportunity to close the gap between in-office and at-home sessions.

Table 13.3 Advantages of the INTERSTRESS (Therapist)

Advantages of the INTERSTRESS (Therapist)	
Better assessment	The following indexes help the therapist to redirect the therapy: - Indexes will be taken from biosensors which connect the stressful situation to changed physiological parameters and this will orientate the therapy. - Biosensors will track the emotional/heath status of the users. - Markers of stressful experiences will be recorded directly by the patient in the PDA/Smartphone (e.g. by pressing a button) to orientate the therapy process. - Cognitive, emotional and behavioural feedback will be received from the *stress related virtual experiences*, helping the therapist to conduct more effective, individually-focused therapy. - Forms will be filled out in the clinical session, on the specific stressful situation "lived" during previous days and on their reactions in dealing with it. - Evaluative questionnaires and experiential tasks will be used to assess if patients have really attained the strategies they were taught.
Decision support	For the session: - Biosensor, VR and PDA outcomes will give information on emotional/heath status so therapist will know the best direction to proceed with in therapy. - A Data Fusion system will represent in an easy-to-interpret way the different data collected. - Cognitive and emotional responses and behavioural decisions taken in the virtual worlds will facilitate therapeutic steps. - In the *stress related virtual experiences*, through the evaluative questionnaires, the therapist will obtain information to know if patients have learned recognition of what causes stress, early recognition of stress symptoms, and stress reduction exercises and get information needed to succeed. For the Therapy: - The number of times the avatar steps in and intervenes will be an index of the learning and autonomy level of users. Then the therapist will submit patients to the exploration of new environments to further improve their coping skills. - A Decision Support System (DSS) will provide specific cues during this learning.
Repository of clinical cases	- Physiological outcomes will be collected through a wireless Personal Biomonitoring System (PBS) tracking different biological parameters (respiration rate, heart rate, heart rate variability, etc). - Modules (i.e. control, data acquisition, data filtering and feature selection may be grouped recursively in order to share common properties and functionalities of entity modules belonging to the same type. All base modules manage dynamic structures and they are designed to maintain data consistency while the environment state may change. - During the sessions, information will be saved in a database which will help the therapist to take information about users' cognitive, emotional and behavioural responses. - Through evaluative questionnaires, in the *stress related virtual experiences*, therapist will take information on patients' learned capabilities in using relaxation techniques. - Through forms filled out in the clinical session, the therapist will have more information about users' appraisal and behavioural skills related to the stressors.

13.4 Conclusions

In the past decade, medical applications of VR technology have rapidly developed, and the technology has changed from a research curiosity to a commercially and clinically important area of medical informatics technology (Riva 2009b; Riva et al. 2010a). This book clearly underlines this transformation.

However, there is a growing recognition that VR can play an important role in clinical psychology, too.

One of the main advantages of a VE for clinical psychologists is that it can be used in a medical facility, thus avoiding the need to venture into public situations. In fact, in most of the existing applications, VR is used to simulate the real world and to assure the researcher full control of all the parameters implied. VR constitutes a highly flexible tool, which makes it possible to program an enormous variety of procedures of intervention on psychological distress. The possibility of structuring a large amount of controlled stimuli and, simultaneously, of monitoring the possible responses generated by the user of the program offers a considerable increase in the likelihood of therapeutic effectiveness, as compared to traditional procedures.

More, the availability of low-cost hardware and software is opening the VR experience also to individual clinicians. For instance, the NeuroVR platform (http://www.neurovr.org)—a cost-free VR toolkit based on open-source software—allows nonexpert users to easily set up a clinical VE and to visualize it using both immersive and nonimmersive technologies (Riva et al. 2009; Riva et al. 2007, 2011a)

Finally, the reduction in the distance between the virtual and real world allowed by the IR paradigm frames VR in a more contextualized experiential process (Riva 2009a).

Specifically, the clinical use of IR is based on a closed-loop concept that involves the use of technology for assessing, adjusting and/or modulating the behaviours and emotions of the patient in both real and virtual worlds (Riva 2009a; Riva et al. 2010c). On one hand, the patient is continuously assessed in the virtual and real worlds by tracking their behavioural and emotional status in the context of challenging tasks (*customization of the therapy according to the characteristics of the patient*). On the other hand, feedback is continuously provided to improve the skills of the patient through a conditioned association between performance and execution of assigned tasks (*improvement of self-efficacy*).

In general, this closed-loop experience is used as a trigger for a broader empowerment process. In the psychological literature, *empowerment* is considered a multifaceted construct reflecting the different dimensions of being psychologically enabled, and is conceived of as a positive additive function of the following three dimensions (Menon 1999):

- *perceived competence*: Reflects role-mastery, which besides requiring the skilful accomplishment of one or more assigned tasks, also requires successful coping with nonroutine role-related situations.
- *perceived control*: Includes beliefs about authority, decision-making latitude, availability of resources, autonomy in the scheduling and performance of work, etc.

- *goal internalization*: This dimension captures the energizing property of a worthy cause or exciting vision provided by the organizational leadership.

On one side, in the real world, the dynamic behavioural profile of the patient and his/her physiological response to events is collected and assessed through different sensors (e.g. GPS) and biosensors (e.g. HR, SCR). Using this data, both patient and therapist can identify the antecedents and the consequences of any crisis. More, it is even possible to forecast a possible anxiety attack and to provide in real time suggestions and feedback to the patient.

On the other side, VR can be considered the preferred environment for the empowerment process, since it is a special, sheltered setting where patients can start to explore and act without feeling threatened (Vincelli 1999). In this sense, the virtual experience is an "empowering environment" that therapy provides for patients.

Besides, it is unnecessary to wait for situations to happen in the real world because any situation can be modelled in a VE, thus greatly increasing self-training possibilities (Riva et al. 2002). In addition, VR allows the situation to be graded so the patient can start at the easiest level and progress to the most difficult. Gradually, because of the knowledge and control afforded by interactions in the virtual world, the patient will be able to face the real world.

For these reasons, the future of health technology for the treatment of anxiety disorders will probably include two main features: portability and IR. Portability refers to the use of portable devices (tablets and smartphones) to provide VR everywhere. Having the possibility to run a VR system on a mobile device will allow patients to practice the skills learned in the therapist's office by themselves and without limitations.

Currently, the mobile phone supports advanced communicative features such as real-time video communications, audio and the exchange of texts and videos. This innovation will increase in the next few years, so a new generation of hardware accelerated mobile devices will soon be joined by a suite of emerging 3D software standards that give developers the ability to create interactive content and other applications that have not been possible before (Preziosa et al. 2009). More, the creation of two open standards (Ant+—http://www.thisisant.com/—and Bluetooth 4) for connecting biosensors to mobile phones is pushing the development of personal sensors for advanced self-tracking.

This trend is also parallel to the development of online VR worlds, such as SecondLife (http://www.secondlife.com) or JustLeapIn (http://www.justleapin.com).

Compared to the traditional VR worlds, the online worlds appear to have much to offer to exposure-based therapy. Since they allow multiplayer's interactions, the therapist and the patient can share the same online virtual space. This means that the therapist can accompany the patient through a particularly threatening experience just by logging onto a specific website and adopting a preferred avatar. The way of interaction as well as the surrounding environment can be easily modified on the basis of therapeutic needs. In the case of social phobia, for example, after practicing with the therapist within a closed environment (i.e. the therapist's virtual office), the patient can be taken to a virtual world populated by other avatars and asked to initiate a conversation and obtain feedback from them in real-time audio through the use of a microphone. Similarly, patients with agoraphobia can be exposed to a variety of unfamiliar worlds different from those the clinician can provide in an office setting. As reviewed by Gorini and colleagues (Gorini et al. 2008), many environments created specifically for therapeutic purposes are available within the platform of SecondLife. Most of them aim at providing help to patients and caregivers dealing with psychiatric and neurological diseases: Brigadoon, for example, is a private island in which people suffering from Asperger's syndrome may meet each other and have the opportunity to practise their social skills (http://braintalk.blogs.com/brigadoon/2005/01/about_brigadoon.html). With similar goals, Live2Give (http://slurl.com/secondlife/144/210/28) is designed for patients affected by cerebral palsy. A third example of this application is targeted specifically for anxiety symptoms. Starting from a personal experience, Roberto Salvatierra, a medical student with agoraphobia, created a VE to help other people suffering from the same disorder (http://slurl.com/secondlife/neptune/128/110/30). These are just a few examples describing the promising potential of on-line virtual worlds in the field of psychological therapy.

The bridging of mobile devices with online VR worlds is the final goal of the IR paradigm. On one side, the patient will be continuously assessed in the virtual and real worlds by tracking the behavioural and emotional status in the context of challenging tasks (customization of the therapy according to the characteristics of the patient). On the other side, feedback is continuously provided to improve both the appraisal and the coping skills of the patient through a conditioned association between effective performance state and task execution behaviours (improvement of self-efficacy). In sum, from the clinical viewpoint, the IR paradigm may offer the following innovations to current protocols for anxiety disorders:

- *objective and quantitative assessment of symptoms using biosensors and behavioural analysis*: monitoring of the patient behaviour and of his general and psychological status, early detection of symptoms of critical evolutions and timely activation of feedback in a closed-loop approach;
- *decision support for treatment planning*: monitoring of the response of the patient to the treatment, management of the treatment and support to the clinicians in their therapeutic decisions.
- *provision of warnings and motivating feedback to improve compliance and long-term outcome*: the sense of "presence" allowed by this approach affords the opportunity to deliver behavioural, emotional and physiological self-regulation training in an entertaining and motivating fashion.

References

Asukai, N., Saito, A., Tsuruta, N., Kishimoto, J., & Nishikawa, T. (2010). Efficacy of exposure therapy for Japanese patients with posttraumatic stress disorder due to mixed traumatic events: A randomized controlled study. *Journal of Traumatic Stress, 23*(6), 744–750. doi:10.1002/jts.20589.

Barlow, J. H., Ellard, D. R., Hainsworth, J. M., Jones, F. R., & Fisher, A. (2005). A review of self-management interventions for panic disorders, phobias and obsessive-compulsive disorders. *Acta Psychiatrica Scandinavica, 111*(4), 272–285. doi:ACP499 [pii] 10.1111/j.1600–0447.2 005.00499.x.

Beck, J. G., Palyo, S. A., Winer, E. H., Schwagler, B. E., & Ang, E. J. (2007). Virtual reality exposure therapy for PTSD symptoms after a road accident: An uncontrolled case series. *Behavior Therapy, 38,* 39–48.

Borst, G., & Kosslyn, S. M. (2010). Fear selectively modulates visual mental imagery and visual perception. The *Quarterly Journal of Experimental Psychology: QJEP, 63*(5), 833–839. doi:9 19484212[pii]10.1080/17470211003602420.

Botella, C., Quero, S., Baños, R. M., Perpina, C., Garcia Palacios, A., & Riva, G. (2004). Virtual reality and psychotherapy. *Studies in Health Technology and Informatics, 99,* 37–54.

Botella, C., García-Palacios, A., Villa, H., Baños, R. M., Quero, S., Alcañiz, M., & Riva, G. (2007). Virtual reality exposure in the treatment of panic disorder and agoraphobia: A controlled study. *Clinical Psychology & Psychotherapy, 14,* 164–175.

Botella, C., García-Palacios, A., Guillen, V., Baños, R. M., Quero, S., & Alcañiz, M. (2010). An adaptive display for the treatment of diverse trauma PTSD victims. *Cyberpsychology, Behavior and Social Networking, 13,* 67–71.

Cornwell, B. R., Heller, R., Biggs, A., Pine, D. S., & Grillon, C. (2011). Becoming the center of attention in social anxiety disorder: Startle reactivity to a virtual audience during speech anticipation. (Research support, N.I.H., Intramural). *The Journal of Clinical Psychiatry, 72*(7), 942–948. doi:10.4088/JCP.09m05731blu.

Côté, S., & Bouchard, S. (2005). Documenting the efficacy of virtual reality exposure with psychophysiological and information processing measures. *Applied psychophysiology and Biofeedback, 30,* 217–232.

Cotè, S., & Bouchard, S. (2009). Cognitive mechanisms underlying virtual reality exposure. *Cyberpsychology & Behavior: The impact of the Internet, Multimedia and Virtual Reality on Behavior and Society, 12*(2), 121–129.

Craske, M., & Barlow, D. (2007). Panic disorder and agoraphobia. In D. H. Barlow (Ed.), *Clinical handbook of psychological disorders: A step-by-step treatment manual* (4th ed., pp. 1–64). New York: Guilford.

Damasio, A. R., Grabowski, T. J., Bechara, A., Damasio, H., Ponto, L. L., Parvizi, J., & Hichwa, R. D. (2000). Subcortical and cortical brain activity during the feeling of self-generated emotions. *Nature neuroscience, 3*(10), 1049–1056.

Deacon, B. J., & Abramowitz, J. S. (2004). Cognitive and behavioral treatments for anxiety disorders: A review of meta-analytic findings. *Journal of Clinical Psychology, 60*(4), 429–441.

Difede, J., Cukor, J., Jayasinghe, N., Patt, I., Jedel, S., Spielman, L., et al. (2007). Virtual reality exposure therapy for the treatment of posttraumatic stress disorder following September 11, 2001. *The Journal of Clinical Psychiatry, 68*(11), 1639–1647.

Emmelkamp, P. M. (2003). Behavior therapy in adults. In M. Lambert (Ed.), *Handbook of psychotherapy and behavior change* (5th ed., pp. 393–446). New York: Wiley.

Franklin, M., & Foa, E. (2007). Obsessive compulsive disorder. In D. H. Barlow (Ed.), *Clinical handbook of psychological disorders: A step-by-step treatment manual* (4th ed., pp. 164–215). New York: Guilford.

Freedman, S. A., Hoffman, H. G., Garcia-Palacios, A., Tamar Weiss, P. L., Avitzour, S., & Josman, N. (2010). Prolonged exposure and virtual reality-enhanced imaginal exposure for PTSD following a terrorist bulldozer attack: A case study. *Cyberpsychology, Behavior and Social Networking, 13,* 95–101.

Gamito, P., Oliveira, J., Rosa, P., Morais, D., Duarte, N., Oliveira, S., & Saraiva, T. (2010). PTSD elderly war veterans: A clinical controlled pilot study. *Cyberpsychology, Behavior and Social Networking, 13*(1), 43–48.

Gerardi, M., Rothbaum, B. O., Ressler, K., Heekin, M., & Rizzo, A. (2008). Virtual reality exposure therapy using a virtual Iraq: Case report. *Journal of Traumatic Stress, 21*(2), 209–213. doi:10.1002/jts.20331.

References

Glantz, K., & Rizzo, A. A. (2003). Virtual reality for psychotherapy: Current reality and future possibilities. *Psychotherapy, 40*, 55–67.

Gorini, A., Gaggioli, A., Vigna, C., & Riva, G. (2008). A second life for eHealth: Prospects for the use of 3-D virtual worlds in clinical psychology. *Journal of Medical Internet Research, 10*(3), e21.

Hazlett-Stevens, H., & Craske, M. (2008). Live (in vivo) exposure. In W. O'Donohue & J. Fisher (Eds.), *Cognitive behavior therapy—Applying empirically supported techniques in your practice* (2nd edn.). New York: Wiley.

Heimberg, R., Dodge, C., Hope, D., Kennedy, C., Zollo, L., & Becker, R. (1990). Cognitive behavioural group treatment for social phobia: Comparison with a credible placebo control. *Cognitive Therapy and Research, 14*, 1–23.

Hodges, L. F., Anderson, P., Burdea, G. C., Hoffmann, H. G., & Rothbaum, B. O. (2001). Treating psychological and phsyical disorders with VR. *IEEE Computer Graphics and Applications, 21*(6), 25–33.

Krijn, M., Emmelkamp, P. M. G., Olafsson, R. P., & Biemond, R. (2004). Virtual reality exposure therapy of anxiety disorders: A review. *Clinical Psychology Review, 24*(3), 259–281.

Krijn, M., Emmelkamp, P. M., Olafsson, R. P., Bouwman, M., van Gerwen, L. J., Spinhoven, P., et al. (2007a). Fear of flying treatment methods: Virtual reality exposure vs. cognitive behavioral therapy. *Aviation, Space and Environmental Medicine, 78*(2), 121–128.

Krijn, M., Emmelkamp, P. M, Olafsson, R. P., Schuemie, M. J., & van der Mast, C. P. G. (2007b). Do self-statements enhance the effectiveness of virtual reality exposure therapy? A comparative evaluation in acrophobia. *Cyberpsychology & Behavior: The Impact of the Internet, Multimedia and Virtual Reality on Behavior and Society, 10*(3), 362–370.

Landon, T. M., & Barlow, D. H. (2004). Cognitive-behavioral treatment for panic disorder: Current status. *Journal of Psychiatric Practice, 10*(4), 211–226.

Malbos, E., Mestre, D. R., Note, I. D., & Gellato, C. (2008). Virtual reality and claustrophobia: Multiple components therapy involving game editor virtual environments exposure. *Cyberpsychology & Behavior: The Impact of the Internet, Multimedia and Virtual Reality on Behavior and Society, 11*(6), 695–697.

McLay, R. N., McBrien, C., Wiederhold, M. D., & Wiederhold, B. K. (2010). Exposure therapy with and without virtual reality to treat PTSD while in the combat theater: A parallel case series. *Cyberpsychology, Behavior and Social Networking, 13*(1), 37–42.

McLay, R. N., Wood, D. P., Webb-Murphy, J. A., Spira, J. L., Wiederhold, M. D., Pyne, J. M., & Wiederhold, B. K. (2011). A randomized, controlled trial of virtual reality-graded exposure therapy for post-traumatic stress disorder in active duty service members with combat-related post-traumatic stress disorder. *Cyberpsychology, Behavior and Social Networking, 14*(4), 223–229.

Menon, S. T. (1999). Psychological empowerment: Definition, measurement, and validation. *Canadian Journal of Behavioural Science, 31*(3), 3.

Michael, T., Zetsche, U., & Margraf, J. (2007). Epidemiology of anxiety disorders. *Psychiatry, 6*(4), 136–142.

Olatunji, B. O., Cisler, J. M., & Deacon, B. J. (2010). Efficacy of cognitive behavioral therapy for anxiety disorders: A review of meta-analytic findings. *The Psychiatric Clinics of North America, 33*(3), 557–577. doi:S. 193-953×(10)00044−4 [pii]10.1016/j.psc.2010.04.002.

Opris, D., Pintea, S., Garcia-Palacios, A., Botella, C., Szamoskozi, S., & David, D. (2012). Virtual reality exposure therapy in anxiety disorders: A quantitative meta-analysis. (Research support, Non-U.S. Gov't). *Depression and Anxiety, 29*(2), 85–93. doi:10.1002/da.20910.

Parsons, T. D., & Rizzo, A. A. (2008). Affective outcomes of virtual reality exposure therapy for anxiety and specific phobias: A meta-analysis. *Journal of Behavior Therapy and Experimental Psychiatry, 39*(3), 250–261.

Perez-Ara, M. A., Quero, S., Botella, C., Baños, R. M., Andreu-Mateu, S., Garcia-Palacios, A., & Breton-Lopez, J. (2010). Virtual reality interoceptive exposure for the treatment of panic disorder and agoraphobia. *Studies in Health Technology and Informatics, 154*, 77–81.

Powers, M. B., & Emmelkamp, P. M. G. (2008). Virtual reality exposure therapy for anxiety disorders: A meta-analysis. *Journal of Anxiety Disorders, 22*(3), 561–569.

Preziosa, A., Grassi, A., Gaggioli, A., & Riva, G. (2009). Therapeutic applications of the mobile phone. *British Journal of Guidance & Counselling, 37*(3), 313–325.

Price, M., & Anderson, P. L. (2012). Outcome expectancy as a predictor of treatment response in cognitive behavioral therapy for public speaking fears within social anxiety disorder. *Psychotherapy, 49*(2), 173–179.

Price, M., Mehta, N., Tone, E. B., & Anderson, P. L. (2011). Does engagement with exposure yield better outcomes? Components of presence as a predictor of treatment response for virtual reality exposure therapy for social phobia. (Randomized controlled trial). *Journal of Anxiety Disorders, 25*(6), 763–770. doi:10.1016/j.janxdis.2011.03.004.

Pull, C. B. (2005). Current status of virtual reality exposure therapy in anxiety disorders: Editorial review. *Current Opinion in Psychiatry, 18*(1), 7–14.

Pull, C. B. (2008). Recent trends in the study of specific phobias. *Current Opinion in Psychiatry, 21*(1), 43–50.

Ready, D. J., Gerardi, R. J., Backscheider, A. G., Mascaro, N., & Rothbaum, B. O. (2010). Comparing virtual reality exposure therapy to present-centered therapy with 11 U.S. Vietnam veterans with PTSD. *Cyberpsychology Behaviour and Social Networking, 13*(1), 49–54. doi:10.1089/cyber.2009.0239 [pii].

Reger, G. M., & Gahm, G. A. (2008). Virtual reality exposure therapy for active duty soldiers. *Journal of Clinical Psychology, 64*(8), 940–946.

Riva, G. (2009a). Interreality: A new paradigm for e-health. *Studies in health technology and informatics, 144*, 3–7.

Riva, G. (2009b). Virtual reality: An experiential tool for clinical psychology. *British Journal of Guidance & Counselling, 37*(3), 337–345.

Riva, G., Molinari, E., & Vincelli, F. (2002). Interaction and presence in the clinical relationship: Virtual reality (VR) as communicative medium between patient and therapist. *IEEE Transactions on Information Technology in Biomedicine, 6*(3), 198–205.

Riva, G., Gaggioli, A., Villani, D., Preziosa, A., Morganti, F., Corsi, R., & et al. (2007). NeuroVR: An open source virtual reality platform for clinical psychology and behavioral neurosciences. *Studies in Health Technology and Informatics, 125*, 394–399.

Riva, G., Carelli, L., Gaggioli, A., Gorini, A., Vigna, C., Corsi, R., & et al. (2009). NeuroVR 1.5—A free virtual reality platform for the assessment and treatment in clinical psychology and neuroscience. *Studies in Health Technology and Informatics, 142*, 268–270.

Riva, G., Algeri, D., Pallavicini, F., Repetto, C., Gorini, A., & Gaggioli, A. (2010a). The use of advanced technologies in the treatment of psychological stress. *Journal of CyberTherapy & Rehabilitation, 2*(2), 169–171.

Riva, G., Raspelli, S., Algeri, D., Pallavicini, F., Gorini, A., Wiederhold, B. K., & Gaggioli, A. (2010b). Interreality in practice: Bridging virtual and real worlds in the treatment of posttraumatic stress disorders. *Cyberpsychology, Behavior and Social Networking, 13*(1), 55–65. doi:10.1089/cyber.2009.0320 [pii].

Riva, G., Raspelli, S., Pallavicini, F., Grassi, A., Algeri, D., Wiederhold, B. K., & Gaggioli, A. (2010c). Interreality in the management of psychological stress: A clinical scenario. *Studies in health technology and informatics, 154*, 20–25.

Riva, G., Gaggioli, A., Grassi, A., Raspelli, S., Cipresso, P., Pallavicini, F., & et al. (2011a). NeuroVR 2—A free virtual reality platform for the assessment and treatment in behavioral health care. *Studies in Health Technology and Informatics, 163*, 493–495.

Riva, G., Waterworth, J. A., Waterworth, E. L., & Mantovani, F. (2011b). From intention to action: The role of presence. *New Ideas in Psychology, 29*(1), 24–37.

Rizzo, A. A., Difede, J., Rothbaum, B. O., Mclay, R. N., Reger, G., Gahm, G., & et al. (2009). VR PTSD exposure therapy results with active duty OIF/OEF combatants. *Studies in health technology and informatics, 142*, 277–282.

Robillard, G., Bouchard, S., Dumoulin, S., Guitard, T., & Klinger, E. (2010). Using virtual humans to alleviate social anxiety: Preliminary report from a comparative outcome study. *Studies in Health Technology and Informatics, 154*, 57–60.

Rothbaum, B. O., & Schwartz, A. C. (2002). Exposure therapy for posttraumatic stress disorder. *American journal of psychotherapy, 56*(1), 59–75.

St-Jacques, J., Bouchard, S., & Belanger, C. (2010). Is virtual reality effective to motivate and raise interest in phobic children toward therapy? A clinical trial study of in vivo with in virtuo versus in vivo only treatment exposure. *The Journal of Clinical Psychiatry, 71*(7), 924–931. doi:10.4088/JCP.08m04822blu.

Steuer, J. (1992). Defining virtual reality: Dimensions determining telepresence. *Journal of Communication, 42*(4), 73–93.

Tortella-Feliu, M., Botella, C., Llabres, J., Breton-Lopez, J. M., del Amo, A. R., Baños, R. M., & Gelabert, J. M. (2011). Virtual reality versus computer-aided exposure treatments for fear of flying. (Comparative study randomized controlled trial research support, Non-U.S. Gov't). *Behavior Modification, 35*(1), 3–30. doi:10.1177/0145445510390801.

Vincelli, F. (1999). From imagination to virtual reality: The future of clinical psychology. *Cyberpsychology & Behavior: The Impact of the Internet, Multimedia and Virtual Reality on Behavior and Society, 2*(3), 241–248.

Wallach, H. S., Safir, M. P., & Bar-Zvi, M. (2009). Virtual reality cognitive behavior therapy for public speaking anxiety: A randomized clinical trial. *Behavior Modifications, 33*(3), 314–338. doi:0145445509331926.[pii]10.1177/0145445509331926.

Wallach, H. S., Safir, M. P., & Bar-Zvi, M. (2011). Virtual reality exposure versus cognitive restructuring for treatment of public speaking anxiety: A pilot study. (Research support, Non-U.S. Gov't). *The Israel Journal of Psychiatry and Related Sciences, 48*(2), 91–97.

Waterworth, J. A., Waterworth, E. L., Mantovani, F., & Riva, G. (2010). On feeling (the) present. *Journal of Consciousness Studies, 17*(1–2), 167–178.

Wiederhold, B. K., & Wiederhold, M. D. (2003). Three-year follow-up for virtual reality exposure for fear of flying. *CyberPsychology & Behavior, 6*(4), 441–445.

Wiederhold, B. K., & WIederhold, M. D. (2008). Virtual reality for posttraumatic stress disorder and stress inoculation training. *Journal of CyberTherapy & Rehabilitation, 1*(1), 23–35.

Wiederhold, B. K., Jang, D. P., Gevirtz, R. G., Kim, S. I., Kim, I. Y., & Wiederhold, M. D. (2002). The treatment of fear of flying: A controlled study of imaginal and virtual reality graded exposure therapy. *IEEE Transactions on Information Technology in Biomedicine, 6*(3), 218–223.

Wolpe, J. (1958). *Psychotherapy by reciprocal inhibition*. Standford: Standford University Press.

Wood, D. P., Murphy, J., McLay, R. N., Koffman, R., Spira, J. L., Obrecht, R. E., & et al. (2009). Cost effectiveness of virtual reality graded exposure therapy with physiological monitoring for the treatment of combat related post traumatic stress disorder. *Studies in Health Technology and Informatics, 144*, 223–229.

Index

A
Abdominal breathing, 263
Acrophobia, 7, 78, 79, 119–121, 130–132, 134, 137
After effects, 37
Agency, 14–17, 67
Agoraphobia, 3, 7, 65, 71, 145, 150, 158
Animal phobia, 108, 119
  in virtuo exposure for other, 105, 106
  key variables involved in, 91–94
Animation, 129, 200, 250–253
Anxiety sensitivity, 150, 154, 175
Arachnophobia, 7, 91, 99, 105, 110, 111, 113, 131
Augmented reality (AR), 105, 108, 129, 273
Avatar, 25, 80, 191, 199–203, 221, 225, 273, 278
Aviophobia, 65, 66, 71, 78, 81, 160
Avoidance, 28, 75–78, 84, 96, 106, 113, 124, 132, 133, 146, 158, 173, 190, 196, 237
  of enclosed spaces, 145, 153
  of flying, 74
  of heights, 119
  of shopping alone, 150
  of spider, 92, 108, 109

B
Behavior avoidance test, 93, 96, 98, 101, 108, 121, 123, 126, 128, 130, 155, 194, 198
Being there, 20, 22, 137, 267
Biofeedback, 5, 71, 83, 111, 216, 242, 265

C
C-automatic virtual environment *See* CAVE
Case formulation *See* Conceptualization
CAVE, 28, 126–132, 200–202
Children, 107, 112
  in virtuo exposure with, 103, 104

Claustrophobia, 7, 65, 66, 78, 79, 146–150, 152, 154, 155, 158, 160
Cognitive behavior therapy, 6, 66, 78, 82, 92, 121, 132, 165–167, 169, 173–179, 189, 190, 193–198, 204, 205, 238–241, 254, 263
Cognitive restructuring, 67, 72–78, 109, 120, 125, 131, 132, 146, 149, 154, 158, 160, 166, 169, 171, 190, 193, 215, 245
Comorbidity, 163, 164, 188
Computer-Aided vicarious exposure, 95, 96
Conceptualization, 21, 95, 111, 155–158, 237
Context, 10, 12, 21, 35, 36, 49, 52, 58, 82, 91, 93, 110–112, 120, 159, 167, 201, 205, 246, 252, 254, 273, 274, 277, 279
Cortisol, 130, 134, 135
Cost, 5, 85, 108, 196, 262, 274
Cultural differences, 81, 203
Cybersickness
  assessment, 41, 42, 47, 50, 51, 110

D
D-Cycloserine, 133, 134, 140
Degrees of freedom *See* DOF
Desensitization, 121, 160, 211, 261
  presence and, 27, 28
  Development of a virtual environment, 246
  evaluation, 252, 253
  modelization, 248, 249
  needs and goals, 246–248
  scenario development, 246
  scripting, 251, 252
  texturing, 250, 251
Disgust, 91–93, 98, 104, 110, 111, 245, 247
DOF, 38, 45, 78, 110, 126, 129, 132, 133, 136, 137, 140, 247
Driving simulator, 38, 53–58, 176

E

Ecological theory of motion sickness, 40
Ecological validity, 21, 39, 73, 178
Emotion regulation, 164
Exposure parameters, 25–29, 74–77, 81–85, 109–112, 128, 155
Eye-tracking, 196

F

Fear of enclosed spaces, 147, 149, 158
Fear of flying, 65–70, 74–78, 83, 85, 113, 253
Fear of heights, 66, 69, 78, 119, 121, 124, 135, 139, 140, 155
Fear of public speaking, 191–194, 197, 204, 205
Fear of spiders, 91, 92, 103, 108, 112, 265
Functional MRI (fMRI), 24, 25, 92, 145

G

Gender differences, 48, 51, 57, 146
Generalized anxiety disorder (GAD), 7, 235, 236, 242, 265

H

Habituation, 47, 53, 66, 74, 149, 244
Haptic, 10, 97, 98, 105, 107, 111, 247, 251, 261, 267
Harvard business review, 261
Homework, 109, 124, 154, 155, 158, 159, 169, 195, 242, 253, 274
HMD, 10, 27, 28, 36–39, 45–49, 52, 70–78, 98, 99, 101, 105, 108–110, 124–132, 136–140, 148–150, 152, 155, 157, 193, 196, 200–202, 212, 213, 217, 229, 242–245

I

Illusion of nonmediation, 10, 13, 14, 24, 205
Immersion, 6, 10, 47, 70, 76, 83, 102, 111, 124, 128, 132, 138, 157, 196, 205, 244, 245, 251
Immersive tendencies, 76, 83
In virtuo exposure
    definition of, 4
InterReality, 273, 278
Interoceptive exposure, 146, 164, 167, 171, 173, 175

L

Lightmaps, 251

M

Mental acts, 236
Milgram's experiment replicated, 201

Mixed reality, 273
Mobile devices, 242, 274, 275, 278, 279
Modeling, 5, 67, 121, 226, 252
Modelization, 247, 248, 250
Motion capture, 250
Motion simulator, 75
Motion tracker, 74, 76, 78, 98, 106, 110, 126, 130–133, 140, 148, 150, 198
Motivation, 18, 103, 104, 112, 152, 166, 267
Motor vehicle accidents, 7, 160, 213
Multisensory integration, 10, 25, 76

N

Nausea, 37, 41, 56, 122, 138, 170, *See also* Cybersickness
Negative side effects, *See* Cybersickness; Side effects; Simulator Sickness
Neutralization, 190, 238

O

Obsessive-compulsive disorder (OCD), 7, 236–238, 266
Ownership, 14

P

Panic disorder, 3, 7, 65, 71, 113, 145, 150, 153, 158, 266
Pharmacotherapy, 187, 189, 204
Physiological arousal, 27, 71, 152, 159
Physiology, 71, 74, 159, 160, 261, 262
Pit room experiments, 136–139
Polygons, 250
Posttraumatic stress disorder (PTSD), 3, 7, 65, 145, 211
Postural instability/control, 35, 37, 39–41, 120, 123, 124
Presence, 6, 9–12, 190–195, 223
    copresence, 202
    and emotions, 25, 26
    impact on treatment, 12, 82, 126–129
    layers of, 18, 20
    measuring, 20
    subjective measurements of, 20–23
    versus immersion, 9
Prevention, 99, 110, 151
    of PTSD, 221–223, 225, 226

R

Realism, 75–77, 126–129, 134–138, 193, 194, 199–202
Repetitive behaviors, 236
Response prevention, 240

S

Safety seeking behavior, 147, 148, 186, 188, 190
Scripting, 251, 252
Self-efficacy, 28, 71, 78, 94, 101, 102, 111, 113, 121, 155, 263, 274, 277, 279
Sensory conflict theory, 36, 37, 39, 47
Side effects, 35, 36, 47, 85, 157
Simulator sickness, 37, 38, 40, 42, 57, *See also* Cybersickness;
Sleep, 104, 235
Social anxiety disorder (SAD), 187–191, 193–199, 205
Software, 53, 72–75, 84, 99, 106, 107, 153, 194, 251, 277
  available, 80, 81
Sopite syndrome, 40
Stereoscopic (3D) television, 192
Stereoscopy, 126, 130
Stress inoculation training (SIT), 66, 215, 221, 224, 263, 274
Suspension of disbelief, 261

T

Tactile augmentation, 97, 98, 105
Texture, 108, 110, 138, 250
Therapeutic relationship, *See* Working alliance
Treatment mechanism, 92–94, 110, 111, 121, 128, 187, 193

U

Uncanny valley, 202–204

V

Virtual humans, 191, 196, 199, 202, 205

W

Working alliance, 195
Worry, 163, 235, 237–239

CPSIA information can be obtained at www.ICGtesting.com
Printed in the USA
LVOW10*2123091214

418020LV00007B/146/P